THE MODERNIZATION OF AGRICULTURE: RURAL TRANSFORMATION IN HUNGARY, 1848-1975

Joseph Held

EAST EUROPEAN MONOGRAPHS, BOULDER
DISTRIBUTED BY COLUMBIA UNIVERSITY PRESS, NEW YORK

1980

EAST EUROPEAN MONOGRAPHS, NO. LXIII

Joseph Held is Associate Professor of History
at Rutgers University

Library of Congress Card Catalog Number 79-56526
ISBN 0-914710-60-5

Printed in the United States of America

CONTENTS

ACKNOWLEDGMENTS

I owe the Rutgers University Research Council a great deal of appreciation for providing me a Faculty Study Leave during the 1978-1979 Academic Year which enabled me to complete the necessary work for this study. I also want to thank the participants who contributed their valuable time and effort to make this volume a reality. Further thanks are due to professor Gyorgy Ranki of the Historical Institute of the Hungarian Academy of Sciences and Peter Hanak of the same institution for their encouragement and help in bringing this work to a completion.

The staff of Alexander Library at Rutgers University, especially Neha Weinstein, provided much needed help in locating material used in the composition of Part IV; the difficulties of translating an entire Hungarian essay into English would have been impossible without expert help from Ivan Volgyes. A special thanks is due to Miss June Johnson for the clerical help that she provided. Finally, my wife, Margaret, was not only patient and understanding at a time when pressures seemed to pile on me without end, but did some of the drawings for this volume. Her help was, therefore, a *sine qua non* for this book.

I would like to thank the International Research and Exchanges Board [IREX] for providing me with funds for travel to Hungary, without which this project could not have been completed.

INTRODUCTION

The origin of this volume goes back to several scholarly conferences. The first of these, organized by Professor Ivan Volgyes at the University of Nebraska in Lincoln in 1976, brought together some of us interested in exploring the modernization of Hungarian society for the first time. The papers presented at this conference became the bases of studies included in a panel under the chairmanship of Professor Jerome Blum of Princeton University at the Washington Conference of the American Association for the Advancement of Slavic Studies in the fall of 1977. Finally, during a trip by the editor to the Historical Institute of the Hungarian Academy of Sciences in the summer of 1978, Dr. Antal Voros, a member of the Institute, graciously consented to join the authors of the book. Thus, the present work represents close cooperation not only between scholars of different disciplines, but also of two continents.

The problem of modernization, which is the subject of this volume, is a controversial issue, widely debated by scholars.[1]

The major points of difference seem to be related to divergent approaches to the theory of modernization. According to Dean C. Tipps, the major approaches fall into two categories: one includes "critical variable theories" of conceptualization, equating modernization with a single type of social change. The other approach consists of "dichotomous theories" that consider modernization "as a process by which 'traditional' societies acquire the attributes of 'modernity.'"[2] Critical variable theories describe the modernization process as the consequence of a single variable factor, usually industrialization, and its consequences, which include the emergence of an urbanized society based on "mechanized" social and personal relations. On the other hand, dichotomous theories are usually based on ideas, rooted in 19th century notions of evolution, viewing societies undergoing modernization in holistic terms. According to these theories, such societies

> change from primitive, subsistence economies to technology-intensive, industrialized economies; from subject, to participatory political structures; from closed, ascriptive status systems to open, achievement-oriented systems; from extended to nuclear kinship units; from religious to secular ideologies, and so on.[3]

The authors of this volume have no desire to become embroiled in these disputes. But they certainly have no wish to equate the modernization process with one of its single factors, such as industrialization. By focusing on agriculture in the modernization process, they want to make clear their conviction that it was also a component of change in the transformation of society as a whole. Furthermore, they would probably have little objection to discussing the Hungarian process of modernization up to the mid-20th century in terms of the Western model. After all, this was the model that Hungarians tried to emulate in that period of their history. Similarly, when discussing the Eastern—Soviet—model of modernization followed by Hungary after 1948, they would probably frown upon any sort of criticism of the modernization process that is based on ethnocentric theories.

The contributors of this volume seem to agree that as far as the modernization of Hungarian agriculture was concerned, the process hinged upon both the mechanization of production methods *and* changing social attitudes towards the concept of modernity. Furthermore, attitudes on both sides of the social spectrum (among the rural population, most of whom were peasants, and among the urban inhabitants) had to change before modernization could proceed. In the Hungarian situation, such attitudinal changes were to come only as the result of wars and social revolutions in the 20th century; the decisive factors *also* included general industrial progress. Therefore, the concept of modernization in Hungary was inseparably linked to the development of ideas among all social strata, where the backwardness of one part seriously hampered the evolution of the rest.

The Hungarian case of agricultural modernization also presents at least two peculiarities of development. The first of these was the fact that the modernization process began under the control of the Habsburg bureaucracy following the Revolution of 1848-1849. Thus, modernization of agriculture served the interests of the Habsburg Emire as a whole, often in contradiction to specific Hungarian national interests. It was true that modernization gained considerable speed after the Compromise of 1867, when Hungary reached partial independence within the Empire. But when full independence was achieved after World War I, the process of modernization slowed down considerably.

Losses of natural resources and manpower during the war and the partitioning of Hungary among the Successor States and Romania were among the reasons for this phenomenon. On the other hand, modernization of agriculture gained new momentum after 1945, and especially after 1948, when Hungary was brought into the newly formed Socialist Camp and its affairs were once again controlled by foreigners. Hungary, therefore, presents the case of a state whose agrarian modernization began, and its current phase concluded, under foreign domination.

Another peculiarity concerns the development of the Hungarian peasantry itself during the past 125 years. These peasants were similar yet unlike the peasantry of other East European nations, and were certainly vastly different in most of the manifestations of their life from the agriculturists of South America, Asia and Africa.[4] Their historical experiences—some of which they did *not* share even with the peasantry of the neighboring states—predisposed them to behave in peculiarly Hungarian ways; for instance, in their creation of the *tanya*-system.[5] The "little community" of Robert Redfield had certainly existed in the Hungarian countryside, but it was never so small, homogenous, self-sufficient that distinctive as were the Mexican villages that provided the bases of Redfield's generalizations.[6] Nor were the Hungarian peasants as conscious of what George M. Foster described "the Idea of Limited Good," as were "his" South American rural folks.[7]

In fact, peasant villages in Hungary, and the peasantry in general, were never static or socially and physically immobile in the period under discussion. One major characteristic of this period was continuous change in the rural sphere; the change was fast during part of the 19th century, slowed down during the two-and-a-half decades of the interwar period, and accelerated after 1948. However, "change" did not always mean "progress," especially if we mean better living conditions and greater individual freedom under this term. But change in the rural sphere followed change in the urban areas; it pointed towards the gradual, slow dissolution of peasant communities, the absorption of particularistic social strata into the body politic of the nation. Few among us would be so bold as to maintain that such change was preordained or inevitable.

We cannot foretell the future of Hungarian agriculture or that of the peasantry. Yet, if signs that we have observed prove consistent and long-lasting, we may expect the further dwindling of the peasant population of Hungary, and the eventual disappearance of the peasant way of life in the countryside. In place of the old peasant communities, we can already see the larger outlines of an atomized rural society whose craving for consumer goods—both material and cultural—is no different from that of the urban citizens. The backward peasant village is now largely a matter of the past; modernity with its vulgar mediocrity of culture and artifacts on the one hand, and its increasingly available consumer goods on the other, seems to be here to stay. Whether this new balance will prove "better" in the future than it is in the present will be the task of future historians to explore.

New Brunswick, April, 1979
Joseph Held

NOTES

1. The literature of modernization is enormous and continuously growing. Some of the interesting volumes dealing with this problem are as follows: Cyril E. Black, *The Dynamics of Modernization: A Study in Comparative History* (New York, NY, 1966); David Lerner, *The Passing of Traditional Society* (Glencoe, IL, 1968); Barrington Moore, Jr. *Social Origins of Dictatorship and Democracy* (Boston, MA, 1966); Alex Inkeles and David H. Smith, *Becoming Modern* (Cambridge, MA, 1974); Myron Weiner, *Modernization: The Dynamics of Growth* (New York, NY, 1966); Robert Redfield, *The Primitive World and its Transformation* (Ithaca, NY, 1953); Albert O. Hirschman, *The Strategy of Economic Development* (New Haven, CT, 1959); S. F. Franklin, *The European Peasantry: the Final Phase* (London, 1969); W. W. Rostow, *Stages of Economic Growth* (Cambridge, MA., 1961) and many others.
2. Dean C. Tipps, "Modernization Theory and the Comparative Study of Societies: A Critical Perspective," *Comparative Studies in Society and History* 15 (1973), 203.

3. *Ibid.,* 204. See also, Samuel Huntington, "The Change to Change: Modernization, Development and Politics," *Comparative Politics* 3 (1971), No. 3, 294.
4. On this issue, see Ferenc Erdei, *Parasztok* (Peasants) (Budapest, 1976), 2nd ed., 203-6.
5. A discussion of these issues will be undertaken in chapter 3 of Part VII of this work.
6. Robert Redfield, *The Little Community: Viewpoints for the Study of a Human Whole* (Chicago, IL, 1955).
7. George M. Foster, "Peasant Society and the Image of Limited Good," *American Anthropologist* 67 (1965), No. 2, 293-315.

PART I

THE EMANCIPATION AND ITS IMPACT ON THE HUNGARIAN PEASANTRY IN 1848-1850

Peter Hidas

East of the River Leitha, East of Vienna

Revolutionary fever gripped France in February, 1848. News and rumors from Paris created ferment in the minds of those who were clamoring for power. The Hungarian nobility was no exception. Dispatches from the French capital coupled with reports of peasant risings east of the River Leitha, made the Magyar ruling class deliver the ultimate gift to its charges: land. Not even the reluctance of the Viennese government could impede the increasing velocity of the emancipation process.

Louis Kossuth, leader of the parliamentary opposition, initiated the liberation of the peasantry at the Hungarian Diet of 1847/48. At that point many of his supporters were reluctant to include all Hungarians in the ancient constitution. They also debated the wisdom of a complete and compulsory redemption without guarantees of compensation as a satisfactory solution to their socioeconomic and political woes.[1] The news of the February Revolution in Paris sufficiently impressed enough delegates in Pozsony (Bratislava), the seat of the Hungarian Diet, to allow passage of Kossuth's Oppositional Declaration in the form of a Petition, without any hindrance from vacillating party members. The Upper House demurred. When on March 9, 1848, the rumor of a peasant rising reached Pozsony (a rumor possibly manufactured by Kossuth and spread by his followers), the Lords hastily approved the Petition's pro-peasant parts but stiffened their resistance to political reform.[2]

Young radicals, comprised mainly of law students who assisted the delegates, now moved to exert pressure on their reluctant masters. Young people appeared armed at the Diet and conducted a torchlight parade to celebrate the Viennese Revolution of March 13. The next morning each aristocrat found a threatening note at his seat in the Chamber of the Upper House. The admonition was reinforced by sabre rattling in the galleries. Meanwhile, a passenger ship arrived from Budapest, where a mostly peaceful demonstration had taken place on March 15, which soon became the symbol of the Magyar Revolution. On March 18, both Houses approved a bill terminating the nexus between lord and bonded peasant.[3]

To prevent meddling by Vienna and to enhance the repute of his newly formed government, Prime Minister Count Lajos Batthyany ordered the immediate distribution of the text of the new bill (which, as yet, had no royal assent) to local authorities who were, in turn, to brief the peasants. Vienna, after some hesitation, approved the bill. On April 9, 1848, all peasants in Hungary became free in their persons and eight and a half million out of nine million received legal ownership of land without charge.[4] This was surely a revolution from above.

After twenty years of indecision, national unity became urgent and opportune for the nobility. The peasantry had to be won over or neutralized during the quest for firm political control over Transleithania.[5] In fact, the history of the peasantry in Hungary during the first half of the nineteenth century had little in common with the political history of the Habsburg empire. The continuous struggle for power between

Vienna and the Hungarian nobility resulted in the Age of Reform in the Danubian basin and the birth of Magyar national consciousness. But the peasants viewed the struggle dispassionately. At times, one or the other antagonist fell under the illusion that the uncommitted peasants were on its side and, subsequently, converted this illusion into an actual threat towards its opponent. Both sides offered economic concessions to the peasants in return for their loyalty.

At the end of the eighteenth century, Joseph II transformed the purely feudal relationship of lord and peasant into a mixed economic and feudal relationship. By 1835, the peasants also received concessions from the Hungarian Diet: they could commute their dues and services for money rent, some noble privileges were eliminated completely, and the competence of the Patrimonial Courts was restricted. During the early 1840's, the Diet authorized self-emancipation with compensation.[6] In 1846, Kossuth and his fellow liberals opted for compulsory emancipation with compensation and government participation. Vienna also urged pro-peasant legislation but was regularly blocked in the Upper House. By 1848, only 280,000 acres of land were removed from the Lords' jurisdiction. But this amounted to no more than 1.89% of the arable lands. By the time of the emancipation, the common land was already partitioned and consolidated in 16% of the villages and in 24% of them the process had begun but was not completed.[9] The old economic edifice was crumbling, albeit in slow motion.

Priority was still given to political matters by both the Magyar nobility and the Viennese government. Only in 1848 did the former decide on radical social change. In that year, international developments temporarily paralyzed the Habsburgs but the revolutions abroad could have inflamed the peasants, the other potential antagonists of the Hungarian ruling class. Emancipation was to make the aristocracy and the gentry masters in their own house.

The April laws of 1848, which included the emancipation decrees, declared the peasants debt free owners of the lands previously used by them. The government promised on the nation's honor to compensate the former lords. The clergy abandoned, without indemnification, the collection of the tithe and the lords relinquished the *robot* (corvee). The Patrimonial Courts of the landlords were abolished. The peasant became legally a citizen. The gains for the people of the land were enormous. From the 25,900,000 acres of plowed and meadow land in Hungary, the peasants immediately received without charge 55% of the total.[10] These were only holdings that were entered in the cadastres during the reign of Maria Theresa (urbarial lots). In addition, the peasants acquired an estimated 3,640,000 acres of clearings and non-urbarial remainder (unregistered but *de facto* urbarial) lands, plus an unknown quantity of forests, pastures, and vineyards.[11] The families of 1.4 million formerly bonded peasants received clear titles to these lands. All holders of urbarial lots became owners. Bond peasants without urbarial lots numbered 800,000 plus their families. Over 600,000 were awarded a house and a small lot. Close to 100,000 peasants rented land from the lords' allodial holdings before the reform; the law sustained the set contracts and these peasants did not receive free land. Of the remaining 100,000 agricultural worker families up to 10% continued to rent non-allodial lands.[12] Since the new laws cancelled all feudal debts the peasants could view their economic future with optimism.

As citizens, eligible peasants were enfranchised. Their 582,262 votes consisted a potentially strong political force in balancing the weight of the 617,521 noble and urban middle class votes.[13] Local government actually came under the influence of the villagers.[14] The thousand-year dream of the peasantry was now partially fulfilled.

A minority of peasants did not draw economic advantages from the April Laws. Land rental contracts, signed previously between individual peasants or peasant communities and the landlords or the Treasury, remained valid. The allodial holdings were not considered for distribution. The tithe on vineyards was maintained and small royal privileges, such as the making and selling of wine, beer, and spirits, hunting, fishing, milling and local retailing rights were retained by the nobility. The April Laws left unsettled the status of the village commons, the cleared lands and the self-liberated villages. Eventually, problems arose as to the interpretation of the emancipation laws, the applicability of previous court decisions and the practicality and political feasibility of enforcing tithe payments, collecting regular taxes, protecting the former lords' commercial monopolies and the collecting of ordinary land rents in a war-torn country.

There can be no question as to the great benefits the Revolution brought the Hungarian peasantry. The change was revolutionary since there was a fundamental alteration in the ownership of the better part of the arable land and the legal status of the overwhelming majority of the population. Whether the new regime met the expectations of the people of the land is another question. Most recent authors scrutinize the moral stance of Vienna, Budapest or the nobility of 1848; however, few contemporaries took a critical look at the motives of the peasantry before the defeat of the Kossuth regime.[14] It is not accidental that the punctilious recent study of Janos Varga on the struggle for emancipation and its achievement had little to say about the share of the peasantry in that struggle. In fact, it was nil. There were no uprisings, demonstrations or attacks on manor houses. The villagers refrained from going to market when townsfolk became politically hyperactive. The Hungarian countryside retained its serenity. On receiving the news of emancipation the liberated peasants were mostly surprised and confused.[15]

There were occasional celebrations but some suspected trickery. The non-Magyar peasants had the least amount of confidence in the legislation of the new all-Magyar national government. Largesse was acknowledged but old grievances lingered on in the minds of the peasants only to surface once anarchic conditions threatened to overtake most of Hungary. County and borough chiefs and stewards on large estates were temporarily confused and uninformed on questions of law and authority. The radical intellectuals tried to wrestle political power away from the county gentry in local assemblies, German burghers organized pogroms against their Jewish competitors and the peasants decided to redress pre-1848 illegal land rearrangements and "unjust" court decisions. But in most cases, peasant activism remained with the law. The sanctity of property was duly respected. The peasant did not wish to meddle in the conflict of the king and the lords. He only wanted to set straight his affairs with his former landlord.[16]

The map of the peasant movements of 1848 and 1843 indicates that the main causes of conflict between landlord and peasant were over the use of the common ley rights and learings. The grieved were often well-to-do peasants. In Transdanubia, where many of the mammoth estates were located, the landless made few attempts to improve their lot. Owners and renters of vineyards, former serf-peasants with unit lots were the ones who, driven by both justice and greed, opted for arbitrary redress. Invasion of allodial holdings was rare. Professor Szabad's map identifies two such occurrences in Transdanubia, two in northeastern Hungary, six in the "storm corner" south of the Koros River, but none in Transylvania, Croatia or the Borderlands. Szatmar County was one of the hotbeds of dissatisfaction. The Ministry of Justice received more written complaints from this county than from all others combined.[17] But the government was not to blame. Between 1836 and 1848, the nobility, with various excuses, deprived the peasant population of fifty percent of its rustic holdings, which then were converted into or exchanged for allodial lands. Consequently, emancipation had a greatly reduced impact on Szatmar. The Minister of Justice, fearing renewed conflict in neighboring Rumanian counties, sent commissioners into the area to force both sides to observe the new laws and protect the peasantry from further inequities.[18] Restoration of order and national unity were the cornerstones of the Hungarian government's domestic policies.

Now committees were sent to the countryside to explain the April Laws.[19] Even the most radical intellectuals, including

Mihaly Tancsics, spoke out against class struggle.[20] Patience and legal solutions were advocated. The writers Gereben Vas and Janos Arany urged the peasants to defend the Revolution.[21] The unity campaign was reinforced with the organization of the National Guard, which, together with the few available imperial units, restored order in Hungary. The first National Guard formations were composed of former citizens' guards, revolutionary youth and wealthier peasants. Owners of less than half sections of land were not invited to enlist. Neither were the Slovak peasants of Pozsony, Saros and Zemplen counties, the Serbs of Pest and the Rumanians of Krasso, Torontal, Bihar and Zarand, because they were considered hostile to the national cause. Pre-1848 freemen Magyar peasants—*Kunok, Hajduk* and *Jaszok*—flocked to the colours. In June, martial law was declared. By mid-summer social peace reigned again. The Kossuth government was now ready to widen the base of the Revolution. On August 13, the cabinet introduced the volunteer system. Now any male over 18 could join the National Guard. After St. Michael's Day, more and more peasants agreed to serve since the land had been prepared for the next Spring.

In the autumn of 1848, the revolutionary government organized a volunteer national army. All healthy Magyar citizens between the ages of 18 and 40 were recruited. Peasants composed two-thirds of the first volunteer regiments. For the whole army, the average hovered between 55 and 60 percent.[22] The percentage was, indeed, below the population-ratio of the peasantry, but not low enough to support claims of failure of the national unity policy or of peasant indifference in 1848.[23] There was mass opposition to Jelacic's Croat imperial forces which invaded Hungary in September. Kossuth on his recruiting agricultural towns was received with enthusiasm, trust and loyalty demonstrations.[24] A basically volunteer armed force of 130,000 amply demonstrated that national unity was achieved in the first year of the Revolution.[25] From this unity, however, the Slovak, Rumanian, Serb, Croat and Ruthene peasants were excluded. A minority of the Magyar peasants refused to back Budapest unless their economic demands were met. Certain villages attempted to blackmail the government by offering recruits for concessions.[26] But the majority were willing to defend the Revolution. By the middle of 1849, however, three factors appeared to change the attitude of the loyal Magyar peasantry. First, the defense of the Revolution became a war of independence, in fact, a war to protect the gentry state. Then, the murderous civil war, the continuous presence of various armed forces, threatened many communities with physical annihilation or, at least, economic ruin. Finally, the advancing imperial armies promised to respect the emancipation laws and leave the peasants in peace, while Kossuth was drafting more and more young farmers into the army in areas under his jurisdiction.

In Bekes County, the revolutionary army was employed to suppress rebellious peasants; several of their leaders were hanged.[27] In Transylvania, only the Szekely border guards remained loyal to Budapest. Both Magyar and Rumanian peasants resisted their former lords' authority and their occasional illegal demands. Few Transylvanians joined the Hungarian army.[28] Many drifted into the enemy camp. For a long year civil war raged in Transylvania. Villages were razed during the autumn of 1848. Contractuals who refused to fulfill their obligations were often expelled from the land.[29] In June, 1849, several peasant agitators were executed in Transdanubia. These incidents had cumulative effects. Cracks appeared in the edifice of national unity.

At the invitation of the Austrian government, a Russian army of over 100,000 men invaded Hungary in the Spring of 1849. On May 18, the Hungarian cabinet proposed that Governor Kossuth proclaim a crusade against the intruders. The Magyars were implored to rise *en masse,* pray, fast, and arm themselves. The clergy was to give spiritual guidance to the holy cause. Peasants were encouraged to form guerilla units and adopt a scorched-earth tactic.[30]

There was little response from the weary populace. During its retreat, the Hungarian Northern Army met with indifference. At times, the soldiers could not buy bread from the villagers.[31] Young men took to the forests to avoid the Kossuth levy.[32]

Commissioners assigned to Russian and Austrian troops advised the Hungarian population that there would not be a return to the pre-1848 property arrangements and that the Viennese government would assist the people in retaining the fruits of the Revolution.[33] The Imperial Patent of July, 1849, reassured the peasants concerning the legality of their newly-acquired liberties and lands.[34] This agitation contributed to the alienation of the peasantry from the anti-Habsburg Kossuth government. When the Hungarian forces temporarily retook Transdanubia from the advancing Austrians, the peasant movements revived. The stern counter-measures of the Hungarian administration reinforced class antagonism in the countryside.[35]

The returning imperial armies imposed new hardships on the populace. Vince Szentivanyi, Chief Commissioner of the Pest District, noted that due to the many campaigns there was a need for urgent governmental action to prevent the spread of the misery and impoverishment of the peasantry. The situation was critical, he remarked, because the army was using the population's essential draft animals and did not leave enough grain for the bread supply of the people.[36] The ire of the peasantry now enveloped General Haynau's soldiers too.

Despite disappointments, 1848 turned out to be a glorious year for the peasant population of Hungary. The defeat of Kossuth did not signify the defeat of the Revolution. The social program of the Hungarian liberals was safeguarded during the years of political counter-revolution by the economic liberalism of Vienna and the determination of the emancipated peasantry. Liberation enabled the Hungarian peasants to enjoy the many advantages brought by the economic boom of the 1850's and the 1860's.

NOTES

1. JanosVarga, *A jobbagyfelszabaditas kivivasa 1848-ban* (The Successful Struggle for the Liberation of Serfs in 1848) (Budapest, 1971), 15-19.
2. *Ibid.,* 34-43. See also, C. A. Macartney, *The Habsburg Empire 1790-1918* (London, 1968), 337.
3. Varga, *op. cit.,* 150, 70, 75, 138.
4. *Ibid.,* 167.
5. Robert A. Kann, *The Multinational Empire: Nationalism and National Reform in the Habsburg Monarchy 1848-1918* (New York, 1970), 1:118.
6. Zoltan Horvath, *A jobbagyvilag alkonya Sorpon megyeben* (The Decline of the Age of Serfdom in Sopron County) (Budapest, 1976), 11. See also, Maria Loranth, *Adatok az urberi karpotlas tortenetehez 1848-1853* (Documents for the History of Urbarial Compensation (Budapest, 1927), 3; Macartney, *op. cit.,* 247.
7. Loranth, *op. cit.,* 4-7.
8. Varga, *op. cit.,* 340.
9. Pal Sandor, *A birtokrendezesi periratok* (Documents of Suits of Consolidation) (Budapest, 1973), 28. See also, Antal Voros, et al, *A magyar mezogazdasag a XIX.-XX. szazadban* (Hungarian Agriculture in the 19th-20th Centuries) (Budapest, 1976), 42-3.
10. Varga, *op. cit.,* 167.
11. Pal Sandor, "A XIX. szazadi parasztbirtok vizsgalatanak problemai es ujabb eredmenyei a felszabadulas utani irodalom tukreben," (Problems of the Exploration of Peasant Holdings and the Latest Results in Light of the Post-Liberation Literature) *Agrartorteneti Szemole* 10 (1968), 105.
12. *Ibid.,* 115. See also, Varga, *op. cit.,* 339.
13. Gyorgy Spira, "Parasztsagunk es az elso magyar forradalom nemesi vezetese," (Our Peasantry and the Noble Leadership of the First Hungarian Revolution), *Szazadok* 82 (1948), 120. C. A. Macartney is obviously mistaken

when he states that "peasants, workers and tradesmen together secured a bare 2% of ther mandates," *op. cit.*, 378, unless he refers to the social background of the elected parliamentarians. The nobility dominated the elections numerically, but to secure the complete mastery of electoral districts elections were held during the week when peasant voters were in the fields.

14. Istvan Szabo, ed., *A Parasztsag Magyarorszagon a kapitalizmus koraban 1848-1914. Tanulmanyok* (The Peasantry in Hungary in the Age of Capitalism 1848-1914. Studies) (Budapest, 1965), II:573 and 593. See also, Oszkar Sashegyi, ed., *Munkasok es parasztok mozgalmai Magyarorszagon 1848-1867. Iratok* (The Movements of Peasants and Workers in Hungary 1848-1867. Documents) (Budapest, 1959), 9.

15. Sympathy for the working classes or for national aspirations could easily color one's view of the past. Edsel W. Stroup in a recent work on 1848 denies the revolutionary nature of events in Hungary, and praises the nobility for its judicious reformism and unselfishness, *Hungary in Early 1838: The Constitutional Struggle Against Absolutism in Contemporary Eyes* (Buffalo, NY, 1977). George Handlery in "Revolutionary Organization in the Context of Backwardness: Hungary's 1848," *East European Quarterly* 4 (1972) March, 57, accuses the liberals of not solving the land question, and Macartney, *op. cit.*, 72, claims that "relatively little land was distributed under the 1848 reform." Kann states that the Hungarian liberals failed because of their disregard for social misery and national discord; *op. cit.*, 120. Ferenc Erdei wrote in 1943 in "A szabad parasztsag kialakulasa," (Emergence of the Free Peasantry) *Sorsunk* 3 (1943) Nos. 7-12, 691, that actually only 600,000 peasants could enjoy the benefits of the emancipation. Between 1945 and the mid-1960's, Hungarian historians were anxious to show the predominance of class struggle in history, the impoverishment of the peasantry, and the selfishness of the

nobility, and the proper behavior of the peasants. According to Jozsef Nagy in *A Heves megyei munkasmozgalom kezdeti szakasza* (Early Period of the Workers' Movement of the County of Heves) (Eger, 1956), 3, the peasants hardly received anything from the Revolution. In Lajos Fur's view in "Jobbagyfold, Parasztfold," (Serf-Land, Peasant Land) in Szabo, *op. cit.,* 71, the landless *zseller* gained nothing in 1848; Gyorgy Szabad states in Erik Molnar ed., *Magyarorszag tortenete* (History of Hungary) (Budapest, 1964), I:494, that 40% of the former Hungarian serfs received a mere one-third of the arable lands. The re-examination of available data, inspired by a new intellectual atmosphere in Hungary, made also possible the revaluation of the history of the Revolution of 1848. The pioneering studies of Pal Sandor in *Agrartorteneti Szemle,* Janos Varga, *op.cit.,* Urban Aladar's *A nemzetorseg es a honvedseg szervezese 1848 nyaran* (The Organization of the National Guard and the Army in the Summer of 1848) (Budapest, 1973), and the work of Antal Voros following this essay are based on modern computations of data and are free of deliberate distortions.

15. Varga, *op. cit.,* 118, 287.
16. Gyozo Ember, *Magyar parasztmozgalmak 1848-ban* (Hungarian Peasant Movements in 1848) (Budapest, 1948), 59. See also, Tibor Toth, *A mernyei uradalom a feudalis rend utolso szakaszaban* (The Estate of Mernye during the Last Phase of Feudalism) (Budapest, 1978), 92-3.
17. Istvan Barta, "A kormany parasztpolitikaja 1849-ben," (The Peasant Policy of the Government in 1849) *Szazadok* 89 (1955), No. 6, 857. See also, Fur, *op. cit.,* 58.
18. Barta, *op. cit.,* 858.
19. Ember, *op. cit.,* 31.
20. *Ibid.,* 61.
21. Spira, *op. cit.,* 126-36.
22. Urban, *op. cit., 263-8.*

23. *"Many contemporary accounts and reminiscences," writes Macartney, "testify to the widespread indifference to, or ignorance of, the national cause shown by the peasants,* *op. cit.,* 387. Handlery, *op. cit.,* 57, also cites peasant passivity. Gyorgy Spira in *op. cit.,* 141, makes the surprising statement that thousands of poor peasants joined Kossuth's army just to settle acocunts with the nobles after the war, while Barta, in *Szazadok* 90 (1956) Nos. 1-2, 30, hints that pecuniary considerations were not foreign to the new recruits.
24. Barta, *Szazadok* (1955), *op. cit.,* 872.
25. Gunther E. Rothenberg, *The Army of Francis Joseph* (West Lafayette, In., 1976), 32.
26. Barta, *op. cit.,* (1955), 849. Also, Molnar, *op. cit.,* 514.
27. Barta, *ibid.*
28. Molnar, *op. cit.,* 521-3.
29. Barta, *op. cit.,* (1955), 866.
30. *Kossuth Lajos 1848-49 ben, vol. 5, Kossuth Lajos Kormanyzoelnok iratai, 1848 aprillis 15-augusztus 15* (L. Kossuth in 1848. The Papers of Governor L. Kossuth, Apr. 15-Aug. 15, 1849) edited by Istvan Barta (Budapest, 1955), 602-6. See also, Gyorgy Gracza, *Az 1848-49-iki magyar szabadsagharc tortenete* (History of the Hungarian Fight for Freedom in 1848-49) (Budapest, n.d.), 461-8, and Peter Hidas, "the Russian Army in Hungary, 1849," J. G. Purvis and D. A. West, eds., *War and Society in the Nineteenth Century Russian Empire* (Toronto, 1969), 67-79.
31. Lajos Steier, *Hajnau es Paskievics* (Hajnau and Paskievics) (Budapest, 1928), 83.
32. Spira, *op. cit.,* 557; Molnar, *op. cit.,* 540.
33. *Gyujtemenyet a Magyarorszag szamara kibocsatott legfelsobb Manifestumok es Szozatoknak, valamint a cs. kir, hadsereg foparancsnokai altal Magyarorszagban kiadott hirdetmenyeknek* (Collection of Manifestos Issued by the Highest Authority and Proclamations for Hungary, and Declarations of the Imperial and Royal High Commanders in Hungary) (Buda, 1849), 19.

34. Ibid., 113 FF. Also, *Az ausztriai birodalmat illeto birodalmi torveny es kormanylap* (The Austrian Empire's Law-and Government-Journal) (Vienna, 1849), 110 FF., and (1850), 1694 FF.
35. Spira, *op. cit.*, 550, and Barta, *op. cit.*, (1956), 41.
36. Magyar Orszagos Leveltar, *Az Abszolutizmuskori Leveltar, "Szentivanyi Vince Pesti ker. fobiztos,"* (Hungarian National Archives, Archive of the Age of Absolutism, Vince Szentivanyi, Commissioner of the District of Pest) D 77/1848/4238.

PART II

THE AGE OF PREPARATION: HUNGARIAN AGRARIAN CONDITIONS BETWEEN 1848-1914

Antal Voros
Translation by Joseph Held

SURVIVAL OF TRADITIONAL PRODUCTION METHODS AND WAYS OF LIFE 1850-1867

1. The Balance Sheet of the Emancipation of Serfs in 1848

The "Spring of Peoples" in 1848 made short shrift of the Hungarian feudal system. The storm of European revolutions reached the Habsburg Empire and its component, the Hungarian state, as well. The Hungarian Diet, meeting in Pozsony (Bratislava) had been debating the possibility of lightening the feudal obligations of serfs since 1847. At first, it seemed that even the mildest reform efforts by the liberal-minded segment of the nobility would be thwarted by a combination of the conservatives and Viennese court. But the revolutions in Pest and Vienna in March encouraged the liberals to increase their pressure and the frightened conservatives and the court—both scared by the spectre of the spread of popular movements—felt compelled to concede to their demands. The results were better than even the wildest hopes of the liberals. Within a few short weeks after March 15, the legislature introduced a new governmental system based on popular representation, a responsible Hungarian ministry, laws for general taxation, and declared the immediate abolition of serfdom.

The emancipation laws decreed that serfs using urbarial lands—as these were defined in the legislation of Maria Theresa in 1767—no longer owed obligations to the lords and the church. These obligations were substantial: they included on an average 104 days of manual labor or 52 days of *robot* (corve) with horses and a wagon per serf lot per year, the *nona pars* or the ninth of the harvest due to the landlords, and the tithe to be paid to the church. The serfs were also obliged to pay a one florin *census* a year per family, and had other smaller obligations as well.[1] Now the urbarial serfs who, only a day or two before, were compelled by law to perform these services, became, at a stroke of the legislature's pen, the owners of the land which they used. On the other hand, peasants who worked on non-urbarial lands (mostly manorial properties) that did not come under the emancipation laws, were to continue paying their obligations as required by their agreements with the landlords.

What did in fact the emancipation mean in terms of statistics? According to relatively accurate statistical sources, there existed 1,366,749 peasant families in Hungary and Transylvania who, before the emancipation, lived in partial or full dependence on their use of urbarial lands. These peasants all became free by the laws of emancipation. Of them, 568,673 families (divided between 539,753 families using serf-lots and 29,920 families of landless peasants, *zsellerek*) or 43.7% of all peasants, became owners of the land used by them. Of the 798,076 families of landless peasants, about 100,000 families experienced little change in their economic conditions. The other 600,000 families lived in houses and used small parcels of land (*belsoseg*) that now became their own property. On the other hand, the 100,000 families mentioned above, had neither houses nor gardens of their own. The subsequent subdivision of common grazing and forest lands between peasants and landlords provided the 600,000 families with one-eight sections of grazing or forest lands each (between 6.4-30.8 acres of grazing, and 2.8-11.2 acres of forest lands respectively), available for some sort of agricultural activity.

Even before emancipation, 365,400 acres of grazing and forest lands from the commons came into peasant hands through private arrangements. Now the emancipation laws provided the peasants with 14,351,400 acres. At the same time, the peasants were freed of a total of 11,717,000 days of obligatory *robot* with horses and 12,373,000 days of manual labor, not to mention the still unknown amount of the crops that were included in the ninth of the harvest and the tithe and other obligations.

We cannot evaluate the results of the emancipation of serfs in Transylvania, (legislated in June, 1848, with provisions that were similar to those passed in Hungary). The urbarial obligations of serfs had not been regulated in that province as they had been in Hungary and, therefore, the size of urbarial lots and the amounts of peasant obligations varied almost by landlord and by village. However, contemporaries estimated the total amount of land coming into peasants hands through the emancipation laws as having been between 2,240,000-2,380,000 ares, including grazing lands.

We must also remember that compensation for the landlords' losses was to be undertaken by the state. Compensation, therefore, did not burden the peasantry alone, since the necessary funds were to be derived from general taxation to which everyone was to contribute.[2] This was a notable difference in comparison with the post-emancipation situation of the serfs in other countries where the peasants alone had to bear the burden of the landlord's losses.

2. The Illusions of a Generation and Reality

Before 1848, the liberal reform generation, struggling for the abolition of feudal institutions, lived under the illusion that the freeing of peasants from feudal burdens would bring about a sudden improvement in agricultural practices. They hoped that production methods of primitive self-sufficiency would be quickly transformed into a system based on individual peasant smallholders of a capitalist kind. A comparison with Western agricultural conditions, founded on free peasantries, helped to strengthen these beliefs. But the reformers usually failed to look very closely at the historical processes that influenced the development of West European peasant economies. They believed that only two motivating forces existed for furthering progress, namely, "freedom and property." As one of the reformers remarked, "there is a magic force in the idea of private property, a force that frightens away indolence, awakens all the slumbering powers of labor and sows the seeds of moral ennoblement."[3]

But the expected transformation actually proved to be a much slower process than the liberal reformers hope for. Although there were numerous reports after the first few months of the emancipation, suggesting a great upsurge in peasant initiative, later statements confirmed the fact that these reports were reflecting only a passing enthusiasm for the revolution. The experiences of the 1850's were soon to show that "freedom and private property" were insufficient forces by themselves to alter life styles and methods of production that were inherited from ancient times. The journals of the 1850's and 1860's, especially those dealing with economics on a professional level, contained continuous complaints about the peasants' continuing to work their lands the same way as they had done in the age of the *robot* and the ninth of the harvest (*dezsma*). They observed that peasants refused to earn extra money and spent their free time in a "frivolous manner." Such complaints came from all areas of the country. For instance, the reporter of the *Economic Journals* from Moson County in Western Hungary stated that:

> While we observe with satisfaction the advantages, namely, the emancipation from bondage, which our peasants now enjoy, we at the same time see that they are as yet unable fully to appreciate their new opportunities and increase their well-being. Emancipation, although considered by the peasants to be a treasure-chest, still cannot be opened by them on account of their mental blocks . . . .[4]

From Baranya county in southern Hungary a similar report was received:

> There seems to exist some sort of dull lethargy, a monotonous weight pressing upon the economic conditions of the entire population. When searching for the causes of this, we inadvertently stumble upon the fact that a people lacking leaders or well-wishers willing to take on leadership, has become incapable of extricating itself from its prvious stagnant status, unable to rise by itself to a level required by the times, even in the matter of economics . . . .[5]

In the Transylvanian county of Nagy-Kukullo, folklorist researchers discovered the words of a song half a century after emancipation by which the peasants summarized the significance of liberation this way:

> Thank God, we can now rest, We no longer have to do *robot; Dezsma, robot* are now lost, We can now be merry . . . .[6]

A former Rumanian serf from Arad County remembered that:

> We are happy to no end that the *robot* and the *dezsma* had been abolished . . . . We ate and drank . . . . at the expense of the 'skin of the fat bear' " . . . . Two years had passed in this manner when the chief judge came to complain that now we had to pay taxes . . . .[7]

A Bavarian economist, Heinrich Ditz, who was sent by his government to Hungary in the mid-1860's in order to study agriculture, reported similar impressions. Ditz travelled throughout the most important grain growing region of the country, the Great Plain, and he summarized his findings this way:

> A population that used to work only upon the command of its lord is often dizzied by freedom that it suddenly acquires, and often believes that freedom simply means that it does not have to serve another even for money.... The enjoyment of freedom, therefore, goes to its head as does wine. Thus, after the abolition of feudal relations, the peasants were reluctant to work any more for their former landlord, partly because of their desire for complete independence, partly out of irresponsibility. but a few acted this way for the reason that they wanted to pay more attention to their own properties.[8]

In spite of emancipation, the Hungarian peasant continued to work "according to ancient, extensive methods" (*more patrio*).[9] Ditz remarked further that he "hoped that his readers would not mistake his words to feel that he is a supporter of feudalism, or that he regards the freedom of labor and land as harmful." He only wanted to point out the unpleasant consequences of a transitional period, and his charges are probably not as serious so that they would warrant the renunciation of freedom that is behind this change.[10]

Mihaly Tancsics, who rose from serfdom to become a radical writer and was incarcerated in 1847 (only to be liberated by the March revolution), provided a criticism of the peasantry similar to that of Ditz. Tancsics was the most radical spokesman of peasant interests during the revolution, proposing the expropriation of estates over 1,420 acres in size in 1849. But he wrote a book in 1858 for the former serfs, entitled *Bordacs Elek a gyalog arendas* (Elek Bordacs, the Renter on Foot), advocating the use of advanced agricultural methods. Tancsics illustrated, through the life of his hero, the process by which a landless *zseller,* rented a significant parcel of land and in turn was able to buy the property in a few short years from income derived through rational organization of his production. Tancsics suggested to his fellow peasants that their advancement depended upon their willingness "to get things done, to do them diligently, to be able to be parsimonious, and being able not to throw money away on useless things and fads."[11]

Tancsics considered that the causes of irrationality in organizing agricultural production and in peasant life in general lay in the fact that the peasants became owners of their land "only yesterday," and "what are nine or ten years in the life of a people? Habits have become ingrained in thousands of years." He said; "How can such habits be discarded in a few years?"[12]

The authors of these sources, the utopian-radical Tancsics, the liberal Ditz, and the reporters of county newspapers realized that, although 1848 ended feudalism in Hungary, the past proved much too strong a force in peasant life. What sort of mental and moral conditions, what kind of world views dominated peasant thinking when they so suddenly entered the new bourgeois society?

The feudal system in Hungary—as in the other societies of East Central Europe—actually impeded the development of rational thinking among the peasants, or, as contemporaries were fond of saying, "it retarded the development of work-ethics." The liberal generation of the Age of Reforms faced this problem while struggling for the emancipation of the serfs. Its members often demonstrated the effects of the feudal system on the work-ethics and the diligence of the peasants. For instance, in 1843, the *Magyar Gazdasagi Egyesulet* (Hungarian Economic Association) offered a prize for competitive essays analyzing the problem of the ways the *robot* and *dezsma* retarded the development of agriculture in general, and the rational production methods of the serfs in particular. Three winning essays were published in 1845 under the common title *Robot es dezsma erkolcsi es anyagi, mezo-es statusgazdasagi tekintetbe* (Robot and Dezsma from the Points of View of Ethics, Material Status, Agriculture, and General Conditions).[13] I am going to quote a few short lines from this work below, since the authors provided excellent summaries and explanations of the mental and moral conditions characterizing Hungarian peasants under the feudal system.

First of all, the authors had suggested that the damages caused by the urbarial system were partly mental and partly economic. They contended that the serfs were forced into "a perpetual mental childhood" by the system, since they were not permitted to develop independent initiatives, the basis of the material improvement of their conditions. To the question as to why this happened, one of the authors replied:

> The serf was constantly working for the lord, or trying to fulfill his obligations to the county and others. Thus, he was not in control of his own time; since he was unable to start anything on his own initiative, and since he was constantly interrupted in whatever he was doing, he became accustomed to following orders without which he would not lift a finger . . . . This is the explanation for his somberness, his abhorrence of innovations, behind the latter of which he always suspects efforts to harm him . . . . but the major damage was caused to his ethical and moral standards; one finds laziness in first place among his faults. Diligence is usually awakened in man by the expectation of gain; since the work of the peasant is badly paid and since he cannot go far even at the price of his sweat and blood, he becomes fond of just doing nothing . . . . to all this one must add the tremendous corruption that accompanies the collection of the *dezsma*. One should not be surprised, therefore, that the *robot* kills all mental powers, diminishing the capacity of men who were born free, depriving them of self-respect, and initiative. It corrupts their morals, throws them at the mercy

> of base-spirited supervisors and steals their best time of life away. We must insist that the *robot* does even more damage to the serf's spirit and his morals than it does to his material well-being.[14]

Besides the *robot,* the ninth of the harvest (*dezsma*) was the most significant of the feudal burdens carried by the peasants. "It would be difficult to decide," argued the authors of the above quoted work, "if they would rank the material or mental effects of the *dezsma* as more serious:"

> The merciless nature of the *dezsma* system is shown in that it is a burden not so much on the land, as it hinders the diligence of the peasants which, being a beneficial force, would be a duty of all to preserve. The collectors of the *dezsma* do not consider which part of the harvest was provided by the labor and diligence of the agriculturist, and which was given by capital . . . . they do not consider what is rightful and what is not. The *dezsma* creates another evil for agriculture; the peasant who can figure things out for himself does not even want to consider investment (in his land) . . . . We can safely assert that as long as the *dezsma* system exists in our country, it is not in the interest of the peasant to spend time and effort in improving his land, because the *dezsma* takes away the larger part of his net income. Instead of providing an incentive for the agriculturist to improve his land, it actually punishes him if he does so.[15]

Equally serious were the moral damages caused by the *dezsma* system:

> When the serf gives up the ninth or the tenth of his harvest to his lord, if he were diligent, he undoubtedly is cheating himself, and if he were lazy, he cheats the landlord. In the first case, he gives up the fruits of his diligence which his lord does not own; in the second, the lord does not receive

> that which he could expect.... Under such conditions it is not possible for the serf not to be lazy. It follows that in countries where similar systems exist, the land is left in a poor condition at the expense of the national economy.... Avoiding any more exertion than it is customary, the serf entrusts everything to nature. The *dezsma* keeps the mind of the peasant in an eternal state of stagnation; guiding him away from the path of rational methods in agriculture, it forces him to remain in his accustomed ways ....[16]

These were the reflections of the members of the liberal reform generation. It is possible that the liberals, serving a noble cause, painted a somewhat darker picture here and there, than was warranted by real-life conditions. But the interrelations that they discovered did bring us to a better understanding of the complaints about the behavior of the peasantry during the 1850's and 1860's. They provided a plausible explanation for the complaints and charges concerning the laziness and indolence of the former serfs who, even if the labor demands of their properties would have permitted it, would not go to work for their former landlords even for money. In the peasants' mind there was an entirely different conception underlying the idea of working for others than that of free workers in a bourgeois society. There were, for them, the memories of humiliations and servitude that were parts of his concept; the remembrance of times when the supervisors of the lords stood behind them with a stave in hand, prodding them to work.

Perhaps time, the Great Healer, had the greatest effect on these problems; sources from the 1870's no longer contain similar complaints about peasant behavior. Material incentives proved to be a stronger force by then, than past memories of humiliation. But what was involved here was the fact that even working for the former landlords did not alter the life style of the peasants, a style which was lived according to ancient unwritten laws by the people of former serf villages.

3. Traditional Agriculture

What we said about the system of *robot* and *dezsma* above tends to explain the fact that, before 1848, serf-peasant methods of production did not progress beyond the three-field system. This was the method used in most areas of the country. Deviation from the method on a larger scale existed only in Transylvania, where an even simpler method, the two-field system, was followed. The peasants refused to alter the essential elements of these systems during the agricultural boom following the Napoleonic wars even in areas nears towns and cities where the nearby markets could have logically caused such a change.[17]

The three-field system was enforced by the village authorities: every peasant was required to plant autumn wheat in one part of the field, spring grains in another. The time for planting and harvesting was also determined by the authorities before 1848; in areas where the lands of the lord and the peasants were intermingled, the time of work in the fields was determined by the former. Furthermore, the dates on which various tasks were to be undertaken were also influenced by ancient customs, including the "right time" to graze cattle on harvested lands. This was required by the fact that by the time harvest came around, the common grazing lands were usually bare of any vegetation, and the quickly growing stubble provided food for the animals.[18]

The major problem with the three-field system was not only in that it excluded one-third of the lands from production each year, but that it was geared exclusively to the production of grain crops. Because of various periods of growth, the system did not leave room for fodder and root crops. These were, therefore, grown mainly in small parcels near the gardens, and they were not included in the compulsory rotation of the three-field system. Although the Viennese authorities decreed several times during the 19th century that no *dezsma* could be collected by the lords from crops grown on formerly fallow lands, these decrees seldom resulted in the changing of "black fallows" into "green" through the planting of root crops and fodder. There was no change since a break with the three-field system would have required a complete transformation of the methods of production.

In fact, there was a close interrelation between the production of grains and the methods of animal husbandry. Fallow lands were necessary not so much in order to secure grazing lands but to permit the regeneration of the land through rest. If they were to plant in the fallow lands, the peasants would have had to provide fertilizers for them sooner or later. This was practically impossible under the given practices of animal husbandry.

Hungarian animal husbandry emphasized cattle raising. Data from 1842 show that of all animals cattle amounted to 49.5%; the ratio of horses was 12.4%, that of hogs 20.6% and of sheep 17.5%.[19] Sheep raising was done mostly by the landlords, while hogs were raised largely by the peasants.

East of the Danube River and on the Great Plain, cattle raisers still followed semi-nomadic methods. The village herder drove the cattle into the grazing grounds in early spring, and brought them back after the first snow. Similar methods were followed in the mountainous areas. Special grazing grounds were provided near the villages for the draft animals (*okortilos*) that could be reached quickly when the animals were needed. West of the Danube, these practices no longer existed. Here the herder drove the cattle into the fields every morning and brought them back at dusk. No matter how poor the grazing lands had been, however, no extra fodder was provided for the animals during the grazing season in either area. Only on a narrow strip of the Western part of the country near the Austrian border, did cattle receive fodder at night after their return from grazing. In areas where oak forests existed, hogs were fattened on acorns during late summer, and only about a month before slaughter were they brought into the village and fed grains and corn to eliminate the bitter taste of their lard.[20]

These methods of animal husbandry had one tremendous advantage, namely, they required minimal costs, since fodder was needed only during the winter. Their major disadvantage was that they produced very little fertilizer. This was especially evident in areas east of the Danube River. Since the given methods of animal husbandry provided little natural fertilizers, the peasants had no choice but to leave one-third of the lands fallow each year.

The circle was, therefore, complete. This was a closed system whose links could not be separately improved. The actual choice was between the complete abandonment of the system or its maintenance as a whole. That the serfs did not choose the first alternative was, in our opinion, entirely understandable.

Since 1848 lifted the burden of feudal obligations from athe peasants, eliminating the obstacles to diligence and initiative, improvements could soon be expected. But it took three decades before the existing system began to fall apart. Not even the tremendous increase of demand in grains that followed the revolutionary era in Europe could effect immediate changes.[21]

Agricultural experts believed in the early 1850's that the peasantry's continuing adherence to traditional methods was the result of the fact that their holdings were in small strips scattered throughout their villages' lands and that this could be changed only by consolidation. (In the three-field system each peasant holding had to be divided into three parts, located in various areas of the village's lands.) It was usual to have even the grazing lands divided into several small parcels; the practice was justified by the argument that the peasants had to share equally from good as well as poor lands.

The Patent of 1853, issued by the absolutist government in Vienna, ordered the partitioning and distribution of grazing and forest lands between the lords and the peasantry. The process was permitted to run parallel with the consolidation of peasant properties, if requested by the landlord or the majority of the peasants in question. But hopes for improvements in methods of agriculture were not fulfilled even through this process. The peasants insisted everywhere that the new lands be distributed in three parts. They justified their demand by various arguments in different localities, including some that were based on the fertility of the lands or on the problems caused by possible natural catastrophes. The latter argument was indeed valid, since hail storms and other catastrophes were known to effect only part of the lands at one time. But the major reason was in each case the insistence on the continuity of traditional methods of agriculture. These methods brought prosperity for the peasants as a result of the growing demands for grain.[22] When it was suggested that they obtain insurance against fire and hail storms, their answer was that "such catastrophes were God's punishment against which it would be foolish to buy insurance."[23] Thus, the free possession of private property and the influence of the agricultural boom were insufficient by themselves to bring about fundamental changes in the traditional methods of peasant production.

4. Traditional Life Style and Mentality

We tried to show above that the method used by the peasants in working their lands when society entered its bourgeois phase was a logical, closed system which could not be improved piecemeal. The peasantry formed and transmitted its knowledge and experience in this system; its entire life style conformed to it; its customs and habits as well as the division of labor within the family were part and parcel of this system. Each phase of peasant production was also regulated by superstitions rooted in ancient traditions, or was performed according to the perceived meaning of natural phenomena such as the turning of the new moon, or a full moon, sunrise or sunset.[24] In fact, the peasants had no opportunity to acquire better expertise in agriculture even if they wanted to.[25] Neither were their former landlords providing a better practical examplem, since the methods used by the former were on an even more primitive keel during the 1850's and 1860's. A great deal of the landlords' properties were actually rented to peasants; former serfs who were unwilling to work for their lord for wages, were quite ready and willing to rent his properties.[26]

The three-field system had its own comfortable rhythm of work. After the completion of the spring sowing, the planting of a few root crops required some work. But this was followed by many days of idleness until the time for the first hoeing arrived. In early summer, haymaking was followed by the sweaty days of the harvest of grains. A second hoeing of the root crops or the cutting of hay demanded some more labor from peasant families. After that came the autumn harvest, and some more ploughing and planting. Then came winter rest during which the peasant only had to feed his animals twice a day, including the cattle driven in from the grazing fields. This cycle provided an ample number of work-free days for the peasants. A few additional days were required for tending the vineyards—pruning, hoeing, tying and harvesting the grapes—in areas where soil and climatic conditions provided room for grape growing.

This cycle was called by the people "turning," (*fordulis*) and the work required by it could easily be performed through a work-rhythm to which they had become accustomed during the feudal age. The rhythm was aptly described by a folklorist of Gocsey in Zala County, when he reviewed the period of the 1850's and 1860's:

> The small areas cultivated by the people were not tilled properly .... Their cattle were in the grazing grounds from early spring to the first snowfall; thus, the owners had little fertilizers for their land and even when they did have some—not knowing its real value—it remained largely unused. When the time for ploughing arrived, the owner picked up the yoke for the oxen, walked out to the meadow to take his animals out of the herd, caught them with some difficulty, and returned them to the herd after his work was done. The people of Gocsey were lazy and indolent during this time. They were reluctant to work. There was little appreciation of the value of labor among them. Their daily preparation for work took such a long time that they actually spent only five hours working ....[27]

The division of labor within the peasant family reflected this comfortable work rhythm. The specific tasks demanded from various family members were defined by age and sex, and regulated by the requirements of the fields and notions of self-sufficiency.[28] Contemporary sources unanimously assert that women contributed very little to field work. They worked in the fields only during the harvest and haymaking, especially if the two tasks coincided in time because of unusual weather conditions. The situation of young men was similar. Sources from many areas of the country pointed out that 20-year olds did not yet know how to use a scythe. Their first participation in ploughing, planting and harvesting the crops tended to have the character of initiation into manhood.[29] There was some retrogression in this sense in comparison with pre-emancipation times. At that time, 16-year old boys were liable for service to the lords. They also had to begin paying taxes at the age of 16. In fact, it was general practice to send teenagers to perform a family's fuedal obligations to the lord. After 1848, therefore, the labor of these young men went unused.[30]

Women's working hours were spent mostly in and around the house. However, their tasks demanded a great deal more work than those of the peasant households of our times or even of the 1930's. First of all, the clothing of the family was mostly homemade. Only specific pieces of a man's suit or a woman's dress, such as the richly decorated sheepskin jackets (*cifra szur*) or the heavy fur coats of the men (*bunda*) and the shoes of both sexes were craftsmen-made. The raw materials for everyday clothes, bedsheets, and table cloths used on specific occasions—such as baptisms or weddings—were usually manufactured at home by the womenfolk. The production and preparation of hemp and flax for these goods were women's work and required a great deal of time. In some areas of the country, especially in Transylvania, emphasis was on the weaving of wool. The value of a peasant women was judged throughout Hungary by her skills not only in cooking, but also in spinning and weaving. The growing well-being of the peasants that stemmed from the increasing Western demand for agricultural goods was soon reflected in their dressing habits.

Folk-dresses were poorly made and had few decorations before 1848. The flowering of folk-art in clothing began only after emancipation; the people then introduced rich variations and colors into their many-layered dresses that varied in their patterns in every region of the country. This was the folk-art that was so much admired by the folklorists at the end of the century, by then a disappearing art. Although the basic materials for women's dresses—linen, chiffon, cotton, velvet and silk—were increasingly factory-produced, the preparation of patterns used on scarves, blouses, skirts and petticoats, their drafting and the actual embroidering, demanded months of patient labor. Similar care was needed for the making of bedsheets, pillow cases and table cloths.[31] A girl who finished elementary school had hardly any other task until her wedding than the preparation of these articles for her trousseau.

We admire the surviving pieces of folk-dresses in museums and other collections today as a manifestation of the people's artistic talents. But the historian must note that the time required for their creation was way out of line with requirements of bourgeois progress. These dresses, as well as the decorations used in beautifying the peasant homes, were not functional, and the beds of the "clean room" with their towering loads of pillows and down-filled covers expressed more the vain pride of a peasant family than its realistic needs.

According to custom, the basic material and number of holiday dresses or suits that a peasant possessed expressed both his wealth and social position in the village. Those who did not dress appropriately became the center of gossip. The outward manifestations of life were regulated by customs, paralleling the regulations imposed on people working the fields, regardless of the requirements of bourgeois developments in society. But while the peasant dressed in richly decorated costumes that required a great deal of time to produce, their houses were often made of adobe with windows the size of a fist, usually permanently closed. The contrast was an illustration of the vanity of peasants that was coupled with primitive modesty.

There existed similar irrational contrasts in almost every area of peasant life. Often the beginning, and always the conclusion, of major phases of work in the fields—the harvest of grains or of grapes—gave reason for gaudy celebration. Days before these holidays, the women began to cook and prepare food, and to air out the proper clothing.[32] Family celebrations, such as baptisms or weddings, became expressions of senseless vanity—of boasting of the family's wealth. The length of a wedding (usually lasting from a Tuesday or a Wednesday to the end of a respective week) and the number of guests invited both demonstrated the wealth of a family. Custom turned the preparation for a wedding into a rigid ritual, beginning with the asking of a girl's hand in marriage, to the invitation of guests, to the actual ceremony. Everyone concerned was obliged to show off one's wealth and ability. For such a wedding, hogs were slaughtered, lambs, calves and chickens were put to the knife, and wines and liquers flowed freely.[33] The expenses involved in the wedding, to which often an entire village was invited, usually destroyed the financial balance of a peasant family for years to come. But this was usually a well-kept secret in the village. Customs, the unwritten laws of peasant communities, were stronger than a sensible approach to these issues.

Folklorists have uncovered the rich material manifestations of this peasant world, but they usually described only the surface appearances. They were reluctant to explore the deeper relations of peasant life with the age in which this culture emerged. But others did discover the problems below the glittering surface and were not reluctant to voice their criticism of the frivolous side of peasant life. For instance, Tancsics did not hesitate to admonish "peasants like himself" for their propensity to spend their funds on "gaudy nonsense" and on "useless knick-knacks," to scold them for following fads that often led to financial ruin. "Disasters or natural catastrophes can affect anybody," he stated, "and at such times the one who is in trouble should ask for help. But," he observed:

> people often get into difficult situations not because of natural disasters, but on account of their recklessness, and then they have to borrow money. It is true, on the other hand, that recklessness is an unfortunate trait in itself. Many people, when they are not pressed by want, do not consider the fact that 'there are more days than sausages,' and they eat and make merry as long as the good days last . . . .[34]

Ditz explained the absence of parsimony among the peasants by two historical causes. Since, for a long time, the peasants had no opportunity (or need) to invest in their properties, they became accustomed to spending their funds in an easy manner. At the same time, since there was no export market for Hungary's agricultural goods, "these goods were worth only as much as they could be used by the producers themselves." Although the real value of such goods is now being recognized, "customs prove to be more enduring than the market price of goods, and although parsimoniousness is twice as important today as before, the ingrained habits (of the people) have a greater force . . . ."[35]

Descriptions of peasant life in this period usually provide a contradictory picture. Vanity and boasting of one's wealth was paralleled by everyday drabness; reckless spending and the destitution were two sides of the same coin. The notion that "time is money" had not yet been recognized by the peasants. They simply did not know how to budget their time, just as they had no notion of the significance of saving money, or of the value of rational organization of their methods of work. Observers are almost unanimous in reporting from every area of the country and about every peasant stratum that when a peasant was sure that the survival of his family was secure for a given year, he would not work any more. According to Karoly Galgoczy, an agricultural report:

> The Hungarian peasant became accustomed to the notion that he would work only as much as was absolutely necessary for his survival. But we are not speaking here

> of the characteristics of a single ethnic group, since Slovak, Serbian and Rumanian peasants living in Hungary acted in a similar manner.[36]

A common consequence of the lack of interest in work was that available labor depended upon the changing amount of grain crops. The sources paint a similar picture about attitudes before and after 1848. "It is typical of the agricultural daily wage-earners of this area," reported an observer from Debrecen, "that when the harvest is bountiful . . . they do not work as much as when the crops are poor. After all, they have their bread (at such times)."[37]

Such complaints are especially frequent in the year 1869, since at that time the "blessings of heaven" (as the peasants called the harvest) were especially good two years in a row. Not only were dwarf-holders who otherwise had to work for daily wages to supplement their income so described, but so were wealthier members of the peasantry.[38] The statistician Karoly Keleti wrote about the peasants of the Great Plain that they usually harvested their crops with their families in a bad year. But if the crops were good, "they hired sharecroppers whom they not only paid very well, but wined and dined with good food and plenty of alcohol."[39]

A reporter describing the environs of the city of Gyor stated that at the time of the harvest of grains, especially if there was a good crop, even small landholders "who could complete th harvest and other work by the use of family labor . . . hire special sharecroppers and other workers."[40] The peasants were unable to break out of such attitudes even when they experienced bad years: two decades following 1848, have brought little change in this. Karoly Keleti, quoted above, followed up his description of the life of smallholders in the Great Plain this way:

> When the harvest is completed and the second hoeing of the corn is done—which is often neglected—the autumn grains are planted in land that is superficially scratched.

> Then, he can start his winter indolence. This is interrupted only by feeding the cattle and sheep, when heavy snow drives these animals from the grazing grounds. I am saying "heavy snow" because otherwise the animals are staying outside even during the Christmas week, grazing on the tobacco stubbles, and the peasant worriedly shakes his head when the animals have to be brought in before New Year's Day for he has so little fodder for them .... He is enticed to go out to his lands only by the singing of the lark when he does ploughing and planting, and when these tasks are finished in a couple of weeks, his work consists of a little hay-making and corn planting until harvest time arrives. On the other side of the Danube River, the life of a smallholder peasant is not much different, except he may pick up the ax during wintertime .... But he does this only in order to secure his firewood, otherwise he is not interested in working for wages. On the other hand, if he had a good year, no matter how good the wages the larger landowner offers him, he will not care even if all the firewood rots in the forest. He will not have his animals tire out by shipping wood ....[41]

Centuries-old habits and customs were, thus, stifling initiative and diligence among the peasantry of Hungary.

Unwritten laws regulating everyday life in the villages were closely tied to the financial standing and social status of the peasants. The stratification of the former serfs, in a sense, paralleled that of the nobility. The nobles were stratified into the artistocracy, the common nobles and the "nobles with seven plum trees," the latter possessing practically no land at all. In turn, Karoly Keleti complained of the "surprising spirit of castes" characteristic of the peasantry all over the country. This spirit dictated that "the owner of a half-plot look down upon the landless peasant; and the owner of six oxen is a big man in the village to whom even the judge would not talk with his hat on his head."[42]

The former serfs carried the burdens of their memories; this was especially reinforced by the contempt by which the ruling classes treated the peasantry, whose very name, "peasant," had a derogatory connotation. In turn, the consciousness of a common fate among the peasantry found expression in attitudes towards the "better ones." The lawsuits that followed the partitioning by forest and grazing lands unified the peasants in opposing the lords, but these came to an end by the 1860's. The final boundaries between peasant and lordly lands having been established, the time was ripe for the peasantry to embark on its own independent way of life.

In the new situation memories of the past slowly began to fade. There emerged the consciousness that peasants who possessed more land than others could not be the equal of those who had less. Thus, the decisive factor in determining peasant status increasingly became the amount of land possessed; this, in turn, depended upon the amount of land with which the emancipated peasants entered the new era. But memories faded slowly; even at the turn of the century the size of lands was still measured by the old serf-lots, whether they were full, half, or quarter-lots. Customs also dictated the forms of social intercourse based on individual wealth alone; almost like Spanish etiquette, the rank of a village peasant in his community determined the way he was greeted by others or the way his betters or inferiors addressed him. Village customs rigidly prescribed not only the type of holiday dress or suit a peasant should wear if he were the owner of a "full lot," but also the place of his seat in the pews of the church, the way he should pay homage to others, etc. It did not behoove the son of a landless peasant to prove stronger in the customary wrestling competitions between young people than the son of the owner of a "full lot." If this did happen, village gossip immediately began about the young man: "what does this beggar's son want?" In other words, those who "received more from God" were expected to be superior in every facet of life to those who received less.

The caste-spirit would not permit the breaking of customs in the villages. It tolerated only stereotypes and inspired the rejection of individuals who aspired to a better life, to a more advanced existence. Competition could exist only among equals. The knowledge or diligence of an individual was not considered as a basis for the measure of his worth. Under the existing conditions of agricultural methods, there was little opportunity indeed for such attitudes to become dominant in the countryside. On the other hand, there is plenty of evidence to show that the individual peasant who tried to break out of the stifling hold of these customs by his diligence, by more conscientious work, was hindered in his efforts at every turn.[43] The most common methods of maintaining inherited status among equals was the marriage of their children to each other, and in some areas of the country, methods of birth control that permitted the birth of only one child per family.

5. The Shady Sides of Development

Despite the negative aspects of this balance sheet, the impact of emancipation and the following agricultural boom was formidable. Favorable prices paid for grain encouraged the peasants to produce higher volumes of crops. They began to break up lands that came into their hands after the partitioning of the grazing and forested areas. Added to these were the drained lands which they acquired after the regulation of the larger rivers. Ditz aptly pointed out that despite the long, depressing period that followed emancipation, "if Hungary occupies a different position in feeding the rest of Europe today then before 1848, this can largely be attributed to the liberation of land and working hands."[44] This assertion seems to have been proven by the land surveys of the time. According to one of these taken during the first years of the period (as a basis for the planned new land tax), the area of Hungary's ploughlands—including Croatia and Slavonia—consisted of 23,521,158 acres; in 1867, this number rose to 25,724,440 acres.[45] The increase amounted to 2,203,282 acres, or 9.4% of the entire area.

This meant that increased production volumes came from the

expansion of the area of ploughlands. However, the expansion came at the expense of the better grazing grounds, further restricting the bases of animal husbandry. We must remember that the knowledge that the maintenance of steady production volumes demanded a parallel development in animal husbandry was quite widespread by that time. but contemporary censuses show that the number of animals remained relatively stable in this period, perhaps there was even a slight decline in their numbers. Compared to the growth in the size of the ploughlands, this meant a serious upsetting of the balance.[46]

The agricultural journal, *Gazdasagi Lapok* (beginning its publication in the 1850's) wore a motto alongside its title: "Let us bring a correct balance into our agriculture!" But this admonition did not help much, since every monetary interest, including the agriculture boom and the abolition of custom barriers between Austria and Hungary in 1850, encouraged increased production of grains. We can add—as we have triedto show previously—that such increases in grain production were possible because they fitted into the traditional methods of production of the peasants quite well; they did not need new methods or large investments in capital and labor. The boom came at such a propitious time (or, perhaps, at such an unfortunate moment) that the entry of the peasantry into the system of large-scale production did not induce a break with traditional life-styles.

But the disadvantages of traditional methods began to come to the fore more and more frequently. A characteristic factor of monocultural production is a lop-sided exploitation of the lands. The replenishment of the land became, therefore, an extremely important factor in this period. The problem was especially acute in the central regions of the country where grain production assumed the largest proportions. In Csanad County, for instance, 77% of all ploughlands were planted with wheat; in Bekes County 66%, in Csongrad 58%, and in Torontal 54%.[47] Therefore, taking into consideration the continuing survival of the three-field system, wheat was often planted in the same lands in consecutive years. Since these regions also lacked forest and, thus, firewood, the peasants used dried manure as fuel.[48] Since the soil was not treated correctly in any case (even the plough only scratched the surface), the results depended not so much on peasant labor as on the vagaries of climate. The extreme variations of climate in the Great Plain often resulted in drought from the month of May until the harvest. This destroyed the hopes of many producers. (The 50-year average rainfall in this territory was between 550-580 millimeters per year, or 22-23.2 inches.)[49]

Average crop yields, therefore, widely varied. Ditz collected a great deal of material illustrating these averages in the 1850's and the first years of the 1860's. According to his notes, the average yield of one *hold* (1.42 acres) in autumn wheat ranged between 4.8 and 22.3 *mero*,[50] which meant that at the lower amount it did not even return twice the weight planted.[51] These averages were actually not much better than those recorded in the late 1820's and early 1830's. Nature and the changes in climate do influence the size of crops everywhere, but with intensive production methods and a considerable investment of capital and labor, the producer can mitigate the effect of these factors. This was obviously not the case in Hungarian agriculture during this period.

In fact, the Hungarian peasant regarded nature as being regulated by God; it was easier for him to ask for God's blessing than to work harder to deserve it. The peasant of the Great Plain excused his own negligence and his refusal to plough his land deeper and more than once a year by the argument that if drought came, his work would have been wasted anyway. "Wherever nature is obliged to work alone, and the agriculturist wants to play only the role of an observer and then harvest the results," noted Ditz, "he should not complain about the fickleness of nature."[52]

The expansion of production through extensive methods only strengthened peasant beliefs that the basis of their well-being and advancement in life was not intensive production and more diligence, but the possession of large tracts of land. The lucky peasant who was able to save some money and was emboldened in his expectations by a few years of good harvest, invested his money in land — if available— but he did not invest anything in improved production methods.[53] He did not listen to the advice of agricultural experts; "grab little, but hold on to it fast; do not multiply (your holdings), but work more diligently!"

The extreme fluctuations in the volume of yields caused similar changes in prices. This, in turn, had an impact on the exporters, since they could never be sure that they were to be able to buy what they needed at a steady price. According to data derived from the Grain Exchange in Budapest, it was common for prices to vary by 50% from year to year, despite the fact that even more extreme fluctuations were somewhat mitigated there. In fact, price variations were much greater in the countryside.[54]

Before 1848, the Hungarian grain trade was insignificant. Because of bad roads, grain commerce had to rely upon water for transportation, using especially the river road of the Danube. Demand for grains was significant only along the transportation routes. In areas distant from major trade arteries, the peasants usually kept their harvest in their atticks or in underground storage after a good year. If harvest was bad, most peasants had enough grain left from previous years to save them from starvation, and some of the wealthier ones could even lend some to their less fortunate fellows. However, in the 1850's, there developed a stratum and network of merchants encompassing the entire country, providing opportunities for the peasants to trade. They were instrumental in connecting the peasants who continued to think and produce in traditional ways with the developing capitalist markets.

In 1853, the *Pesti Gabona Csarnok* (Grain Market of Pest) was established, fulfilling the role of an exchange and, in 1864, it was turned into a full-fledged stock- and commmodity exchange. Customary rights that had developed in the grain trade were now incorporated into the rules of this exchange, eventually to be adopted in the grain trade in all areas of the country.[55]

The emergence of the new commercial network increased the peasants' chances to sell their produce, but it also increased opportunities for indebtedness. Most grain trade in the countryside was in the hands of Jewish traders who, during the feudal age, were forced into commercial activities by the laws that excluded them from crafts and other occupations. As renters of innkeeping rights (owned by the lords), grocers, and travelling salesmen, they provided the needed goods for the villages before 1848.[56] Mihaly Tancsics praised their diligence, parsimoniousness and foresight in a short book written in 1830 and published in Kolozsvar (it was eventually confiscated by the authorities). He offered them to the peasants as examples to emulate, in contrast to the frivolousness of the nobility.[57]

In the 1850's, the attention of merchants turned towards the grain trade. They used their usually small capital to buy and market the increasing volume of grains that became available. This was a risky business because of the price fluctuations. By the mid-1850's, voices were being raised against these Jewish merchants, accusing them of unscrupulous and usurious practices that were allegedly ruining the peasantry. Articles were published in various journals and these were not free of covert or even overt anti-Semitism. A journalist of *Gazdasagi Lapok* (Economic Journals) reporting on the backward methods of peasants in Somogy County in 1854, remarked that those who could afford it would even sell their manure instead of spreading it on their lands. He concluded his report by saying that he could name entire villages where at least one-sixth of all inhabitants were deeply in debt to the local Jewish innkeeper. In his follow-up report dated February 1855, he stated that because of the bad harvest in the previous year, many former serfs had no bread left.[58]

We could cite similar reports from almost every area of the country. Historical literature dealing with usury usually explained this phenomenon as the consequence of the lack of capital and the generally backward nature of village finances. We may add that usurers could be found not only among the Jewish merchants but among all social groups. But, because of their occupational experience, Jews were represented among the usurers by a higher proportional percentage.

In examining the relations between peasant methods of production and life style, we found this explanation for usurious practices less than fully satisfactory. We actually discovered the roots of this problem in contemporary social relations. We must also question, if everything that was labeled "usuary" could really be considered as such.

Before 1848, the customary forms of loans among the peasantry consisted of grains. Lending actual cash to each other was rare. The former serfs were hard put to acquire cash, and if they could do so, they did it at usurious rates, which was only natural in the capital-poor country. But self-sufficient peasant households were seldom forced into such a dangerous predicament, except if natural catastrophies struck them, or if they had to share an inheritance in kind, or wanted to purchase a piece of real estate. After a bad harvest, the needy obtained loans in the form of produce. The repayment of such loans was regulated by decade-long practices. These customs could be considered usurious in our sense of the term, but no one at that time would think them to be so. For instance, a loan of bread grains given in the spring was usually charged "interest" of 25% at the time of harvest. Such a seemingly high "interest" was justified by the argument that grains had a higher moisture content right after harvest than at springtime, and that the lender was entitled to receive compensation also for his handling and transporting the loaned produce. The same interest rates were charged by philanthropic organizations at that time, including the Seed Savings Association. The rates varied somewhat by region, but the lowest were between 17-20%[59]

Before 1848, the lack of commercial opportunities forced the peasant serfs to retain some reserves from each year to the next for fear of a bad harvest. However the boom of the 1850's brought about changes in these practices. Now every peasant was eager to sell his surpluses down to the last ounce. This was also encouraged by the constantly rising taxes and the increasing needs of rural families for non-agricultural goods. In the case of more courageous peasants, the desire to purchase land forced them in the same direction. Reserves for a possibly bad year were retained only by a few peasant families. The grain merchants did retain some reserves as noted by the report from Somogy county quoted above, but these wre not very extensive.

The village merchants were, of course, quite familiar with the unwritten customs of lending goods. But they also had to consider the price fluctuations on the modern capitalist markets, since their livelihood did not depend solely on their lending activities. Therefore, they demanded not only "one-fourth" of interest at harvest time (which only covered their weight-loss in the case of grain loans), but they also asked for the price difference between the spring- and the freshly-harvested grains, the latter of which was always lower.[60] This was the so-called usurious practice condemned by those who refused to accept the changes in marketing practices. Thus, the Jewish merchants who had accepted the new rules of business life of bourgeois society, were called usurers. The concept itself was, therefore, extended to cover activities that have been the actual consequences of evolving commercial life.

There existed islands of exception to the usual methods of peasant production practices. There were reports from Vas and Sopron counties near the Austrian borders that reflected differences with traditional practices. According to these reports, the peasants of this region not only planted root crops and fodder on a large scale, but they also fertilized their lands on a regular basis (every five years).[61] Karoly Glagoczy who explored this area wrote in 1857 that wherever he went, "if it were not too early in the morning or not too late at night," he could not find the peasant landowners at home, since they were all busy working their fields. In their free time, the same people busied themselves by brickmaking, not only for their own use, but also for sale.[62] The environs of the city of Szombathely and the surrounding districts were described by him as an area where each village was "a small, diligent workshop/"[63]

Contemporaries described villages with a German population (settled during the 18th century) in similar terms. On the basis of his experiences on the Great Plain, Ditz generalized by saying that in Hungary "the Germans practiced only intensive agriculture."[64] But this generalization was nullified by the example set by the peasants in Moson county, where German peasants followed extensive methods just as their Hungarian neighbors did. On the other hand, it was true that in the Bansag, and in the majority of German-settled villages along the banks of the Danube River, intensive methods of production were practiced as early as the 1850's. The greater diligence and more rational life-style of the Germans were usually contrasted by the backwardness of the Hungarian, Serbian and Slovak peasants. The obvious differences were usually explained by the fact that the Germans came to Hungary during the 18th century from areas where agricultural practices were already in a more advanced stage than in their new homes.[65] According to Tancsics,

> The German settlers have diligence in their blood . . . Their ancestors carried the seeds of diligence along from their earlier homeland; since they possessed smaller parcels of land there and the population was more numerous, they were forced by their circumstances to exert themselves more . . .[66]

It was in this period, however, that the fruit and vegetable cultures of the market towns of the Great Plain, those of Kecskemet, Nagykoros, Mako, and Szeged began to develop, making the evolution of their peasants diverge from those of the rest of Hungary. The lack of control over these towns by the lords (probably due to early agreements to permit the towns to redeem their feudal obligations), provided opportunities for their freer development. The large open areas owned by these towns (*pusztak*) were famous for their semi-nomadic animal husbandry (*ridegmarhatartas*). By the beginning of the 19th century, the dwarfholder-peasants of these towns were already producing vegetables, fruits, and grapes. The increasing tax burdens of the towns after 1848 forced their leaders to seek higher incomes from their *pusztas* (about 50,877 acres in aggregate size) than the income that they derived from animal husbandry.[67] But each town followed a different path in its quest for funds. Szeged rented its lands out in small parcels; Kecskemet partitioned its holdings and sold the plots to its citizens; Mako divided and sold only its grazing lands; here even landless peasants were able to obtain 2-3 acres each.[68]

After getting the land, the smallholders expanded truck farming and fruit production from nearby areas to more distant lands. The towns began specializing in specific products; Nagykoros became the center of cucumber growing, Kecskemet produced fine apricots, Szeged grew red peppers and Mako onions. In place of the customary biweekly cattle fairs, Kecskemet developed a lively fruit market by the 1860's. Although the production of fruits and vegetables became a veritable craft in these towns, it could not gain an immediate significance in their economies (mostly because bad transportation and a restricted internal market). But it did show the way to future progress.[69]

But the evidence of these "green oases" did not fundamentally change the generally dismal picture projeted by the methods of production usually practiced by the Hungarian peasantry. The period following the Compromise of 1867, had to face the fundamental issue as to how much the peasantry was to be able to cast off the yoke of the past.

NOTES

1. One serf lot consisted of one *hold* (1.42 acres) of household plot and between 22.7 and 53.2 acres of ploughland, depending upon the county and the quality of the land in question. Such a lot also shared between 8.5 and 31.2 acres of meadows or grazing land. The meadows and forests were usually shared between landlords and serfs. The partitioning of the latter were ordered by the Patent of 1853, the process extending to the early 1860's. Serfs who possessed less than one-eighth of a lot were called *hazas zsellerek* or landless serfs with a house.

2. Janos Varga, *op. cit.,* 337-46. The statistical data following was taken from this work.
3. Janos Hetenyi, Pal Kiraly and Adolf Ploetz, *Robot es dezsma* (Corvee and Tithe) (Pest, 1845), 357.
4. *Gazdasagi Lapok* (Economic Journals), March 29, 1855.
5. *Falusi Gazda* (Village Landowner) Aug. 24, 1858.
6. Lajos Fur, *op. cit.,* 1:33.
7. In Gyula Varga, "A parasztsag munkaeszkozei," *Ibid.,* 1:314.
8. Henrik Ditz, *Ungarische Landwirtschaft.* Translated by Gabor Halasz as *A magyar mezogazdasag* (Pest, 1869), 108.
9. *Ibid.,* 84.
10. *Ibid.,* 108.
11. Mihaly Tancsics, *Bordacs Elek a gyalog arendas* (Elek Bordacs, the Renter on Foot) (Pest, 1878), 2nd ed., 52.
12. *Ibid.,* 55.
13. Karoly Galgoczy, *Az Orszagos Magyar Gazdasagi Egyesulet tortenete* (History of the National Magyar Economic Association) (Budapest, 1880), 61-2.
14. Hetenyi et al., *op. cit.,* 49-59 and 69.
15. *Ibid.,* 94-5.
16. *Ibid.,* 112.
17. The ploughland of each village was divided into three equal parts (dulo). Spring grains were planted in the first, autumn grains in the second and the third was left fallow each year. The last of these parts was used for grazing and, simultaneously, the animals fertilized it. In the next year's cycle, the fallow land was planted with autumn grains and spring grains were planted in the place of previous year's autumn grains. The third section was left fallow. In each part of the land every peasant family had one share.
18. About this system and its modifications see the more detailed work by Istvan Balogh, "A paraszti gazdalkodas es technika" (Peasant Ways and Techniques) in Szabo, *op. cit.,* 1:351-75. See also, Peter Gunst, Tamas Hoffman, (eds.) *A magyar mezogazdasag a XIX.-XX. szazadban*

(1848-1949) (Hungarian Agriculture in the 19th-20th Centuries) (Budapest, 1976), and Antal Voros, *A magyar mezogazdasag a kapitalista atalakulas utjan* (Hungarian Agriculture on the Way to a Capitalist Transformation) (Budapest, 1976), 74-89.

19. Gyula Benda, *Statisztikai adatok a magyar mezogazdasag tortenetehez, 1767-1867* (Statistical Data for the History of Hungarian Agriculture, 1767-1867) (Budapest, 1973), 133.
20. See a detailed description of animal husbandry in Voros, *op. cit.,* 109-31.
21. *Ibid.,* 28-37.
22. Emil Simonffy, "A paraszt es a tagositas," (The Peasantry and the Consolidation of Land) in Szabo, *op. cit.,* 1:207-34.
23. Quoted by Balogh, *op. cit.,* 1:358.
24. *A magyarsag neprajza. A magyarsag szellemi neprajza* (The Folklore of the Hungarians. The Spiritual Folklore of the Hungarians) (Budapest, 1937), 4:248-86. This volume is based on research conducted largely before 1914, and contains the descriptions of an assorted number of superstitions related to about every facet of life. If one examined only this one collection, one would come to the conclusion that peasant methods of production were guided solely by superstitions. Unfortunately, one of the weaknesses of Hungarian folklore research, reflected in this work, was that researchers did not consider the difference between superstitions that they only heard about and those that were still functional at the time of the survey.
25. Balogh, *op. cit.,* 2:500-27.
26. Voros, "*A magyar . . .* op. cit., 53.
27. Ferenc Gonczi, *Gocsej, s kapcsolatosan Hetes videkenek es nepenek osszevontabb ismertetese* (Gocsej, the Area of Hetes and Its Environs and People, a Summarized Description) Kaposvar, 1914), 557.
28. Balogh, *op. cit.,* 1:357.
29. *Ibid.,* 358.

30. Views about the work of young peasant lads are well expressed by the popular song of the time rendered here in an imperfect translation;

> "The owner is not one who has a nice daughter, but is one who possesses six oxen. Oxen in the yoke; his boy in the inn; that is what befits a young man at the age of twenty."

31. There is a definitive description of folk dress in the first volume of *A magyarsag neprajza, op. cit.,* 381-435. About the relations between folk art and production methods in this period see Antal Voros, "A paraszti munka es eletforma jellegenek valtozasai a Dunantulon, 1850-1914," (Changes in the Character of Peasant Work and Style of Life in Transdanubia, 1850-1914) *Tortenelmi Szemle* (1966), 172.
32. *A magyarsag neprajza, op. cit.,* 4:248-86.
33. *Ibid.,* 186-211.
34. Tancsics, *op. cit.,* 83.
35. Ditz, *op. cit.,* 156-7.
36. Many similar reports are quoted by Balogh, *op. cit.,* 1:360.
37. *Ibid.,* Note 21.
38. *Erdelyi Gazda* (Transylvanian Landowner), Apr. 30, 1869.
39. Karoly Keleti, *Hazank es nepe* (Our Country and Its People) (Pest, 1871), 148.
40. Ipoly Feher, *Gyor megye es varos egyetemes leirasa* (General Description of the County of Gyor and the City) (Budapest, 1874), 266.
41. Keleti, *op. cit.,* 148-9.
42. *Ibid.,* 152.
43. Voros, "A paraszti munka," *op. cit.,* 172-3.
44. Ditz, *op. cit.,* 99.
45. Benda, *op. cit.,* 245-7 and 262, 375, 408-9. We included data from Hungary, Transylvania, Croatia-Slavonia and the Military Border. The inclusion of Croatia-Slavonia was suggested by the existence of the Military Border; in 1873,

when the Border was abolished, part of it was attached to Croatia and the other to Hungary proper. We do not know the exact amount of land given to each; therefore, we included the entire territory in question in this survey.

46. Voros, *A magyar mezogazdasag, op. cit.*, 115.
47. Keleti, *op. cit.*, 92.
48. Ditz, *op. cit.*, 9.
49. Jozsef Hajas and Imre Razso, *A mezogazdasag szamokban* (Agriculture through Numbers) (Budapest, 1955), 40.
50. Ditz, *op. cit.*, 283-4. One *mero* equalled 62.5 liters.
51. Keleti, *op. cit.*, 87.
52. Ditz, *op. cit.*, 209.
53. *Ibid.*, 84. See also, Izidor Maday, "Feladataink foldmuvelesunk emelese korul," (Our Tasks for the Upgrading of Our Agriculture) *Foldmuvelesi eredekeink*,May 7, 1877.
54. Voros, *A magyar mezogazdasag, op. cit.*, 28-9, and Ditz, *op. cit.*, 299 and 322.
55. Voros, *A magyar mezogazdasag,* op. cit., 28.
56. Gyorgy Szabad, "A hitelviszonyok," (Financial Conditions) in Szabo, *op. cit.*, 2:201-2.
57. Mihaly Tancsics, *Pazardi* (The Wasteful One) (Pest, 1873), 2nd ed.
58. *Gazdasagi Lapok,* May 18, 1854, and Feb. 8, 1855.
59. Szabad, *op. cit.*, 2:202.
60. Orszagos Leveltar, *Foldmiveles- Ipar-es Kereskedelemugyi Miniszterium Leveltara.Altalanos Iratok,* (1867), 2. tetel (National Archives, Archive of the Agricultural-Industrial- and Commercial Ministry. General Papers.) 2nd Fascicle. For the system and the general practices of lending products by grain merchants this is the best collection for the period after the Compromise of 1867. The regulations listed include requests by cooperative societies for seed savings for the approval of their charters. Since the decree of the Austrian government of the 1850's set the maximum rate of interests that could be charged, the Ministry usually objected to the high rates proposed by the cooperative associations. Letters included in these

papers point out the serious differences in weight between spring- and freshly-harvested grains.

61. *Gazdasagi Lapok,* March 7, 1851.
62. Karoly Galgoczy, "Rabakozi utazasom," (My Trip to the Raba District) *Falusi Gazda,* Nov. 10, 17 and 24, 1857.
63. Karoly Galgoczy, *Magyarorszag- a Szerb-Vajdasag s a Temesi Bansag gazdasagi statisztikaja* (Economic Statistics of Hungary, the Serb Voivodina and the Bani of Temes) (Pest, 1855), 171-2.
64. Ditz, *op. cit.,* 84.
65. Balogh, *op. cit.,* 1:381.
66. Tancsics, *Bordacs, op. cit.,* 55.
67. Bela Lakos, "Kecskemet gazdasagi fejlodese," (The Economic Evolution of Kecskemet) *Huszadik Szazad,* 1913.
68. Ferenc Erdei, *Varos es videke* (city and Its Countryside) (Budapest, 1971), 273.
69. Karoly Galgoczy, *Nagykoros varos monografiaja* (The Monography of the City of Nagykoros) (Budapest, 1896), 550-1.

II

THE DISSOLUTION OF THE TRADITIONAL PEASANT WORLD, 1867-1890

1. The Compromise and Peasant Political Rights

The Compromise of 1867 ending political absolutism in Hungary, resulted in the stabilization of the country's legal situation and the restoration of constitutional politics. But it hardly touched the life of the peasantry; in fact, everyday life went on in its accustomed channels. However, with the restoration of political liberties, several possiblities opened up for the creation of various peasant organizations and cooperatives. The peasants could have used these openings for the improvement of their material existence if they could have acquired the necessary information.

Owners of at least one-fourth of a former serf-lot were now enfranchised, and they could be elected as participants in national politics. But in the parliamentary elections (held every four years), the peasants usually voted for candidates who provided the most merriment and food and drink during the campaign. Half of the membership of the autonomous village administrations was elected by all the house- and landowners, while the other half consisted of the *virilistak,* that is, people who paid the highest taxes in their community.[1]

However circumscribed the authority of these autonomous organs had been, the elections usually brought into the open all sorts of simmering antagonisms in the villages, disturbing the calm and order of the communities often for months to come. Besides the political rights of the peasantry, we want to attribute great significance to the fact that the new constitution secured the possibility for the creation of all sorts of associations such as landowners' circles, collectives, breeders' associations, reading circles, etc. Although the activities of such groups were legally permissible during the previous absolutist period, the authorities usually suspected political motives behind their establishment. Thus, the approval of organizational bylaws as, for instance, grain-lending collectives (usually established by village priests), was usually dependent upon the political attitudes of their leaders. The approval required so much red tape that people were usually reluctant to become involved. Now the Compromise removed most of these obstacles. However, in order to take advantage of the new organizational opportunities, changes in peasant thinking were absolutely essential.

2. The Improvements in Financial Conditions in the Countryside

After 1867, foreign capital, always sensitive to political circumstances, began to show unprecedented interest in investment possibilities in Hungary. Parallel with this, local capital derived mainly from internal sources (especially from the grain trade) began to assume a greater role in the establishment of financial institutions. A boost was provided initially by the removal of restrictions in interest rates in 1868, the Hungarians following a precedent set by Austria. In 1867, only 107 lending institutions existed in Hungary with 10,722,000 florins of capital and 71,563,000 florins in savings deposits. By 1890, there existed 1,255 such institutions, with 121,737,000 florins of capital and 548,000,000 in savings deposits.[2]

The elimination of the restrictions on interest rates in the capital-poor country created a gold mine for usurers and rural banks, as well as for provincial savings and loan associations. Interests of 20% and more were frequently charged in backward areas of the country; thus, a law of 1877 decreed that no interest of more than 8% a year could be mortgaged or legally enforced.[3] In response to public pressure, another decree (issued in 1883), patterned on similar Austrian legislation, stated that

> at the time of giving a loan it will be a breach of the law to take advantage of the irresponsibility, difficult conditions, inexperience, etc. of the borrowers; (it will be unlawful) to secure advantages and promises of the sort which, because of their insatiability, would result in the ruination of the borrower.[4]

The new law further decreed interest rates above 8% annually to be a criminal offense and denied them legal protection.

This law curtailed usury to some extent, but the elimination of such practices was due primarily not to legal restrictions, but to improvements in the general financial situation, and changes in peasant thinking and life-style.

By the end of the 1880's, savings and loan institutions in the central and western parts of the country were lending money at 6-8% interest rates to peasants.[5] However, in the backward eastern and northeastern areas of Hungary the law failed to have the desired results.

3. The Development of the Transportation Network

A fundamental criterion of further increases in agrarian production was, by the end of the 1860's, the creation of an infrastructure for the transportation of goods. This was demanded by medium- and large landholders (who were looking out for their own interests) who had regained their leading political role in the country. At the center of this process were the railroads. Railroad building had already begun before 1848; however, it slowed down during the absolutist era, the network growing from a length of 178 kilometers in 1848 to a measly 2,285 kilometers by 1867. The new constitutional government did everything in its power to speed up railroad construction. The legislation secured a considerable return on invested capital, and if the expectations of the builders were not realized, the differences were paid by the state. As a consequence, the railroad network was extended to 11,399 kilometers by 1890.[6] The backbone of the future Hungarian railroad network had, therefore, been established. The main lines reached out of Budapest like the spokes of a wheel over nearly every area of the country. However, the lines thinned out when they reached the outlying provinces.

But the growth of the railroad network did not diminish the importance of the waterways. The significance of the Danube River transports was and remained especially great. Navigation of the river was declared free for all nations by an international congress in 1865. Consequently, the Danube Steamship Company transported 12.5 million quintals of goods in 1868, and an average of 16.5 million quintals a year between 1886-1890.[7]

There was also a new interest in flood control, including the regulation of the waterways, something that was entirely neglected during the absolutist era.[8] As a result of the regulation of the Danube and the Tisza Rivers and their tributaries, 3,174,000 hectares (6,221,040 acres) of new lands were opened for cultivation.[9]

4. Education

The constitutional government also began to create a new network of educational institutions for agricultural improvements. The only secondary institution for such training was located at Magyarovar where the agrarian technicians of the entire monarchy were trained. This situation came about as the result of the closing of the *Georgicon*, originally established by Count Gyorgy Festetics in 1797, an institution that fell victim to Habsburg absolutism in 1849. Although the Viennese authorities reopened the *Georgicon* just before the Compromise, this institution alone could not make up for all the neglect of two decades. Between 1868 and 1894, new secondary institutions were, therefore, founded in eastern Hungary, at Debrecen, Kolozsvar and Kassa. They were intended to educate a new generation of agrarian technicians, attuned to local conditions. Besides the five secondary schools, six lower level institutions were created—theso-called agriculturists' schools—aimed at educating young peasants in the new agrarian techniques through a two-year program.

The idea behind the establishment of these schools was to educate young people who were then expected to return to their villages in order to transmit their knowledge to local peasant landholders. But these hopes were in vain. The peasantry showed little interest in the schools provided "for them." Those who did attend, seldom decided to return to their villages after graduation, and accepted supervisory jobs in large estates instead (*Botosispan*).[10] In fact, most peasants continued to insist that agriculture could not be learned at school; the educated ones were not expected to return to their village to a despised peasant life.

As a consequence, a much greater role was assumed by elementary schools in spreading agricultural knowledge. The law of 1868 decreed not only that every child between the ages of 6-12 had to go through school, but it also stipulated that natural science be taught with special attention to local conditions. Agricultural and gardening instructions had to be related in these schools to practical life. But the law presupposed the existence of trained teachers capable of providing such instructions. In fact, the subject in question was included in the curriculum of teacher-training institutions only in the year of the law's enactment, and its results did not begin to appear until the 1880's.[11]

Another consequence of the law on education was the increase of literacy rates among people over six years of age. The ratio grew from 44.5% in 1870[12] to 53.2% in 1890.[13] These numbers, however, do not reveal the significantly wide variations in the literacy rates in various regions. For instance, in 1870, the ratio in the Transdanubian counties—except Baranya, Somogy and Zala—was over 65%. On the other hand, in Transylvania, it was only 21.3%. There were counties in the latter region where only about 10% of the population was literate.[14] These differences were somewhat reduced by 1890. And yet, in contrast to the 69.1% literacy rate in Transdanubia, it was only 32.9% in the three Transylvanian counties of Hunyad, Kis-Kukullo and Kolozs. The rate was especially low in eastern Hungary in general, and especially in Maramaros County.[15] Similar differences in development could be observed in almost every facet of peasant life in the various regions of Hungary.

5. The Agrarian Crisis and the Beginnings of Modernization

The agrarian boom had lasted for years after the Compromise and had necessitated the expansion of extensive methods of production on most ploughlands. Although the rapid development of transportation expanded traditional European markets into world-wide centers of trade, the competition of American wheat had not yet resulted in lowering the prices in Hungary during the 1870's. Because of a consecutive series of natural disasters—drought, spring frosts, the grain rust—average crop yields remained relatively low, but the market of the Monarchy remained secure for Hungarian agricultural goods. The Hungarian grist mill industry—especially the mills of Budapest—succeeded in producing an excellent quality of flour from the steely Hungarian wheat that the other European mills had been reluctant to use only a couple of decades before because of its hardness. In 1862, only 440,000 quintals were exported; by

1869, exports of this kind of flour reached 2 million quintals a year.[16] This, in turn, created an increasing demand for Hungarian wheat. In the 1870's, the threat of overseas competition was not yet a reality. Extensively produced grains needed little work and capital investment and were still profitable.

However, by the end of the 1870's, the worry-free period of agriculture had come to an end. Wheat prices began to fall in the early 1880's and they remained low for almost two decades. Wheat prices between 1867-1895 were as follows:

1867-1870	21.3 florins/quintal (220 lbs.)
1870-1875	25.2 florins/quintal (220 lbs.)
1876-1880	22.6 florins/quintal (220 lbs.)
1881-1885	20.6 florins/quintal (220 lbs.)
1886-1890	16.1 florins/quintal (220 lbs.)
1891-1895	16.4 florins/quintal (220 lbs.)

The price of the other important Hungarian grain crop, rye, also declined and agriculture as a whole entered a period of crisis. Now the peasant producers had no other choice but to turn to more intensive, more rational methods of production. This process, which had had some feeble beginnings in the previous decades, really accelerated in the 1880's. But while in the previous period national agrarian production (with the variations discussed above existing between western and eastern Hungary) was generally on the same technical level, now the intensity of modernization was varied greatly by region. Some areas progressed very rapidly, others remained stuck in the traditional system. The previous universality of production methods was now changed into a kaleidoscopic pattern. This was also reflected in the life-style of people existing in the various regions.

The process of modernization began in the western areas of the country and the process gradually spread towards the Great Plain. But by the time it reached this region, the process began to slow down. For the most part, modernization left the eastern part of the country relatively untouched during the 1870's and the 1880's. The process was reflected in the following changes:

1. the system of land usage was altered from the three-field system to a system of regular crop rotation;
2. the use of fertilizers became a general practice;
3. changes in tools and techniques were introduced;
4. the methods of animal husbandry were fundamentally altered by a new emphasis on dairy cattle breeding and the improvement of live stock.

Before we can proceed to an analysis of the disappearance of the old system of land usage, let us look at the statistics of ratios between fallow and ploughlands during the 1870's and 1880's, on the basis of five-year averages:[18]

Year	Total land area in 1,000 acres	Percent	Fallow lands in 1,000 acres	Percent	Fallow land ratios
1871-1875	19,879	100	4,351	100	21.9%
1876-1880	21,943	110.4	4,535	104.3	20.6%
1881-1885	22,089	111.2	4,058.4	93.3	18.4%
1886-1890	22,342	112.4	3,748.7	86.2	16.8%

These numbers show that the growth of the size of the ploughlands slowed down in the 1880's. This was the result of the fact that producers increased their ploughlands by increasingly resorting to the breaking-up of fallow lands. However, the situation varied by region. The fallow lands were systematically tilled in the good soil regions of the Great Plain. However, this did not always mean the advancement of the cause of modernization in this area, only that the change of wheat-corn rotation was followed, which was another method of robbing the soil.[19] The most balanced progress occurred in areas west of the Danube River-line; here the ratio of the fallows was reduced to 13-17% of all ploughlands by 1890. In these territories the three-field system was replaced by a more rational method of crop rotation combining root crops, fodder and grains. But the north and northeastern perimeters of the country, from Maramaros to the Transylvanian Haromszek counties, still followed the old system: here fallows continued to make up 40-50% of the ploughlands in the 1890's. This was incontrovertible proof of the survival of the medieval two-field system.[20]

Wherever the peasants changed over to a method of crop rotation, they needed fertilizers to maintain the productivity of their lands. In the previous decades, one of the general complaints was that the peasants did not use even the limited amount of fertilizers that they derived from their animals. A significant change occurred during the 1880's. Economic specialists in the counties (and provincial newspapers alike) reported that the fertilization of lands every four or five years became a general practice among the peasantry and only the treatment of manure was still inadequate. Low grain prices forced the peasants to increase the productive capacity of their lands; reports of increasing use of fertilizers were now coming in from regions even where the three-field system continued to survive. Several reports contended that the peasants went so far as to buy manure when it was available.[21] Peasants who admired a steam plough at a large estate in Baranya county remarked that "it is a good tool, but its one great disadvantage is that it does not lay manure."[22] On the other hand, complaints continued to be received from the largest grainproducing area of the country, the Great Plain, that, just as decades before, manure was still being used as fuel. The adherence of the peasants to this ancient custom was "explained" by the assertation that when the weather was wet, wheat stalks were bent down to the ground in the freshly fertilized land, so that it was more secure to use methods of the ancestors than to experiment with new ones.[23]

In general, the peasantry of the Great Plain regarded the regular fertilization of the lands as a dangerous invention. At the same time, peasant landholders of the western countries increased the productivity of their lands by sometimes using chemical fertilizers. For instance, in Sopron Country, the peasants took notice of the excellent results achieved by the estates of the local sugar refineries through the use of such fertilizers. In one village they turned to the local teacher to find out for them the way they could acquire the stuff. In another village, they began experimenting, on the advice of the supervisor of the local estate, with chemical fertilizers. In Vas County the leaders of the local agricultural association were surprised to hear that the peasants of several villages in their county were using chemical fertilizers. These associations were usually the protectors of the interests of medium-and large estates and, in general, cared little for peasant agriculture. However, the association in Vas County proved to be an exception. When its leaders found out about the peasant initiative, they established stores of chemical fertilizers at the larger railroad stations where peasants could buy what they needed. The secretary of the association then proceeded to deliver several lectures in the villages about the types of chemical fertilizers in existence and their most advantageous use. The monthly journal of the group published articles on the subject, The results were soon evident; in 1882, only 200 quintals were acquired by them through the efforts of the association. This development must be measured against the fact that private traders also began to sell chemical fertilizers in the villages. According to some estimates, their trade came to three times the amount sold by the association. In Sopron and Vas Counties, the experiments with chemical fertilizers usually began in areas where the soil was poor. Only by increasing average yields could the peasants maintain their existence at the prevailing low grain prices[24] in these areas.

Similar regional variations existed in the modernization of agricultural tools and equipment. The speed at which modern equipment was adopted depended upon rational considerations. The changes were fastest in cases when the technical superiority of the new tool or equipment was immediately obvious and their price was not significantly higher than that of the old tools. This was what happened, for example, with the steel plough. In 1872, 48% of the existing 1,109,000 ploughs were still made of wood. In Transylvania, the percentage was even higher; in 1872, it was 98%[25] By the time agricultural statistics came into their own (in 1895), this typical wooden tool of feudal agriculture almost completely disappeared from use so much so that it was not even counted. The statistics differentiated only between steel ploughs with iron or wooden superstructures. With the steel plough, the land could be worked easier and by the use of fewer draft animals. Thus, by the 1890's, gone was not only the wooden plough, but also the concept of the "landholder of six oxen," a notion that previously expressed a high rank in the village community.

The changeover from the use of the sickle to that of the scythe was a much faster process. But in the eastern and northern regions of the country where grain production was somewhat limited, sickles were continued in use for the harvest even at the turn of the century. The adherence to tradition in this case was "explained" by the argument that sickles did a cleaner job, little of the grains were lost, and when wheat stalks were bent by the wind, they were easier to cut with a sickle than with the scythe.[26] Usually, the women used the sickle at harvest, while men did the easier work of collecting the grain stalks. Harvesting with the scythe was, on the other hand, hard work, dictating a much faster rhythm to the men; women in this case did the collecting of the stalks.[27] In Transylvania, public opinion was against the use of the scythe in harvest. The major argument against it was that it took away the jobs from day laborers.[28]

Harvester machines were considered only as tools of the future; there were few of them even in large estates—according to the survey of 1895—and peasant landholders had even fewer. The survey counted altogether 3,040 such machines of which only 772 (25.4%) were in peasant hands.[29]

On the basis of statistics of agricultural firms compiled in 1895, the following changes occurred in the mechanization of small holds under 142 acres in size (by region):

in absolute numbers and percentages

Region	number of smallholds and %	steam threshers and %	capstan threshers and %	planters and %	hoes and %	fodder shredders
Right bank of Danube	378,368 18.3%	678 25.9%	22,618 51.4%	5,730 29.7%	16,134 23.7%	51,383 32.5%
Small Plain & western Highlands	264,792 12.8%	193 7.4%	9,921 22.5%	2,830 14.7%	1,366 2.0%	62,282 39.3%
Lands between Danube-Tisza Rivers	263,445 12.8%	740 28.3%	2,502 5.7%	2,707 14.0%	11,288 16.6%	15,734 9.9%
Left bank of Tisza	285,636 13.8%	236 9.0%	878 2.0%	1,620 8.4%	4,950 7.3%	3,785 2.4%
Right bank of Tisza (eastern Highlands)	204,503 9.9%	76 2.9%	4,264 9.7%	374 1.9%	2,562 3.7%	19,183 12.1%
Tisza-Maros triangle Banat, Bansag)	256,731 12.4%	540 20.6%	1,475 3.3%	2,437 12.5%	27,506 40.4%	3,692 2.3%
Transylvania	416,122 20.0%	154 5.9%	2,373 5.4%	3,615 18.7%	4,307 6.3%	2,314 1.5%
Hungary altogether	2,069,597	2,617	44,031	19,313	68,113	158,373

In contrast to the small number of mechanical harvesters, a surprising factor in these statistics was the relatively large number of threshers. Typical for the growth of their number was the fact that while in 1872, only 2,416 steam threshers and 3,198 capstan-driven ones were used,[31] by 1895, their numbers increased to 8,920 and 46,800 respectively. Of all these the peasants owned 2,617 (29.3%) and 44,031 (91.4%).[32] This expressed not only the desire of the peasants to modernize their techniques, but it also refleted the emergence of a new stratum of village entrepreneurs. The statistics did not even provide an accurate number of the steam threshers in use, since they did not record the machines used by landless peasants, or associations and cooperatives.[33]

It was understandable that the peasants quickly accepted the mechanical threshers since they did a much better job than traditional tools used by hand or driven by horses. Characteristic of the rapidity of this transformation was the fact that a reporter of economic conditions prevailing in Csik county spoke of the use of "shared steam threshers" while still deploring the peasants' use of the sickle in harvest.[34] By the 1890's, hand-threshing or threshing with horses characterized only isolated smallholds in the mountains or in the *tanya* system of the Great Plain. The large number of capstan-driven thresher cabinets in use in the western regions of the country showed the early beginnings of modernization of agrarian techniques in these areas. These machines which the peasants were buying were, in turn, replaced by steam threshers in the early 1890's, and these were owned by entrepreneurs.

The statistics also reflect regional production characteristics in the high ratio of mechanical planters and hoes used by peasants in the fertile areas between the Danube and Tisza Rivers and in the Bansag. Here the three-field system was changed to a rotation of wheat and corn crops. But the continued backwardness in every area of mechanization of the regions east of the Tisza River was striking. The most balanced growth in machinery occurred in Transdanubia, and in the peasant landholds of the left bank of the Danube River in the Small Plain. In comparison with other regions of the country, the number of fodder shredding machines was very large here, and the situation was also similar with grinders and turnipshredders. Animal husbandry had played a considerably larger role in these areas than in the central and eastern areas of the country.

Agricultural experts of this period argued repeatedly that the expansion of the size of ploughlands in the interest of grain production, without a similar expansion of animal husbandry, would lead agriculture to a dead end. They pointed out that under the Hungarian conditions cattle breeding was not only the most profitable branch of animal husbandry (because of its threefold use in providing meat, milk and draft power), but that intensified cattle breeding would lead to the development of the entire agriculture in an intensive direction. But the rationality and persuasiveness of this argument did not sink into peasant minds until the beginning of the agricultural crisis. However, statistics dealing with the number of animals do show the growing role of cattle breeding in animal husbandry:[35]

	1870	1884	1895
horses	1,819,052 21.8%	1,748,895 20.2%	1,972,448 20.0%
cattle	4,490,905 53.8%	4,879,039 56.4%	5,829,018 59.2%
sheep	1,320,770 15.8%	1,059,483 12.3%	752,668 7.7%
hogs	714,706 8.6%	960,727 11.1%	1,289,314 13.1%

The greatest problem in cattle raising was the problem of breeds. Until the 1870's, the breed most generally raised in the country was that of the gray or Hungarian cattle. These cattle were acclimatized, resistant to sickness, and good draft animals. But the animals were, at the same time, poor providers of milk and slow in growth; in other words, they did not return a fair amount of the invested fodder in the form of produce. They were profitable to keep only under circumstances of extensive agricultural production methods. Animal husbandry could not depend on this breed at a time when the fallow lands were being broken up for plough. New breeds were needed whose returns for the invested fodder would be more favorable. The large estates had already been experimenting with various imported, colored Alpine breeds; peasants in the western regions near the Austrian borders were also trying out various mixed breeds. In the 1880's, the government decided to speed up the transformation and imported Simmenthal cattle from Switzerland. This breed seemed eminently suitable to Hungarian conditions.[36] According to three consecutive contemporary surveys, the ratio of various breeds of cattle changed between 1870 and 1895 as follows:[37]

	1870	1884	1895
Hungarian breed	90.8%	78.3%	64.4%
Swiss breeds	7.5%	19.3%	33.3%
Bisons	1.7%	2.4%	2.3%

The introduction of new breeds became more rapid in the 1880's. In 1884, in the western counties such as Pozsony, Nyitra, Sopron and Vas, 66.7%, 65%, 75.5% and 67.7% of the cattle, respectively, belonged to new, intensively raised, fodder-fed western breeds. At the same time, the ratio in the Great Plain and Transylvania was only around 5%. By the 1890's, in the four western counties mentioned above, plus Tolna County in Transdanubia (especially around the market town of Bonyhad), new, more productive breeds were developed and their products were gradually becoming known on the Austrian markets.

What prompted the quick spread of colored western breeds of cattle was the condition of the market. When grain prices began to decline in the 1880's, the price of cattle showed a rising tendency despite minor fluctuations. The price of live cattle on the Viennese market between 1867 and 1895 was as follows (in hundredweights):[38]

1867-1870	47.5 crowns	1881-1885	47.5 crowns
1871-1875	49.4 crowns	1886-1890	51.6 crowns
1876-1880	48.2 crowns	1891-1895	53.1 crowns

Favorable prices were coupled with increased demands, and this was reflected in rising Hungarian exports. According to the statistical surveys that began in 1882, Hungarian cattle exports doubled within a decade. The increases are shown in the following table:[39]

1882-1886	92,292 heads were exported (100%)
1887-1891	157,629 heads were exported (163.7%)
1892-1896	199,420 heads were exported (207.1%)

With the introduction of new breeds, the production of animal husbandry had significantly increased. But the rapidity of transformation remained uneven in the various regions of the country. While on the west bank of the Danube River 80% of the cattle consisted of Western breeds in 1895, the ratio remained less than 10% in the eastern areas of the Great Plain and in Transylvania.

Wherever the peasants introduced the western breeds, they had to increase the production of fodder crops; then, in turn, they had to give up the three-field system. Cattle raising became, therefore, the "heavy industry" of agriculture, and its impact included the elimination of patriarchal production methods. The transformation that began at the western perimeters of the country rapidly moved east in Transdanubia, but when it reached the line of the Danube River, it lost the momentum. The new possibilities of marketing dairy products were to help in rekindling the transformation during the last decade of the century.

6. Treasure Hunters and Treasure Finders. The Crisis of Traditional Peasant Ways of Life

This short survey of the process of modernization provides a glimpse of the fact that the people of the villages in western and central Hungary were slowly entering the threshold of *embourgeoisment.* It was a process that raised the fortunes of some, and lowered those of others. This was also the process through which the formerly self-sufficient peasantry of the feudal period gradually emerged as small capitalist producers. Marketing possibilities, now altered by the agrarian crisis, and new production methods demanded that the peasantry adopt a new view of the marketplace. But the retarding factors of the past (whose existence encompassed many peasant generations), coupled with the general suspicions of the peasants towards any innovation, proved to be stronger in a large part of the country than the forces of progress. But everyone had to respond to the challenge posed by the overseas producers one way or another. Wherever the peasants decided to respond, they did succeed, after a few years of struggle, in creating better conditions of life for themselves. On the other hand, wherever traditions proved stronger, they continued to vegetate despite the fact that they had to work harder than ever before.

The population of the country grew from 13.6 million in 1869 to 15.6 million in 1890. The ratio of people who made their living from agriculture, however, remained basically the same. According to historical statistics, this ratio was 73-75% in 1869 (including producers and their dependents) of the total population. By 1890, the ratio declined to 67.4%.[40] The increase of the population was, therefore, absorbed largely by industry and trade as well as the rapidly growing ranks of public employees. If we recall the data on the changing ratios of fallow and ploughlands, we may add that, by the 1880's, a relatively stable number of agricultural producers had to work 3,064,700 more acres of land than they did in the early 1870's. Thus, even a superficial comparison will clearly show that, by the end of the 1880's, agriculture demanded more work and more intensive production from the same number of producers.

After this short foray into statistics, we can return to the title of this subchapter. (It must have raised the eyebrows of the reader!) The title, in our view, expresses the beginnings of social mobility among the peasantry as well as changes in thinking and life-style that were behind the mobility. We have documents going back almost to the beginning of the century showing that there existed a series of legends about treasures found or robberies committed that were woven around peasants who succeeded in rising out of the common herd by their abilities. In a novel by Miroslav Krleza, entitled *The*

Glembay Family, for instance, the emergence of the family was connected to the murder of a jeweller, providing the capital needed for advancement in the 1790's. In the biography of Mihaly Tancsics (born in 1799), there is a story about his serf-lot owner father who wanted to stop the decline of his fortunes by finding buried treasure. He received news of a girl living in a nearby village who was the seventh child of her parents, having been born at new moon. She was thus supposed to be able to locate buried treasure and show its hiding place to interested parties. The girl was secretely summoned to Tancsic's house, wined and dined and paid in advance for her service. But they dug in the area that she indicated in vain; they found no treasure.[41]

How far the roots of such beliefs go back in time, and if there were a kernel of truth in them is immaterial from our point of view. However, it is significant that the peasants of feudal society believed that finding hidden treasure was, for them, one of the very few possibilities for material advancement, and that their superstitious imagination created a whole series of rituals around this concept. These beliefs lasted way beyond 1848, and even the newspapers in the 1850's noticed the increase in the number of treasure hunters. Towards the end of the 1860's, treasure hunting grew with feverish intensity, but the fever soon declined. After the turn of the century, only legends had survived about wealthy, fortunate peasants who had succeeded in laying the foundations of their success by finding hidden treasure.

Folklorists have provided expert descriptions of the "rules" of treasure hunting and the procedures followed by "seers." But the deeper relations of this phenomenon with social history have not yet been explored.[42] Let us, therefore, look at this problem as a rapidly developing and just as rapidly fading symptom of a changing age.

With the birth of free peasant property at the end of serfdom, the concept of losing one's property also became a reality. When the results of the harvest depended more on nature's will than on the work of the producer, and when the extreme fluctuation of crop yields influenced prices, the peasant who could not think ahead and who was wasteful could easily fail. At the same time, the possibilities of rapid advancement were also there. He who realized the possibilities of breaking with the leisurely work-tempo of the age of serfdom, of thriftiness, and who kept an eye on price changes, could acquire wealth even if he followed traditional methods of production. Such a man could break out of his inherited status in a few years. More opportunities were offered in areas where the peasants discarded the three-field system that curtailed individual initiative than in areas where they did not.

Historians rightfully criticized the statistics of the Age of Dualism in Hungary, (prepared at various times), since their varying methods and differing points of view make it impossible to survey peasant social mobility. However, statistics, contemporary local reports, and official statements agree almost unanimously that "there was a great deal of buying and selling among the urbarials" after the emancipation.[43] Real-estate data in the statistical yearbooks from the 1870's support such generalizations. From contemporary reports,[44] and novels dealing with village life in this period, as well as from the latest monographs on local history, it is also evident that many former noble landholds came into peasant hands. This was the result of the nobility's disdain for work and their reckless disregard of changed economic conditions. By the early 1880's, a new upcoming stratum of peasants emerged alongside of those who inherited their status in the villages.

The village was, however, still in the grip of traditional values; it looked at the advancing peasants with a jaundiced eye. According to the conviction of the majority of peasants, advancement could only be the result of personal luck or of the coercion of others; gossip thus began about those who succeeded. It was said that "this one had discovered hidden treasure, that one had connections with highwaymen or was a robber himself," and so on. Public safety, what there was of it in the 1860's, provided a semi-realistic background for the gossipers. There were only a few well-to-do peasants behind whose backs such talk was not heard. But the imagination of the people (still influenced by past superstitions) was gripped most of all by the ancient variety of the basis of success, that of finding treasure. Those who found the going difficult under the new economic circumstances, or who were heading directly towards personal failure, often tried to force a change in their fortunes by looking for hidden treasure. There was a glut of "seers" and "lookers" who, according to popular belief, had the ability to locate buried treasure.[45]

The contemporary press reported from almost every region of the country the operations of a flood of treasure seekers. Their beliefs were supported by the fact that in a country that was repeatedly ravaged by armies, many archeological discoveries were made during railroad constrution or during the breaking-up of fallow lands. But sometimes even in the regularly ploughed lands peasants turned up gold and silver jewelry and coins. This must have had some correlation with the increased use of heavy steel ploughs and deeper ploughing. The *Archeologiai Ertesito* (Archeological Reporter) often published news by local correspondents at the end of the 1860's and in the 1870's reporting archeological finds. The journal also reported that there was a mood of "digging up mounds," and of "looting" in the countryside,[46] and it proposed to have a law issued to punish the "looters."[47]

No matter how carefully and in what deep secrecy the treasure hunters worked, many cases of discovery became known. The championship of treasure hunting could probably be claimed by the village of Patosfa in Somogy County where, according to the reports of a journal in the year of the Compromise, 50 credulous men were digging for treasure with great diligence, looking for the loot that was to lay the foundations of their happiness.[48]

However, the fever of treasure hunting subsided rapidly by the 1890's; correspondingly, the belief in the treasure-locating ability of the seventh child faded.[49] The disappointment of the treasure hunters, the spread of the influence of general education, and the good examples of rationally-thinking peasants, all contributed to the gradual decline of illusions of advancement by finding treasure.

7. The Dissolution of the Traditional Peasant Way of Life.

The conserving force of rigid, unwritten laws of peasant life began to lose its influence in the 1870's and 1880's. The transformation was everywhere related to the abandonment of the three-field system, and it started only in regions where this had taken place. For us, changes in the system of production appear to be a simple, logical step. In real life, however, it amounted to reckoning with centuries of traditions, and change was achieved through years of painful reappraisals, resulting in heated arguments and hostilities in the villages. In fact, the interests of various peasant strata had clashed in the process of transformation. The initiators of change were usually the dwarf- and smallholders, possessing a few *hectares* of land. For them it was a matter of economic survival to use every square foot of land in the competitive situation. (The very same stratum was involved in creating the vegetable and fruit cultures of the market towns of the Great Plain.) Their families provided the necessary labor force for intensive production. On the other hand, the wealthier peasants swore by the traditional system exactly because of their need for an increased labor force. This was especially true in villages where the common grazing grounds had been distributed among the peasants and broken up for ploughlands. Where would the peasants be able to graze their animals, and under whose supervision, if the fallow lands were denied to grazing? There were a great many arguments about this issue in the western regions where intensive cattle raising became widespread. "Lately, however," as an expert described the agricultural conditions of Somogy County,

> lands that were usually left fallow and fertilized only fitfully during the winter and spring months are now being planted with fodder crops; but this does not happen in a smooth way, since in many villages the common grazing lands had already been broken up by the plough and the fallows served as a substitute. When a few people plant the fallows with grain, where shall the cattle find grazing grounds? From this, chaos results that often causes a great deal of dissatisfaction.[50]

The interests of the upper stratum of the peasantry coincided with those of the landless *zsellers* possessing only garden lands in the villages, since the law—at least until the introduction of decrees regulating local police forces in 1894—stated that in matters of land usage, the voice of the majority of the landowners was to be decisive. The dwarf- and smallholder were, thus, able to enforce their interests since they usually constituted the majority in the villages.

The fact that the poorer elements in the villages were able to enforce their will over that of the wealthier peasants had a devastating effect on the traditional caste spirit, a shock from which it never recovered. The complaints of the lot-owners were described by a reporter of the Transdanubian journal, *Gazdasagi Lapok:*

> The more intelligent members of the population (that is, the wealthier ones; *AV*) noticed the abnormal situation and began to speak up at the village-houses, and even took their case to the counties. But even there they could not achieve the retention of even one single hectare for the fallows . . . . There was no way to create order in the villages because the owners of one or two hectares had a vote equal in weight to those who possessed one or two lots . . It was only natural that those who possessed less land would vote down the wealthier ones who desired order . . . .[51]

In this report the wealthier peasants are made to appear the guardians of the old, the customary, in one word, "order." They were opposed by those who wanted something different, more modern. (The rich peasants finally succeeded in changing the situation; the law of 1894, regulating the local policing of the fields, stipulated that village land usages should be decided upon by a weighted vote in favor of the larger property owners.)[52]

There had been arguments in the villages before, indeed, but the voice of the community usually prevailed in the most important matter of peasant life, the method of production, as long as the three-field system existed. After that, everyone had to act according to his best knowledge. Each peasant had to make up his own mind as to what sort of crop rotation he wanted, how to secure fodder for his animals, and how to maintain the fertility of the land, to mention only the most obvious issues. Individual ability and talent began to weigh heavily in the balance of peasant life.

The opportunity for transformation was provided in the 1870's and 1880's not only by the coercive forces of economics, but also by another important factor, namely, generational change. Customarily, the dominating person in the peasant family was the oldest male. He gave out daily work assignments, decided upon the methods to be used in work, controlled income and determined necessary expenses. This was the case even when he could no longer directly participate in the work of the family because of his age.[53] The generation that had grown up in serfdom and brought the attitudes of that era into the new period, was beginning to be replaced in the 1870's and 1880's by the new generation born after 1848. This new generation felt not only the crisis of peasant life, but was also unable to assimilate a great many norms whose bases were the conditions of which it had no personal memories. Although this generation, too, learned its agricultural know-how from its elders, it was more open to new ideas. When its members observed a technique that they judged to be advantageous, they did not hesitate to adopt it.[54] (For instance, we have evidence that many of them were reading the journals of county economic associations.)[55]

After the introduction of the compulsory draft in 1869, many members of the new generation of peasants had the opportunity to see various areas of the Monarchy. During their travels, they had opportunities to observe agricultural methods that were better—or worse—than those used in Hungary. Positive as well as negative experiences widened their horizons. The new generation included many who were now becoming heads of their families; they recognized the fact that the comfortable work-tempo of a vanished age, and the unthinking spending-practices characteristic of it, were an impediment to their success in life.

New peasant attitudes and behavior patterns began to emerge in the 1880's, patterns that were to characterize peasant life until recently. The extremes were represented by two types of upwardly mobile peasants: one was hard-working, often miserly and ruthless with himself and others, usurious towards his fellow villagers in need. The other type was also hard-working but had wider horizons, was willing to take risks (often failing in his endeavors but always willing to start anew). One guarded his money in his chests at home because he was by his very nature, suspicious even of the local savings and loan association, or because he saw in these associations unwelcome competitors. He was unwavering in following the traditional production methods and was weary of innovations and risk-taking. The other type was, on the other hand, observant, always looking out for new methods, new enterprises to enter, new machinery with which to increase his income. The latter was active in organizing peasant associations (for buying steam threshers, for instance), or peasant cooperatives during the 1890's. The usurious type, especially if he moved up from lower ranks, represented the old caste-spirit that was already in decay, while the other type did not care too much for the unwritten laws of the village. One was dedicated to conservation, the other to innovation, or even to breaking out of peasant status altogether. The first type existed mainly in the grain-growing regions of the Great Plain, while the latter were more numerous in the western regions of the country.

We said that these two types represented extremes in attitudes; in fact, the majority of the peasantry developed attitudes somewhere in between, remaining cautious in their thinking and behavior. The tumultuous events of the previous decades, the examples of failure resulting from adherence to traditional methods, and the ups-and-downs of agricultural prices, made them conclude that they would have to think twice before spending their money, even if they had more on account of the increase of the volume of their crops. Such attitudes were strengthened not only by past examples, but also by the very real angers that threatened the existence of smallholders working only a few *hectares* of land. If some natural disaster (drought, a hailstorm, sickness of his animals) forced extraordinary expenses on the smallholder, his financial balance was so badly affected that it could be straightened out only with great difficulty. The failures of some of the courageous experimenters often counselled caution for the rest: peasants who adhered to traditional attitudes often pronounced severe and humiliating judgment on such people: "it was not enough for him what he was born into, and this is the consequence," was usually the judgment, voiced openly, or behind his back. The contemptuous judgment of the village was often more difficult to bear than the material consequences of bankruptcy.[56]

Surviving traditional peasant attitudes continued to suggest that agriculture was not an occupation, not a craft; it was something that could not be learned; someone had to be born into it and to grow with it, just as children grow into their fathers' clothes. Agriculture and peasant existence constituted a destiny according to these attitudes, one which had to be accepted by those who had been born into it since they had no other choice.

At the same time, cautious villagers watched the peasant entrepreneur. His innovations, if they were successful and needed little investment, were duplicated by the entire village within a few years. In fact, good examples were more important in expanding peasant expertise than were the best lectures or journal articles. This was also emphasized by contemporary writers; our illustration of the use of chemical fertilizers above was a case in point. But if an innovation or an experiment failed in a village, then the cause of progress was stifled for years to come. For example, if the experimenter did not spread his fertilizers on the land in good time, and his results were meager, judgment (that could not be appealed) was immediately pronounced on him. The activities of dishonest traders also contributed to the strengthening of cautious peasant attitudes towards innovation. In regions where new techniques were being introduced and accepted, there soon appeared a host of con artists who, for instance, offered chemical fertilizers for a few pennies less per kilogram, that had lost their power. The economic association of Vas County warned the village readers of its newspaper about the activities of such unscrupulous agents.[57] There were also large numbers of fraudulent sales of agricultural machinery. Many agents carried prepared agreement forms which they induced the naive peasants to sign. In return, the latter received unordered machines and equipment.[58] These were only a few of the many important factors that shaped peasant attitudes, and these attitudes were often different in various regions or even in individual villages.

While caution did survive in the western counties of Hungary, attitudes tending towards entrepreneurship gradually prevailed. But similar transformation in attitudes occurred only in villages surrounding the capital city and the environs of the market towns where garden culture was fortunately advanced. In descriptions of the prevailing economic conditions of various counties published in the 1890's, great differences in methods of peasant agriculture and attitudes were well illustrated. For instance, the author of the monograph on Sopron County observed that "the period during which the people of even the best agricultural regions were ruined" ended by the 1870's:

> with the arrival of the 1880's, it appeared that the wheel of fortune made a full turn. Land prices began to be good

> once again, the number of usurers declined, and forced public sales and bankruptcies that used to be everyday occurrences became rarer . . . .[59] There is not even a trace of the fallows system any more in our country; the peasants freely rotate their crops according to their belief that they would get more of less crops. In most of the lands in our county—whose counterparts elsewhere are left fallow—the peasants are producing fodder crops. We have such well-to-do peasants that their counterparts would be hard to find elsewhere, even if we do have some poorer ones. But the well-to-do have few debts, and if they have some, it is the result of their buying of real estate. The unspeakable misery of the 1870's has been overcome and capital is being accumulated . . . . The small properties that came into the hands of merchants are now being gradually returned to their former owners.[60]

According to this author, a "tremendous factor" in this process of change was the "proverbial vitality" of the peasants of Sopron County that induced them to learn methods of fattening cattle. After discussing the skill of the traders among the German and Croatian-speaking population of the county, he states that the Hungarian-speaking peasants:

> do not lack brains, a practical sense, and even the ability to trick someone, and they take advantage of these character traits in every instance when selling their products . . . . Their greatest desire is (to possess) real estate and land, in whose tilling they show unparalleled diligence and a desire to learn. For these reasons every change that is related to the productivity of their land leaves a deep impression on them.[61]

But there is quite a different picture provided in the monograph on Zemplen County, located in the northeast, extending from the Polish border to the valley of the Tisza River. The smallholders, the author of the monograph stated, practiced a "robber-economy:"

On the backward, extensively-worked lands, profitability is minimal; alcoholism and usury are rampant in every part of the country. . .[62] The local economic association tried to stop the process that produced wide-spread indebtedness by attempting to establish village self-help-savings and loan associations. However, its attempts failed because of the indolence and ignorance of the people . . . .[63]

Finally, let us illustrate our point with a few excerpts from the monograph on Csanad County; this will show the differences in attitudes of people living in a wider region. The former urbarial peasants of this county whose soil was very fertile, were, according to the author:

> diligent, but not very receptive to innovation . . . . They were especially desirous of buying land from their savings; if this were not possible, they wanted to obtain rentals.[64] They practiced extensive methods of production. They planted grains in two-thirds of the lands and corn in the rest. They liked to buy machinery and form associations for the purpose of acquiring threshers, but because of the bad impact of low grain prices, many of them became impoverished.[65]

In contrast to this, the author stated that the people of the market town of Mako were being enriched, and if the saying "there is no poor man in Mako" was not literally correct, it was at least typical of the area. In Mako, the main emphasis was on grain production, but the people also produced huge amounts of onions and other vegetables. Onion production was the basis of the income of the poorer segment of society: "there were years," the author asserted, "when this income came to 500-600,000 florins, mainly from the export of onions to foreign countries. Part of the population also used to sell this product as travelling merchants."[66] Besides vegetable products, the people of Mako also grew grapes. When they realized that the local wine was not competitive on the market, they began growing table grapes and they proved so skillful in the trade that they shipped their grapes as far as Berlin.[67] The author described the attitudes of the people of Mako this way:

> they are extraordinarily diligent workers, and they are thrifty; they also possess an excellent business sense. They often ship the produce of their gardens to distant places, such as England, in great quantities. Here, at home, they can sell their excellent vegetables and fowl for advantageous prices. They obey the decrees of authorities if lawful, but will not abide coercion. The priesthood has little influence over them. They eat well, but they are not alcoholics, and will drink wine only as long as their own supplies last. The drinking of liquor is being restricted to an ever-shrinking circle . . . .[68]

In this contemporary characterization we find no trace of attitudes typical of former serfs. Similar description could probably have been given of the peasants of Nagykoros, Kecskemet, and other market towns whose people developed intensive production methods in their areas. In these regions the typical peasant of the 1880's was characterized by Ferenc Erdei, the outstanding sociologist of Hungary a half century later, as "the group that developed the closest traits of *embourgeoisment*," a group that "was completely liberated from peasant traditions, and which, therefore, felt the least of the crisis of peasant life."[69]

It is not very difficult to discover in this charactrization a democratic consciousness that, according to Erdei, was typical of the people of the market towns. The labor-intensive agriculture in these areas provided steady incomes for dwarfholders and landless workers alike at a time when work opportunities were available for them only in the summer months elsewhere. It was not an accident, therefore, that the centers of the agrarian socialist movements that emerged in the 1890's were in the villages of the Great Plain, and there was no trace of these movements in the market towns where intensive agricultural methods were practiced.

We attempted to illustrate the changes in life-style and attitudes among the peasantry in three different regions, and tried to provide a classification of four types of peasants. These were: (a) the peasants of western Transdanubia, gradually turning to animal husbandry, being in the process of *embourgeoisment* but still retaining a great deal of peasant traditions; (b) the peasants of the market towns of the Great Plain, creating an agriculture based on truck-farming, acquiring bourgeois attitudes; (c) the people of the Great Plain outside the market towns, remaining stuck with traditional agricultural methods, struggling with the crisis of production, and remaining strongly traditional in attitudes; (d) the peasants of the northeast and east, hardly touched by the changes, continuing their traditional feudal life-style, backward, living off usurious loans, often escaping into the haze of alcoholism.

The transformation of peasant life-style and attitudes was, therefore, already in process in the 1880's in large areas of Hungary. New possibilities for progress were to be opened up, as further regions were to become affected by the changes in the decades of the turn of the century. Some regions, however, remained locked in their traditions. Thus, the regional differences were to continue to exist well into the future.

NOTES

1. Bela Sarlos, *Kozigazgatas es hatalompolitika a dualizmus rendszereben* (Administration and Power Politics in the System of Dualism) (Budapest, 1976), 104-107.
2. Gyula Vargha, *A magyar hitelugy es hitelintezetek tortenete* (History of Hungarian Finances and Financial Institutions) (Budapest, 1896), 529-30, 538-9, 550-1.
3. Gyorgy Szabad, "a hitelviszonyok," (Financial Conditions) in Szabo, *op. cit.*, vol. 2, 206-10.
4. Magyar Penzugy, 1881, June 3.
5. *Magyar Statisztikai Kozlemenyek, Uj folyam* (From now on, MStK UF) (Hungarian Statistical Review, New Series), vol. 16.

6. Vilmos Sandor, *Nagyipari fejlodes Magyarorszagon* (The Development of Heavy Industry in Hungary) (Budapest, 1954), 25-6.
7. Antal Voros, *A magyar mezogazdasag, op. cit.*, 22.
8. "Az 1878, evi oktober 17.-ere hirdetett orszaggyules nyomtatvanyai," (Printed Records of the National Diet of October 1878) *Kepviselohaz-Iromanyok* vol. 16 (Budapest 1880), 270.
9. Jeno Kvassay, *A Duna- es Tiszavolgyi armentesito tarsulatokra vonatkozo statisztikai adatok* (Statistical Data Related to the Flood Control Associations of the Danube and Tisza River Valleys) (Budapest, 1900), X.
10. Antal Voros, *Ovar, Ovar* . . . (Budapest, 1968), 37-45, 50-2, 55-7. See also, Arpad Balazs, *Magyarorszag mezogazdasagi szakoktatasi intezmenyei* (Agricultural Educational Institutions of Hungary) (Budapest, 1896), 154, 163-4.
11. Istvan Balogh, "A paraszti muvelodes," (The Education of Peasants) in Szabo, *op. cit.*, vol. 2, 537.
12. Karoly Keleti, *Hazank nepe* (Peoples of Our Country) (Pest, 1871), 358.
13. *Magyar Statisztikai Evkonyv* (Hungarian Statistical Yearbook) (From now on, MStE), 1901, 301.
14. Keleti, *op. cit.*, 360-1.
15. *MStE,* 1901, 301.
16. Keleti, *op. cit.*, 200.
17. *MStK, Uj Sorozat* (From now on, US), vol. 44, "Arstatisztika" (Price Statistics), 7-10.
18. *Ibid.*, vol. 66, 44X; "A magyar korona orszagainak 1900-1915. evi mezogazdasagi termelese," (Agricultural Production of the Countries of the Hungarian Crown between 1900-1915).
19. Sandor Matlekovics (ed.), *Magyarorszag kozgazasagi es kozmuvelodesi allapota ezereves fennallasakor* (The Conditions of Public Education and Economics in Hungary at the One-Thousandth Anniversary of its Existence) (Budapest, 1897), vol. 6, 278-82.

20. *A magyar korona orszagainak mezogazdasagi statisztikaja. Mezogazdasagi termeles* (Agricultural Statistics of the Countries of the Hungarian Crown. Agricultural Production in the Years 1895 and 1896), (Budapest, 1897), 5.
21. Voros, *A magyar mezogazdasag, op. cit.,* 84-5.
22. *Gazdasagi Neplap* (People's Economic Journal) (Pecs), September, 1883.
23. *Bacskai Kisgazda* (Smallholder of Bacska), December 24, 1903.
24. Voros, *A magyar mezogazdasag, op. cit.,* 87-8.
25. Gyula Varga, "A parasztsag munkaeszkozei," (Tools of the Peasantry) in Szabo, *op. cit.,* vol. 1, 322.
26. Imre T. Nagy, *Csikmegye kozgazdasagi leirasa* (Economic Description of Csik County) (Budapest, 1902), 21.
27. Varga, *op. cit.,* 320.
28. T. Nagy, *op.cit.,* 22.
29. *A magyar korona orszagainak mezogazdasagi statisztikaja. A gazdasagok megoszlasa jelleg es nagysag szerint* (Agricultural Statistics of the Countries of the Hungarian Crown. The Distribution of Firms According to Size and Characteristics) vol. 4 (Budapest, 1900), 57X.
30. *Ibid.,* 91-7, 291-303.
31. *MStE,* vol. 2 (1874), 152-7.
32. *A magyar korona orszagainak, op, cit.,* vol. 4, 63-64X.
33. *Ibid.,* 56X-7X.
34. T. Nagy, *op. cit.,* 22.
35. *A magyar korona orszagaiban az 1870. ev elejen vegrehajtott nepszamlalas eredmenyei a hasznos haziallatok kimutatasaval egyutt* (The Results of the Census of 1870 in the Countries of the Hungarian Crown, Including the Survey of Useful Domestic Animals) (Pest, 1871), 482-517. See also, *Magyarorszag hasznos haziallatai az 1884-ik ev szeptember havaban eszkozolt felvetel alapjan* (The Useful Domestic Animals of Hungary Based on the Survey of September, 1884) (Budapest, 1884), 16-7; *A magyar korona orszagainak, op.cit.,* vol. 1, "Az osszeiras fobb eredmenyei" (Major Results of the Survey), 114X.

36. Orszagos Leveltar, FIK, Altalanos Iratok (National Archives, General Documents), 1881, tetel 1229 and 2445.
37. See note 35 above.
38. *MStK US,* "Arstatisztika" (Price Statistics), 44 (1913), 150.
39. *Ibid.,* 63. See also *A Magyar korona orszagainak 1882-1913. evi kulkereskedelmi forgalma* (Foreign Exports of the Countries of the Hungarian Crown) (Budapest, 1923), 36X.
40. Tibor Kolossa, *Statistische Untersuchung der sozialen Struktur der Agrarbevolkerung in der Landern der Osterreichisch-Ungarischen Monarchie. Die Agrarfrage in der Osterreichisch-Ungarischen Monarchie, 1900-1918* (Bucharest, Rumania, 1965), 142.
4.1 Tancsics, *op, cit.,* 37.
42. *A magyarsag neprajza, op. cit.,* vol. 2, 425-6.
43. Istvan Orosz, "A differencialodas es a kisajatitas," (Differentiation and Expropriation) in Szabo, *op. cit.,* vol. 2, 142.
44. Istvan Tisza, *Az agrarius kerdesrol. Tisza Istvan osszes munkai* (About the Question of the Agriarians. Collected Work of Istvan Tisza) (Budapest, 1923), 358, 364-5.
45. Gyula Wieder, "Kincsaso babonak es raolvasasok," (Treasure-digging superstitions and Cants) *Ethnographia* 1912, 29-34.
46. *Archeologiai Ertesito,* 1870, 195.
47. *Ibid.,* 1872, 21.
48. *Magyar Neplap,* 1867, Nox. 161-2.
49. Samu Borovszky, *Bacs-Bodrog megye monografiaja. Magyarorszag varmegyei es varosai* (The Monography of Bacs-Bodrog County. Hungary's Counties and Cities) (Budapest, n.d.), vol. 1, 344.
50. Imre Szechenyi, *Somogy megye* (Somogy County) (Budapest, 1895), 13.
51. Jozsef Francsics, "Salus rei publicae," *Gazdasagi Lapok,* September 29, 1889.
52. Antal Hampel (ed.), *Magyarorszag foldmuvelesugyi igazgatasa* (Agricultural Administration of Hungary) (Budapest, 1913), 51.

53. Varga, *op. cit.,* 318.
54. *Ibid.,* 317.
55. *Egyesuleti Ertesito* (newsletter of the Association) (Szombathely), January, 1890 and March, 1891. See also, *Gazdasagi Neplap* (Pecs), April, 1884.
56. Zsigmond Moricz, in his *Novel of My Life,* described this sort of behavior among village peasants.
57. *Egyesuleti Ertesito* (Szombathely), September, 1888.
58. Varga, *op. cit.,* 316-7.
59. Pal Berenyi, *Sopron megye* (Sopron County) (Budapest, 1895), 240.
60. *Ibid.,* 249-50.
61. *Ibid.,* 239.
62. Geza Ballagi, *Zemplen megye* (Zemplen County) (Budapest, 1895), 160-1.
63. *Ibid.,* 194.
64. Jeno Gaal, *Csanad megye* (Csanad County) (Budapest, 1895), 123.
65. *Ibid.,* 129-30.
66. *Ibid.,* 124.
67. *Ibid.,* 108.
68. *Ibid.,* 99.
69. Ferenc Erdei, *A magyar paraszttarsadalom* (Hungarian Peasant Society) (Budapest, n.d.), 124.

III

THE DEVELOPMENT OF NEW LIFE STYLES AND A NEW MENTALITY

1. Incentives of Modernization

By the 1890's, new directions in agricultural production reached a point at which some producers could not only disregard the consequences of periodic price fluctuations (resulting from overseas competition) but were able to increase their income. But the west-Hungarian type of production, based on intensive cattle breeding, and that of the Danube-Tisza region based on vegetable and fruit growing, were no longer stimulated exclusively by the market of the Monarchy, regulated by a system of common tariffs, but by the rapidly developing Hungarian capitalist system.

The population of the country, 15.26 million in 1890, continued to increase despite extensive emigration; it reached 18.26 million in 1910.[1] At the same time, the ratio of the agricultural population decreased from 67.4% to 62.4%.[2] Thus, the internal market for agrarian goods increased considerably. The segment of the population that lived from industry and trade, and the six million civil servants, proved to be important consumers of agricultural produce.

During this period, the population of Greater Budapest increased from 0.56 million to 1.1 million people.[3] The population of other cities beginning the process of industrialization (such as Pozsony, Gyor, Pecs, Miskolc, Nagyvarad, Temesvar, etc.) reached or passed 50,000 people each. The growing demand for fruits and vegetables by the cities created a ring of gardening villages not only around Budapest, but also around other cities (on a somewhat smaller scale, of course) by the 1880's. There were, however, growing problems with milk supplies; the large estates as well as small independent proprietors were unable to satisfy the demand.[4]

At first, the Economic Associations of the counties tried to create new forms of cooperation for the marketing of milk; by the 1890's, however, the Ministry of Agriculture became convinced that the demands of Budapest for dairy products could be satisfied only through the organization of the regular marketing of milk, produced by distant village-cooperatives.[5]

The true motivating force for intensive cattle breeding became, therefore, not the demand for meat, but for milk. The peasantry of Moson County (in the neighborhood of Vienna) became the suppliers of dairy products through cooperative marketing to the Austrian capital by the end of the 1890's. The peasants of this county, located in the Small Plain, originally possessed urbarial lots larger than the national average. However, they were, until the 1890's, bogged down in extensive production of grain crops, using the old three-field system, despite the demands of nearby Vienna for agrarian goods. Within a decade, however, the county developed rapidly through the modernization of its dairy production.[6]

The problem was that the expanding market of the Monarchy continued to demand flour as well as beef cattle and swine. According to statistics, 77.4% of all wheat exports and 59% of flour went to the Austrian markets. By 1897-1901, the Austrians bought 98% and 85.1% of wheat and flour respectively.[7] Most exports of other wheat products also went to Austria.

But changing prices provided incentives for the expansion of animal husbandry, especially cattle breeding. The changing index of prices between 1891-1910 were as follows:[8] (1871-1875=100)

Years	wheat	cattle	swine
1891-1895	65.1	107.6	85.6
1896-1900	72.9	116.6	89.9
1901-1905	66.8	132.6	98.3
1906-1910	88.8	152.7	123.2

Thus, the price of wheat had not come close to the averages of 1871-1875 even by the end of this period, despite the fact that, in 1906, an agreement between the Austrian and Hungarian governments established high protective tariffs (a minimum of 6.30 and a maximum of 7.5 crowns per quintal) to exclude foreign competitors from the Monarchy's markets.[9] The consequence was the rise of the price of this commodity.

According to export statistics, the demand for the most important Hungarian agricultural product at that time, wheat, was exceeded by demands for beef cattle. The ratios of wheat, flour, cattle and swine in Hungarian agricultural exports changed according to the index of 1892-1911 as follows:[10] (18821886=100)

Years	wheat	flour	cattle	swine
1892-1896	105.5	177.7	207.1	132.0
1897-1901	78.6	178.2	300.1	61.2
1902-1906	97.7	218.3	389.0	76.3
1907-1911	79.5	207.5	362.3	98.3

The volume of wheat export, compared to the yearly average of 5.24 million quintals in 1882-1886, fell to 4.17 million quintals. It was true that this was balanced by the growth of flour exports from 3.39 million to 7.04 million quintals, although the data included wheat imported from the Balkans that entered Hungary under special arrangements with the Hungarian mills. (This wheat averaged about 1.1 million quintals a year.) The decline of swine exports seemingly contradicts our previous statement about the growing demand for Hungarian meat products. However, the decline did not result from a decrease in market demand, but from the swine plague which reached Hungary in 1895, devastating the swine herds.

We must also mention the rapid increase of poultry exports. The production of fowl was almost exclusively in the hands of small peasant proprietors. The value of Hungarian exports of eggs, poultry and feathers averaged about 22.5 million crowns a year between 1882-1886; in contrast, it reached 78.9 million crowns in 1907-1911,[11] while, at the same time, the value of wheat exports was 97.9 million crowns.

The significance of railroad transportation of grain continuedease, and the railroads occupied a central place in providing incentives for agrarian modernization. The railroad network increased by 8,000 kilometers between 1890 and 1913, expanding from 11,399 to 19,484 kilometers in length.[12] Parallelis, transport costs became lower. The lines running from the capital city to the peripheries of the country were increasingly tied in with local tracks. This made it possible for villages that were located 100 or more kilometers away from the cities to market their perishables, especially their dairy products. While a few decades before, the prices of grain in distant provinces were half as much as those paid in the capital city (due to high transportation costs), now the price differences between the countryside and the cities were negligible.

The expansion of the railroad network, therefore, provided incentives for agricultural modernization, or at least it was an important factor in the process. The increase in the number of financial institutions, on the other hand, provided the financial foundations for the transformation. In contrast to the 1,255 such institutions existing in 1890, by 1913, there were 5,014 of them in the country.[13] The growth of village savings and loan associations was especially conspicuous. In 1890 only 591 such institutions existed,[14] and their operations were not geared to provide credits for agricultural use. The organization of *Reiffeisen*-type savings and loan cooperatives was a more suitable step to provide credit for the peasantry. Count Sandor Karolyi, himself a large estate owner, the leader of the political opposition to the contemporary liberal government of Hungary, furthered the cause of these institutions. Karolyi and his political friends sensed that the survival of the traditional peasant life style could contribute to great social tensions. Thus, they tried to help the changes along by the formation of savings and loan cooperatives. But they were only partially successful; they created only 157 such institutions by 1893, and these were all under the close supervision of Karolyi's group.[15] The reason for the slowness of this process was, according to Karolyi, that "those whom they wanted to address, whose interests they wanted to protect, namely, the people, did not understand their language."[16]

The liberal government reacting at least partly to the agrarian socialist movement of the 1890's, began to search for sociopolitical means to reduce the dissatisfaction of agricultural workers and poor peasants. In 1894, two high ranking administrators of the Mininstry of Agriculture were sent to the Great Plain to study existing social conditions. The outcome of their study included the suggestion that the state should provide strong support for the establishment of savings and loan associations in the villages.[17]

These factors constituted the background for the enactment of the law for the organization of the *Orszagos Kozponti Hitelszovetkezet* (National Central Office of Credit Cooperatives or *OKH*) in 1898. The major task of the central office of the future savings and loan associations was to be the organization of village branches, and the securing of their working capital. The government supported the venture by underwriting one million crowns worth of shares, and the large credit institutions in Budapest contributed by buying another million's worth.[18] This was a signal that these institutions considered it their task to help the social mission of the Association.

Such support, thus, became at least partly an administrative matter. The government was especially interested in the Association's branches in the distant provinces. This was the explanation for the fact that the number of branches was almost higher in the provinces than in the more advanced regions. The number of savings and loan associations belonging to *OKH* was 712 in 1899, and in 1913 it was 2,425; their activities covered 7,761 villages or over 61.8% of all the settlements in Hungary. The amount of credits which they extended to borrowers increased from 25.4 million to 279.6 million crowns in the same period of time.[19]

One could conclude from the wide territorial dispersal of these institutions that the various levels of development characterizing different regions in Hungary were being gradually eliminated. But we get a different impression when comparing the amount of capital, the number of shares purchased, and the amount of money deposited in these institutions. In 1909, 18.8% of all cooperative savings and loan institutions existed in Transdanubia, and 17.5% in Transylvania. But 30.8% of all shares and deposits held by the associations were in Transdanubia and only 4.4% were in the hands of the Transylvanian cooperative associations.[20]

These institutions (under the supervision of *OKH*) provided loans at interest rates that corresponded to those charged by the Austro-Hungarian Bank, adding 1-1.5% as handling charges. Including these charges, the annual interest rates came to 5-7%.

The government achieved only partly what it considered the social mission of the savings and loan associations in the backward regions of the country where help was needed the most. The activities of these institutions were hampered by the fact that they presupposed a relatively high level of general education on the part of the membership. The members were expected to oversee the activities of the officers. Wherever this was not the case (especially in the most backward regions), the possibility of corruption emerged. For instance, in Csik County, where the associations were all members of *OKH* (having been founded by government help), they turned to usurious practices. The officers simply used the capital of these institutions to lend money at usurious rates of interest.[21] In contrast, the associations in western Hungary, where the level of education was generally higher, often requested the central office to reduce its interest rates since the local associations provided loans at lower rates to their customers.[22]

Among factors that helped the modernization of agriculture, the level of education generally available for the rural population was also important. We must consider data on literacy as the best way of determining this level. Among people of six years of age or older the literacy rate increased from 53.2% in 1890, to 68.7% in 1910. But this represented the national average; there existed considerable differences between eastern and western Hungary in this respect. In contrast to a literacy rate of 81.8% in Transdanubia, the rate was only 56.9% in eastern Hungary. In Transylvania it was only 50.5%. In one of the most highly developed west Hungarian counties, Moson, the literacy rate was 88.9%, and in Zala County it was 75.1%. The most developed Transylvanian county, Brasso, boasted of 82.3% literate people among those six years of age and older, but in Szolnok-Doboka County the rate was only 28.6%. The least literate county in Hungary was Maramaros where only 26.8% of the population could read and write in 1910.[23]

Statistics do not provide information on the contents of elementary school curricula. The six-year elementary schools and the one-day-a-week courses of three-year refresher schools were able to provide the necessary information for the peasantry to support agrarian modernization. But it was exactly in the most backward areas where the schools were unable to fulfill the demands of the law on elementary education (introduced in 1868). In the scattered settlements of the mountainous regions, children were generally unable to attend school with the onset of winter. Furthermore, the villages or religious organizations that were running the schools in these districts were too poor to hire well-trained teachers who demanded higher salaries.[24] The untrained teachers that they were able to obtain usually taught only reading, writing, and some elementary mathematics. Although there were only 886 such teachers in these schools (in the 1907-1908 school year), their number was sufficiently large to impede real progress.[25] While in the country as a whole (with the exception of children in the cities) 52% of the children completed four years of elementary school, in the backward areas their number was considerably lower.[26] The education provided by elementary schools was, therefore, hardly more than a smattering of knowledge of reading and writing, and this was certainly no longer sufficient to enhance the process of the modernization of peasant production methods in the first decades of the 20th century.

2. Modernization and Traditionalism

Although the tempo of the modernization of peasant production methods somewhat increased after the 1890's, the advances remained uneven in the different regions of the country. Changes occurred at the most rapid rate in western Hungary, while the eastern areas were showing a slow, sluggish progress. On the other hand, the half century of capitalist development left the northeastern and eastern areas of the country practically untouched. The latter regions continued to use production methods characteristic of the feudal age, although there was some progress in the adoption of some power tools such as the steel plough and mechanical threshers. The differences in developmental levels thus, not only continued to exist, but in some instances they were even aggravated.

Changing market conditions were reflected in the slowing down and then again speeding up of the expansion of the ploughlands and the simultaneous construction of fallows. But the new expansion never reached the size of that of the 1870's. The changing ratio between ploughlands and the fallows was, in 1891-1915, as follows (five-year averages):[27]

Year	Total Ploughlands in 1,000 hectares		Total Fallows		
	hectares	index	hectares	index	%
1871-1875	10,463	100	2,290	100	21.9
1891-1895	12,007	114.8	1,697	74.1	14.1
1896-1900	11,970	114.4	1,458	63.7	12.2
1901-1905	12,280	117.4	1,287	56.2	10.5
1906-1910	12,780	122.2	1,158	50.6	9.1
1911-1915	12,967	123.9	1,149	50.2	8.9

The growth of the size of the ploughlands, following upon the stagnation of the 1890's, resumed after 1906, when grain prices became favorable once again (following the imposition of new custom duties). The increases were the largest in eastern Hungary and the Bansag,[28] that is, in the regions where onesided extensive grain production dominated agriculture during the previous decades. The hope was alive once again among the producers of these regions that the good old days of worry, free grain production were coming back. Thus, in eastern Hungary and the Bansag extensive production methods remained dominant. On the other hand, in western Hungary, more modern methods, including a more varied crop rotation system, came to characterize peasant production. This was evident in changes in planting practices. In these areas grain crops took up 61.9% of the ploughlands in 1891-1895; by 1911-1915, their ratio decreased to 56.9%. At the same time, the share of the root crops increased by 3.5% and those of fodder by 3.1%[29] The speed of the spread of intensive production methods as illustrated by the changing ratios of fallows and fodder crops between 1891 and 1911-1915, was as follows:[30]

Region	Fallows in % of ploughlands		Lands planted with fodder crops in % of all lands	
	1895	1911-1915	1895	1911-1915
Transdanubia	10.0	4.0	13.0	13.8
Northern Highlands and Small Plain	14.4	7.8	10.6	12.3
Between Danube-Tisza Rivers	8.3	3.9	6.5	7.0
Northeastern Highlands	18.2	15.0	8.8	10.5
Eastern Hungary	15.0	13.2	8.4	9.2
Bansag	3.7	3.7	4.9	5.7
Transylvania	23.6	20.6	6.9	8.2
Entire Hungary	12.51	8.9	8.5	9.5

This table illustrates the fact that the direction of agricultural developments differed in the Great Plain and western Hungary. The large size of fallow lands in the former region indicates that the three-and-two-field systems continued to hinder there the introduction of more rational methods. We have data about villages from 1902 and 1908 where traditional land usages remained in force. In 1902, 28.6% of all settlements continued to enforce the three-or-two-field system, and their ratio was still 26.4% six years after.[31] In 1908, the ratios in the various regions of the country were as follows:

Region	Number of villages	Three or two-field systems, %	Free villages
Transdanubia	2,699	8.1%	91.9
Northwestern Highlands and Small Plain	2,235	7.4%	92.6
Between Danube-Tisza Rivers	537	13.6%	86.4
Northeastern Highlands	2,223	43.3%	56.7
Eastern Hungary	1,456	49.4%	50.6
Bansag	1,050	19.6%	80.4
Transylvania	2,362	41.4%	58.6
Entire Hungary	12,362	26.4%	73.6

This illustrates the fact that about 40% of the villages in eastern Hungary continued to use land in a manner that hindered modernization. The process of modernization had actually slowed down in eastern Hungary in the early 20th century. The causes included the peasants' insistence upon continuing the traditional, customary methods of production; they also included laws such as that which regulated the policing of the fields (*mezoori torveny*), issued in 1894, that included provisions about land usage.

Although the law, and especially its provisions dealing with its execution, favored the elimination of the traditional system, and it even prevented its reintroduction wherever it was already given up, it also had deleterious effects. It stipulated that in villages where the traditional system survived, a meeting of all landowners was to decide by a two-thirds majority as to which system they wanted to follow.[32] According to contemporary accounts, many villages then decided to free themselves of the yoke of the past. But the law also decreed that wherever the owners decided to maintain the three-or-two-field systems, they could not discontinue this practice for the following six years, or two turns of the system.

Discontinuance was then made subject to so much bureaucratic red tape that the peasants (who did not like to have too much contact with the authorities in any case) usually remained locked into the system.[33] In this case, therefore, the legislation itself became a hindrance to modernization.

Chemical fertilizers gradually assumed a growing significance in the agriculture of Hungary. The aggregate production of this type of fertilizers by small firms reached 2 million quintals by 1910.[34] The new producers conducted a fervent campaign of advertisement to propagate the advantages of their products, paralleling the activities of the Economic Associations of the counties. But they were unable to alter regional characteristics; these were part and parcel of peasant life, and were reinforced by the agrarian boom of the 1879's.

Survey's were conducted about the spread of the use of chemical fertilizers in various counties, based on the deliveries of these products.[35] Accordingly, in some western counties, 14-16 kilograms (30.8-35.2 lbs.) of chemical fertilizers were used on an average for every *hold* (1.4 acres of land). But the averages declined towards the east of the country; on the Great Plain the average was only 5 kilograms (11 lbs.) per *hold* and in Transylvania it was only 1.7 kilograms (4.1 lbs.). Even these numbers do not fully illustrate the true nature of regional differences in fertilizer use, since they do not include about 0.5 million quintals of chemical fertilizers that were imported from Austria and Germany after 1905. These imports were used, according to an expert, "mostly in the western counties," since the foreign producers could not compete with Hungarian firms in eastern Hungary because of their higher transportation costs.[36] In the western counties, therefore, the true average of chemical fertilizers used on ploughlands, was closer to 30 kilograms per *hold* (66 lbs.) a year, and in this the region was closer to countries with a more advanced agricultural system than that of Hungary.

The worst practices in fertilizer use existed in eastern Hungary. Dried manure was still used for heating fuel in these regions despite the arguments and efforts of agricultural experts to discontinue the practice. One problem was that the arguments of experts could hardly reach the peasants who lived on scattered settlements on the Great Plain. The only known method of increasing production was, for most of these peasants, the expansion of the size of the ploughlands. Their average yields usually reflected the backwardness of their production methods. For instance, in the much poorer Transdanubian soil, the average yearly yield of autumn wheat in 1906-1911 was 13.8 quintals per hectare (2.9 acres); in contrast, the better soil of eastern Hungary yielded only an average of 11.8 quintals a year in the same period and that of Bansag 12.1 quintals. The differences were even greater in 1901-1905. During the ten years in question the average yield of wheat in Transdanubia grew yearly by one quintal (220 lbs.) per hectare. In eastern Hungary the increase was only 30 kilograms (66 lbs.), while in the Bansag the yield decreased by 40 kilograms (88 lbs.) per *hectare.* We should also note that because of better soil treatment, a more rational crop rotation, and the more frequent use of chemical fertilizers in Transdanubia, the difference of yields in the best and worst years was only 4 quintals per hectare, while this difference came to 5.7 quintals in eastern Hungary and 6.3 quintals in the Bansag.[37]

Regional differences were probably the smallest in terms of the available technology in agriculture. Moreover, the differences could be explained at least partly by objective factors, not by the subjective elements inherent in peasant mentality. Unfortunately, no surveys were taken—except in the case of mechanical threshers—that could be used as evidence for the spread of technology after 1895. But it was significant for both a correct treatment of the soil and the more economical use of draft power that the Hohenheim-type iron ploughs were gradually exchanged for the various types of Sack-ploughs during the 1890's. In the case of the latter, the depth of the ploughing was regulated by a simple lengthening or shortening of a chain that connected the axle with the barrow of the plough, never altering the straight line of its progress in the soil. Accoring to expert estimates, the older ploughs completed the ploughing of 0.28 hectares a day, while the Sack-plough did 0.4 hectares.[38]

The actual increase in the number of small machines used by the peasants could only be estimated on the basis of their imports. This import was 80% higher in 1909-1913 than in 1896-1900.[39] The import of machinery from the United States continuously increased after the turn of the century, signifying peasant demands for better tools; in the 1910's, this import made up fully one-third of all such imports.[40] Similarly, the import of mechanical planters doubled,[41] while the local production of these machines reached 1,200 a year.[42] Mechanical harvesters were imported in large numbers after the harvest strikes of 1905 and 1906, 88% of these machines coming from the United States.[43] These served as a threat against possible strikes of agrarian workers on the large estates.[44]

Qualitative improvements were achieved in viniculture after 1890. In the mid-1880's, the area planted with grapes was 368,000 hectares. This area decreased to 195,000 hectares by 1895, following the destruction caused by the philoxera-infection,[45] and increased once again to 326,000 hectares by 1913.[46] The infection destroyed in a few years over 50% of the historical viniculture of Hungary, the destruction reaching 80% of the vineyards in Tokaj.[47] Thousands of small producers lost their way of making a living from one day to the next.

The government tried to help the producers. At first their taxes were forgiven; then, after 1895, they were provided loans for the replanting of their vineyards. The government also established special nurseries on the sandy soil of the Great Plain, using imported American grapes (that proved immune to the infestation) and hardier local varieties. The new foundations for a revived Hungarian viniculture were, thus, established. The American varieties, of course, had to be mixed with European grapes in order to provide wine that suited Hungarian tastes.

During the tremendous effort of reconstruction not only were better varieties of grapes established in the Hungarian vineyards, but production technology itself was completely transformed. The better varieties of grapes needed more expert handling. Planting had to be preceded by better soil treatment; the vines had to be grafted and regularly fertilized. They needed several hoeings a year, expert pruning and several sprayings. In consequence, viniculture became almost a separate agrarian craft. The old ways were still sufficient to produce wine for home consumption, but not enough to fulfill the demands of the market.

The discovery that vines grown in sandy soil were largely immune to the philoxera infestation, actually contributed to changing the character of sandy areas between the Danube and Tisza Rivers. Many of these areas were useless for agriculture before. About 70,000 hectares (203,000 acres) of new vineyards were planted in this region after 1890, the process being spurred on by the higher price of wine. The work was done mostly by small proprietors from the market towns and villages of this area, as well as by former owners of vineyards from other regions whose grapes were destroyed by the philoxera infestation.[49] These people later were to be called the "heroes of the sand."

Truck farming also made great strides along the northern line of the Danube River and in the Gyongyos-Hatvan area. The truck farms supplied vegetables for the capital city of Budapest, now having more than a million people. The needs of this city could no longer be satisfied by the existing gardens of these villages. Thus, very large areas of ploughlands were turned over for this purpose. According to surveys that covered only the most important vegetable varieties, 150,800 acres were used in 1895, and 402,000 in 1913 for this purpose.[50] Specialization made it possible for the peasants of this region to acquire such expertise in producing vegetables and some fruits that even scholarly experts of gardening were amazed. The agriculturists who were concentrating on the production of onions, melons or green peppers were no longer peasants in the traditional sense of that term, but rather capitalist entrepreneurs. However, the transmission of their knowledge was done by the traditional method of fathers teaching their sons the secrets of their craft.

While in the region around Budapest and of the emerging other cities truck gardening was the major means of change from the traditional to modern methods of production, in western Hungary, cattle breeding provided the incentives for change.

Here the peasants concentrated on cattle breeding; it provided 60-70% of the income of small-and medium landholders (owning between 6-60 acres each).[51] This form of modernization did spread from west to south, and even to Transylvania. But the trend was not strong enough to change the extensive production of grains that was practiced in the Bansag, or the two-and three-field systems of the Transylvanian villages. In fact, rising grain prices after 1906 even reduced the significance of animal husbandry in the Bansag.[52]

The significance of cattle breeding was, however, underlined by the increase in the number of animals raised. According to surveys conducted in 1895 and 1911, the distribution of major animal breeds was as follows:[53]

Animal	1895	%	1911	%
cattle	5,829,018	59.2	6,184,264	60.4
horses	1,972,448	20.0	2,001.431	19.6
sheep	752,000	7.7	769,771	7.5
hogs	1,289,314	13.1	1,283,284	12.5

The 6% increase in the number of cattle illustrated in this table seems relatively insignificant. But when we consider the fact that the export of cattle between 1902 and 1911 increased by a yearly average of 162,000 animals, the real effect of this process becomes evident.

Higher productivity in cattle resulted from the establishment of improved breeds. In 1895, 64.4% of the animals still belonged to the slowly-developing, poor milk-producing grey Hungarian breed. By 1911, only 30.3% of the animals were of this breed and peasant smallholders owned only 27.9% of these cattle. In the various regions of the country peasants possessingan 142 acres of land held the following ratios of Hungarian gray breeds in 1911:[54]

Region	Percent
Transdanubia	3.6%
Northwestern Highlands and Small Plain	0.4%
Between the Danube and Tisza Rivers	35.1%
Northeastern Highlands	23.4%
Eastern Hungary	58.9%
Bansag	21.6%
Transylvania	41.7%
Entire Hungary	27.9%

This table also reflects the advancement of modernization in the various regions of Hungary. The dichotomous nature of the modernization process in the region between the Danube and Tisza Rivers is also evident. In this region, the small-and dwarfholders increasingly turned to intensive garden- and viniculture, while the richer peasants continued their extensive grain production. The rapidly developing, good milk-producing western breeds of cattle needed intensive care and a great deal more fodder than the Hungarian breed; their raising was possible only in areas where the entire system of agrarian production was changed.

In fact, the efforts of the peasants were being more and more concentrated on animal husbandry in western Hungary. According to estimates based on surveys in 1895, only 53.5% of the agricultural lands were held by small-and dwarfholder peasants; yet they raised 78% of all the major animal breeds and 77% of all the cattle.[55] By 1911, the aggregate size of peasant landholdings was somewhat increased; but their share in the major animal breeds also increased to 80%. This illustrated the fact that peasant production began to correspond to market conditions with some regional variations. However, there was also another motivating force in this process, namely, the rapid development of a marketing network for dairy products, especially milk.[56]

The periodic crises of the dairy supplies of the capital city of Budapest (and the agrarian socialist movements of the 1890's) induced the Ministry of Agriculture to think about the creation of an organized system to market the dairy products of the villages, patterned on Danish methods of marketing co-operatives. "In order to counterbalance social movements," wrote an official entrusted with the supervision of milk production in the Ministry, "every effort that could provide work and an extra income for smallholders should be encouraged."[57] The Ministry, thus, began to search for a region where intensive animal husbandry had reached an advanced stage, the western breeds of cattle were already accepted and a "spirit of enterprise" existed among the peasants. It also wanted a region where some compelling factor existed that would force the reluctant peasants into accepting something "new" such as a cooperative marketing association. The first three conditions existed in Baranya County, in its historic grape-growing region in the Mecsek mountain range. Here the breeding of good dairy cattle was already well advanced and the peasants had already been involved in several enterprises. The compelling factor was represented by the destruction by the philoxera infestation of the vineyards.[58]

However, despite the presence of these factors, it took months of arguments and intense efforts to form the first village-marketing cooperative for dairy products in early 1895. The peasants were reluctant to pay even one forint for a share, since they expected the cooperative to fail. Finally, the store of the cooperative was opened in a former press-house.[59] It took another half-year to establish the next cooperative in a neighboring village, reflecting the continuing mistrust of the venture by the peasants.[60] But the favorable year-end reports of the cooperatives ended the reluctance of the peasants in other nearby villages to enter cooperative arrangements. The original first cooperative established in a village of 80 houses paid off in a year all the expenses that it had incurred, and distributed nearly 12,000 forints among its members. This was equal to an income which the peasants derived from their vineyards only in exceptionally good years. The news of success spread like wildfire. The Ministry of Agriculture began receiving numerous requests for advisors for the establishment of new cooperatives. By 1897, there existed 42 cooperatives in the villages of Baranya County. "Now we have milk instead of wine; although the men do not drink it, they probably make more money out of it than they previously did from their wine," reported the journal of Baranya County in 1898.[61]

A year later a similar organizing effort began in Moson County. Within a decade, the dairy marketing cooperatives of this region acquired an international reputation. The organizer of this region was Professor Imre Ujhelyi of the department of animal husbandry at the Agricultural Academy of Mosonmagyarovar. In 1894, Ujhelyi studied animal husbandry in Bavaria, Switzerland, and Austria; he discovered that the peasantry of these countries, working under expert direction, raised the standards of their animal husbandry to a very high level. In contrast, he observed the backwardness of animal husbandry in his own county, which was way behind even that of Sopron and Vas Counties. The peasants of the latter regions received twice as much money for their cattle than those of Moson. Furthermore, the landholders of the latter possessed much more land on an average than the Transdanubian peasants. In Moson, the comparatively large peasant holdings were extensively worked and in many areas the three-field system continued to survive.

Thus, Ujhelyi started his organizing efforts under difficult conditions. He visited the villages of the county on weekends, lecturing about the advantages of modern methods of cattle breeding. In 1896, he was instrumental in organizing the county's cattle-breeders' association which immediately began the registration of simmenthal-type animals. He seemed tireless; he organized milking-contests to prove that there were wide differences between individual milk-cows even of the same breed, establishing the principle of selectivity. His association took steps to acquire the appropriate breeding bulls. The first dairy cooperative association was established by Ujhelyi in 1900, and this was followed by many others. Their early activities were supervised by the young professor; he signed their delivery contracts, examined the activities of each cooperative closely, especially if there were complaints from Vienna about the quality of the butter which they delivered to the Austrian capital. He introduced the practice of systematically checking the calorie content of fresh milk, thus, eliminating the possibility of cheating. The procedure in question also enabled the cooperatives to check the work of the butter-makers, since the calorie content of milk enabled them to predict the amount of butter that could be expected. In order to be able to compete with the Danish producers, the cooperatives obtained pasteurizing machines in 1908 and pasteurized their butter. Some of the cooperatives marketing raw milk, began to experiment with cheese making under Ujhelyi's prompting, and when they found that this product was more profitable than milk, they turned to cheese making on a large scale.

Such expert direction and advice soon had its results in the successes of the dairy cooperatives and in cattle breeding. Within a decade, the entire cattle stock in the county had been transformed. This was the more remarkable, since the large estates in the county—and in Hungary in general—still continued their practice of regarding the outward appearance of cattle as their most important characteristic. Milk-producing capability was regarded as secondary to appearance. Ujhelyi argued for just the opposite: "we are producing for our pockets, not for our eyes," he said in his campaign to win the peasants to his ideas. He also worked hard to convince the peasants of the importance of cattle registration. The eventual results included not only the doubling of the actual value of cattle held by the peasants of the county, but also a tremendous increase in income derived from dairy products. In 1900, the average income per milk-cow was 62 crowns! In the early 1910's, the most valuable breeding bulls in Hungary were being produced by the villagers of Moson County, since they were able to show (through the registry) the milk-producing ability of their cattle. By then, the buyers included some of the largest estates of the country. The owners of these estates themselves began to apply Ujhelyi's principles in their own cattlebreeding programs.

The cattle-breeders' association of Moson, when it was conceived, took notice of the entire agricultural system. After its first successes, the association began to take steps to modernize the entire system. Thus, improved seeds of fodder crops were distributed free of charge among villagers who were willing to experiment with them as early as 1898; the first quintals of chemical fertilizers were similarly given away. Each of these programs was buttressed by expert practical advice about the use of seeds and chemical fertilizers. Within a decade the villages that were still using the three-field system in the 1890's became showcases of the most intensive agricultural production, using chemical fertilizers.[62]

Thus, the process of modernization, starting in two opposite corners of Transdanubia, spread very rapidly in western Hungary; but it remained basically confined to this region. In 1900, there existed 246 dairy cooperatives; in 1905, their number grew to 540, and in 1910, to 549.[63] Of these, fully 52.8%, 61.3% and 63% respectively were located in Transdanubian areas. It was true that many more cooperative associations were established, but many were also dissolved.

There were two major reasons for the failure of individual cooperatives: one was the lack of expert direction, and the other included the activities of private entrepreneurs. One precondition of the cooperatives' success was the participation of the village intelligentsia (teachers and village priests) in the common venture. They were the only ones capable of conducting the correspondence of the association, taking care of accounting and the inventories, and performing the general administrative duties. Wherever such cooperation was absent, the cooperative was soon dissolved.[64] After the successes of the first cooperatives were disseminated, private capitalists also took notice of the possibilities inherent in the marketing of dairy products. In many villages, private entrepreneurs began organizing marketing, often indirectly contributing to the dissolution of established local cooperatives. In the final count, however, it did not matter who organized the marketing network. The real significance of the creation of the network was in not only securing a significant new source of income for the peasants, but also in modernizing cattle breeding and, as its corollary, the modernization of the entire agricultural system.

The influence of the cattle-breeders' association of Moson county reached beyond the confines of this administrative district. Reports of its success were soon noted not only in the local papers but also in national publications. Ujhelyi himself propagated the result in local and even foreign scholarly journals. Thus, in the early 1900's, delegations of peasants, often under the leadership of their parish priests and teachers, came to visit the villages of Moson County and to observe the results of the new type of agriculture. In a decade and a half, over 1,200 peasants visited these villages.[65] The visits—and the reports of the papers—convinced many peasants that the establishment of producers' and marketing cooperatives was a sure way to increase the level of their knowledge and production. The cattle breeding practices of the peasants of Moson also aroused the interest of foreign experts. Up to the outbreak of World War I, 297 such experts from various countries visited the cattle breeders' association. In the summer of 1914, 18 veterinarians from the United States, attending the London congress of their profession, undertook a "little detour" to observe the breeding practices of the peasants of Moson County.[66]

Here we attempted to provide an outline of the tempo and speed of modernization in the different regions of Hungary. We would like to emphasize the fact that this cannot be more than a bare outline of the process that was much more colorful and varied than could be fully described in this short summary. Even in regions where modernization was at the most advanced stage, there continued to exist areas where the peasants still adhered to traditional production methods. Moson county as a whole was backward for a long time, then its people suddenly embarked on a very rapid process of modernization. The peasants of two neighboring counties, those of Sopron and Zala, also began their modernization process in the 1890's. In contrast, the peasants of Tolna County who were equally recognized for their advanced cattle breeding methods, as well as those of Baranya County, were not unanimous in their approach to modernity. Areas in Tolna, especially the Sarkoz, and others in Baranya, including the Ormansag, continued to retain the traditional agricultural system. Transylvania as a whole was hardly touched by half a century of capitalist developments, while the production methods of its Saxon peasants were as modern as those of the peasants of the most advanced regions of Transdanubia. It seems safe to say, however, that as far as Hungary as a whole was concerned, the agrarian crisis of the last decades of the 19th century began to force the peasantry onto the path of modernization.

3. The New Life Style

The pages of contemporary journals provide an interesting reflection of the wide varieties in peasant life styles between the 1850's and 1860's and that of the turn of the century. By 1900, the papers speak about intense labor from dawn to dusk that the peasants had to perform in contrast to the comfortable work-rhythm of the mid-19th century. The old complaints about the peasants' reluctance to work for wages have been exchanged for complaints about the lack of work opportunities and the lack of income. Instead of the proverbial lazy, neglectful peasant, the reports speak of diligent people intent on their work, some of them failing to achieve their goals only because of their lack of expert knowledge of agriculture. By the turn of the century we find exactly the sort of peasantry that the liberals thought they were fighting for at the time of their emancipation.

The expansion of the size of the ploughlands, a new crop-rotation system, practices of intensive animal husbandry were all phases of work that demanded more systematic labors from the peasants. This meant that, with the exception of one or two winter months, the labor force of the peasant family was constantly occupied. The increased need for labor thoroughly changed the peasants' life style within a few decades, a life style that was characterized shortly before by naive folklorists as "idyllic." In place of the old ways of work and leisure, of the colorful but vain social practices, a more rational but certainly less colorful, often more monotonous but, materially, certainly more secure existence was created.

Before we proceed with an analysis of the changed life style, let us briefly review the yearly labor needs of peasant landowners practicing intensive animal husbandry, and producing fodder and root crops on their lands. The snows had hardly melted at the end of winter when the diligent peasant was already out in his field, clearing the meadow and grazing areas, pulling out weeds and briars. When he completed this task, the ploughlands were already dry enough to begin spring planting. He was in a hurry; he had to spread the manure that accumulated at his house during the winter on the lands that were to receive the root crops. This task took quite a few days to accomplish; then he was pressed by time to put the corn, potatoes and turnip seeds into the ground.

If the weather were favorable, and these tasks did not drag out for too long, then the peasant had a few days to catch his breath at the end of April or early May. This was the perfect time to build new dwellings, when the neighbors were able to get together to help out each other. By the end of May, work in the fields began anew, and the peasants had little time to waste until the completion of the autumn harvest. First came the hoeing of potatoes, corn and the turnips; when these jobs were completed, haymaking, including the drying and transportation of the hay, began. All these tasks were still in process when time arrived for the second hoeing of the root crops; the family members usually split the tasks since time was neversufficient to do everything at once. Once the harvest of grains was completed, the peasants immediately began preparation for the autumn ploughing before the weeds had a chance to grow too big, and the land had dried out too much. Then the second planting of silo corn and turnips had to be quickly completed. Following this, the transportation of the grain to the barn had to be done. By then, the threshers were already at work in the village, the neighbors helping each other out with the threshing. One member of the family usually worked at the machine, while the others began to transport and spread the manure that accumulated in the yard or the house since the spring. By that time the month of August was coming to its end and a second cutting of hay was necessary. When this was completed, the great autumn rush really began, since this was the time for the harvest of the root crops and of autumn ploughing. In October, the newly produced manure was spread on lands reserved for spring wheat or next year's root crops. In November, the peasant continued the autumn ploughing. Usually, the arrival of autumn rains or the first winter snow literally forced the landholder off his fields.

The completion of the agricultural season was no longer followed by a comfortable, pipe-smoking period of winter rest. The winter feeding of animals included the preparation of fodder, the grinding of turnips and other tasks that were much more labor-intensive than the old ways, when the animals wintered on not much more than hay and a little straw. If the weather were not too uncomfortable, the peasant took up his ax and saw and went to the nearby forest to cut next year's firewood. There was also more work to be done during the winter months. For instance, the peasant had to repair his tools, his baskets and other containers.[67]

This description is only an outline of the tasks a peasant had to perform after he turned to his modern ways of production. His work varied according to the types of crops that he produced.

For instance, we have not yet mentioned viniculture in this list; it also demanded plenty of work from early spring to late autumn, including pruning, several hoeings, spraying, etc. Nor have we discussed the situation in the vinicultural areas of Tolna and Baranya Counties where the first dairy co-operatives were founded at the time when the philoxera-infestation destroyed the vineyards. In fact, reports from these regions noted that the advances in cattle breeding and dairy farming in general had slowed down in the early 1900's because the peasants gradually replanted the vineyards and returned to their previous occupation.[68] Similar processes were noted by an expert in the Gyongyos-Matra wine producing regions; in fact, in all these areas the available labor force of individual peasant families proved inadequate for the simultaneous production of grapes and intensive cattle breeding.[69]

The problem was that if the peasants had left just one phase of work incomplete, for instance, if they ran out of time and did not prepare the land properly for ploughing, or left out the second hoeing, the consequences were less produce at harvest time.

Tasks around the house during the summer months also multiplied because of the needs of intensive animal husbandry. Previously, most animals practically lived out on the grazing grounds from early spring to late autumn and only occasionally received some fodder at night if the grazing happened to be poor. (At times of drought, for example.) However, with the introduction of intensive animal husbandry, the animals had to be fed three times a day; they had to be watered frequently, and cleaned at least once a day. They also had to be provided with clean straw and the cows had to be milked. These tasks considerably increased the labor demands on the family. From spring to late fall, the peasants were compelled to transport green fodder (alfalfa, clover, etc.) for their animals every day in order to increase their production. All this had to be done each day at early morning before they went out to the fields, or late at night after they had returned.

The peasant family that practiced modern agricultural methods therefore was compelled to devote more time to its tasks than before. This turned the traditional division of labor upside down. The new division of work that developed in peasant families consisting of three generations (grandparents, parents and children), provided plenty of work for everyone, according to age and physical ability (excepting, of course, the infants and the feeble old). The hardest work in the fields was now performed by family members between 18 and 60 years of age (perhaps the upper-age limit was somewhat closer to 50). The older folks took care of the animals in the stalls and barns, helped by the children. If previously we have noted that younger peasant lads were not required to work in the fields during the 1870's and 1880's and that they began such labors only upon reaching manhood, now the situation had completely changed. The tasks that were now entrusted to young people gradually increased according to their age. A child who had reached his tenth year was already considered a member of the family's labor force. After school, these children helped out by grazing cattle (by holding on to them at the end of a rope) on the side of roads, in order to utilize every bit of grass. They helped their parents at the watering of the animals and at haymaking; they were entrusted with such tasks as the twisting of straw ropes at harvest time. As they grew, their tasks multiplied; by the time they were 17 years old, they were full members of the labor force of their families. Moreover, the reputation of a young man in the village was now determined not only by the size of his family's holdings, but also by his diligence and ability to carry on work in the fields.

However, the greatest change in the family's labor force, one that had a tremendous impact on the entire life style of the peasantry, occurred in the tasks that women were now asked to undertake. Modernization, the change of the methods of production meant, from a social point of view, that the peasants entered the road to *embourgeoisment.* Yet the tasks that a peasant women had to perform greatly differed in character from those required of a bourgeois woman. For instance, the women of independent craftsmen or merchants, not to speak of government officials, had as their exclusive task, homemaking. They rarely participated directly in the business activities of their husbands. In contrast, the peasant woman became increasingly involved in production. In this, there was little difference between peasants who practiced intensive animal husbandry or those who emphasized intensive crop-rotation in the Transdanubian lands, and the peasants of the Great Plain involved in truck gardening. Nor were peasant women different in this sense in the extensively grain-producing regions of eastern Hungary. None of the peasants could afford not to use their women in production.

The tasks of keeping the house clean, of cooking, watching the infants, the raising of fowl, now belonged to the grandmothers. The time of older girls and young women was increasingly taken up by work in the fields. Except ploughing and the actual cutting of grain, there was hardly a task that women did not perform alongside of the men. Of the household duties, only the most difficult ones, such as carrying water for the kitchen, the baking of bread or washing the clothes, fell to the younger women. Most of all, they were required to produce vegetables for the family in the household garden; they also planted beans and peas in the field between the lines of corn. This was the generation of women who had still to trouble itself with the planting and preparation of flax and hemp for their strong thread and to spin and weave the thread into garments during the winter. This last task was a remnant of a previous style of life and there was little profit in it; yet, every woman tried to continue doing it, since this was an important criterion in judging her diligence.

The entering of peasant women into agricultural production on a large scale is akey to the understanding of the disappearance of the outward signs of the traditional life style within a couple of decades. The family holidays that used to last for days and were organic part of the traditional life style, the ornate baptism of infants, the colorful wedding ceremonies, or the preparation of multi-layered folk costumes, were originally tasks mainly for women. Now there was simply no time for such "amusements."

The folklorists generally explained the decline of folk art during this period by the increasing availability of industrial products. But it should suffice to note that the basic material on which the folk art designs were created was mass-produced by industry as early as the 1850's and 1860's. The collectors of folk art pointed out the real reason much more succinctly than the folklorists for the disappearance of this art. When they questioned the peasants, they usually received the reply that the peasants had no longer any time left for folk art. One folklorist who explored the regions of Hetes in Zala County, where the traditional white folk costumes were quickly abandoned, summarized his findings this way: "The preparation and cleaning of the white garments . . . took so much time that they could no longer do them under the new conditions of life. They finally gave in to the temptation of buying the cheap products of industry." He further wrote: "this is a process of changing tastes, a corollary to the changing notions of the value of time. The destruction of folk art has been especially evident during the last ten years; the most characteristic pieces of folk costumes typical of this region have been completely abandoned."

In the region of Lendva in Zala county, the abandonment of folk costumes was explained as the result of the fact that "their preparation and cleaning took too much time," and in the busy period of that time when work in the fields was pressing on the peasants "they hardly had time even for dying." In the same region another folklorist described the changed work-ethics of the people this way:

> In the past, the diligent, aspiring worker, one who had achieved something through his own efforts, was hardly tolerated; he was condemned and his property stolen or destroyed. Now the opposite of this is true; it is the lazy man who is being condemned . . . .

This observation accurately described the differences between the traditional work-ethic (surviving from the feudal age) and the new relations to work that developed among the peasants during the 1890's. The same researcher later remarked:

> Those who neglect their tasks or do them in a superficial manner are judged by the people as working as if they still were performing the *robot;* the main efforts of the people are now directed towards fulfilling their tasks in time, in the best possible way . . . .

Contemporary observers made similar observations in other areas of the country. For example, the historian of Baranya County asserted about the people of the Hegyhat region in the 1890's that their twenty-year old sons did not really know how to use a scythe just a few decades before. Now, however, even the children must share in the work, and that there is a saying that "he who is able to drink the 'juice' of the grapes should also be able to hoe the vine." Their women do not get bogged down with work in and around the house, but they labor in the fields. In this area that was populated by German and Hungarian peasants:

> 20 to 25 years before, if a wagon went through the village in the early morning hours, we could be sure that it was driven by a German hurrying to work; the Hungarians waited for the bright morning before leaving their house. Now, however, it would be completely wrong to assume such a thing . . . .[70]

In Nyitra county, the abandonment of traditional folk costumes was explained the same way: "the hard physical work that must be performed throughout the summer and winter months takes up so much of the time of the girls that they are compelled to give up their traditional folk-art work."[71]

If we projected the regions on a map from the period before World War I where the folk costumes and other traditional elements of peasant culture still survived, and matched this with a map of the regions where the traditional three-field system continued to exist, we would show basically the same areas. This was the case in Sarkoz in Tolna County, in the Ormansag in Baranya County, both of which became later famous for their folk art. A similar situation existed in Komarom County where, according to the historian of the region, only in the northern areas did folk art survive.[72] Other sources pointed out that in this area the three-field system also survived.[73] We know that in the northern reaches of Nyitra County the German settlers retained their folk costumes, their week-long weddings, as well as their traditional methods of production.[74]

In the central regions of Hungary, one could observe a similar dichotomous development. In the northern areas that were connected to the cities by the Budapest-Miskolc railway line, and where truck gardening was added to the viniculture of the region, "the changes completely transformed folk art, altering its original forms and colors." In contrast, the areas north to the Matra and Bukk mountain chains, in the lands of the Paloc folks, the peasants not only preserved their traditional methods of production, but also the folk costumes of their ancestors.[75] We could go on citing similar examples all the way from Bereg County in the north through Kolozs and Brasso Counties in Transylvania in the southeast, and down to the Bansag, illustrating the correlations between the survival of traditional production methods and folk costumes.

It is only apparently contradictory to this statement to point out that in some villages where the peasants reaped the benefits of modernization (as in those around Budapest) many typical pieces of folk garments continued in use. This was especially true in villages that may be called "ethnic islands (in Slovakia, for instance.). But the basis of such survivals was the exceptional well-being of the peasants in these villages; in fact, they no longer produced the garments themselves but had them prepared by others.

In order to complete this picture, we should get a glimpse of peasant life style in Csik county in Transylvania. We mentioned above that in this region a very primitive method, based on the two-field system, continued to survive. The expert of the county's economy, a person who is still highly regarded for his accurate observations by Transylvanian historians today,[76] stated that there were few agrarian wage-earners in the area. On the other hand, the number of families possessing only a few *hectares* of land was relatively large and they should have been available to work for wages in their own village or elsewhere. However, this large stratum of peasants who made up the majority of the population of the county, was "choosy and finicky" and its members could not be compared with "regular agrarian workers" in diligence or stamina. These "reluctant workers," continued the expert,

> who had a little land at home, sometimes came together, loaded their wagons, and travelled to other regions to look for easy work that paid well. While there, they worked for a couple of days, but when they made enough money for the return trip, they packed up and went home. They liked to go to Wallachia since they worked there for daily wages which were relatively high, and where the supervision of workers was not as strict as in here or in Hungary. Thus, they seldom went to work in inner Hungary. We must also note the fact that the Szekely worker does not like to do piece work, and he favors jobs where he can work together with a large number of his fellows. In this way there is always a chance for taking a little rest without reducing one's income, for one gets paid by the day. This was the reason for the fact that, during the construction of the Transylvanian railroad lines, the earth-workers and stone-cutters were workers from outside of the province. One could not find one single Szekely doing those jobs; there has never been a Szekely willing to move earth by wheelbarrow for piece-wages.[77]

This discussion corresponds to our own general description of conditions in the rural sphere right after emancipation in the first chapter of our study. The Szekely peasants continued to shun the work-ethics demanded by capitalist production methods.

The same author provided a description of methods used by the Szekelys who worked their own lands. These corresponded to practices that were common in inner Hungary a half century before. The comfortable work rhythm and collective work were even more widespread here than they were elsewhere in Hungary. The strong dependence on collective work was a consequence of the technical backwardness of agriculture in general. But the need for such practices no longer existed for the Szekelys since the tools of modern technology were available for them if they so desired. But they continued to cling to their traditions even after these had lost their original functions; their emphasis was still not on the speedy completion of work, but on opportunities for mutual visitations that the collective work practices implied. Almost every task that took time to complete, such as the harvest, the spreading of manure in the fields, the transportation of firewood, the soaking of hemp in preparation for spinning, all were done in common:

> In the late morning (almost at noontime) the collective begins its work; the members work little, but they eat a lot and drink even more. Such work is done almost every week since each neighbor has almost always something to do, but the value of the work performed never co-responds to the considerable expenses for the one who has to provide the provisions.[78]

Besides such collective "work," the family holidays of baptism and weddings remained formidable events. Even uninvited guests were welcome at the wake for the dead, and better-off families usually slaughtered a cow to provide food for the guests who came to pay final respect to the dead. Fairs and weddings provided other opportunities for visitations. Our author had stated that in the 61 villages of Csik County 700 fairs were held during one year (averaging 11.5 fairs per village!) and each of the fairs drew 5-6,000 visitors in the sparsely populated region. He estimated that each Szekely peasant lost 130 work days a year to these fairs.[79]

Szekely folk costumes had shown changes at the turn of the century, paralleling those of inner Hungary during the 1850's and 1860's. Until that time, the basic material for folk garments was produced exclusively at the Szekely home. By 1900, this was no longer the case. Although the Szekelys continued to weave flax, hemp and wool, the use of manufactured materials—especially for the dresses of women—became widespread. Thus, although the original function of folk costumes was lost, the garments were still produced, but they now reflected only superficial vanity. The girls, as our author had stated, were no longer embroidering home-woven Szekely linen by home-dyed yarn, but they worked on linen that was produced in the factories of Brasso and used silken threads.

As we have observed in the case of modernization in general, we also found contrasting practices in peasant life style, separating central and western Hungary from the eastern regions. In the latter, there continued to exist a mixture of the old and the developing new styles, providing for often sharp contrasts. In regions where modernization was more advanced peasants' tasks following closely upon one another, left little free time for fairs or the holding of wedding celebrations lasting for several days at a time. Here the peasants participated in the Sunday services of their churches almost half asleep, and lectures about proper agricultural techniques could only be given on Saturday evenings or on Sundays. But it would be wrong to attempt to explain the transformation of peasant life style by the increased work load of modernization production alone. Together with technical modernization, peasant mentality had also changed.

NOTES

1. Peter Hanak ed., *Magyarorszag tortenete, 1890-1918* (History of Hungary, 1890-1918) (Budapest, 1978), 405.
2. Tibor Kolossa, *Statistische Untersuchung der sozialen Struktur der Agrarbevolkerung in der Landern der osterreichisch-ungarischen Monarchie. Die Agrarfrage in der osterreichisch-ungarischen Monarchie, 1900-1918* (Bukarest, 1965), 139.
3. Hanak, *op. cit.*, 406.
4. Ede Egan, *Magyarorszag tejgazdasaganak es tejtermelesenek mai helyzete* (The Current Status of Hungary's Dairy Farming and Milk Production) (Budapest, 1885), 42-3.
5. Orszagos Leveltar, *FoldmuvelesiMiniszterium Leveltara* (National Archives, The Archive of the Ministry of Agriculture; from now on, *FMLT*) *Altalanos Iratok* (General Papers), (1894), Fascicle 16, 27,660.
6. Antal Voros, "A belterjes gazdalkodas es az allatenyesztes Moson megyeben, 1896-1914," (Intensive Production and Animal Husbandry in Moson County, 1896-1914) *Agrartorteneti Szemle,* (1964) Nos. 1-2, 84-109.
7. *MSTK, US,* vol. 62, "A magyar korona orsszagainak kulkereskedelmi forgalma, 1882-1913," (The Exports of the Countries of the Hungarian Crown) 22x-29x.
8. *Ibid.*, 44.k. "Arustatisztika," 7-10 and 150. (Price Statistics)
9. Hanak, *op. cit., 298.*
10. *MSTK US,* vol. 63, 30x-39x.
11. *Ibid.*, 106-7, 111, 118.
12. *Magyar Statisztikai Evkonyv* (*MSE*), (1913), 210.
13. *Ibid.*
14. *Ibid.*, 1893, 231.
15. Karoly Schandl, *A magyar szovetkezes negyven eve (Forty Years of Hungarian Cooperatives) (Budapest, 1938), 10-21.*
16. *Karolyi Emleklapok* (Memorial Pages of Karolyi) (Budapest, 1908), 18.

17. Mihaly Dekany, *A mezogazdasagi munkaskerdes* (The Labor Problem in Agriculture), (Budapest, 1895), 45-8.
18. Schandl, *op. cit.*, 42-3.
19. *Ibid.*, 63. The sum which was calculated in *pengos* by the author was calculated by us in crowns. 1 *pengo*= 0.86316 crowns.
20. *MSTK,* vol. 35, 138-154; "A magyar korona orszagainak hitelintezetei, 2894-1909."
21. *Csiki Gazda,* June 18, 1901.
22. *Moson Megye leveltara. Bezenye kozseg hitelszovetkezetenek iratai. Igazgatosag* (The Archive of Moson County. The Savings and Loan Association of the Village of Bezenye. Directory) July 10, 1905.
23. *MSTE,* (1911), 26.
24. Geza Ballagi, *Zemplen megye* (Zemplen County) (Budapest, 1895), 217-8.
25. *MSTK US* vol. 31, 57 and 290-9, "A magyar korona orszagai nepoktatasugyenek fejlodese," (Budapest, 1913). (The Development of Public Education in the Countries of the Hungarian Crown.)
26. *Ibid.*, 62.
27. *MSTK US,* vol. 66, 44. We changed the basis of the data from *holds* to hectares.
28. *Ibid.*, 2-18.
29. *Ibid.*, 45 and 30-7.
30. *A magyar korona orszagainak mezogazdasagi statisztikaja,* vol. 3; "Mezogazdasagi termeles az 1895. ex 1896. evben" (Agricultural Statistics of the Countries of the Hungarian Crown; Agricultural Production in 1895 and 1896) (Budapest, 1897), 4-13, and *MSTK US* vol. 66, 30-37. In the case of the 1880's, we used the data of only one year, since as it turned out at the time of the survey of 1895, the earlier data were incomplete.
31. Jeno Gal, ed. *A Magyar Tarsadalomtudomanyi Egyesulet Altal 1910-1911 evekben tartott birtokpolitikai szaktanacskozmany* (Conferences of the Hungarian Social Science Association in 1910-1911 Concerning Landownership Policies) (Budapest, 1912), 665.

32. Antal Hampel, ed. *Magyarorszag foldmuvelesugyi igazgatasa* (The Agricultural Direction of Hungary) (Budapest, 1913), 51-61.
33. *Ibid.*, 65-6.
34. Bela Dorner, *A kereskedelmi tragyak tortenelme, gyartasa es hasznalata* (The History, Production and Use of Chemical Fertilizers) (Budapest, n.d.,) 67.
35. Tade-usz Matlaszkovszki, *A szuperfoszfat nemzetgazdasagi fontossaga Magyarorszagon* (The Importance of Super-phosphates in the Hungarian National Economy) (Budapest, 1913), 31-2.
36. *Ibid.*, 27.
37. *MSTK US* vol. 66, 56-82.
38. Lajos Fur, "A kapitalista mezogazdasagi termeles megszilardulasa a szazadfordulon," in *A magyar mazogazdasag a XIX-XX. szazadban* (Budapest, 1976), 181-2.
39. *MSTK US* vol. 63, 309-11; the import of steam threshers, straw elevators, harvesters and mechanical ploughs and their parts and the steam ploughs were listed separately in the statistics.
40. *Ibid.*, 308.
41. *Ibid.*, 310.
42. Zoltan Sarkozi, Gabor Szilagyi, Jozsef Szekeres, *A Mosonmagyarovari Mezogazdasagi Gepgyar tortenete* (History of the Argicultural Machinery Factory at Mosonmagyarovar) (Budapest, 1968), 48 and 76.
43. *MSTK US,* vol. 63, 310.
44. Fur, *op. cit.*, 206.
45. *A magyar korona orszagainak, op. cit.*, 28-30. vol. 3.
46. *MSTE,* (1913), 94.
47. *A magyar korona orszagainak, op. cit.*, 29-30. vol. 3.
48. Fur, *op. cit.*, 248-52.
49. Between the Danube and Tisza Rivers, the area planted with grapes grew from 56,000 hectares (162,400 acres) in 1895, to 126,000 hectares (365,400 acres) in 1913. See *A magyar korona orszagainak, op. cit.,* vol. 1, "Major Summaries of the Surveys," 116. See also, *MSTE,* (1913), 93.

50. *A magyar korona orszagainak, op. cit.*, vol. 3, 3. See also, *MSTE,* (1913), 87.
51. Rezso Karoly, *Mezogazdasagi uzemviszonyok es eredmenyek* (Budapest, 1909), 75-93.
52. In the Bansag, there were 65 village dairy cooperative associations in 1907; of these, 35 were dissolved by 1913. *MSTE,* 1907, 124, and 1913, 103.
53. *A magyar korona orszagainak, op. cit.*, vol. 1, 114. See also, *MSTK US* vol. 41, 3, an "A magyar korona orszagainak allatletszama 1911-ben," Part I, 10. The results of the two surveys were somewhat changed by the fact that the first was conducted in November and the other at the end of February in the respective years. This meant that the slaughtering of the hogs did not yet begin in November, and it was already completed by the end of February.
54. *MSTK US* vol. 51, Part II., 12.
55. *A magyar korona orszagainak, op. cit.*, vol. 4; "A gazdasagok megoszlasa" (The Classification of Farms), 41.
56. *MSTK US* vol. 51, 12.
57. Janos Sierban, "A falusi tejszovetkezetekrol," *Tejgazdasag,* Feb. 24, 1898.
58. Vince Nagy, "Beszamolo a tejszovetkezeteink mukodeserol," *Ibid.*, Dec. 24, 1896.
59. *Ibid.*, Feb. 3, 1895.
60. *Ibid.*, Dec. 24, 1896.
61. "Juniusi Tudositas," (Report from June) *Gazdasagi Neplap* (Pecs), June, 1899.
62. Voros, *op. cit.*, in *Agrartorteneti Szemle,* 1964, 84-109 and 313-43.
63. *MSTE,* 1900, 110 and 1910, 122-3.
64. *Az 1907. evi elso orszagos tejgazdasagi kongresszus naploja* (Records of the First National Dairy Product Congress in 1907) (Pecs, 1907), 40-5.
65. Sandor Kecskes, Miklos Miko-Kovacs, *Ujhelyi Imre* (budapest, 1978), 117.
66. Imre Ujhelyi, *Jelentes a Magyarovari Szarvasmarhatenyeszto Egyesulett 1914/14. evi mukodeserol* (Report of

the Activities of the Cattle Breeders' Association of Magyarovar in 1913-1914) (Magyarovar, 1914), 5.

67. Antal Voros, "A paraszti termelomunka es eletforma valtozasai a Dunantulon 1850-1914," (Changes in Peasant Production Methods and Life Style in the Transdanubian Region) *Tortenelmi Szemle* (1966), No. 2, 176-8.
68. "Tenyeszallat Dijazasok," (Prize Winning Animals) *Gazdasagi Neplap* (Pecs), July, 1911, Dec., 1911 and January, 1912.
69. Jozsef Molnar, *Nagyrede tortenete, 1850-1945* (The History of Nagyrede, 1850-1945) (Nagyrede, 1976), 36.
70. Voros, *op. cit., Tortenelmi Szemle,* 1966, 178-80.
71. Benedek Banner, "Nyitra megyei Sagkozseg . . ." (The Village of Sag in Nyitra County) *A Magyar Nemzeti Muzeum Neprajzi Osztalyanak Ertesitoje,* 1911.
72. Samu Borovszky (ed.), *Komarom varmegye* (Komarom County) (Budapest, n.d.), 168-9.
73. *Gazdasagi Kozlony* (Komarom), April, 1940, 3.
74. Samu Borovszky (ed.), *Nyitra varmegye* (Nyitra County) (Budapest, n.d.) 265-6. See also, Istvan M. Richter, "Lakodalmi szokasok a nyitramegyei nemet falvakban," *Ethnographia* (1904), 432.
75. Samu Borovszky (ed.) *Heves varmegye* (Heves County), (Budapest, n.d.), 204.
76. Imre Kozan, *Fekete Ugar* (Black Fallow Land) (Bukarest, 1978), 8-9.
77. Imre T. Nagy, *Csik megye kozgazdasagi leirasa* (The Description of Csik County's Economy) (Budapest, 1902), 42.
78. *Ibid.,* 17.
79. *Ibid.,* 34-5.

PART III

Bela K. Kiraly

PEASANT MOVEMENTS IN THE NINETEENTH CENTURY

I

ORGANIZED POLITICAL PEASANT MASS MOVEMENTS SINCE 1867

1. Introduction

Hungarian peasant mass movements of the nineteenth century were much influenced, if not pre-conditioned, by certain traditions of the past as well as by the socio-economic status of the peasants brought about by the emancipation of the serfs. Inherited from the past was the tradition of violence and of village self-government, as well as the legacy of semi-servile and free peasants from a broad sector of the rural population.

The tradition of violence was established with the Dozsa peasant rebellion of 1514.[1] This peasant war generated a myth of Dozsa himself and of the heroism of peasant warriors fighting the lords unto death for their rights and dignity. This myth has prevailed in folklore, in literature and in the arts, and has become vivid in times of crises. It received a new lease on life exactly prior to and during the era under discussion through the work of such literary giants as Baron Jozsef Eotvos, Sandor Petofi, Endre Ady, Gyula Illyes and others.[2] These poets and others reviewed the heroic and mythical figure of Gyorgy Dozsa and euologized his rebellion.

Violent movements of discontent were not rare in Eastern Europe. Three such major peasant movements in recent times, one in Hungary and two in neighboring countries, deserve mention. The peasant plague revolt in Northern Hungary (Slovakia) of 1831, the insurrection in Galicia in 1846, and the bloody peasant rebellion in Rumania in 1907,[3] all have had a profound effect on the Hungarian peasants. This is true despite the fact that all these peasant movements of discontent ended in failure and were followed by bloody vengeance by the lords and the state. In fact, all peasant movements in Hungary (and elsewhere) were defeated as soon as the state had time to catch up with events and mobilize its armed forces. The peasants suffered from a lack of organization on a national scale, the Dozsa war having been the only exception. Their acts of violence had only a local thrust and were staged principally for the elimination of grievances rather than the overthrow of the system. The movements in general lacked a cohesive ideology. One exception was the peasant movement in the upper Tisza region in the early 1790's,[4] which produced a surprisingly progressive, informed, and well-publicized program.

Beside the legacy of violence, modern Hungarian peasant movements were also inspired by the traditions of village self-rule. Even at the height of the feudal era, many Hungarian villages possessed a certain degree of self-government. Some of the village councils and village headmen were elected by the respective village community. Usually the council members were elected directly; the peasants elected several candidates and the lords appointed one of them as headman. The peasants' control over their own affairs was significant. Equally important was the legacy of semi-servility which flourished in large territories, mostly in the Great Hungarian

Plain. These territories were depopulated and devastated during the Ottoman rule and the War of Liberation (1683-1699) which expelled the Turks from Hungary. To bring the land back to cultivation, the lords settled farmers on these lands from Hungary or from abroad, mostly not as serfs but as contractual peasants. The size of the lands thus gained by the peasants was larger, and the terms easier, than in other sectors of the country. By the late eighteenth century these areas were fully populated and the value of working farmhands declined. Subsequently, the lords attempted to retract what they had given but met with resistance. Although the resistance was gradually overcome, these peasants retained at least some of their prerogatives. Their individual, legal, and economic rights remained more extensive than those of the serfs in other parts of the country. This semi-servile, semi-free peasantry in the Great Hungarian Plain had greater self-confidence and was more militant in protecting its dwindling rights than was true of their fully servile brethren.

The most militant, the most self-conscious peasant movements in late nineteenth and early twentieth-century Hungary were launched in these areas. Not the most hungry but the most self-conscious; not the poorest, but those with rising expectations, were the builders of political movements, and of revolutions. That was true even more regarding the large communities of fully free peasants. The peasants of the *Hajdu* towns, the *Jasz* and *Kun* districts, and the *Szekelys,* were free peasants who sent representatives to the national Diet. It must also be remembered that pre-1848 Hungarian society was stratified into four estates and not three, as in the West. The third estate was the lesser nobility, in itself extremely stratified. It contained the *bene possessionati* (the gentry); the *possessionati* (the smallholder or dwarfholder nobility), and the landless *bocskoros nemesek* (moccasined nobles).[5] This third estate contained a considerable proportion of Hungary's society, not matched in any other immediate neighboring country, except in Poland.

At the end of the feudal era there was one nobleman in Hungary for every 20 commoners; in contrast, for one nobleman in Bohemia, there were 828 commoners, in the Habsburg Alpine Provinces 350, in Lombardo-Venice 300, and in Galicia 68.[6] This proportion of dwarfholders and landless nobles was important since, after the emancipation of the serfs, many of these poor nobles were either absorbed into the state or county bureaucracy or were educated and became professionals. A large number of them remained in the village and faded into the peasantry. However, they retained their voting rights. Having had a long tradition of playing a political role, these enfranchised farmers now became avtive in the movements of their newly adopted class. Andras L. Achim, the first genuine peasant leader of a twentieth-century peasant movement in Hungary, was one of them.[7]

These traditions were important, but so were the objective political, social, and economic circumstances established by the acts of emancipation.

The noted "April Laws" (promulgated on April 11, 1848) emancipated the serfs[8] but the legislation was somewhat obscure and contained many loopholes. Some of the remnants of feudal privileges of the lords were not touched by it. Although Ferenc Deak presented a draft intended to eliminate these shortcomings,[9] the revolutionary events swept it away. Eventually, the emancipation of the peasants and a partial elimination of the remnants of feudalism were accomplished by the counter-revolutionary regime of Bach. On March 2, 1852, the *Urbarial Patent*[10] was issued, but that decree repealed much less of the remnants of lordly feudal privileges than did the "Deak-draft." These were the circumstances under which conditions in rural Hungary were established after the emancipation.

It must be borne in mind that the Emancipation Act, as well as the *Urbarial Patent*, were drafted and promulgated without the consultation and/or cooperation of the most interested party, the peasantry. It should not be surprising that the emancipation provided provisions that did not benefit the peasantry. Forty-five percent of all the arable land remained the property of the former feudal owners and 55 percent became peasant property. Part of the latter gradually changed hands and become the property of the bourgeoisie. 1,538,096 serfs and *inquilinus* families were emancipated, out of which only 46.6 percent became owners of various tracts of lands (only 36.8 percent owned parcels large enough to produce for the market), and 57.4 percent were emancipated without any land whatsoever (7.1 percent were emancipated even without owning a house to live in).[11] In short, emancipation made all of the peasants legally free citizens but left a majority of them in abject poverty. Nor could they find a better life by moving into the towns:[12] because of the lack of industrial development, they were forced to continue their miserable life as bravely as they could in the villages.

These conditions created a protracted agrarian social crisis in Hungary throughout the entire era under discussion. The crisis was heightened by several factors, including the general European agrarian crisis of the 1880's during which overseas grain exporters of East India, Argentina and Canada gradually pushed Hungary out of her formerly lucrative Western markets. The wholesale price of Hungarian grain dropped from its peak in 1873, of 14.76 florins per quintal (220 lbs.) to 9.12 florins per quintal in 1899.[13]

The pauperization of the peasantry and the indebtedness of their lands grew by leaps and bounds. But the great landlords were also in trouble. They tried to save themselves by increasing the entailment of their lands and simultaneously borrowing heavily. These two trends showed this development:[14]

	Land mortgages in florins	Entailed lands in hold (1 hold = 1.42 acres)
1867	86,568,521	
1870		463,325
1894	618,868,752	
1900		2,360,000

The difficulties of the peasants were further aggravated by the method of taxation. They paid three to five times more taxes than did the great landlords. Thus, many became bankrupt and had to sell their lands. During the last quarter of the nineteenth century smallholder peasants lost 4,620,000 acres of land. During this same period, the ratio of rural proletariat rose by 27.3 percent and a half million peasants emigrated overseas. Peasant holdings were gradually subdivided in every generation until the share of families became minimal.

The economic conditions created by the Act of Emancipation were miserable and the political status of the peasantry was not much better. The "April Laws" enfranchised only 6.7 percent of the population. That figure was further cut back by the post-*Ausgleich* electoral law of 1874 to 5 percent. Only the electoral act of 1910 increased it again to 8 percent.[15]

The electoral law of 1874 restricted electoral rights to peasants in the villages holding approximately 8.4 to 14 acres. The electorate for village offices was much broader. All males from the age of twenty who paid state taxes at the same locality for the preceding two years were enfranchised, except seasonal workers hired for an entire economic year, farm hands, and domestic servants. However, the prerogatives of this very broad electorate in the villages were tempered by the regulation that 50 percent of the village council was to be elected by the entire electorate. The other 50 percent was to be elected exclusively by the *virilistak* (those citizens who paid the highest taxes) from among themselves. The list of *virilistak* was compiled by the district magistrate (*foszolgabiro*), an office traditionally held by the representatives of the gentry, who were not always objective in making the compilation. The village government, consequently, was at least partly in the hands of the richest peasants.

There was one area in Hungary which played an important role in peasant politics. The *Viharsarok* (Csanad, Csongrad, and Bekes counties) or Storm Center contained a great proportion of the conscientious, militant, politically-oriented peasant population. The area included exceptionally large peasant villages. As one observer remarked, "the struggle of the rural proletariat against the system of the great landowners and great capitalist coalition was launched from Bekes county. Its main basis remained for a half century the *Viharsarok* . . ."[16]

Historians have been justly puzzled about the causes of this peculiarity of the *Viharsarok,* and no unanimous consent has yet been reached on the main causes of peasant militancy in the area. All the major causes of peasant movements of discontent, such as the tradition of violence, of village self-government, of free and semi-free peasantry, were present here as in other parts of Hungary. The agrarian crises struck this area just as other sectors of the country, perhaps more severely. In the late nineteenth century, while the average mortgage on a *hold* (1.42 acres) of arable land was 16.62 to 19.74 florins, in the *Viharsarok* in Bekes county it was 27.95, and in Csongrad county 49.26 florins, more than double the average.[17] This indebtedness increased the speed of sale of peasant lands. Consequently, the increase in the number of the agrarian proletariat was greater here than in other areas. The presence of large peasant towns and massive settlements of navvy men created concentrations of people which facilitated the organization of their movements. The navy men emerged with the large-scale public works projects such as railroad building, the regulation of rivers, and the soil removal works needed in the building of large towns and factories undertaken after 1867. Since this kind of work provided for employment for a considerable time, the navvy men became permanently detached from agricultural work and constituted a very specialized stratum of the rural proletariat. They usually concluded contracts in large labor units often comprising several thousand navvy men. As they became accustomed to being organized for labor, so they became accustomed to voicing their political or economic demands jointly. They travelled widely since their skills were needed throughout Hungary and abroad, and their outlook as a result became much broader than that of the peasants. At the end of the nineteenth century, about 200,000 to 250,000 navvy men were located in the *Viharsarok,* where in many towns they made up the majority of the population. Their social position among the peasants was respected and their pride and militancy combined with strong organization made them a factor in peasant movements inconsistent with their small numerical ratio.[18]

These were the conditions, then, in Hungary, in the late nineteenth century when the first mass movements for agrarian democracy were organized by the peasants. The rumblings began as the Bach regime fell and the political life of the country was started anew. In this early stage (the period of the negotiations for the *Ausgleich* of 1867), the protest may be considered as a proto-peasant democratic movement. Yet, this brief flare-up is important since many aspects of peasant democracy surfaced at this time. Subsequently, the main democratic peasant movements evolved in five consecutive stages, all of them having their own characteristics, organization, ideology and leadership. Self-contained unto themselves, all five movements were different from both those which preceded and those which followed.

The first organized movement was an Agrarian-Socialist one, launched by the Social Democratic Party, and directed by non-peasant leaders. The Social Democratic Party tried to harness this movement so as to serve the interest of industrial labor rather than that of the peasantry. This effort remained unsuccessful (Istvan Varkonyi and Vilmos Mezofi's organizations). The second wave called itself an Agrarian-Socialist movement. It was led by a genuine peasant and served exclusively the interests of the poor peasantry (Andras L. Achim's party). The third stage emerged simultaneously with Andras L. Achim's party, but championed mostly the interests of the smallholders and the rich peasantry. This movement was absorbed after World War I by the political organization of the old regime and lost its significance for the peasantry (Istvan Nagyatadi Szabo's Smallholders' Party). The fourth wave was the Independent Smallholders' Party of the interwar years which, continuing the traditions of Istvan Nagyatadi Szabo, concentrated on the problems of the smallholders and rich peasants. This movement, too, was taken over by the men of the old regime. Only during the years of World War II did genuine peasants assume its leadership. By then, it was too late: the party went to its doom under the totalitarian pressure of the Soviet-sponsored Communist regime in 1947 (the movement of Gaszton Gaal, Dr. Tibor Ekhardt, Zoltan Tildy and Ferenc Nagy). The last two movements will fall outside the scope of this part of the book.

2. The First Flare-up: The Proto-Democratic Peasant Movement of Janos Asztalos.

The first effort to organize a democratic peasant movement in Hungary occurred at the time of the *Ausgleich*. It originated in Kecskemet, one of the large peasant towns of the Great Hungarian Plain. Its leader was Janos Aszatalos. This proto-democratic movement faced the fundamental problem of Hungary's dualist political structure. The electoral system contained such high property qualifications that only rich peasants were enfranchised to elect members of Parliament. The rural proletariat remained without the right to vote. The basic issue was whether the regime would be willing to change the extremely disadvantageous political, social, and economic conditions of the rural proletariat, and to integrate the peasantry into society as full-fledged citizens.

It should be stated in advance that dualist Hungary did not effect the needed change. If peasant organizations concentrated upon the problems of the rich peasants, these peasants could lend the organization political power, since they had the right to vote. For them, it was possible to adopt an evolutionary reform policy, especially since the demands of the rich peasants were not extreme and could be solved without resorting to violence. The case was different concerning the rural proletariat. They could hardly offer open political support to a reform movement since they were disenfranchised. But as this was the stratum of society most unjustly treated, the only course open for it was violence, nay, even revolution.

The populist writer and peasant leader, Peter Veres, expressed the paradox by remarking that the system did not leave the poor peasant any other alternative than "liberation [by force] or ruination. . ."[19] The Asztalos movement posed this question for the first time. It is surprising that the Hungarian peasant movements of the late nineteenth and early twentieth centuries did not become more radical and violent than they were.

After the fall of the Bach regime, political life in Hungary picked up momentum in the early 1860's. The peasants were quick to sense the change of the political atmosphere and initiate their own activities. The rural proletariat which did not have the possibility of agitation within a legal, political framework, resorted to extra-parliamentary organizations. Peasant "Clubs," "Democratic Circles," and "Reading Circles" emerged throughout the country. No matter what name these organizations adopted, they were the focus of discontented peasants. The halls of clubs buzzed with heated discussions and with plans. Peasants who were politically astute, however, were not satisfied with political activities of a merely local character. Efforts were made to achieve greater results through a national coordination of the activities of the clubs and to arrange for the political support of a major political party.

To realize the first goal, the *Magyar Ujsag* (Hungarian Journal) proposed on its pages of January 3, 1868, to create a set of by-laws for the Democratic Circles with the aim of grouping the Circles into an ideologically unified undertaking on the national level. The ideology behind this proposed set of by-laws was clearly democratic. The second goal, cooperation with an existing political party, obviously pointed towards the "Party of the Extreme Left" which championed the Kossuth traditions. It seemed natural to the peasants, for whom Kossuth represented a social Messiah, that a party which proclaimed itself the flagbearer of the Kossuth heritage would, by its very nature, represent the interests of the peasantry. But it did not take long for the peasants to become bitterly disappointed in their expectations.

The "Party of the Extreme Left" was quickly put to the test of whether to represent the majority of the peasantry who were disenfranchised (thus powerless to send representatives into Parliament, and who could be satisfied with nothing less than radical or revolutionary changes) or the rich farmers (the minority of the peasantry) who could send representatives of the Party to Parliament, and who would be satisfied with less. The party selected the second solution and, as early as 1868 changed its name to the "The Party of [18]48." This change of name represented a change in fundamental policy: it meant the abandonment of radical, social platforms and the concentration on futile and often demogogic constitutional issues. The rural proletariat became slowly aware of this change. However, long after the party abandoned the cause of the rural proletariat, the poor peasants remained loyal and continued to see the Party as their only hope.

It was in the year of transition, in 1868, that the short-lived Asztalos movement emerged. Janos Asztalos was a lawyer who had recently settled in Kecskemet. He championed the cause of the poor peasants in clubs, in the courts, and wherever else he had a chance to do so. He selected the most intelligent, the most talented peasants in town, and trained them in organization and leadership. He supplied them with publications on national issues, and with evidence of the utter corruption of local administration officials. Asztalos, with the aid of his clients (who gradually grew into a band of comrades), organized local chapters of Democratic Clubs and reading circles in Keckskemet and in the outlying districts of the city. He himself travelled, spoke, wrote, and drafted platforms indefatigably. As his organization grew, its fame spread throughout the country.

In early 1868, the platform of his movement was crystalized. It contained an attack on the political-social structure of dualist Hungary. It demanded the elimination of the remnants of feudalism by certain changes in property laws. It contained a demand for the amelioration of the social and economic status of the poor peasantry, and a demand for democracy. The platform also included a plea to the masses to join mass movements for direct political action in the attainment of all these goals. In short, the Asztalos platform, which aimed for political democracy and social change, based its policies on the needs of the landless agrarian laborers. As the masses he attracted and the goals he sought were fundamentally different from the partisans and the platform of the "Party of [18]48," the two movements inevitably drifted away from each other.

In April 1868, Asztalos issued one of his most remarkable manifestos. Although this appeal represented his most extreme call for democracy and radical social reform, it still advocated gradual change and remained inside the framework of the existing legal system. The platform was democratic and evolutionary but, since it was mainly addressed to the problems of the disenfranchised peasantry, it was really a revolutionary platform. That was indeed the regime's interpretation.

After this Manifesto it was obvious to the ruling classes that if the Asztalos movement were permitted to develop, the government would have to introduce radical reforms or face violence. Since they dared not let things develop so far, the authorities had Janos Asztalos arrested on April 13, 1868. Arrest of his lieutenants followed shortly: in Kiskunfelegyhaza, thirty were arrested; in Hodmezovasarhely fifteen; in Szeged and Kecskemet arrests were also made. All the halls of the Democratic Circles were closed, their documents, publications, and proclamations were confiscated. The movement was crushed before it could take on national proportions. In any case, before the arrests, the movement's finances were already shaky and its social basis was too restricted. Yet, up to the emergence of the Agrarian-Socialist movements of the 1890's, the Asztalos movement mobilized the largest mass of peasants for the purpose of direct, political action. It revealed an inherent strength among the peasant masses and pointed to the fact that, with skilled leadership, good organization, and a clear ideology, the peasant masses could eventually become a political power.

3. Agrarian Socialism: General Framework

The first major wave of peasant democratic action after the suppression of the Asztalos movement was initiated by the Social Democratic Party of Hungary. At first, the Socialists' inherent reluctance to tackle peasant problems was the source of much confusion, disagreement, and shifts of policy by the socialist leaders. However, after a long debate, a leading party theoretician, Arnold Daniel, came up with a general policy that stated:

> Any popular movement that is class conscious and is based on internal democracy can be incorporated into the framework of Social Democracy provided that it tends to increase the forces of production by raising the living standards of the working people, that it consolidates the laborers into organizations, that its success depends on confrontation with one single class of employers, and if all these conditions are fulfilled, provided that it would make its members susceptible to socialist propaganda. These conditions should be kept in mind when judging any program for farm laborers.[20]

The fact was that the labor movement simply could not afford to ignore the rural proletariat if it really wanted to strive for democracy in Hungary.[21] But how far the industrial workers' party should take up the cause of another social group was as vexing a question in Hungary as it was elsewhere in the West. Would a government of landlords, which has already shown acertain tolerance toward labor organizations in the cities but which was extremely sensitive about any rural movement, suppress the still weak industrial labor movement if it were extended into the countryside? On the other hand, how could labor alone, without peasant support, work for democracy? What political power could be derived from activities in the countryside where the poor peasants who were interested in supporting Socialism were not enfranchised and the rich peasants who were, were afraid of Socialism? Should the Socialist movement work toward its ideal goals, or struggle for the social, political and economic betterment of *all* the oppressed? Should it run the risk of being completely suppressed in turn, or should its policy be opportunistic, restricted to the industrial proletariat alone, in which case it would be permitted legally to function. If this latter alternative were chosen, should the party openly turn its back on the rural proletariat and so gain a lease on its life in the industrial areas while losing prestige in the countryside, or should it pay lip service to the problems of the rural proletariat, without backing it up with action, in which case it might still be tolerated by the ruling classes but lose credibility in both rural and urban areas?

Such dilemmas resulted, not surprisingly, in a confused and indecisive policy. As a consequence, most of the radical peasant movements sooner or later repudiated the leadership of, and even any contact with, the Social Democratic Party. Two initiatives in particular contributed to their position. The first was the political activities of Istvan Varkonyi and his "Independent Social Democratic Party," the other was those of Vilmos Mezofi and his "Reorganized Social Democratic Party." Both of these considered themselves "Agrarian Socialist" movements, but an analysis of their programs and political activities (as will be shown later) makes it clear that in a strict sense neither of them was Socialist. Neither was a Marxian Socialist movement. They were "Agrarian Socialist" movements only in the broadest possible sense of socialism as "any economic doctrine that challenges belief in the sanctity of private property and favors use of property for the public welfare."[22] For every socialist movement in Hungary challenged the sanctity of the system of land ownership and sought to change it into one that promoted public welfare. This challenge to the system of land ownership was deeply rooted in the mind of the peasants, who firmly believed that they had been cheated at the time of emancipation and that much of the land owned by the landlords was morally, legally, and in justice theirs.

The cradle of all these agrarian socialist movements was the National Alliance of Farmworkers (*Foldmunkasok Orszagos Szovetsege*), a branch of the Social Democratic Party.[23] It was headed by Sandor Csizmadia, who was also a member of the Central Committee of the Social Democratic Party. Whatever ups and downs the agrarian socialist movement went through during the following decades, whatever the relationship between the individual peasant organizations and the Social Democratic Party, the National Alliance of Farmworkers continued to exist, reaching a peak of importance—and its demise—in the post-World War I revolutions.[24]

4. Istvan Varkonyi and the Independent Social Democratic Party

The first peasant party in name and substance was a political organization sponsored by the Hungarian General Labor Party (*Magyar Altalanos Munkaspart*) under the leadership of Istvan Varkonyi, a self-made, successful businessman.[25] Varkonyi was interested in the problems of the rural proletariat. His ideas were close to socialism of the anarchist version, but he was rather obscure and confused. He entered the Social Democratic Party not for ideological but pragmatic reasons.[26] He aimed to carry out his peasant reform programs legally, within the framework of the party. Its ideas and purposes came nearest to his own, and no other party would have let him act so freely.[27] The Social Democratic Party included in its 1890 platform the statement, "Modern social developments necessitate the socialization of arable lands."[28] This was the first official exposition of a manifestly socialist agrarian policy in Hungary. The party actually fostered grass-roots peasant movements of discontent by supporting the "Reading Circles," "Democratic Clubs" and similar rural organizations. These local groups busied themselves with reform projects, most of which demanded better working conditions. Only a few wanted land reform.[29]

These projects were scarcely socialistic, nor did they advocate violence, but the government crushed them all as socialist movements. Their easy suppression brought home the fact to the organizers that better organization and a clearer program were needed to transform the peasants' discontent into an effective political force. Both were offered by the Social Democratic Party which, in December 1895, issued a "Manifesto to the Rightless People of Hungary." The manifesto advocated that working people, including the peasants, should bring massive pressure on the government to grant universal suffrage by secret ballot, and to open the road toward a democratic form of government. The manifesto was printed in great numbers and circulated all over the country, particularly in the *Viharsarok.* Simultaneously, to give an organizational framework to the peasant movement, it was decided on December 25, 1895, to call a "Rural Workers' Congress." In the drafting of the manifesto and the organization of the congress, the key figure was Istvan Varkonyi. The congress met on May 24, 1896, and action was begun to set up an even wider party network and to establish an organization to fight for peasant interest on the lines of a trade union. It seemed that a legal, nationwide, well-organized, and well-led peasant democratic mass movement with a definitive platform was about to emerge.

These hopes were dashed by a sudden change of leadership in the Social Democratic Party. The Marxist leadership, which had wholeheartedly supported Varkonyi's efforts to organize the peasantry, was eliminated[30] and the new leadership decided to tone Varkonyi down. Behind the decision was the realization that the government would tolerate a legal industrial workers' party and an industrial trade union but not any similar organizations among the rural population. The Social Democratic leaders assumed that if they were to go along with the Varkonyi movement, not only would the regime crush the peasant movement but also the industrial workers' organizations. To save the latter, they were ready to sacrifice the former. Thus, the Social Democrats continued to give lip service to the organization of the peasants but placed every possible obstacle in Varkonyi's way. As a result, he became disillusioned and realized that there was no way his movement could remain within the framework of the Social Democratic Party.

Thus Varkonyi and the Social Democrats organized separate and competing agrarian socialist congresses. The Socialist Party's took place in Budapest in January 1897. Varkonyi called his first congress to convene in Cegled in February 1897. At the latter, leaders of the agrarian proletariat discussed the possibility of forming their own organization. Varkonyi's second congress, held on September 8-10, 1897, saw the creation of the Independent Social Democratic Party[31] under his personal leadership. Varkonyi's journal, *Farmer* (Foldmivelo), became the voice of the new party.[32] The former secretary general of the Social Democratic Party, Pal Engelmann, was enchanted by the new organization.

> "The revolutionary movement of the industrial laborers," Engelmann wrote, "proceeds from West to East. The peasant Social Democratic movement in Hungary allows us to hope that the revolutionization of the rural proletariat will move from East to West and that the two waves rushing toward each other from opposite directions will sweep away the system of exploitation of man by man."[33]

The enthusiasm of Engelmann, the revolutionary dreamer, the mass appeal of Varkonyi's movement and Varkonyi's own impeccable devotion and energy were one side of the coin; the other was more ominous. The new party had to fight for survival on several fronts. The Social Democratic Party, for one, declared total political war against him, dubbing him the "divider of the labor movement." The regime was no gentler and took vigorous measures to nip the movement in the bud. Varkonyi responded with equal energy. He mobilized the farmworkers and moved the scene of battle to the countryside by organizing a strike of harvesters. The struggle was greatest in the *Viharsarok.* Neither force nor massive numbers of strike-breakers from Slovak and Rumanian villages could break the backbone of the movement. To save the grain from rotting where it stood, the landlords surrendered in many areas and offered unprecedented benefits to the farmhands in the form of new harvest contracts. In the short term the first direct mass action of Varkonyi and his new party was outstandingly successful.[34] The second congress of the Independent Social Democratic Party which followed the harvest strikes consolidated the party by solemnly severing all ties with the Social Democrats. The congress also promulgated the most comprehensive peasant reform program in the history of peasant movements in Hungary up to that time.

The program included the expropriation of all church and state-owned lands and their division into 7.5-acre-units to be leased to landless peasants and dwarfholders; it advocated the expropriation and distribution of all other estates over 142 acres in area, "since it is contrary to human dignity for man to serve man in a servant-master relationship . . . all such relationships are to be repealed." It wanted the restriction of working hours to a daily maximum of twelve, with overtime paid at a higher rate; the prohibition of child labor; a universal, free educational system; a progressive system of taxation;[35] the reorganization of the multinational state of Hungary into an alliance of its different nationalities; and the denial of taxes and army recruits to an oppressive state. The attack on the state as an institution by denying it taxes and army recruits was an anarchist tenet very characteristic of the party's ideology. However, it was not Varkonyi's doing. The anarchist aspects of the party's ideology which considered both the state and the organized church as ultimate evils were the contributions of Jeno Henrik Schmidt, a philosopher and close friend and collaborator of Varkonyi. Schmidt subscribed to the "Christian nonviolent social revolution" of Leo Tolstoy's school of thought. In fact, Schmidt was in close correspondence with Tolstoy, whom he regarded as his master.

Schmidt advocated a nonviolent campaign to attain the party's goals by persuasion, and favored bringing as much information and education to the peasants as possible to combat the influence of the organized church. He preached the "replacement of the church's slavish idolatry and religious superstitions with the genuinely free spirit of Christ, which alone can liberate the world."[36] This idealistic Christian anarchism did little to promote the party's political goals, but did contribute to the spread of sectarian beliefs, already widespread beyond the Tisza River. Inside the party Schmidt opposed the routine centralism and discipline demanded by a modern party:

> "We do not rule, we do not exercise patriarchal control; rather do we work to wake our fellow men from the deep sleep of ignorance. We have one single weapon—knowledge, which lays low all rule, privilege and power that endorse oppression, exploitation and subjugation."[37]

Such views were utterly utopian in late nineteenth century Hungary.

Varkonyi's movement was exciting, and though short-lived, it raised high hopes and inspired in its followers undeniable idealism, devotion and enthusiasm. But it was already under heavy attack during the winter of 1897. The Roman Catholic Church issued pastoral letters condemning the movement. The regime declared martial law in the areas where Varkonyi was active. Arrests, imprisonment, confiscation of documents, temporary bans on the journal, *Foldmivelo,* were included in the arsenal of persecution. Parliament in 1898 passed an act outlawing harvest strikes.[38]

The regime's violence elicited peasant counterviolence in early 1898. There were land seizures in the *Viharsarok* and beyond the Tisza River. Varkonyi announced in *Foldmivelo* on February 11, 1898, that the Independent Social Democratic Party would hold its congress in Torokszentmiklos on May 6-8. The agenda would include "practical problems involved in the matter of publicly and privately owned landed properties",[39] that is, the redistribution of land. The regime banned *Foldmivelo* and indicated Varkonyi on four counts for "press offenses." Varkonyi was arrested in Vienna, extradited to Hungary, sentenced to four months in jail and fined 400 florins. The convening of the congress was prevented by thesimple expedient of arresting the delegates and banning all travel across the country. This was the end of Varkonyi's organization.

Varkonyi's movement typified many of the merits and shortcomings of agrarian socialism in Hungary. It concentrated too narrowly on the problems of the rural proletariat, neglecting Hungary's other social strata. This was, however, the result of social and political circumstances. Actually, no social group that was endowed with political rights was about to share them with the rural proletariat. Nor would any such group jeopardize its own rights by allying itself with those whose political struggle would be opposed to the last both by the great landlords and the upper bourgeoisie.

The moribund party reappeared briefly when Varkonyi himself resurfaced during the constitutional crisis of 1905-6. The solution of the crisis, however, left the old regime in power in Hungary and there was no place for Varkonyi and his agrarian socialist movement. Like Asztalos' movement it had ceased to be a political force, and only its memory would have any effect on future events. It had however, proved that a radical peasant reform movement could be, and for that matter should be, organized independently of the Social Democratic Party. It had shown that the creation of a mass peasant movement was possible in Hungary and with a progressive platform the peasant masses could be induced to support direct political action. Finally, and most pathetically, it had demonstrated that the old regime was unwise, stubborn and inflexible, and could not be expected to yield to reasoned arguments or peaceful demands.

For the fundamental changes needed in Hungary's social, economic and political system only one road was left open—revolution. It is strange to observe that so few activists have come to this final conclusion, despite the fates of the Asztalos movement in the late 1860s and the Varkonyi movement in the late 1890s. There was also a more opportunistic lesson to be drawn, namely, the goals had to be adjusted to the existing rigid circumstances. This meant that the peasants' just demands had to be toned down. This was the lesson taken to heart by the next peasant movement.

5. Agrarian Socialism: Vilmos Mezofi and the Reorganized Social Democratic Party

As Varkonyi's movement was disintegrating, a new agrarian socialist movement was formed under the leadership of Vilmos Mezofi. At first, the members of Varkonyi's movement who survived persecution drifted aimlessly. Some joined the Social Democratic Party; others went into "front" organizations where they could function legally; a few went underground. Agrarian socialism as a consolidated movement went into eclipse until November 1, 1899, when it was given a second lease on life with the publication of a new journal, *Szabad Szo* (Free Voice), by Balint Arvai, a shoemaker in Szentes. The publisher soon hired a professional journalist to run the paper, Vilmos Mezofi, a member of the Social Democratic Party.[40]

Mezofi was not simply out to edit the newspaper. He intended to use *Szabad Szo* and the movement that was forming around it to gain influence inside the leadership of the Social Democratic Party. In exchange he offered to bring the journal and the peasant movement into the party fold. For various reasons, including personality conflicts and fear of the government, the Social Democratic leaders felt that absorption of the peasant movement would be a liability rather than an asset and Mezofi was turned away. He and fifteen other leaders quit and decided to organize their own party.[41]

On April 16, 1900, the first convention of the new party met in Budapest. Two hundred delegates attended. They included a number of industrial workers, an indication that Mezofi had more in mind than establishing a peasant organization. Indeed, some trade unions and, for approximately one year, the entire Social Democratic Party in the province of Transylvania joined Mezofi. This amalgam called itself the Reorganized Social Democratic Party *Ujjaszervezett Szocialdemokrata Part*).[42]

The new party's first pronouncements, policy statements, and actions seemed radical enough for Engelmann, the Marxist former secretary general of the Social Democratic Party. He decided to lend his support, just as in 1897 and 1898 he had backed Varkonyi's party. But this initial radicalism and internationalism gradually gave way to Hungarian nationalism. The party also developed a moderate economic program favoring the smallholders, rather than the rural proletariat.

On January 1, 1901, *Szabad Szo* and the party headquarters were moved from Szentes to Budapest. In the general elections of 1901, the party put up candidates in twenty-eight constituencies. The candidates dramatically illustrated once again that in Hungary nonpeasants habitually sought to represent a rural electorate: six of them were shoemakers, one was a paper merchant, one an industrial worker, one a merchant, two were carpenters, one was a commercial agent, two were locksmiths, one was a newspaperman, two were clerks in private businesses, two were motormen, one was a house painter, and two were bricklayers. Only two of the twenty-eight were peasants.[43]

Of course, the transformation of the party from a radical agrarian socialist political organization into a moderate one did not occur overnight. The party's second convention in

Szentes in April 1901 still adopted a fairly radical social-reform platform. It advocated the expropriation of all entailed estates. This would have contributed to the distribution of an enormous amount of land to the peasants on the basis of long-term leases. A substantial prosperous peasant community could have thus taken the place of the existing system of *latifundia*.

This plank was similar to the proposal of Varkonyi's party five years earlier. Consequently, the endowment of so many landless peasants with land would have opened the franchise to a great rural mass even without changing the property qualifications under the existing electoral laws. The platform also proposed the establishment of a government fund for the expropriation of small peasant properties for tax arrears or other debt, if these properties supported those who worked them and produced no marketable surplus. Finally, the 1901 program called for progressive taxation instead of the regressive system in force.[44]

By 1903, this eminently radical platform was gradually abandoned. In this year Mezofi and his party openly sided with the Marxist revisionist ideas of Eduard Bernstein. Mezofi held the party together by the force of his eloquence. He had become a towering figure in the peasant movement, just as his predecessor, Varkonyi. Under his tutelage the party congress of 1903 took a revisionist socialist stand. It passed a resolution stating:

> Whereas the foremost goal of Social Democracy must be to make communal property the means of production; whereas land, being one of the means of production, is considered ripe for socialization; whereas this alone could be expected to free long-suffering humanity from material misery; notwithstanding, to achieve this final goal, that is, the socialization of the land together with the other means of production, /the party/ would not sacrifice the present.

Instead, the party advocated gradualism as the means to achieve necessary social reforms.[45]

Bernstein and his revisionism were probably appropriate policies in Germany at that time, for peaceful change was feasible there through parliamentary means and Bernstein was himself a legislator (1902-06, 1912-18, 1920-28). But there was no such possibility in Hungary. To achieve radical political, social and economic changes by peaceful means in Hungary in Mezofi's time meant their indefinite postponement. To advocate such a platform, was, therefore, political suicide for Mezofi and the Reorganized Social Democratic Party, and it was a disaster for the rural laborers. From that time on, indeed, the party no longer encouraged the peasant masses to take direct political action.

As the party abandoned the peasants' cause so did the agrarian proletariat abandon the party. Some historians have considered this fundamental change to be a matter of *realpolitik* similar to the Social Democratic Party's *volte face* in 1898. Others have charged Mezofi with outright betrayal of those who invited him in good faith to be their leader.[46]

Whatever the motivations of Mezofi's decision were, his party turned into an organization directed towards the smallholders, who took the place of the rural laborers. The gradualist approach became even more pronounced after several Calvinist ministers joined the party. Dezso Balthazar, the dean of Calvinist ministers, Dezso Varga and Tamas Ozy were the first. All became party publicists, making it more and more socially acceptable. The party's increasingly pacific character was compensated for by its growing strength in village government, including in the *Viharsarok*. In 1903, members of the Reorganized Social Democratic Party were elected to the councils of twenty-nine villages. To accelerate this trend the party drafted a special "Village Platform" for these members. This platform made it their duty to work for universal suffrage, nationalization of the school system (or rather, its declericalization), a village health insurance scheme, and progressive taxation—in fact, a fairly progressive democratic political program. The following year the party was even more successful. More villages elected party members to their councils. In Csongrad and Bekes counties in the *Viharsarok* several members of the Reorganized Social Democratic Party were elected to the county assemblies, hitherto the exclusive preserves of the landed gentry. Among them was the man of the future, Andras L. Achim,[47] who was elected to the Bekes County Assembly.

1905 was the peak of the Reorganized Social Democratic Party's influence. At the general election that year Vilmos Mezofi and Andras L. Achim were both elected to Parliament on the party platform. There was, however, a gap between the two legislators' views. Vilmos Mezofi continued his drift toward a more and more conservative position, while Achim gallantly championed the cause of the rural proletariat. He militantly demanded fundamental political, economic and social changes in Hungary.[48]

6. The Genuine Peasant Party of Andras L. Achim

Andras L. Achim,[49] with the creation, on March 11, 1906, of the *Magyar Fuggetlen Szocialista Parasztpart* (Hungarian Independent Socialist Peasant Party, hereafter referred to as Peasant Party) founded the first true peasant party, led by men of rural stock like himself. This, among other things, was what gave the party its extraordinary significance.[50] This Party's official organ was *Paraszt Ujsag* (Peasant Journal). In 1905, Achim was returned to Parliament as a Reorganized Social Democratic party member and scandalized Mezofi, his party leader, by a maiden speech in which he demanded radical land reform.[51] In the 1906 general election Achim ran as a candidate of his own Peasant Party and won. He started his activities in the new Parliament with even more radical reform proposals. Widespread harvest strikes in the *Viharsarok* were then blamed on him though they were not of his making. As a result, the *Kuria* (Supreme Court of Justice) annulled his parliamentary mandate for "incitement to insurrection and class antagonism."[52] His prosecution generated great fame and prestige for him. The national press habitually referred to him as "The Peasant King of Bekescsaba."[53] Suits against him continued. At one hearing Achim declared from the dock:

> A society that assures comfortable property and political standing for only a handful or for a few thousands of privileged people is sick. /It/ is immoral. It cannot rightfully demand that any decent person hold it in respect. Agitation for alteration of such a society cannot be considered a crime, for the eternal law of nature and of faith, both demand that justice and equality shall prevail on this earth.[54]

It was to the credit of the judicial system that Achim was acquitted[55] on this occasion.

At Whitsun, 1908, the Peasant Party held a huge congress attended by the most diverse Hungarian and non-Hungarian peasant organizations and spokesmen from approximately half of Hungary's administrative districts.[56] A gathering of representatives of such a wide cross-section of Hungary's ethnically and economically different peasantry was epoch-making. So, too, was the program they adopted. They demanded political democracy, substantial social reforms, reform of education and of church-state relations, welfare legislation, land reform measures, protection of the peasants' interests by *ad hoc* organizations as well as national legislation, certain modifications in Austro-Hungarian relations, and fundamental reform of the national defense system. Since this was the first fundamental political program drafted by peasants for peasants and since, according to several contemporary political and social scientists, it could be interpreted as an embryonic form of a peasant ideology, the platform merits analysis in some depth.

The first demand was for democracy through a Parliament "truly representing the people." For this, universal, direct, equal suffrage by secret ballot should be granted to everyone twenty years old or more, "regardless of sex, religion, nationality, profession, native tongue, or property status," including even the illiterate, for illiteracy was not a fault of the individual but of the state. Another safeguard for democracy and truly popular representative legislation was the abolition of the House of Lords. The first demand also sought abolition of the so-called Slave Act and Whipping Post Act,[57] both of which were condemned as utterly unjust, representative of class privilege, and violations of the human dignity of those subjected to them. As "democracy really means nothing without a proper system of justice," cheap and efficient adjudication and free legal counsel for the poor were demanded. The central and local administrations should be completely overhauled by repealing the privileges of the *virilistak* and by electing officials at all levels of government by the same system of universal suffrage as members of Parliament were to be elected. There should be genuine community control over the local administrations, and freedom of speech, of the press, of assembly and association, and the communication of ideas should be guaranteed.

The second group of demands referred to social changes. By the introduction of progressive taxation, the lot of the poor was to be improved at the expense of the rich. Income up to the level needed for subsistance was to be exempt from taxation. A law "for the protection of the home" was to be enacted to prohibit expropriation or complusory auction of a family home and of the means by which a working man earned his living.

Related to these social reforms was the land reform program. According to it, no one in Hungary should be permitted to own more than 14,200 acres of land. Those who did were to be required by law to parcel out the excess land to peasants on long-term, low-interest leases. The lessees were to pay their rent through the state and their leases were to be irrevocable so long as they kept their terms. The avowed goal of this land reform was to create jobs and earning opportunities for the rural proletariat and to make agriculture more intensive in Hungary. No foreigner was to be allowed in the future to purchase land.[58] Landowners residing and spending their earnings abroad were to pay double taxes. To intensify agriculture further, the Great Hungarian Plain should be irrigated by a new canal system. Lastly, the existing, unjust system of subsidizing the owners of flood areas for their losses should be eliminated and a system introduced based on equal justice for all.

To protect the peasantry, the program proposed legal guarantees of the freedom of labor for the benefit of the rural proletariat and a radical reduction in inheritance taxes for the benefit of smallholders. A national network of peasant organizations was to be established. A state supported credit system was to be set up to aid smallholders in debt or facing economic disaster. The parcelling-out of land would be brought under state supervision and labor laws would be passed to protect the rural worker. Fishing and hunting laws should be reformed to extend to the peasants and the village communities a fair share of these potential sources of income.

In the area of welfare legislation, a rural laborers' pension system was proposed as well as state protection for old or bankrupt peasants. Village health services were to be nationalized, and state-supported free medical care and free prescription drugs would be given to poor peasants, "for the health of the nation should be the responsibility of the state."

Free public education was demanded, and talented children from peasant families were to be educated at state expense. The party declared itself "not an enemy of the church or of religion," and advocated educating young people in "religious morality." It also suggested that the state should support the churches financially on the basis of the enactments of the 1848 revolution.

The program condemned the traditional parties' excessive involvement in efforts to change the relationship between Austria and Hungary. It advocated a radical turning away from this "constitutionalist" issue and concentration instead on social legislation. The one "constitutionalist" demand it made was that Hungary should become a separate and independent customs area. It also proposed that conscription should be reduced to one year's active service with financial compensation for those with families to support during their military service. The Standing Army was to be abolished and a People's Army, a kind of national militia, to be organized for the defense of the nation.[59]

It is most fortunate that Oszkar Jaszi's journal, *Huszadik Szazad* (Twentieth Century), the most progressive publication of its time, printed the entire program immediately after its promulgation, and invited readers and a dozen experts on peasant politics and sociology in Hungary to comment on it. There can be no better judges of the program than those contemporary statesmen and political and social scientists. Subsequent issues of *Huszadik Szazad* carried their comments, gave the editor's views and published Andras L. Achim's own concluding remarks and answers to criticism.[60]

The monthly journal requested answers to the following questions: Could the entire peasantry be amalgamated into one single party? Was the platform a proper program to establish such a party? If the entire peasantry could not be fused into such a single party, which strata could be? What should the party's relationship be to the already existing political parties? The answers were all well-disposed towards the new party, and only one expert pronounced mildly hostile views. All of them expressed opinions that were to help Achim and his colleagues to refine their program rather than discourage them.

It was pointed out by several correspondents that the extreme stratification of the peasantry, from landless rural proletariat to very well-to-do farmers, was a serious obstacle to a unified party organization. Some even questioned whether the very concept of a "peasant class" or the "peasantry" was valid or reasonable. Nevertheless the majority agreed that even the poorest landless laborer who lived and worked on the soil was nearer to the rich peasants, who did the same, than to the industrial proletariat, whose way of life was utterly different. In consequence, the concept of the "peasantry" was not so irrational after all.

Several writers criticized the proposed maximum landholding of 14,200 acres. Estates of this size and larger comprised only 7.5% of Hungary's arable lands, much less than was needed to satisfy the land hunger of the rural proletariat. On the other hand, estates of more than 1,420 acres accounted for 49% of the areable lands. The redistribution of estates over the lower limit would give land to all those who had to hire out their labor. In this case, the owners of the *latifundia* would face an acute labor shortage and would have to sell much of their lands anyway. Hungary would be irrevocably transformed into a land of intensively cultivated smallholdings, orchards and market gardens.[61]

Objections to the plan were raised for the lack of any provision for the establishment of cooperatives, which would be the only way the peasants could prosper after a major land reform. Many commentators also disliked the program's support for the church. Others considered the program too narrowly peasant-oriented. They felt it had missed the opportunity to become a national reform plan in scope and attractive to broader sectors of society. It was stated that Achim expected too much of a class-oriented state which, by its nature, was hostile to programs like that of the Peasant Party. On the other hand, many critics considered the party to be too moderate for the rural proletariat and too radical for the smallholders and the rich peasants.

In his answer Achim dealt positively with the criticism. He contended, however, that the peasantry was already politically mature and aware enough to act on its own behalf independently of any other class. He said that under the present circumstances the Peasant Party had to be a radical political organization. Finally, he acknowledged that, while the platform was far from being scientific, precise, or all-encompassing, it nonetheless expressed the peasants' wishes and was a product of the peasants' thinking, and these, after all, were the foundations of any ideology fitting a peasant movement. He promised a vigorous campaign to bring the program to fruition.[62]

In 1910, Achim was elected to Parliament for the last time. His election was followed by a murderous campaign of character assassination against him.[63] The outcome was a tragic confrontation between him and the two sons of his rival, Dr. Endre Szilinszky (Gabor and Endre, Jr.) who shot him to death. They were, however, acquitted by every court up to the *Kuria* (the supreme court of the realm). After Achim's death, the Peasant Party rapidly disintegrated under relentless government pressure. "In the cemetery at Bekescsaba, the earth fell not only upon Achim's coffin, but also upon a beautiful revolutionary initiative."[64] In the longer run Achim's death was even more devastating. As Tibor Erenyi correctly suggested, such a man was badly to be needed in 1918. Had the peasantry had Achim as a leader then, their aspirations would probably not have been sold out during the revolutions of 1918-1919 and thereafter.[65]

NOTES

1. Gyorgy Dozsa, A *Szekely* (Szekler) petty nobleman, was appointed by Cardinal Tamas Bakocz, Primate of Hungary and Archbishop of Esztergom, to command a crusade against the Ottomans. On April 24, 1514, a banner was granted to Dozsa blessed by Pope Leo X himself. Nevertheless, the campaign turned into the widest spread and bloodiest peasant war in Hungary's history. The defeat of Dozsa'speasant army in the same year was followed by a brutal execution of the leaders and of countless rebels. The peasants were from that time on subjected, in all respects, to the lords. The principles and practices of this subjection were compiled in Istvan Verboczi's (also Werboczy) famous book the *Tripartitum,* published in 1517 in Latin and subsequently republished several times in Latin and in Hungarian. No law or publication ever influenced more permanently, effectively, and adversely the fate of Hungary's peasantry than did the *Tripartitum.*

2. Baron Jozsef Eotvos (1813-1874), liberal statesman, writer and twice Minister of *Kultus*. Sandor Petofi (1823-1849), Hungary's poet laureate, a revolutionary in 1848-49. Endre Ady (1877-1918), radical "Westerner," writer and poet. Gyula Illyes (1902-), one of the "village explorers," Hungary's current poet laureate. See Antal Szerb, *Magyar Irodalomtortenet* (History of Hungarian Literature) Budapest, 1958), 181, 357, 358, 383, 348 and 437.
3. Bela K. Kiraly, "The November Insurrection and the Hungarians," *Antemurale* 14(1970), 229-52. See also, Stefan Kieniewicz, *The Emancipation of the Polish Peasantry* (Chicago, Ill., 1969), 113-27; Henry Roberts, *Rumania: Political Problems of an Agrarian State* (New Haven, Conn., 1951), 4-21.
4. Bela K. Kiraly, *Hungary in the Late Eighteenth Century: the Decline of Enlightened Despotism* (New York, 1969), 212-33.
5. *Ibid.*, 24-43.
6. Gyula Szekfu, *Harom nemzedek. Egy hanyatlo kor tortenete* (Three Generations. The History of a Declining Age) (Budapest, 1920), 74.
7. Geza Feja, *Viharsarok. Az Also Tiszavidek foldje es nepe* (The Storm Corner. The Land and People of the Lower Tisza Region) (Budapest, 1937), 49.
8. Acts IX, X, XI, XII, XIII, XV, 1848. *Corpus juris hungarici, 1836-1868* (Quoted below as *CJH*), 232-7.
9. The full text is in Janos Beer, (ed.) *Az 1848/49. evi nepkepviseleti orszaggyules* (The Diet of Popular Representation of 1848-1849) (Budapest, 1954), 621-32.
10. *Reichsgesetzblatt, 1853,* 201.
11. Gyula Merei and Gyorgy Spira, *Magyarorszag tortenete, 1790-1849* (The History of Hungary, 1790-1849), 3 vols. (Budapest, 1961), 3:411. The landless rural proletariat contained 45.9% of the ethnic Hungarian peasantry, 36.8% of the Serbian, 30.2% of the Slovak, 27.9% of the Rumanian, 25.4% of the German, 20% of the Ruthenian, and 19.8% of the Croatian peasantry. In other words, the Hungarian

landlords pauperized mostly the Hungarian peasants, not primarily the peasantry of the ethnic minorities of Hungary. See Mihaly Kerek, *A magyar foldkerdes* (The Hungarian Land Problem) (Budapest, 1939), 132. For definitions of the terms, serf, *inquilinus,* and related other technical data see Kiraly, *Hungary . . . op. cit.,* 213 and following.

12. Seventy % of the population of Hungary lived in the rural sphere in 1860, and 69% in 1900. For the lack of domestic industrial development, agriculture also remained backward; in 1902, 30% of the peasantry still used obsolete methods and 70% cultivated their lands with more modern procedures. See Ferenc Poloskei and Kalman Szakacs, *Foldmunkas es szegenyparaszt mozgalmak Magyarorszagon 1848-1948* (Movements of Agrarian Laborers and Poor Peasants in Hungary, 1848-1948) (Budapest, 1962) 2 vols., 1:108, 112.
13. Pal Sandor, *A XIX. szazadvegi agrarvalsag Magyarorszagon* (The Agrarian Crisis of the End of the 19th Century in Hungary) (Budapest, 1958), 14.
14. Poloskei and Szakacs, *op. cit.,* 1:118.
15. Acts V and XVII of 1848, *CJH, 1836-1868* 223-30, 251-2. Act XXXIII of 1874, *CJH 1872-74,* 314-32. See also, C.A. Macartney, *History of Hungary, 1929-1945* (New York, 1956), 2 vols., 1:11.
16. Poloskei and Szakacs, *op. cit.,* 1:163-4.
17. *Ibid.,* 1:118.
18. *Ibid.,* 1:161. Two major recent publications cover the same subject as this study does; Dezso Farkas, *A magyarorszagi Szocialdemokrata Part es az agrarkerdes 1900 and 1914 kozott* (The Social Democratic Party and the Agrarian Problem in Hungary between 1900 and 1914) (Budapest, 1973), and Peter Gunst and Tamas Hoffman (eds.), *A magyar mezogazdasag a XIX-XX. szazadban* (Hungarian Agriculture in the 19th-20th Centuries) (Budapest, 1976). See also, Peter Hanak, "Short Survey of Recent Literature on Hungarian Economic History," *The Economic History Review,* 2nd Series, 24(1971), Nov., 667-79.

19. Peter Veres, *Az Alfold parasztsaga* (The Peasantry of the Great Plain) (Budapest, 1944), 4th ed., 88.
20. Arnold Daniel, *A magyarorszagi foldmuvelo szocializmus feladatai* (The Tasks of Agrarian Socialism in Hungary) (Budapest, 1906), 9.
21. Arnold Daniel, *A kultura elso forrasa a foldmuveles* (The First Source of Culture is Agriculture) (Budapest, 1907), 33.
22. *The Columbia Encyclopedia* (New York, 1959) (2nd ed.), 1844.
23. The Hungarian labor movement was born in 1869. In 1872, the old trade guilds were finally abolished but the freedom of trade organizations was introduced only in 1884, and only in the form of a common organization of employees and employers. In 1869, however, the *Pesti Altalanos Munkasegylet* (General Laborers' Association of Pest) had been founded, and the following year the *Altalanos Munkas Betegsegelyzo Penztar* (General Laborers' Health Insurance Society) was set up. In 1876, Leo Frankel, a former Commissioner of the Paris Commune of 1871, returned to Hungary and started to organize the labor movement itself. He arranged the first Social Democratic Congress in Hungary in 1878. The party that was formed by him was called the Party of the Disenfranchised. In 1880, several Socialist factions were united in the *Magyar Altalanos Munkaspart* (General Hungarian Labor Party); that was also the year in which trade unions became free to organize and did so. The party was represented at the founding congress of the Second International. In 1890, it assumed the name, Social Democratic Party of Hungary. Its official journal was *Nepszava* (People's Voice).
24. Zoltan Bodrogkozy, *A magyar agrarmozgalmak tortenete* (The History of Hungarian Agrarian Movements) (Budapest, 1919), 72.
25. Istvan Varkonyi was born in Cegled in 1852. In 1889, he moved to Budapest, joined the *Magyar Altalanos*

Munkaspart and became a member of its Central Committee.

26. Bela Szanto, *A magyar munkasmozgalom 1914-ig* (The Hungarian Workers' Movement up to 1914) (Budapest, 1947), 143.
27. Poloskei and Szakacs, *op. cit.,* 1:181-2.
28. Bodrogkozy, *op. cit.,* 48.
29. Szanto, *op. cit.,* 143.
30. Including the Marxist revolutionary secretary general, Pal Engelmann.
31. Szanto, *op. cit.,* 142-3.
32. The first issue of the *Foldmuvelo* was published on August 29, 1896.
33. Poloskei and Szakacs, *op. cit.,* 1:260.
34. Szanto, *op. cit.,* 146-7.
35. Poloskei and Szakacs, op. cit.,1:274.
36. *Foldmuvelo,* Dec., 1899. See also, Poloskei and Szakacs, *op. cit.,* 1:338.
37. *Ibid.,* 1:340.
38. Act II., 1898 in *CJH 1898,* 5-19.
39. Poloskei and Szakacs, *op. cit.,* 1:290, 297; Szanto, *op. cit.,* 148.
40. Poloskei and Szakacs, *op. cit.,* 1:326; Bodrogkozy, *op. cit.,* 77.
41. Bodrogkozy, op. cit., 77.
42. The temporary union of some trade union organizations was an important factor, for rather like the British labor movement, there was a high degree of integration between the Social Democratic Party and the trade unions in Hungary.
43. Bodrogkozy, *op. cit.,* 77, Note 32.
44. Poloskei and Szakacs, *op. cit.,* 1:329.
45. *Ibid.*
46. Szanto, *op. cit.,* 157. The success of the Reorganized Social Democratic Party during its radical phase can be gauged by the number of representatives who attended its congresses;

at the 1901 congress in Szentes, 51 villages sent 127 delegates;
at the 1902 congress in Mezotur, 107 villages sent 168 delegates,
at the 1903 congress in Nagyszalonta 263 villages sent 505 delegates.

These numbers represented a fourfold increase in three years. Bodrogkozy, *op. cit.,* 79.

47. Poloskei and Szakacs, *op. cit.,* 1:333.
48. Bodrogkozy, *op. cit.,* 79.
49. Andras L. Achim was born on March 16, 1871 in Bekescsaba. His father owned 143 *hold* of land (203.6 acres), to which the son added between 1,420 and 2,800 acres of rented land. The family was of minor noble origin and had descended into the peasantry. Achim completed six years of secondary school and went on to educate himself. The most recent biography of Achim was written by Jozsef Domokos, *Achim L. Andras* (Budapest, 1971). See also, Feja, *op. cit.,* 48-9. The other peasant leaders soon to follow Achim were from the Transdanubian region and included Istvan Nagyatadi Szabo, Janos Meyer, Lajos Mohacsi, all of whom came from the same social stratum. See Istvan Kiraly, "Achim L. Andras, a demokratikus parasztpolitikus," (Andras L. Achim, the Democratic Peasant Politician) in Ferenc Poloskei and Ferenc Szabo, (eds.) *Achim L. Andras Emlekkonyv 1871-1971* (Commemorative volume on A.L.A.) (Bekescsaba, 1972), 52.
50. Commemorative speech of Istvan Bencsik at the centennial celebration of Achim's birth at Bekescsaba, March 14, 1971, in Poloskei and Szabo, *op. cit.,* 11. "Becoming a member of the Bekes county Assembly started Achim on his political career." Bodrogkozy, *op. cit.,* 8.
51. *A Kepviselohaz Naploja* (Minutes of the Lower House of Parliament), 1906-11, 2:195. See also, Istvan Kiraly, *op. cit.,* 53, 57, 61.
52. Bodrogkozy, op. cit., 87; domokos, *op. cit.,* 142-52.

53. Janos Tibori, "Achim L. Andras a bekescsabai szegeny-parasztsag elen," (A.L.A. as the Leader of the Poor Peasants of Bekescsaba) in Poloskei and Szabo, *op. cit.*, 82-3.
54. Photostatic copy of Achim's own defense among the appendices in Poloskei and Szabo, *op. cit.*
55. Tibori, *op. cit.*, 83.
56. Istvan Kiraly, *op. cit.*, 62; Domokos, *op. cit.*, 199-213.
57. Acts II, 1898, and XVI, 1907, respectively. See Dezso Sulyok, *A magyar tragedia* (Hungarian Tragedy) (Newark, NJ., 1954), 327.
58. This was the first time that the platform of any peasant movement had called for the curtailment of land ownership by foreigners in Hungary. It reflected a dissatisfaction at the increasing amount of land purchased by foreigners which could have been allocated to local landless peasants. In 1900, 436 foreigners owned 2.84 million acres of land in Hungary, half of it timberlands. Of these landowners 69.4% were Austrians, 14.4% Germans, 4.4% Swiss, 2.2 Frenchmen, 2.2% Italians, and the rest were English, Dutch, Rumanian, Greek, Serbian, Russian, Belgian and American. The estimated landholdings of foreigners in 1914 were 4.26 million acres. Kerek, *op. cit.*, 129.
59. The entire text was published in *Huszadik Szazad* (Budapest) 9(1908) No 8, 130-3. See also, Tibori, *op. cit.*, 84; Domokos, *op. cit.*, 199-232.
60. *Huszadik Szazad,* 9(1908), Nos. 7-9, 44-50, 130-3, 135-42, 228-43, 308-14; Domokos, *op. cit.*, 214-32.
61. *Ibid.*, 9(1908), No. 7, 130-3.
62. *Ibid.*, Nos. 7-9, 44-50, 130-33, 135-6, 228-43, 308-14.
63. Tibori, *op. cit.*, 88-9; Domokos, *op. cit.*, 315-38.
64. Feja, "Commemorative Oration," in Poloskei and Szabo, *op. cit.*, 22.
65. Tibor Erenyi, "A szocialista munkasmozgalom es Achim L. Andras," (The Socialist Workers' Movement and A.L.A.— in Poloskei and Szabo, *op. cit.*, 127, See also, Domokos, *op. cit.*, 348-51.

PART IV
THE DANCE OF DEATH: WORLD WAR I AND THE HUNGARIAN PEASANTS

Peter Hidas

IV.

"Loss and gain are brothers twain"
(Russian proverb)

1. Introduction

As Austria-Hungary entered World War I, a number of economic decisions had to be formulated for an efficient conduct of the war. Once the intitial call-up was completed, the government had to offer some solution to the problem of labor shortages in the countryside which now replaced the chronic unemployment of the pre-war years. Allied blockade, poor harvests in Austria, and fighting in Habsburg soil further challenged the economic policy makers in both halves of the Empire. Immediate attention had to be paid to financing mobilization, paying for the transport, equipment, ammunition, clothing and food supplies of the armed forces.

The Tisza government at Budapest has often been accused in the past of attempting to achieve autarky: it was called selfish, creatinga quasi-independent, inward-looking agricultural policy.[1] But the fate of the Hungarian peasantry between 1914 and 1918 has so far escaped the attention of western historians.[2] Consequently, a good economic history of Hungary during World War I remains unwritten. A few preliminary observations, based on old and new evidence, will perhaps clarify some major aspects of Hungarian economic policies and provide an introductory study about the people of the soil during the war years.[3]

2. The Background

The grandchildren of the pre-1848 bonded peasants, who were soon to be slaughtered and maimed (or enriched) as a result of the Great War, were a very different breed of men than the serfs and *zsellers* of Hungary's yesteryears. Seventy years of social and economic progress, especially during the two decades preceding World War I, significantly improved the economic status of the agricultural population. Those who stayed on the farm produced more and received increasingly higher prices for their crops. Some of the poorest left for the cities to become industrial workers while others emigrated abroad to make their private fortunes (or misfortunes), thereby easing the social pressures on the countryside. Nevertheless, enough extra hands remained to provide soldiers for the Austro-Hungarian Army.

During the war close to 20% of the Hungarian population fought in the ranks. Of the warring countries only Germany surpassed this ratio.[4] Magyars suffered greatly: 28 young men were killed per 1000 inhabitants.[5] Peasants constituted the largest segment of the draftees, superseding their ratio of the population.[6] The farmhands and other agricultural-worker-soldiers who were not wounded or maimed fared well in the army. They were better fed and clothed than in civilian life. Their cousins in the hinterlands, smallholders and well-to-do peasants, enjoyed the benefits of increased demands for foodstuffs, high prices, government protection, and debt-eliminating inflation. But who were these people?

In 1910, the population of Hungary was about 21 million people. Peasants made up 62.22% of that total.[7] Magyars formed 54.50% of the peoples of the state. The various social categories in the rural sphere more or less corresponded to acreage held or rented.

The great husbandman or rich peasant usually owned between 70-142 acres of arable land, but could possess as little as 28 acres of quality land and as much as 280 acres of less fertile fields. In his stables there was often room for 25 to 30 cattle, in the hen house there were at least 100 fowl. He planted a variety of crops and hired a few farmhands. He was a leading citizen who took a prominent role in municipal and church affairs. The children of the well-to-do farmer were sometimes sent to school and aspired to marry someone of higher social standing. He dreamed of acquiring more land. But generally the great husbandman remained part of the village community in dress, work, speech and recreation. The proportion of Magyar-speaking people was highest among them.[8]

The "middle" peasant landholder owned 28-70 acres of arable land. He was equipped with horses and perhaps a threshing machine, hired farmhands and mingled with his wealthier neighbors. This type was most numerous in Transdanubia, in the Great Plain and the Bansag.[9]

The "good husbandmen" or smallholders were the most numerous and fastest-growing layer of the peasantry in Hungary. Their family farms benefited from the boom years of the previous decades; their large stocks of animals or gardens near some rapidly growing towns and cities secured them a share of the benefits of the Hungarian industrial revolution at the turn of the century.[10]

Two-thirds of the dwarf-holders who owned 1.4-7.5 acres each were Slavs or Rumanians.[11] Some of these lived in Transylvania and northern Hungary. Their marginal holdings were rarely sufficient to support a family and so they usually worked as day laborers or sharecroppers.

In 1914, every fourth person in Hungary belonged to an agricultural laborer family. There were 4,356,316 such workers in the countryside, many of them single and frequently unemployed. Magyars constituted a disproportionately higher number, 2,566,105, of this group.[12] Many poor and unemployed farmhands emigrated abroad or found opportunities in the industrializing cities. Between 1899 and 1913, nearly 1.4 million persons left the country officially. More emigrated illegally. In contrast 3-400,000 immigrants entered Hungary during this period. Villages with a population of 5,000 or less inhabitants lost 2.6 million people out of 12.1 million peasants between 1880 and 1910. Consequently, urban concentrations increased their share of the population from 16.9% in 1890 to 20.4% twenty years later. During this interval, the total population increase was 19.6% but in the countryside the rate was only 6.3%.[13] Notwithstanding, Hungarian agriculture was able to feed the growing cities of the Empire, produce surplus for export while increasing the living standard of the peasant-farmer. Agrarian production was gradually concentrated in the hands of the peasantry.

In 1913, estates smaller than 142 acres each owned only 45.44%, while others larger than 142 acres owned 54.56% of all agricultural properties.[14] In the past these figures were taken in isolation to categorize the agriculture of Hungary as an estate-dominated, Prussian-type economy. Truly, the large estates made 1.24% of the landowners wealthy, but not necessarily a dominant factor in the creation of 54% of the G.N.P., the share of agriculture.[15] Ownership of arable lands, mainly plowlands, combined with the actual use of land are the keys to the problem of dominant factor.

The peasant owned in the form of commons or in some other corporate way 3,661,184 acres of estates over 142 acres.[16] At the turn of the century they rented 32.1% of the estates 142-1420 acres in size each and 24.9% of estates over 1420 acres.[17] The smallholders with a minimum of 7.5 acres of properties steadily increased their share of the ploughlands. On the other hand, the dwarfholders' number gradually decreased. Many lost their land and sank to the level of agricultural workers. Others survived and joined the market economy. In the area between the Danube and Tisza Rivers, 28-55% of their properties consisted of valuable vineyards. Many of the dwarf holders with farms near towns turned to truck farming.[18] The expansion of ploughlands during the second half of the 19th century was the greatest on the dwarf and small holdings. The former increased their plowed areas by 63.5%, the latter by 68.1%.[19] Between 1869 and 1913, arable lands increased by 2.24 million acres and plowlands by 1.96 million acres.[20] The increase was primarily due to the purchasing efforts of the peasantry.

The peasant raised money through increased marketing of his goods, tapping conventional loan sources, and through the peasantry's credit unions. Emigrant peasants sent or brought back enormous amounts of cash from America. This process continued during the war. In Leo Pasvolsky's view, "emigrant remittances represented the most important source of international service income" in Austria-Hungary.[21] Through official channels 200 million crowns were returned between 1899 and 1903, 700 million between 1904 and 1908, and 1,500 million between 1909 and 1919.[22] The peasant used the money to pay his taxes, repay his loans and to purchase parcels from middle and large estate owners.[23] Investing in much machinery was beyond his means but creating a labor-intensive economy was not.[24] The peasant economy gradually shifted towards animal husbandry. By 1911, 79% of the cattle stock, 86.1% of the horses, 79.8% of the hogs and 59.8% of sheep were raised on the under 100 hold lots.[25] The Magyar peasants of the Great Plain kept many large herds.[26] Poultry production was also in peasant hands. Smallholders supplied 85% of the country's milk.[27] Some of the finest grain fields in the world were in Hungary. Between 1870 and 1912, bread grain sown land, however, decreased by 14%. This was the result of the fact that the peasants switched to labor intensive crops but still produced 7/10's of all the country's wheat.[28] Corn production increased by 64% and nearly 8/10's originated from peasants' fields. Potato output doubled and 84% of the total crop was grown by the peasants.[29]

The price index of agricultural production also favored the peasantry. Between 1867 and 1914 prices of manufactured goods declined by 5%, while agricultural goods grew by 40% in value. The price spiral of animal products was most spectacular; it came to 89%.[30] As a historian recently observed:

> Hungary's agriculture at the outbreak of the First World War stood at approximately the same level as that of the Western, Northern, and Central European countries with respect to the quality of production per capita, but it remained substantially behind them in the areas of yields and productivity.[31]

This development was largely due to the fact that the agricultural sector of the economy became largely peasant-dominated. The food supply of the Habsburg Empire rested on the shoulders of the peasants. The dependency became even more acute during World War I. In turn, whatever policies the government introduced on that matter were of vital importance to the peasantry.

3. The War Years

On February 20, 1915, the Tisza cabinet voted for intensified recruiting. This increased the country's contribution to the infantry alone to 1.2 million men. During the war the total number of soldiers in the army fluctuated between 2-3 million. By 1918, at least 8 million men served, of which Hungary's share was 3.8 million.[32] As initial call-ups were concentrated in the countryside, more people were drafted from the villages than from the cities (since most people did live in rural districts), more from Hungary than from Austria. Hungary's contribution (without Croatia) was 44.9% of her men between the ages of 18 and 50 while the Monarchy's was 43.28%.[33] (Hungarians made up 40.96% of the population of Austria-Hungary.)

The high call-up rate created immediate labor shortages in Hungary. The requisitioning of large numbers of horses adversely affected the rural economy. In March, 1915, England introduced the economic blockade of the Central Powers. In the same year the granaries of Galicia and Bukovina were ravaged and production also ceased in the northeastern frontiers of Hungary.[34] The last peace harvest in the Empire was the poorest to date in the century. Despite all these events Hungary's economy remained firm. Production volumes approximated the pre-war level. Furthermore, the agricultural boom of the early 1910's continued during the initial years of the war. What were the roots of this economic "miracle?"

Carlyle A. Macartney rightly credited Prime Minister Istvan Tisza with setting up an efficient machine for harnessing Hungary's resources in the service of the war effort.[35] The initial mobilization supplemented the peace time army of half a million soldiers with an additional 3 million men, half from Hungary.[36] Of the disproportionately large number of young farmhands drafted many were previously unemployed, others had completed or were about to complete the harvest of 1914. Labor shortages became a greater problem at plowing time in the autumn of 1915.

By the summer of 1915, the Minister of Agriculture successfully negotiated furloughs for farm mechanics and engineers. Producers of agricultural implements were encouraged to intensify production and were provided with skilled workers from the Army. The government imported farm machinery and fuel from Austria, Germany, and Switzerland and offered financial aid to farmers who bought machines. From 1915 on, many Serbian and Russian prisoners-of-war labored on the fields of Hungary. These measures helped primarily the well-to-do farmers and large estate owners, but other actions were designed to aid the smallholders. The army commandeered 42% of the country's horse stock but the peasants were allowed to retain a minimum number of draft animals, although not necessarily horses. The government encouraged increased grain production and introduced measures to protect the producers' land and financial stability.

Expired land rent contracts were automatically renewed by law. Moratorium was declared on back payments of farmers on newly settled lands. Municipalities were instructed to secure the sowing of all arable lands with grain crops including the properties of drafted soliders. The Association of Magyar Husbandmen (Magyar Gazdak Szovetsege) distributed seed grains on behalf of the Ministry of Agriculture to boost the next year's crop. In 1915, the Association marketed 123,330 quintals of barley (one quintal=220 lbs), (7.6% of the nation's seed requirement), 92,178 quintals of rye, 50,790 quintals of corn and 7,307 quintals of spring wheat seed. The peasants were given 85,000 quintals of seed potatoes in addition to the potato crops produced by 346 experimental farms. Flax seed was distributed at low prices. Blue vitriol (copper sulphate) was imported from Germany for spraying for grapegrowers and the existing domestic stocks were brought up by the government. The government distributed 20,300 quintals of copper sulphate to vintners in 1915. Bad weather, labor shortages and plant diseases, misuse of barrels by the army, however, countered every effort of the government to increase wine production.

Since 50% of the veterinarians were now in the army, the Ministry of Agriculture provided free serum directly to poor farmers. Stock feed was in short supply after the poor harvest of 1914. To ease the shortage the government negotiated a contract with the major mills according to which the farmers were to receive the mills' surplus bran as animal feed. In 1915, a Bran Center was established to hand over 60% of all bran and other useful industrial wastes. In 1915, the Center sold 1.33 million quintals of bran to peasants. These activities mitigated the moderate fodder shortage which was due to the low stock of wheat straw in 1914, and the low quality of the new hay following the wet spring of 1915. Good crops of oats, barley, corn and potatoes, however, prevented any major dislocation in the fodder business.

The Ministry of Agriculture subsidized the purchase of bulls. Buyers (villages) received free stock insurance for one year. The government also purchased Hungarian and Western cattle for 3 million crowns and sold them to the peasants at an average discount of 20%. Although there was no decline in milk production, the expansion of the last decades was arrested. Increased consumption of milk and the subsequent decline of dairy products resulted in shortages despite imports from Denmark. Also, in 1915, boars were sold to the peasants at close to 40% below the market price to encourage meat production to provide for the increasing demands of the army and the urban centers.[37] In the same year the army returned 10,000 horses for farm use. These measures enhanced production in the agricultural sector of the economy. Financial measures also served to stimulate food production.

The war chest of Austria-Hungary was filled quickly with the green masterpieces of the printing press. On July 23, 1914, there were 2,130 million crowns in circulation backed by a gold reserve of 74.16%. By August 7th of the same year, the government had issued 1,450 million additional crowns of new bills and, by New Year's Eve, Austro-Hungarian banknotes in circulation amounted to 5,137 million crowns without a corresponding increase in the gold reserve.[38] The government now had the funds to finance the war effort. There was no shortage of goods or a lack of confidence in victory to trigger a major inflation. The Swiss money exchange devalued the crown by 10% at the end of 1914 and only a further 20% a year later.[39] International dealers somehow shared the confidence of the Austrian and Hungarian population in the Empire's economy. Consequently, a free market economy would be sustained with a minimum of interference by the government. The army purchased supplies on the open market. German and Austro-Hungarian agents bought 60% of Hungary's horse stock for cash. The commodity exchange at Budapest remained open and active, dealing in futures of cabbage, fats, poppy seed, nuts, potato, cheese, rice seed grains and millet stocks. Only the staple grain trade was restricted.

Maximum prices for wheat and rye were set by local administrations who, however, kept these prices at the high December, 1914 level. In 1913, wheat sold for 22.19 crowns per quintal (monthly commodity exchange price average). Between August and December, 1914, the price of wheat rose from 31.52 crowns to 40.96 crowns. The maximum price for the first half of 1915 was set between 40 and 41 crowns per quintal. During the first six months of 1914, rye prices went from 21.93 to 32.50 crowns per quintal and settled at 32.10 crowns in January, 1915. The December, 1914, prices for barley, oats and corn were 27.64, 25.27 and 21.33 crowns per quintal respectively.[40] The new maximum prices stabilized the grain trade and secured a good income for the agricultural producers.

Staple grain trade was restricted by the War Products Corporation of the government, which was organized in 1915, to coordinate the food supply of the country and the army, and was managed by the country's top grain merchants. They financed the Corporation with the anxious participation of the bankers who wished to mobilize their rapidly growing deposits.[41] The allied blockage caused little damage because Hungary's export-import trade was concentrated in Austria proper where the industrial boom had not been interrupted by the outbreak of the war.

Retail stores in Hungary remained well-stocked with goods. The *Hangya,* the most popular retail chain in the Hungarian villages, had acquired a series of production plants enabling its outlets to maintain a steady flow of merchandise.[42] The per capita cotton supply dropped only from .76 kg. in 1913 to .70 in 1914 and .50 in 1915. Tea consumption actually increased from 19 grams through 23 to 33 grams per capita in the above years respectively. The coal supply for agriculture, including home heating, reached 25 million quintals in 1912 and never fell below that level during the span of the war. The supply of petroleum for lamps dropped by 1/3 in the first year of the war but improved in 1915/16 to 79% of the last peace year.[43] The industrial boom and the maximizing of certain industrial prices, such as lamp oil, also helped to inhibit any serious inflation before 1916.[44]

War widows received 72 to 300 crowns plus 48 crowns per child per year. An additional provisional supplement of five crowns plus one to nine crowns per child per month was available. A war widow with three children could receive 828 to 3700 crowns per year.[45] Zsigmond Moricz's hero in *Poor People* worked for two crowns a day, spend .26 crowns on a kilo of bread, bought a dozen peppers for .10, one liter of milk for .30, purchased a good shovel for 1.40 crowns but could not buy leather boots for 60 crowns.[46]

The peasant spent part of his surplus cash in the store; he also increased his savings in the form of bank deposits. Some of them hid their money around the house or bought more land. Others paid off their old debts or purchased high interest bonds. The government siphoned off from the patriotic public a good share of the war profits with successful sales of eight sets of war bonds. Skillful manipulation of the economy resulted in a sufficient volume of agricultural production for the population of Hungary and the Austro-Hungarian Army, but not for Austria.

The Austrians "never ceased to reproach Hungary for niggardliness on food, its unwillingness to accept equal (and lowly) standards of consumption."[47] The mayor of Vienna publicly accused Hungary of selfishness and demanded action from the Austrian premier. The cost of living in Vienna was indeed up 53% by June, 1915, and had tripled by the second anniversary of the outbreak of the war.[48] Basic food items remained available in Austria only until 1916, when the black market became widespread. The cost of one kilogram potatoes, for example, sold for .16 crowns during the first two winters of the war years. The 1916, black market price was already around .50 crowns, or 28% above the 1915 summer price.[49] But according to the report of the *New York Times* (February 6, 1915), a loaf of bread in Vienna still cost a mere 15 cents. The mayor cried wolf too early.

Austria's agriculture usually produced about 73% of the country's wheat requirement, and the balance came from Hungary.[50] In 1914, the Austrian wheat yield was 95% of the previous year's harvest but in Hungary the yield was only 70%. Wheat export to Austria in 1914 accordingly was reduced to 68%

of the 1909-1913 average. Most other foodstuff exported to Austria was similarly, but not significantly, decreased with the notable exceptions being cattle, hogs, eggs, bacon, lards and processed meats.[51] From 1915 on, Hungary took the lion's share in feeding the whole Austro-Hungarian army. In fact, between 1916 and 1918, the soldiers lived on Magyar bread alone.[52]

Austria's troubles did not originate in Hungary. Hoarding, speculation, and primarily the increasing consumption by close to four million inhabitants-turned-soldiers were the probable roots of the matter.

Hundreds of thousands of peasant-soldiers were better fed and clothed for the first time in their lives. At induction, each soldier received a full uniform, two pairs of boots and an overcoat. Eight million quintals of flour was shipped to the army,[53] giving each soldier a daily flour allowance of .58 kg. including a pound of bread, more than double the per capita flour consumption in Hungary in 1914-15.[54] The soldiers were given meat and coffee daily. Hungarian coffee consumption per capita increased from .56 kg. in 1913 to .66 kg. in 1914 and to 1.09 kg. in the following year.[55] The peasant-soldier was well looked after.

The peasants at home, except for those who lived near the battle front, also fared well. Despite lower production levels their grain crops were worth 27% more in the first year of the war and 40% more in the second year than in 1913-14.[56] Agricultural laborers on state-owned farms received a 30% wage hike in 1915.[57] Labor shortages had a beneficial impact on wages throughout the country. Furthermore, extra profits were made by producers near towns and the Austrian border. In addition, until 1917, American-Hungarians sent large amounts of cash to their Hungarian relatives. In early 1917, a British correspondents forwarded the following dispatch about Magyar peasants:[58]

> Their women wear silk stockings and pay as much as 2 pounds or 3 pounds for a pair of silk slippers. In the village of Abony 6,000 inhabitants put 100,000 pounds in the savings bank during the last two years over and above

> their normal savings of prewar years. They paid as much again in discharge of debts or mortgages, and they are said to have left half a million pounds hidden in their straw stacks and cupboards.

Bank records seem to justify the impressions of the journalist. Deposits in one of Hungary's largest savings banks increased from 476 million crowns in 1914 to 559 million in 1915, 707 million crowns in 1916, and 670 million in 1917 and to 1,179 million in 1918. At the same time new loans declined from 5.9 million in 1913 to 4.8 in 1914 and to .2 million in the following year.[59] Once their loans were paid off the peasants began to search for new lands to be purchased or rented. In 1915-16, 32,396 acres of middle and large estates were parcelled out. Distributed lands increased to 74,360 in 1916-17, and only began to drop off after the Russian Revolution.[60] The sale of middle and large estates grew by 20% from 1915-16 to 1916-17, and by a further 36% for the last year of the war. The most likely buyers were *nouveaux riche* peasants and speculators who, in turn, usually sold to peasants.

But there were other peasants, for whom the war brought immediate hardship. The first Russian offensive interrupted agricultural production in the northeastern counties. In this region of Slovak, Ruthenian and Magyar dwarf holders, requisitioning and the destruction of property often led to starvation. The government provided special relief for the peasants in Saros and Zemplen counties and resettled some of the Magyar peasants in Transylvania but to little avail.[61] The Rumanian invasion of Transylvania and the recovery of the area in 1916 turned southwestern Hungary into a war-ravaged land. Serious food shortages plagued both the northeastern and the southeastern regions of the country until the good harvest of 1918. But since neither of these areas possessed a market-oriented agriculture, the difficulties did not seriously hinder Hungary's grain output.

The Tisza government was able to supply the army and secure adequate food supply for consumers because the wheat consumption by 1916-17 was only slightly below that of the last peace year's and actually surpassed it only by 1917-18.[62] The same phenomenon can be observed in studying the production figures for rye, oats, and barley (see Tables at the end of this essay). Hungary's abattoirs processed a yearly average of 1.24 million cattle between 1911 and 1915. In 1916, because of the fodder shortages, this number dropped to .72 million but by 1917 everything was back to normal; in that year 1.12 million cattle were slaughtered for meat.[63] Potato production, however dropped significantly after the bumper crops of the first two years of the war. Corn growers also failed to maintain pre-war standards (see Tables at the end of this essay).[64]

During 1917-18, the agricultural situation was generally somewhat different from the circumstances prevalent during the first half of World War I and, as a result, the government set maximum prices failed to provide the peasantry with an income they now considered fair. A disparity developed between the price of agricultural and industrial goods. For instance, the cost of soap tripled between 1916 and 1917; the price of a scythe rose 33% between 1915 and 1916, and in 1917 the 1915 price was surpassed by a hefty 135%.[65] Soon a wide gap was formed between maximum prices and actual market values. When in November, 1917, the government's Animal and Fodder Marketing Corporation attempted to reduce this gap through its monopoly, the peasants simply withheld their produce and some even reduced production.[66]

The situation was further aggravated when the government sent troops to the countryside in search of hidden food stocks.[67] County authorities cooperated with crafty peasants and often refused to hand over county stockpiles to the military.[68] The three searches conducted inthe winter of 1917 brought meager results.[69] The following report on the matter was sent to the *Morning Star* (London):[70]

> The first two attempts during this winter to seize from the peasant his scanty little hidden stock proved failures. The proceedings are these: the town or rural authorities, accompanied by gendarmes and followed by a number of

> heavy carts, visit every home from cellar to attic, and carry away everything they can lay their hands on in the way of foodstuffs. Where there is reason to believe a stock has been hidden they even dig holes in the courtyard and garden in search of buried maize or potatoes.
>
> This process, employing many thousands of officials and gendarmes, has been gone through twice within the last ten weeks, and only a very small quantity of provisions was found in each case. The authorities, however, think even now it is impossible that there should not be more hidden grain on the farms, and the food dictator has quietly ordered the inquisition to begin afresh.

There were signs of dissatisfation but the Hungarian economy held and the Magyar peasant remained loyal. There is little substance to May's statement that "in the second half of the war the economy of Hungary staggered from bad to worse."[71] Enough food was produced to feed the army and the population of Hungary to the very end of the war. "Country folk, adept at hoarding and concealment, were getting along reasonably well,"[72] is a more accurate observation. Food in Hungarian cities was rationed only to secure minimum requirements at reasonable prices. The government borrowed 1,000 railway cars from Germany to facilitate efficient distribution of foodstuffs.[73] Potato ration was 3 to 4 kg. per week and it never fell below 1 kg. per person for a week in 1918. More could be bought at the open market for somewhat higher prices. There was grumbling about the poor quality of fats and margarine, about milk shortages, and that the worker had to spend 70% of his wages on food—but, at least, the food was available.[74]

Inflated money could still be used to repay old debts and to pay rent at pre-war prices. Peasants could note with satisfaction that some parliamentarians and church leaders began to talk about a new land distribution project to veterans, war widows and owners of marginal farms. Bishop

Prohaszka's proposal to this effect was shelved, however, possibly because the landless peasants were still at the front and most of the marginal farms were in non-Magyar hands.[75]

Prime Minister Tisza's concerns seldom went beyond narrow national interest. The question of the veterans belonged to the future, but war widows and their children were given pensions and some Magyar peasants received newly parcelled lands in Transylvania.

The Magyar peasant masses shared Tisza's conservatism and nationalism. On the whole, the government well represented their immediate economic interest. They remained loyal soldiers, producers and citizens. Few mutineers and deserters were Magyars. The first wave of returning prisoners-of-war were mainly Slavs and Germans and only a few of them were imbued with revolutionary ideas.[76] Magyars were released in large numbers in mid-1918, on the eve of the collapse of the Austro-Hungarian Empire. By then the Russian Revolution had made its impact on both the returnees and the politicians in Hungary. The countryside, however, remained calm, at least until November, when Austria-Hungary was no more.

The clues for the failure of Austria-Hungary cannot be found in the wheatfields of the Hungarian Plain, The Magyar peasantry, which dominated agricultural production since the turn of the century, maintained the volume of their production at a relatively high level during World War I despite labor shortages in the countryside. Their faith in the Budapest government held firm because the government represented their economic interest. Magyars gained the most and bled the most. Loss and gain became brothers twain.

OWNERSHIP OF AGRICULTURAL PROPERTIES IN HUNGARY IN 1910

Occupational category	Number of properties	Owners as % of total population	Nationality of owners Magyars	non-Magyars
I. ESTATES				
100 holds + (1 hold = 1.42 acres)	71,425	.39%	52,542	18,883
II. PEASANT PROPERTIES				
50 holds to 100 holds	134,687	.7%	73,581	60,836
20 to 50 holds	822,912	4.5%	384.789	438,123
5 to 20 holds	3,511,085	19.2%	1,359.085	2,152,000
under 5 holds	2,437,190	13.4%	951,724	1,485,466
other	30,711	.2%	18,639	12,072
Total	6,936,585	38%	2,788,088	4,148,497
III. AGRICULTURAL WORKERS	4,356,316	23.9%	2,566,105	1,790,211

PRODUCTION AND CONSUMPTION OF STAPLE CROPS IN HUNGARY 1900-1918. Wheat, rye, potatoes.

Years	wheat	rye	potatoes	wheat	rye	potatoes	wheat	rye	potatoes
	production in millions of quintals			net export in millions of quintals			per capita consumption in kilogram		consumption in millions of quintals
1900/05 average	43.2	12.0	44.4	13.3	2.6	.5	117	38	30.1
1906/10 average	43.5	12.4	51.0	11.8	2.9	.3	123	37	37.7
1910/11 average	49.3	13.2	55.9	13.0	3.7	.8	142	36	47.7
1911/12 average	51.7	12.8	50.5	15.0	4.0	.6	142	32	38.4
1912/13 average	50.3	13.5	59.7	14.5	2.9	.9	139	41	51.2
1913/14 average	45.6	13.4	54.5	11.4	3.7	.9	129	35	51.6
1900/14 average	47.3	12.9	53.7	13.3	3.3	.7	132	36.5	42.8

PRODUCTION AND CONSUMPTION OF STAPLE CROPS IN HUNGARY 1900-1918. (Continued)

Years	wheat production in millions of quintals	rye production in millions of quintals	potatoes production in millions of quintals	wheat net export in millions of quintals	rye net export in millions of quintals	potatoes net export in millions of quintals	wheat per capita consumption in kilogram	rye per capita consumption in kilogram	potatoes consumption in millions of quintals
1914/15	32.1	11.5	58.5	3.9	.9	1.2	102	40	46.0
1915/16	42.9	12.1	61.6	3.3	.5	.8	158	46	43.8
1916/17	32.8	9.9	46.3	.6	±0	.2	123	37	25.6
1917/18	36.0	10.5	31.8	.9	.2	±0	138	40	28.6

NOTE: Data in first six columns were rounded to the nearest hundred thousands. Per capita consumption was rounded to whole numbers. Potato consumption was rounded to the nearest hundred thousands. SOURCE: A m. kir. kormany 1915-1918 evi mukodeserol esaz orszag kozallapotairol szolo jelentes es statisztikai evkonyv (Budapest: Atheneum, 1924), pp. 162-163.

PRODUCTION AND CONSUMPTION OF STAPLE CROPS IN HUNGARY 1900-1918. Corn, Oats, Barley.

Years	corn	oats	barley	corn	oats	barley	corn	oats	barley
	production in millions of quintals			net export in millions of quintals			per capita domestic consumption in kilograms		
1900/05 average	32.6	11.7	12.9	1.8	2.0	3.7	30.1	8.1	7.5
1906/10 average	41.6	12.6	14.6	3.0	2.0	3.9	37.7	8.9	8.9
1910/11	54.2	10.8	12.1	5.6	1.2	2.3	47.7	8.0	8.0
1911/12	41.0	13.8	16.6	1.7	2.1	3.1	38.6	10.1	11.8
1912/13	51.0	11.7	15.7	-1.2	1.1	3.0	51.2	8.7	10.8
1913/14	53.6	15.4	18.1	1.1	1.7	3.8	51.6	12.1	12.2
1900/14 average	45.7	12.7	15.0	2.0	1.7	3.3	43.0	10.0	10.0
1914/15	50.3	13.4	14.7	3.4	.3	1.4	46.0	11.5	11.4
1915/16	44.6	12.5	13.0	0	0	.4	43.8	10.9	11.0
1916/17	26.8	13.2	11.7	.4	0	0	25.6	10.7	10.1
1917/18	29.8	8.3	.3	0	0	0	28.6	6.8	6.7

Note: All data were rounded to the nearest hundred thousand. The averages for 1900/14 were calculated from the original tables by the author.

Source: Hans Loewenfeld-Russ, *Die Regelung der Volksernahrung im Krige* (Vienna and New Haven: Holder-Pichler-Tempsky A.-G. and Yale University Press), 1926, p. 61.

DISTRIBUTION OF LAND ACCORDING TO SIZE OF ESTATES

Size of property in holds	Year 1869	1895	1900	1910
0-5	58.85%	54.14%	56.3%	52%
5-50	39.92%	44.34%	41.7%	45.8%
50-100	1.23%	1.52%	1.2%	1.3%
100+	not included	not included	.8%	.8%

DISTRIBUTION OF LAND BETWEEN PEASANTS AND ESTATE OWNERS IN MILLIONS OF HOLDS

Size of property in holds	plowlands		gardens		pastures		vineyards	
	Year							
	1895	1913	1895	1913	1895	1913	1895	1913
under 100	13	14.7	.5	.6	3.2	3.2	.4	.5
over 100	7.9	7.6	.1	.1	1.8	1.4	.06	.06

AGRICULTURAL REAL ESTATE TRANSACTIONS

Middle and Large Estates

	units under 100 holds	*units over 100 holds*
May 1, 1915-April 30, 1916	8,931	421,438
May 1, 1916-April 30, 1917	10,428	502,414
May 1, 1917-April 30, 1918	13,116	682,475

MARKET VALUE OF GRAIN CROPS IN MILLIONS OF CROWNS

Hungary 1913-1916

Years	wheat	rye	barley	oats	corn	Total
1913/14	1,184	241	272	246	804	2,747
1914/15	1,282	357	382	322	1,157	3,500
1915/16	1,589	363	377	350	1,160	3,839

FOODSTUFF IMPORT FROM HUNGARY TO AUSTRIA BETWEEN 1909 AND 1917 IN 1000'S OF QUINTALS

	1909-1913	1914	1915	1916	1917
All grains	13,928.1	10,212.3	5198.6	463.7	276.8
wheat	4,087.1	2,774.0	1,390.1	180.3	79.8
rye	2,732.0	1,778.1	465.8	73.8	6.1
barley	2,046.8	1,671.4	566.2	65.8	9.2
maize	3,178.4	2,946.4	2,661.2	110.3	170.2
oat	1,843.0	1,021.1	90.3	18.0	2.1
flour	7,316.1	5,627.7	2,085.9	567.9	234.2
leguminous plants	147.1	289.9	237.7	70.8	6.3
vegetables	1,519.7	1,032.5	1,607.2	1,233.3	556.3
fruits	354.9	405.7	260.4	199.1	248.4
cattle	327.0	351.1	139.1	42.1	95.0
hogs	595.0	779.7	539.3	396.2	113.7
horses	12.0	13.2	10.2	17.7	44.0
poultry	147.8	132.1	88.0	94.0	97.5
wine	29.2	19.9	10.3	13.6	10.9
milk	704.5	656.0	465.5	315.7	117.99
eggs	162.1	179.4	151.0	169.0	44.5
butter	32.8	21.6	10.5	7.5	4.7
bacon, lards	192.7	200.1	153.7	59.4	61.5
cooking oil	27.2	22.0	5.9	4.5	.4
processed meat	152.9	172.0	120.3	86.6	79.0

SOURCE: Hans Loewenfeld Russ, *Die Regelung der Volksernahrung im Krige* (Vienna and New Haven: Holder-Pichler-Tempsky. A.G. and Yale University Press), 1926, p. 61.

NOTES

1. David Mitrany, *The Effects of War in Southeastern Europe* (New Haven 1936).
2. Surprisingly, the most recent seventh volume of the new ten-volume set *History of Hungary* by Peter Hanak and Ferenc Mucsi (eds.), *Magyarorszag tortenete 1890-1918,* II (Budapest, 1978), 414, Volume 7 of the ten volume *Magyarorszag tortenete* (ed.) Pal Zsigmond Pach (Budapest, 1976-), cited hereafter as MT VII 1 or MT VII 2, contains no economic analysis of the war period.
3. Detailed works on the last years of the Habsburg Empire by A. J. May, *The Passing of the Habsburg Monarchy,* I-II (Philadelphia, 1968); by A. B. Zeman, *The Break-up of the Habsburg Empire* (Oxford,1961),and by Leo Valiani, *The End of Austria-Hungary* (London, 1973) are totally void of data on Hungarian economic affairs. The older Gustav Gratz and Richard Schuller, *Der Wirtschaftliche Zusammenbruck Osterreich-Ungarns. Die Tragodie der Erschopfung* (Vienna and New Haven, 1930) volume has a misleading title, lacks basic economic data and concentrates on economic negotiations between Hungary and Austria.
4. Previously little used basic data was obtained from the Hungarian National Archives, the files of the Hungarian Royal Ministry of Agriculture, OL 1919/472, also identified and cited hereafter as K 178/1919/472 and the readily available but little used yearbook, *A m. kir. kormany 1915-1918 evi mukodeserol es az orszag kozallapotairol szolo jelentes es statisztikai evkonyv* (Report about the Activities of the Hungarian Royal Government and of the General Conditions of theCountry in 1915-1918, A Statistical Yearbook.) (Budapest, 1924), cited hereafter as YEARBOOK.
5. Jozsef Galantai, *Magyarorszag az elso vilaghaboruban* (Budapest, 1974), 167.
6. Anton Wagner, *Der erste Weltkrieg* (Vienna, 1968) quoted

in Gunther E. Rothenberg, *The Army of Francis Joseph* (West Lafayette, Indiana, 1976), 218.

7. Galantai, *op. cit.,* 213.
8. MT VII/2, 414. See Table at end of this essay.
9. *Ibid.,* MT VII/1, 428-431.
10. Ibid., 486; Zoltan Sandor Papp, *A beregdaroci emberek elete a szazadfordulon* (The Life of the People of Beregdaroc at the Turn of the Century) (Budapest, 1975), 68-70; Peter Hanak, *Magyarorszag a Monarchiaban. Tanulmanyok* (Hungary in the Monarchy. Studies) (Budapest, 1975), 379.
11. MT VII/1, 486.
12. *Ibid.,* 486-487; Papp, *op. cit.,* 63-64; Hanak, *op. cit.,* 379.
13. MT VII/1, 489-490.
14. *Ibid.,* 501-502.
15. *Ibid.,* 406-415.
16. Szabo, *op. cit.,* I:130.
17. *Ibid.,* 44-45.
18. *Ibid.,* 19.
19. L. Katus, *Economic Growth in Hungary During the Age of Dualism (1867-1913). A Quantitative Analysis* (Budapest, 1970), *Studia Historica Academiae Scientarium Hungaricae,* "Separatum," 115; MT VII/1, 399.
20. Szabo, *op. cit.,* 21.
21. Voros, *A magyar mezogazdasag, op. cit.,* 163.
22. Szabo, *op. cit.* 130.
23. *Ibid,* II:895.
24. *Ibid.,* I:112.
25. *Ibid.,* 13.
26. *Ibid.*
27. *Ibid.,* 481.
28. *Ibid.,* II: 664.
29. Voros, *A magyar mezogazdasag, op. cit.,* 233.
30. *Ibid.,* 234.
31. *Ibid.,* 241.
32. *Ibid.,* 240.
33. *Ibid.,* 199.

34. Szabo, *op. cit.*, 409-410.
35. Katus, *op. cit.*, 52.
36. *Ibid.*, 68.
37. Galantai, *op. cit.*, 167.
38. *Ibid.*, 214.
39. J. Redlich, *Austrian War Government* (New Haven, CN, 1929), 110; C. A. Macartney, *The Social Revolution in Austria* (Cambridge, 1926), 64.
40. C. A. Macartney, *The Habsburg Empire 1790-1918* (London, 1968), 818.
41. Galantai, *op. cit.*, 167.
42. K 178/1919/472.
43. Pasvolsky, *op. cit.*, 29. See also, Lajos Menczel, *A Pesti Hazai Elso Takarekpenztar Egyesulet szazeves tortenete,* II (100 Years' History of First Hungarian Savings Association) (Budapest, 1940), 46.
44. *Ibid.*, 48.
45. YEARBOOK.
46. Gyorgy Spira and Karoly Voros, *Budapest tortenete a marciusi forradalomtol az oszirozsas forradalomig* (History of Budapest from the March Revolution to the Revolution of Mums) (Budapest, 1978), Vol. IV of *Budapest tortenete* (History of Budapest) (ed.), Laszlo Gerevich, 728-730.
47. YEARBOOK, 92.
48. *Ibid.*, 164-165.
49. May. I, *op. cit.*, 400.
50. *Mese a zold fuvon* (Fairy Tales About Green Grass) (Budapest, n.d.), 249-251.
51. Spira and Voros, *op. cit.*, 740.
52. May, II, *op. cit.*, 701.
53. Gratz-Schuller, *op. cit.*, 184.
54. Wilhelm Winkler, *Die Einkommensverschiebungen in Osterreich Wahrend des Weltkrieges* (Vienna and New Haven, 1930), 92.
55. Leo Grebler and Wilhelm Winkler, *The Cost of the World War to Germany and to Austria-Hungary* (New Haven, 1940), 151.

56. See Tables at the end of this essay.
57. Hans Loewenfeld-Russ, *Die Regelung der Volksernahrung im Kriege* (Vienna and New Haven, 1926), 64; Macartney, *op. cit.*, 818.
58. Gusztav Gratz, *A dualizmus kora. Magyarorszag tortenete 1867-1918* (The Age of Dualism. History of Hungary 1867-1918) (Budapest, 1934), 364; Gusztav Gratz, *The Economic Policy of Austria-Hungary during the War in Its External Relations* (New Haven, 1928), 52.
59. See Tables at the end of this essay.
60. YEARBOOK, 165.
61. See Tables at the end of this essay.
62. K 178/1919/472, 103.
63. *New York Times*, February 2, 1917.
64. Menczel, *op. cit.*, 340-341.
65. YEARBOOK, 34.
66. *Ibid.*, 35-36.
67. K 178/1919472, 110, 150-151.
68. See Tables at end of this essay.
69. YEARBOOK, 65.
70. See Tables at the end of this essay.
71. YEARBOOK, 56.
72. *Ibid.*, 110.
73. *Ibid.*, 103.
74. Galantai, *op. cit.*, 391.
75. Gratz, *The Economic Policy . . . .*, *op. cit.*, 52.
76. *New York Times*, February 2, 1917.

PART V

THE INTERWAR YEARS AND AGRARIAN CHANGE

Joseph Held

I.
IN HISTORICAL PERSPECTIVE

1. Introduction

As we have seen above, the transformation of agriculture in Hungary has been a continuous process at least since the mid-19th century. Although the speed of the transformation (compared to that of the period between 1867-1914) had considerably slowed down during the interwar decades, it never completely stopped and traditional ways of production and life were continuously altered in various regions of the country. This change was part of the gradual transformation of society as a whole; in the countryside, this was refleted in the reorganization of production methods through a gradual mechanization of agriculture, and new peasant cognitions of personal and social relationships. Rural modernization, therefore, reflected throughout this period changes that we usually associate with urbanization and industrialization;

however, other changes were also occurring that were peculiar to the rural sphere.

The consequences of this transformation were often contradictory and uneven. On the whole, there were unquestionable improvements in average crop yields and in the volume of production in general. These provided sufficient food for the urban population and, among other socio-political factors, enabled society to develop without a major revolution. But average crop yields continued to fluctuate widely and they improved less on small peasant holdings than on the large estates. Lopsided agrarian change, coupled with considerable demographic change, and the slow process of urban-industrial progress meant unemployment for large numbers of agricultural workers. Consequently, just as industrialization in the West had ruined the independent craftsman and turned him into an industrial proletarian, in Hungary, the gradual mechanization of agriculture tended to impoverish the small, independent peasant proprietor who was unable to compete with the large producers.

As we have seen in previous chapters, in the 1880's rural unemployment was already an acute problem in Hungary. Although the First World War temporarily "solved" this problem, with the return of peace large-scale unemployment reappeared among the Hungarian rural population. Conditions worsened during the depression in the early 1930's until literally millions of landless peasants were able to find work only during part of the agricultural season, and their incomes were no longer adequate to maintain a decent standard of living.

But agrarian change was not a uniform process in Hungary during the interwar years. In regions close to urban centers, particularly near Budapest (but also around other cities), agricultural production gradually became intensive and well-developed. In these regions the peasants produced vegetable and fruit crops in well-tended large gardens, were busy in developing advanced animal husbandry, and participated in the carrying trades. On the other hand, large villages located far from urban areas, continued to exist in many areas of the country whose population lived under truly primitive conditions. In these villages the peasants continued to work the land as their ancestors had done a century or more before. Their communications with the "outside world" were severely restricted. They regarded "outsiders," namely, city-folks (but also often peasants from other villages), as "strange" and continued to live by age-old social values and standards. In addition, about 400,000 servant families (most of them living on large estates) existed under conditions that could only be described as semi-feudal. Finally, over one million peasants lived in detached households, the *tanyas* of central Hungary, where they provided a lively link between rural and urban environments. Many of the latter were already in transition between traditional peasant ways and a new type of rural-urban existence.

The First World War had given an impetus to agrarian modernization in Hungary indeed, but its after effects were not uniform. In fact, the aftermath of the war witnessed the slowing down of the process of modernization and the postponement of a second agricultural revolution, centering on the mechanization of production methods, well beyond 1945. However, after the war, the increasing influence of mass communications, the newspapers, and especially the two national radio networks, made the people of many rural districts aware of being a part of a larger community, the nation. But the changes did not result in an immediate improvement in the standard of life of the average peasant in Hungary. They may have contributed to increased expectations, but no more, not yet. Basically suspicious of "outsiders," most peasants continued to regard their non-peasant co-nationals with reserve. Peasants generally remained withdrawn, watchfully observing the comings and goings in the "outside world," not expecting any great improvements to come from this world into their lives.

The area of Hungary after the peace treaties of 1919 consisted of about 93,000 square kilometers (about the size of the state of Illinois), with 7.6 million inhabitants. Of this area 18,464,230 acres were agricultural lands. Ploughlands included 13,623,066 acres or 60.2% of the total. The rest were covered by forests, vineyards, orchards, meadowlands, swamps and grazing lands. Five agricultural regions existed in the new state with distinct, individual characteristics. The largest of these was the Great Plain, consisting mostly of lowlands. Transdanubia was mostly a hilly region, while the area of the Left Bank of the Tisza River was third in size and first in poverty. The northern Highlands and the Small Plain were smaller in size than either of the first three regions; the first of these were fertile lowlands, while the second was mountainous country.

Dwarfholders possessing less than 1.4 acres of land (one *hold*) each, numbered 630,000 families. Altogether they owned 5.4% of agricultural land. Smallholders owning 7.5-14.2 acres each possessed 8.6%. Medium holders controlling 20-50 acres each, owned 14.8%, and rich peasants owning 50-150 acres each possessed 22.9% of the land. Finally, large estates over 750 acres each possessed more than one-third of the lands. (36.6%), and were controlled by a relatively small number of people.[1]

Despite slow industrialization, centering mainly in the cities (especially in Budapest), Hungary remained basically an agrarian country throughout the interwar years.[2] Only towards the end of the period (after 1941) did the percentage of the agricultual population dip below the 50% mark. The relatively fast pace of modernization that characterized the last decades of the 19th century had slowed down. Many essential projects were postponed or were not undertaken. As an observer remarked in 1934,

> Just as one hundred years before, the following tasks are still awaiting completion; the renewal of alkaline lands, the improvement of sandy soils, the regulation of the flood plains, the creation of a local road system on the Great Plain, the improvement of navigation on the Tisza River, the problems of the *tanya*-system, a rural house-

> building program, the need of villages for fresh water supplies, rural medical care, etc . . .[3]

Although the author of this statement spoke mainly of life in the Great Plain, his observations were valid, more or less, for most other agricultural regions of Hungary as well. One could have gone further by adding that there was a burning need for land reform, a solution for the endemic rural unemployment would have had to be found, low crop yields on the small farms would have had to be improved. Machinery and chemical fertilizers were badly needed in almost all agricultural regions. Above all, the rigid, hierarchical order of peasant village communities had to change if the modernization of agriculture were to advance. But there was both confusion and a lack of vision about the role of agriculture and the place of the peasantry in a slowly developing Hungarian society.

2. Legacies of the Past.

There were external and internal reasons for these conditions. First of all, the First World War had transformed the international economic order by completely rearranging political and economic boundaries in Eastern Europe. Nearly 7,000 kilometers of new state borders were created with 7 new currencies, each border representing a new customs barrier to trade as well as to international economic cooperation. Secondly, a formerly Europe-centered economic system became truly world-wide in scope, bringing producers who were more efficient than those of Eastern Europe into the competition for agricultural markets. Thirdly, the simultaneous emergence of the Soviet Union and its isolation from the rest of Europe further disrupted the international economic system. Finally, Hungary, having been saddled with severe handicaps by the peace treaties, entered the new era as a defeated, partitioned nation.

After the war, the Hungarian economic system was in shambles. The peace agreements were viciously anti-Hungarian in character, placing Hungary in the rank of international outlaws, isolating the Hungarian state from normal diplomatic life. Their consequences included the partitioning of two-thirds of the former territories of historical Hungary among the Successor States and Rumania, leaving rump-Hungary with one-third of its former lands and 41% of its former population. Hungary legally remained a kingdom; but it had no king, only a regent, Nicholas Horthy (a former rear-admiral of the Austro-Hungarian navy), who ruled a nation without direct access to the seas. The population that numbered about 21 million in 1914, was now reduced to only 7.6 million. About 3 million ethnic Hungarians were "awarded" to the surrounding states without the slightest real guarantee of their minority rights. Therefore, throughout the interwar years no politician or public figure in the new Hungary could survive in public life without adapting his views to the strong, jingoistic nationalism that these conditions engendered among large segments of the population, especially the army, the urban bourgeoisie, the remnants of the gentry and the new state bureaucracy. Another side effect of these conditions was the preoccupation of Hungarian governments with issues of "revisionism," that is, the revision of Hungary's borders. This preoccupation (among other reasons) resulted in the repeated postponement of needed social reforms.

Equally crippling were the provisions of the peace agreements dealing with debt repayments and reparations. Hungary's pre-war national debt was 5.4 billion gold crowns (1 English pound sterling was worth 21.35 gold crowns). Of this amount rump-Hungary was forced to repay 48%. This was way out of line with the ratio of territory and population left for the Hungarian state. In addition, the Reparations Commission ordered all Hungarian national monopolies (on salt, tobacco, the railroads, etc.) to freeze their income for the purposes of reparations; however, just as in the case of defeated Germany, the exact amount to be paid was not set until years after 1919. The looting of equipment from Hungarian factories, railroad stock and livestock by the Rumanian occupying forces in 1919-

1920, severe as the damage caused was, was not considered a sufficiently heavy loss to mitigate Hungary's reparations obligations.[4]

The 7.6 million Hungarians left in the new state desperately needed a new economic system to cope with the changed circumstances. But, since the political order that emerged after 1920 was basically a copy of the old Habsburg system in miniature (with minor variations), and since the ruling elites remained basically the same as before 1914, the economic system that they were to create could not be expected to be a novel one.

The new Hungarian state lost a great deal of its industrial raw-material base to the surrounding countries. What Hungary needed most of all was to sell substantial amounts of agricultural goods in order to support its increased needs for imports in industrial raw materials. There was some hope that this could be done, since Czechoslovakia and Austria continued to buy Hungarian foodstuff in large quantities immediately after the war. But growing bitter political antagonism between Hungary and its neighbors remained a constant factor of interwar life and, therefore, economic cooperation was not a realistic expectation. Furthermore, since most of the East European states had basically agricultural economies after 1918, they were, naturally, more interested in helping their own peasants than those of Hungary. Thus, they gradually raised tariff barriers against Hungarian food exports. Nor could the Hungarians regain their economic balance by increasing their agrarian exports to Western Europe. After World War I, most West European nations were also becoming protective towards their own agriculture, and the Hungarians could not really compete with the efficient producers of North and South America for the shrinking markets.

This situation remained virtually unchanged throughout the 1920's. Thus, at that time, Hungary provided a primary example of a state of retarded economic development. This was the more damaging in that Hungary was actually on the threshold of its industrial revolution when World War I interfered with the process. The war actually interrupted the transformation of the economy into one primarily based on industrial production. All this happened at a time when qualitative changes in industrialization were about to bring changes in social developments, possibly transforming Hungary into a modern European society. Similarly, the war had postponed the second agricultural revolution that could have provided the bases for a healthier development of the nation. Yet, changes in society, including the agricultural sector, had never completely stopped; the period of the interwar years was, therefore, a time of slow transition.

There also developed a time-lag between the evolution of various segments of the Hungarian economy and society during these decades. On the one hand, industrial production in the cities, especially in Budapest, slowly but continuously expanded; although the growth rate was slow (about 1.5% yearly), in two decades it amounted to about 30%. On the other hand, agriculture remained behind in raising average yields in general. The consequences were exaggerated by the tariff policies of the Hungarian governments. These policies contributed to the widening of the so-called agrarian scissor; namely, the prices of industrial and agrarian goods were out of kilter. Between 1924-1939, agricultural prices remained unfavorable in relation to industrial prices. In 1930, for instance, a peasant had to produce 35% more foodstuff if he wanted to buy the same amount of goods as in 1913. Although this ratio fluctuated during the interwar years, it was never favorable for the peasants and the difference was 37% by 1939[5] Only during the Second World War was there a turnaround in the agrarian scissor, mostly due to the increasing demand for food by the Axis armies. What this in fact meant was that industrial progress was financed in Hungary at least partly by the withdrawal of funds from the agrarian sector.

There was also a widening gap between rural and urban living conditions. While life for the majority of urban dwellers was becoming more and more similar to that in the cities of

Western Europe, the conditions in the rural areas remained closer to those of the previous century. This was reinforced by the absence of a vigorous internal market for agrarian goods.[6]

A generally low standard of living, aggravated by the consequences of the war, made the expansion of the internal market doubly difficult. Nor were the unemployed masses of peasants being integrated into the other sectors of the economy.[7]

One of the most troublesome legacies of the past was the existing land tenure system. This system continued to be in the grip of the owners of mammoth estates. Almost 1.2 million peasant families owned altogether 2,283,734 acres of land, while 2,432 individuals and corporations owned 8,053,981 acres. There were many extremely rich aristocrats among the latter whose estates were entailed, that is, could not be alienated.[8] Many large estates rented huge parcels of land to corporations or individual businessmen, the latter of whom were mostly industrialists. More than 47% of the ploughlands of the large estates or over 1,420,000 acres were rented out.[9] Foreigners continued to own large tracts of land in Hungary, their total land possessions coming to nearly 300,000 acres during the interwar decades. Among them one could find members of the former Bavarian royal family, the Princess Klementine Metternich, and the Hohenlohe family.[10]

The large and medium-sized estates employed about 400,000 servant families. Most owners of these estates (including various Christian churches) had close affiliations with banks and industrial firms as well as the government.[11] Their interests were, therefore, well protected.

Most large estates had become capitalist firms during the later part of the 19th century in the sense that they produced primarily for the market. But they were, for the most part, using pre-modern techniques of production. They were as yet unwilling or unable to introduce modern technology on a large scale. Most production on these large estates continued to be performed by manual labor, perhaps with the exception of ploughing and threshing. A scheme for the modernization of

Hungarian agriculture had to include the large estates; thus, their continuing backwardness proved to be an important drag on the entire economic system. However, this was mainly a political, not an economic problem. The political power of the large estate-owners insured them not only against the partitioning of their estates through a possible land reform, but also enabled them to survive economically when they were no longer competitive on the world markets. We may say, therefore, that by supporting the large estates, the Hungarian interwar governments actually voted against the modernization of society.

Another burdensome legacy was the traditional nature of peasant society itself. This was expressed in many ways. Not only were the peasants often unwilling to change age-old patterns of production (because they were not convinced that the proposed changes would benefit them),[12] but their entire system of social relations was dead set against change as such. Undue emphasis on grain production resulted in unreliable yields, yet the peasants in many areas felt compelled to follow them throughout this period.[13] For instance, despite the world economic crisis in the early 1930's, depressing grain prices to unprofitable levels, the size of ploughlands planted with grains hardly changed in Hungary. This was only partly due to a low level of agrarian technology known to the peasants; the major factor was the traditionalism of peasant society itself. The promising changes in peasant thinking, so well illustrated in Part II of this study, came to nothing and fizzled out during the interwar years. As an observer commented in the 1930's,

> the peasant first of all follows the habits of his ancestors, then trusts in his luck. He cannot produce profitably nor can he sell his produce economically on the market . . . Organization is what is missing from peasant agriculture . . . If one tried to organize a factory on the pattern of the farms, he would need an army of workers . . .[14]

We shall have more to say about this issue in the following chapters of this work.

A third fundamental Hungarian problem was that the leaders of the country were largely conservative politicians. Horthy and his friends, including Stephen Bethlen, came from ancient aristocratic families. For them, the Habsburg system of the *Ausgleich* represented ideal political conditions for Hungary. The policies of their government, based on the army, the state bureaucracy and the rural gentry, was anti-reformist at home, and radical in its diplomacy abroad. But few of these politicians (with the exception of Bethlen) were able to rise above their narrow class interests. They ruled Hungary during the interwar years through a mixture of the hereditary principle and a combination of various cliques. Nowhere was their ineptness more evident than in economic policy-making, especially as it related to agriculture.

At least two conflicting tendencies dominated the agrarian policies of the Hungarian governments during the interwar years. One was the realization that the nation's future depended upon the updating of the economic system, the foundation of which appeared to be industrialization. Industry was, therefore, protected by high tariffs, averaging from the mid-1920's on, about 30%[15] In line with this policy the peasants were regarded as a social stratum whose primary function was the economic support of the rest of society. The small agricultural producers were provided with no protection against competition. While the resources of the peasants were freely exploited through the agrarian scissor and direct, regressive taxation, the large estates were provided with government subsidies. On the other hand, many government policies were influenced by a paternalistic and romantic view which held that the peasantry was the "root on which the tree of the nation grew." Thus, while the government pursued a policy of slow industrialization using a system of tariffs injurious to the free development of agriculture, it patronized the peasantry by implementing a spotty welfare policy as circumstances dictated. In essence, the Hungarian government tried to preserve as much of the pre-World War I semi-feudal heritage (which served the supremacy of the aristocracy in politics) as much as possible.[16] This was at the root of the contradictions which prevented a truly scientific, systematic approach to agricultural problems in interwar Hungary. The political authorities were the modern day version of Tancred; they were hesitant, but not compassionate, romantic but not merciful in their approach to the problems of the peasant population of the country.

3. The "New" Foundations.

Conditions remained generally favorable for agriculture in Hungary after the partitioning of the state.[17] In 1919, about 51.3% of the population lived directly from agriculture, and this number remained relatively stable during the interwar years. The climate, continental in character, was influenced in the Central Danubian Basin by Atlantic and Mediterranean currents of air, while cold air masses often entered from Russia. But seldom did either of these currents claim predominance over the climate of Hungary for more than a few days at a time. Humidity was generally low with little rainfall in summer; daily temperatures showed wide variations not only between seasons but between days and nights. The sun shone, on an average, between 1,700-2,100 hours a year, providing generally favorable conditions for growing non-tropical crops. Rainfall varied between 20-30 inches a year, between 12-20 inches of this falling during the growing season. However, rainfall was unevenly distributed; the Great Plain received generally much less than western Hungary. Thus, in the summer months the Plain often suffered extended periods of drought. This alone counted heavily for the different agricultural conditions existing in the various areas of interwar Hungary.

The soil was of varied quality. In the Great Plain, the major grain growing region of the country, the soil included large areas of fertile black loess, but also areas of alkaline lands (1.42 million acres!) and large sandy areas. During the interwar years, there were about 350,000 acres of flood plains and swampy areas in this region, generally useless for cultivation before draining.[18]

The Tisza River valley provided excellent to good soil for grain crops, while in eastern Hungary the lands were generally poorer in quality. Here and on the Great Plain heating fuels were scarce; as we have seen above, the peasants traditionally used dried manure and straw for cooking and heating. Since chemical fertilizers continued to be in short supply, this contributed to the gradual exhaustion of the soil. Eastern Hungary also contained areas of swamps and large sections of alkaline lands that were suitable only for grazing.[19]

In the northwest and the Little Plain, the quality of the soil was excellent, while in the large region of Transdanubia it was good to poor. In the entire area of Hungary that was suitable for agriculture, only 6.5% of the lands consisted of hard soil. More than 75% of the lands were flat. Of the 5 million acres of hilly regions only 200,000 acres had an angle over 20 degrees.

The diversity of crops has always been characteristic of Hungarian agriculture. In the interwar decades, 36 different crops continued to be raised. But this was a haphazard affair; conscious efforts at scientific diversification of crops, taking into consideration the quality of the soil, moisture conditions, the availability of irrigation, transportation and storage facilities, were practiced only on a few farms and in small areas. In 1938, for example, 60.4% of all ploughlands were planted with grains. Only 1.3% were used for garden crops, 6.9% were meadowlands, and 10.4% were used for grazing.[20] Vineyards were cultivated on 2.2% of the lands, and 31 million fruit trees were grown.

Animal husbandry played an important role in Hungarian agriculture. To the west of the line of the Danube River, animal husbandry was better developed than to the east. In 1938, 38% of all agricultural income was derived from animal husbandry, the bulk of this coming from western Hungary. Cattle, swine, horses and sheep were the major types of animal raised. The leading swine raising area was Transdanubia where a heavy emphasis on growing corn crops contributed to this. Sheep were raised in areas where the grazing grounds were inadequate for cattle or horses. Horses remained the major source of draft power in all regions of Hungary during the interwar years, accounting for 94% of all draft power in the country. A great many horses were raised in Transdanubia and the Great Plain, and the areas around urban centers also contributed to horse breeding. Cattle and oxen-drawn transportation continued to prevail in the hilly regions in north- and southwestern Hungary, in the Nyirseg in the east, the Upper Tisza regions and the lower Great Plain districts.[21] Fowl of all sorts added considerably to the income derived from animal husbandry, but not nearly as much as the scientific management of this type of animal could have produced.

However, advances in animal husbandry were very slow in coming. For instance, in 1939, the number of cattle declined by 10.7% as compared to 1924, and that of horses by a smaller margin, by 1.3%. This was balanced by the increase of the number of hogs by a whopping 40.8% during the same period. Compared to the development of animal husbandry in other East European states, however, Hungary's progress was still slow.[22]

The mechanization of agriculture progressed very slowly in the interwar decades. This was especially so in the case of small farms. But the large estates were similarly slow in using machinery. Mechanical ploughs, threshers, and planters were introduced only gradually. The number of tractors reached 6,800 in 1929, and there were only 7,000 of these machines in use a decade later. Few trucks could be found even on the large estates, and practically no harvester combines were available.

Average crop yields were low in comparison with average yields in more agriculturally advanced societies.[23] Chemical fertilizers were sparingly used. According to a survey conducted in 1927, natural fertilizers were employed on 27% of the ploughlands, and chemical varieties only on 1.5%. Although the large estates were more advanced in this than were small peasant holdings, their fertilization program was generally inadequate.[24] The basic problem was that the majority of peasant households did not have enough animals for the production of natural fertilizers, and they were too poor to buy chemical fertilizers on the market.

4. Inflation and Consolidation

The history of the Hungarian economy during the interwar years may conveniently be divided into three distinct periods. The first of these extended from the end of World War I to 1929. The second lasted during the depression years, while the third encompassed the years between 1935-1945.[25] The most important economic events of the first period included a runaway inflation, an attempted land reform and, finally, the consolidation of the Hungarian economy after 1924. Of these three events, inflation and consolidation determined the direction that the Hungarian state was taking during the entire period of the interwar years, while the land reform was an episode that we'll discuss in a separate chapter.

During the last two years of World War I, between 60-70% of the Hungarian national income was consumed by the military machine. There was no way for the Hungarians to absorb expenses of such magnitude even by increased taxation. Therefore, the government resorted to the large-scale printing of paper money. The result was the beginning of an inflationary spiral that seemed uncontrollable.

By the end of the war the paper crown, formerly one of the strong currencies of Europe, was worth only 45% of its pre-war value. The process continued after the war; as an economic historian observed,

> During the summer of 1921, 17.3 billion (paper) crowns were in circulation; in three years, this amount was tripled. In the summer of 1923, 400 billion (paper) crowns were in circulation, and in the spring of 1924, 2,500 billion. The value of the crown plummeted accordingly; until August, 1919, the paper crown was valued at 9.9 for the gold crown; in June, 1921, it was worth 50.7, and by 1924, one gold crown equalled 18,400 paper crowns.[26]

Inflation continued to accelerate after 1920 so that by 1924, prices were totally out of control. In that year agrarian prices were 22,000 times higher than in 1913, while the production of agriculture declined by 25%. Most internal trade was, by then, conducted through barter and Hungary's export markets simply disappeared.

Inflation was closely related to the problem of Hungary's reparations-obligations. The post-war scarcity of goods provided only part of the fuel for the inflationary spiral; a good share of responsibility belonged to the new Hungarian government. This government felt that it had no choice; since the Reparations Commission did not set the exact amount to be paid by Hungary to the victors, inflation was believed to be in the national interest in that it would mitigate the demands of the Allied and Associated Powers.

The Hungarian government did not act solely on its own initiative. It followed the advice it received from a Sir William Good in 1922. Early in that year Sir Good accepted a commission from the Hungarians to act as an intermediary between them and the British government in matters concerning reparations.[27] He suggested that the further weakening of the Hungarian currency would help in lowering the reparations bill, and it would even create conditions in which the Allies would consider offering Hungary financial help. The Hungarians believed that only through foreign investments and loans could they stabilize Hungary's economic system. But, since the income of state monopolies was frozen by the Reparations Commission, and since this income would be needed to serve as collateral for foreign loans, only by settling the issue of reparations could financial stabilization really begin.

Inflation was by no means an unmitigated disaster for every segment of the economy. While ruining the middle class and the industrial workers on fixed salaries, it was also a means of recovery for industries and large agrarian producers. During the inflation the government provided huge loans to the latter which were repaid in the depreciated currency.[28] In the case of the large estates, this was accomplished by a law of 1923:XXIII, establishing state-funded loan-cooperatives for the financial support of estates larger than 142 acres in size. Their offices were dispersed in six regions. The loans given through these offices alone came to 74,336 million paper crowns. Other loans for the large estates were financed through various governmental agencies. Most large estates were able to pay off 1.3 billion gold crowns worth of pre-war debts through these manipulations.[29]

By 1924, the maneuvers of the Hungarian government to tie reparations to inflation began to bear results. The restoration of stability to the Hungarian financial system was considered important enough by the Allies to begin negotiations with Hungary. The League of Nations eventually stepped in and guaranteed a loan to cover government deficits for a 2½ year-period. Originally, the Hungarians had asked for 40-50 million gold crowns in immediate help and 500 million gold crowns in long-term loans. In July, 1924, Hungary received 307 million gold crowns' worth of loans, guaranteed by the League. Revenues from customs on tobacco, salt and sugar provided the collaterals for these loans, and the Reparations Commission finally agreed upon the amount of reparations and the time period during which they should be paid.[30] Hungary accepted a representative of the League as a supervisor of stabilization. The funds thus received enabled the Hungarian government to cover its deficits, stabilize the currency and carry out its plans for the stabilization of the economy as a whole. A new paper money, the *pengo* was introduced by Public Law 1925:XXXV on November 25, 1925, stipulating that it was to become sole legal tender in the state on January 1, 1927.[31] A new national bank had already been established in 1924 with the right to issue money.

Hungary now made a major effort to recapture its former position on the export markets of Europe. But, although prices were now favorable for Hungary's major export, agrarian goods especially grains, the Hungarians did not succeed in expanding their markets in the 1920's. In fact, favorable export prices had an indirectly deliterious effect on most large agrarian producers in Hungary. Since their economic survival, thanks to good prices and government subsidies, seemed secure, most of them postponed the modernization of their production methods. This was a missed opportunity that was not to return until the very end of the interwar decades, and then only under the artificial stimulus of World War II.

A sign that not all was going well was that the indebtedness of agriculture began to increase right after stabilization. By 1926, the aggregate agricultural debt was again over the 120 million gold crown level and it increased further by 30 million gold crowns the following year.[32] Although this was a relatively small amount in comparison with pre-World War I debts in the agricultural sector, the problem was that the new debt increasingly fell on the shoulders of smallholders. But during 1925, the volume of Hungarian agricultural production reached the level of 1913, and the following year it exceeded that level by 3%.

Hungary was one of the agrarian countries of Eastern Europe whose population density was relatively high in comparison with the capacity of its industry to absorb the surplus labor from the countryside. In 1929, population density was 86 people per square kilometers; by 1938, it grew to 93. Demographic increases were sufficient by themselves to neutralize the benefits of increased agrarian production. The large estates, one of the key elements in the agrarian structure, paid very low wages to the huge force of rural labor reserves. Slow industrial progress and rural unemployment, thus, created a vicious circle in which the internal market for agrarian goods remained a severely restricted one. Yet, between 1924 and 1929, a gradual improvement in agricultural conditions did take place even if a large segment of the rural population could not benefit from it. The large estates and even some well-to-do peasants began the gradual improvement of their livestock and plant strains and added a few machines to their inventories. By 1929, there were some 549 mechanical planters and over 24,000 (!) threshers in operation in the countryside. But the small individual proprietors and the landless agricultural workers (the overwhelming majority of the rural population), were in economic difficulties. Their indebtedness greatly increased in this period. In 1928, over 58% and in 1930, more than 65% of all agrarian indebtedness was carried by peasant farms less than 70 acres in size. What was even more troubling was that a great many of the loans that they received simply served to augment their yearly income.[33]

Agricultural daily laborers continued to suffer from unemployment and low wages. Nevertheless, living standards in the rural sphere remained relatively stable. The prices of some industrial goods needed by the peasants even declined. For instance, clothing prices were 7.8% lower in the period and the prices of other essential goods were lower by an average of 2.3% in 1925 than they were in 1920.[34] It was true that in some regions as, for instance, eastern Hungary, improvements were slower in coming than elsewhere. (The special reasons for this will be discussed later in this essay.) On the whole, however, Hungary's agriculture successfully recovered from the effects of the war by 1929.

The general improvements in the life of the population were reflected in the actual increase of average life expectancy. In 1914, the expected life span in Hungary was 40 years. By 1930, it rose to 50 years and in 1941, it reached 57 years.[35] Although the breakdown of average life expectancy by social strata is not available for this period, it is safe to assume that, on the whole, the peasantry also benefited from this improvement. There remained rural areas indeed where mortality rates remained high and life expectancy was shorter. More will be said about the circumstances of life in these areas below.

The hard-won stability came to an abrupt end in 1929 with the depression. The average number of work days available for agricultural laborers (those who were lucky enough to find work) dropped from 200 days to 150 or even 120 days a year. Many of the smallholders were unable to pay their bills and went bankrupt. Living standards in the countryside plummeted, especially since prices for agricultural goods declined disastrously. The situation was to change only after 1934.

5. Land Reform.

An interlude in the inflation-consolidation process was provided by the land reform in 1920. The pattern of land distribution was set by the emancipation of the serfs in 1848 as we have seen in the previous sections of this work. But the original pattern had changed; by 1919, 38% of the peasantry possessed less than 1.4 acres each, sharing altogether 330,400 acres among 630,000 families. This was an obviously unjust as well as unjustifiable situation.

The democratic revolution of 1918 started a series of attempts at reform. The government of Mihaly Karolyi introduced Public Law XVII:1919 in February, 1919. The law stipulated the expropriation of large estates over 700 acres in size, and the redistribution of their land among the peasantry.[36] But this law was not carried out. As Bela K. Kiraly described the process in the previous section above, the Karolyi government fell within less than a month, and the Communist government of Bela Kun suspended its execution. With the overthrow of the Communists in August, 1919, and the restoration of the conservative political system, all possibilities of land reform seemed remote. The large landowners who dominated the government were understandably reluctant to commit themselves to a "dangerous course" which might end up by undermining their political influence as well as economic power.

By 1920, however, there was a feeling of urgency about the reform. Istvan Nagyatadi Szabo pressed his colleagues for the law's enactment. Many of the neighboring East European states were introducing measures giving their peasants the land. Above all, the passive resistance of the peasants to the Hungarian Communist regime created a grudging admiration in the new rulers which eventually found expression in the land reform law of 1920. But the law was hastily prepared; it did not achieve its stated purpose of creating a better pattern of land ownership in Hungary and, above all, it hardly touched the lands of the large estates. In the final count what was really surprising was that there was an attempted land reform at all by a regime that was so closely identified with the large estate owners.

Through Public Law 1920:XXXVI, enacted on December 7, 1920, the following distribution of land took place;

> 83,417 acres were given for building lots to 259,733 persons; 979,067 acres were distributed in the form of small farms among 411,514 persons, each receiving on an average 2.38 acres. Public institutions, including schools, hospitals, and others, received 267,050 acres, and individual agricultural officials (mostly overseers on large estates) acquired altogether 40,000 acres. Further 217,429 acres were distributed among peasant families in the form of low-rent individual farmlands.[37]

As the result of this reform, the share of small farms less than 142 acres in size was in the various regions of Hungary as follows:

> in Transdanubia, their ratio rose from 43.0% to 49% of all landholds; in the northern Highlands, it rose from 39.3% to 44.4%; in the Great Plain from 46.9% to 53.1% of all agricultural lands. In Hungary as a whole, the ratio increased from 44.1% to 50.2%.[39]

Of all the lands held by individual peasant proprietors, 73.9% consisted of ploughlands.

The distribution of landholds after 1920 remained relatively stable throughout the interwar years. Although fluctuations in this pattern did occur, and many smallholders lost their properties before, during and after the depression, on the whole, the pattern changed relatively little.[39]

In contrast to the Hungarian land reform, in Esthonia, 49% of all farmland was redistributed among the peasantry; in Latvia, this came to 46%. In Yugoslavia, 6,200,000 acres were given to 650,000 peasant families, each receiving on an average 9.5 acres. In Rumania, 7.98 million acres were redistributed among 1.4 million peasants, each receiving on an average 6.78 acres.[40] It was true that the reforms in these countries served primarily nationalistic purposes, being aimed primarily at former Russian, Polish or Hungarian landlords in the respective states. But the scale of land distribution was so large that the reforms were beneficial for the peasants regardless of their intention.

In contrast, the Hungarian land reform did not attain a balanced distribution of land ownership-patterns. It was true that the reform raised the number of dwarfholders to 552,000 peasant families. It also increased the number of those who had already possessed land and were now possessing a little more than before. But it reduced the territory of the large estates by a measly 0.3% only.[41]

Furthermore, the new landowners were seldom given their properties in one strip of land. Only 29.6% of the new landholds consisted of one single parcel. The rest were made up, on an average, of 3.9 strips each, one strip being less than ½ acre in size. On top of all this, the strips were usually distributed in widely separated areas, forcing the peasants to spend precious time in travelling from one parcel to the next.[42] The servants of large estates were completely excluded from the reform. After the land reform, about 3 million peasants continued to live a precarious existence.[43]

The new landowners made up 34.5% of all peasant households. Few of them had the funds or the knowledge to take advantage of their new status. Their methods of working the land were generally primitive. Many of them simply planted wheat year in and year out, not because this brought better results, but because wheat has traditionally been the symbol of good life in the villages. Machinery or chemical fertilizers were not available for them[44] It hardly mattered that hard evidence was against extensive grain production on small landholds; tradition was stronger in this instance than even the strongest desire for material advancement.

It should not be surprising, therfore, that average yields as well as production volumes were generally disappointing on the small landholds, despite some exceptional achievements of a few individual owners. In 1930, corn yielded 20% less on these farms per acre on an average than on large estates; potatoes brought 32% less in volume and forage production was 15-17% lower per acre on the small farms. Large estates produced better yields of almost every category of crops, and these results provided powerful arguments for the opponents of further land reform in Hungary.[45]

But comparisons based strictly on average yields were misleading. Such comparisons did not allow for the inequities in support which the two types of landholds received from the government. While the large estates continued to receive guaranteed cheap loans and other help in the form of export subsidies, small proprietors were left entirely to their own devices. Characteristically, the interwar Hungarian governments invested nearly 250 million *pengos* in agriculture, of which 110 million went directly to producers to bolster production, 80 million were spent in price support, and 35 million for land improvements. More than 80% of all these investments went to the large estates!

It should not be surpising, therefore, that not only average yields, but the quality of products put out by the smallholders were generally inferior to those of the large estates. Ignorance of modern methods of packaging and transportation, the lack of knowledge of scientific farming methods, all contributed to the situation. The critic was correct when he remarked that every product from eggs to fattened hogs was lower in quality on the small landholds than on the large estates; "the weed-infested wheat, corn, rye; wet potatoes and mouldy, spoiled grains sold on the market all come from small farms," he stated.[47] However, no one measured the pride of the new landholders in their independence; no one took account of the new spirit of hope among those who became landholders for the first time in 1920; no one gauged the impact of the reform on social peace. In retrospect, however inadequate the reform was, however many of its initial promises remained unfulfilled, the law of 1920 did give new hope for the peasantry.

The government clearly saw this and took further steps during the 1920's and 1930's. For instance, the follow-up law of 1921 confirmed ownership for those who had received land. Another law introduced in 1924, further strengthened the provisions of the land reform. Short-term loans were also provided for smallholders for the purchase of tractors in 1926. But only those who could raise the required collaterals could participate in the latter program. These were provided with three-year term loans at 7% annual interests. In addition, each participant in the program was required to contract to plough between 142-210 acres besides his own property with his new machine. Compensation for this work was set at 5.76 *pengos* per acre. In 1927, the plan was extended to cover the purchase of mechanical planters and ploughs.[47] But the results were uneven; only 70 tractors were bought, although 7,000 small machines were acquired.[48] But most peasants were unable to participate in this program since they had neither the collateral for tractors, nor the money to pay for the ploughing.

Further steps in agricultural reform were taken by the government, but in a rather disorganized fashion. For instance, a law of settlers (*telepitestorveny*) introduced in 1936, projected the redistribution of 378,000 acres of land, and the establishment of a land bank of 210,000 additional acres to provide low-rent smallholds for individual peasant families. The intention was to provide the means for an independent existence for 34-35,000 peasant families. The plan was to extend over a stretch of 20 years.[48] Funding was to be provided by the udgeting of 4 million *pengos* a year (about 800,000 dollars) for the purchase of available land by the government. But in 1936, 1.42 acres of land cost, on an average, 400 *pengos*, and the projected purchase of 588,000 acres would have cost 23.5 million *pengos* that year. The price jumped by 33% the following year, making the plan unrealistic. Eventually, 5,434 peasant families were given smallholds through the provisions of the law, and an additional 3,200 families received small rentals. In 1939, another proposal was introduced in Parliament to increase the number of available small rentals; 142,000 acres were to be purchased in each of every following year for this purpose. But this proposal was rejected and never became law.[50] Beyond this, there was nothing further being done, although several proposals for land reform were formulated, mostly by people outside the government.[51]

In sum, the land reform law of 1920 and the follow-up attempts failed altogether to change the character of land ownership patterns in interwar Hungary. This was mainly the result of the haphazard nature of the government's approach to agriculture. After the reform, the number of smallholders increased indeed, but the ultimate beneficiaries of the reform were the large estates! Not only were these estates protected against partition during the reform, but the growth of the number of smallholders whose properties were too small to enable them to make a living from them served the large estates' interests. These peasants were physically less mobile than the landless agrarian workers and were, thus, available for work on the large estates. The estates then took advantage of the increased number of farmhands available for work, and lowered the wages for all agrarian workers.[52]

This is not meant to say that the Hungarian government had a sinister purpose in mind with the reform law of 1920, or that it openly conspired with the large estate owners against the peasantry at that time. But this government acted in such haste and with such dilettantism that the results were quite the opposite of its intentions.

One question that has been raised by Hungarian historians in relation to the reform of 1920 was this; could the direction of the development of Hungarian agriculture have been substantially altered if a meaningful reform were introduced, parcelling out the land in small quantities to most landless peasant families?[53]

Unfortunately, the extensive land reforms in the neighboring East European states did not provide an unequivocal answer to this question. In my opinion, even really fundamental changes in the landowning patterns alone, *without far reaching social and political changes,* would not have resulted in a healthier evolution of Hungarian agriculture.[54]

We must insist on seeing this issue in its true historical context. The very fact that the land reforms in the neighboring states failed to solve the problems of the modernization of their agriculture, should be a warning for all observers to "change the thinking cap" and see the solution to agrarian backwardness elsewhere. In fact, an agricultural system such as Hungary's, could no longer be improved by quantitative changes alone, which was essentially what the reform of 1920 was about. Since producers' cooperatives were very few,[55] the redistribution of the land and its consequences, including the doubling of the number of smallholders, must be judged to have been a fundamental mistake. Events were to show that the new, small farms were hardly competitive against the large estates, not to speak of the production of the mechanized farms of North and South America.

However, a similar problem confronts those who maintain that the state should have encouraged the large estates more at the expense of the smallholders. But it was no longer a question in Hungary whether small or large farms should make up the bulk of the agrarian system, but whether traditional methods of production could be significantly altered. If the Hungarians indeed wanted a small-farms based agriculture (and the peasantry to tend the smallholds), they would have had to resign themselves to making huge commitments to provide machinery, chemical fertilizers, improved plant strains and animal breeds, road building programs and improvements in storage and transportation facilities and, above all, train a cadre of agricultural technicians to help the peasants in the modernization of their production. But even if they spent most of their national income on such a commitment, they could hardly expect to emerge in a competitive position on the world markets in a reasonably short time without the simultaneous development of industries.

On the other hand, the support of the large estates under the existing conditions was not a real solution to the agrarian dilemma. And here was the real problem for the Hungarian leaders during the interwar years. The fact was that the large estates, capitalist firms that they were, were not really modern agricultural enterprises. They operated under a mixture of modern and pre-modern practices some of the latter of which harkened back to the previous century. Only a radical alteration of their organizational structure and ownership could have induced fundamental changes in their production techniques.

In the final analysis, Hungary's lack of a truly industrialized society, one that could have provided the basis for the mechanization of agriculture and the necessary organizational techniques, characteristic of such a society, was the fundamental problem. However, if such a base had existed, its most important impact would probably have been the consolidation of smallholds into large agricultural firms (not estates), and the absorption of the surplus labor force of the rural sphere into its urban-based industries. Thus, in the land reform, however thorough, could have saved the peasantry as a social class from gradual dissolution.

It did not matter that the large estates seemed more viable forms of agricultural production from the point of view of higher crop yields, or the better quality of the goods that they produced than were the smallholds. Their succeses were largelygovernment subsidies, not to a healthy organic evolution. I am, therefore, suggesting that the Hungarian agricultural system as it existed during much of the interwar years would have had to be completely swept away if the the modernization of society were to be achieved. In view of our historical experiences, such a fundamental transformation could not be brought about by gradual, peaceful change.

6. The Depression.

The crisis of the world economy in 1929 ushered in a period of general depression in Hungary. It created severe constrictions in an already restricted internal market for agrarian and industrial goods. The Hungarian crisis, however, had other causes besides the world depression. To the structural inadequacies discussed above, one must add the absence of a well-thought out governmental policy dealing with the general problems of the agrarian sector of the economy. The traditional character of peasant society, shunning innovations unless these directly and immediately benefited those using them, must also be considered as a contributing factor to the crisis.

Nature itself seemed bent on ruining the Hungarian producers in these years. Between 1928-1935, a series of droughts, interspersed with early and heavy frost, caused the losses that were adding further burdens to an already shaky agriculture. The combination of these factors resulted in a 20% reduction in marketed goods. At the depression prices, the market value of these goods was less than 50% of that of 1930.[56] By 1933, interests paid on agricultural loans amounted to over 25% of the total yearly income of Hungarian agriculture, and the brunt of the burden fell on the smallholders. By that time, 60% of the lands of the smallholders were fully mortgaged in contrast to only 37% of the large estates.[57]

Since the recovery affected various regions in different ways during the 1920's, the effects of the new crisis also varied in different parts of the country.[58] The most difficult conditions existed in eastern Hungary, the area that traditionally suffered during agrarian crises.[59] Here, however, major problems also included some that had little to do directly with the depression.

One of these problems was caused by the transportation system. While Transdanubia and southwestern Hungary (because of their geographical proximity to the Western markets) were not burdened by excessive transportation costs, the producers of eastern Hungary were severely handicapped. Since they were cut off from their previous markets in northern Hungarian cities (now belonging to the neighboring state of Czechoslovakia), they had little choice but to ship their goods to distant markets.[60] What was equally disadvantageous for the eastern Hungarian producers was the closing of the traditional north-south trade routes leading from the Balkans through their area to Poland and further north and east; these roads were now blocked not only by the new state borders created after 1919, but by high custom-walls erected by the neighboring states.[61] In addition, the migrant workers of eastern Hungary lost their jobs in the rich vineyards of the Highlands which were now part of Czechoslovakia.

Eastern Hungary actually recovered from the effects of World War I at a much slower rate than other agrarian areas of the country. The few years of prosperity enjoyed by the producers of Transdanubia and the Great Plain in the late 1920's largely eluded this region. A symptom of this fact was that, by 1930' the debt of east Hungarian producers exceeded that of the year 1913. Large and small estates were equally in debt in this region, and their debts continued to grow. By 1940, 430 estates over 750 acres in size each in eastern Hungary owed taxes over 5,000 *pengos* each to the government, their aggregate arrears amounting to 8.2 million *pengos*.

The tax policies of the government did not help the situation. The taxation rate was based on a uniform tax code which was highly regressive. Thus, the Agricultural Office of eastern Hungary reported in 1934, that every acre of land carried a burden of approximately 25% more in taxes in the region than land in other parts of the country.[63] In fact, taxes were increased during the depression. Between 1932 and 1937, taxes increased by 24% and excise taxes by 32%[64]

The major burden fell once again on smallholders. The results were discouraging; between 1929-1932, 6,000 smallholds were sold at public auction per year in Hungary. But in 1934-1937, the number grew to 7,000 a year. Most of these farms were in the 4.5-10.0 acre category,[65] and a disproportionately large number of them were located in eastern Hungary.

The peasants of eastern Hungary were compelled to sell their goods for prices that were lower by 4-22% than did producers of Transdanubia, while they bought non-agrarian goods for prices that were higher by 7-37%.[66] This was also largely due to the inadequacies of the transportation system. During 1927-1935, the value of agrarian properties in eastern Hungary declined by 6-38%. This was reflected in a serious reduction of the living standards of the peasant population. On an average, peasant families were able to spend 33-49% less on essential goods and services here than they did before 1927.[67]

Somewhat different conditions existed in other regions. For instance, the population of the market towns on the Great Plain were somewhat better off. It will be recalled that the peasants of these towns introduced a market- and garden-based agriculture. The prices of the goods that they produced were less affected by the depression.[68] However, here, too, taxes took away a large part of the income of the peasants. Every farm under 142 acres in size was burdened by 18 *pengos* of land taxes per acre per year in contrast to 11 *pengos* paid by the large estates.[69]

But the depression worsened agrarian conditions everywhere in Hungary. In the Great Plain (outside the region of the market towns) grain production was traditionally the major source of agrarian income, and animal husbandry played a relatively small part. Here the depression was severe. This was reflected not only in the income of smallholders, but in the constantly declining wages paid to the agricultural workers. After 1931, these wages were depressed to a point where they no longer provided support even for the minimal needs of their families. Similarly, the servants on large estates saw their income decline by almost 60%; daily wage earners lost almost 74% of their former income. In the counties of Bihar and Bekes, 12 *fillers* (2.5 cents) constituted the share of each family member of the daily wage earners' income.[70] This led to all sorts of unrest in the rural sphere, especially in eastern Hungary. There were demonstrations and harvest strikes. The Council of Ministers eventually attempted to set minimum wage levels for agrarian workers. But the response of the large estates was simply to employ less workers.[71]

By 1931, the government was at the end of its wits. It had to repay short term foreign loans. There was such a sudden outflow of the country's foreign currency reserves that the treasury was threatened by bankruptcy. The deficits were eventually covered by treasury bills issued by the Hungarian National Bank, but this in itself could not solve the problem. Tight controls had to be imposed on all foreign currency transactions and the country's currency reserves were frozen. However, without being able to sell substantial amounts of goods on the world markets, all these actions could only postpone hard decisions.

Industrial firms suffered less in this maelstrom than did agrarian producers since the protectionist policies mitigated their losses. In order to create a more favorable atmosphere, the government began to promote the sale of agrarian goods on the export markets. It also began subsidizing grain production by providing vouchers worth three *pengos* (60 cents) for every quintal (220 lbs.) of wheat or rye sold and these could be used for the paying of state taxes. The program provided altogether 46-48 million *pengos* in subsidies for grain producers, most of which, however, went to large estates.[72] At the same time, the Hungarians sought the cooperation of Italy and Germany, two powers who were also experiencing great difficulties. This process was rooted in traditional diplomatic ties, and was especially accelerated after 1935, when Gyula Gombos, a former army officer was named Prime Minister of Hungary. He began to seek closer cooperation with Nazi Germany as a possible solution for Hungary's economic problems.

7. The Last Years of Peace.

The depression began to ease somewhat in Hungary in 1934. Production indices of agrarian and industrial goods began to rise once again; the yearly volume of grains gradually increased until, by 1939, it was 29% higher than ten years before. Potato crops increased by 20% and alfalfa by nearly 60% in the same period. By 1940, Hungarian agriculture completely recovered from the effects of the depression, reaching production rates higher than those of the late 1920's. There remained, however, some aftereffects of the depression reflected in the continuously high rate of rural unemployment. Even in 1938, the number was close to 100,000 or about 15% of the agrarian laborers.[73] Wages in the agrarian sector were higher in 1938 than in previous years, but they were still almost 30% lower than before the depression! Furthermore, a steady inflation contributed to a steady reduction of the living standards of wage earners.[74]

Real improvements came only after the outbreak of the Second World War. By then, however, Hungarian agriculture was producing large quantities of goods for the Axis armies. In order to keep up with demands, the government introduced a system of compulsory deliveries of agrarian goods. Because of accelerated conscription, labor shortages also appeared in the countryside. In order to alleviate the need of large estates for labor, the government permitted peasants to pay off their tax obligations by working on these estates. Wages were now fixed in rural areas for the duration of the war, but not prices.

How did the Hungarians (together with the Yugoslavs, Rumanians and Bulgarians) manage to end up in the economic sphere of Nazi Germany, when this was clearly against their national interests? The origin of this process went back to the depression when all these states were short of foreign currency reserves, and their economies tottered on the brink of collapse. Nazi Germany offered a tempting solution to their problems. This was included in the plan produced by Hjalmar Schacht, Germany's Nazi Minister of Economics. The plan suggested that Germany and its partners replace the sale of goods for convertible currencies to each other by a combination of exchanges of goods and clearing agreements. The countries of Eastern Europe were desperate to sell their accumulated surplus foodstuff and were badly in need of industrial goods and raw materials. They gladly accepted the opportunity to do just that when the Germans made their offer. Since the governments of these countries (with the exception of Yugoslavia) were fearful of Soviet Russia and Germany seemed to be the most outspoken opponent of Communism, they had few ideological scruples about trading with Nazi Germany. This was especially true for Hungary.

In November, 1933, a mixed Hungarian-German commission began negotiations for a trade agreement based on the Schact proposals, and quickly put together a package for the signature of their government. The resulting agreements were signed by both parties on February 21, 1934. The agreement opened the German market for Hungarian agrarian goods; 50,000 metric tons of wheat, 75,000 tons of barley and corn, 6,000 fattened cattle and 3,000 tons of pork lard were bought by the Germans in the first year. They also bought a considerable amount of other foodstuffs such as beans, peas, butter, eggs and poultry.[75]

Accordingly, the Germans paid a subsidy of 22 million *pengos* over and above the price of goods delivered which the Hungarian government used to subsidize the producers. This provided payments of 4.2-5.5 *pengos* for each hundredweight of wheat, 4 *pengos* for corn and other subsidies. These were used mainly to help large landowners.

A still largely unexplored area of the history of Hungarian agriculture in the interwar decades is the period between 1938 and 1944, especially the era of the two Vienna Awards, returning some former Hungarian territories to the new Hungarian state. This is, of course, still a highly sensitive subject, obscured by the understandable reluctance of historians to review a currently touchy area of internal and international relations. Here we can only provide a limited outline of the consequences of the Awards, suggesting possibilities for further exploration of this issue.

The first Award was enacted in November, 1938. It returned to Hungary the southern areas of Slovakia with a mixed population of Magyars and Slovaks. The Carpatho-Ukraine was returned in March, 1939, after the Germans destroyed the rump Czechoslovak state. In August, 1940, the second Vienna Award returned parts of northeastern Transylvania to Hungary, where the majority of the population was ethnically Hungarian. The tragedy of these changes was, of course, that they were brought about by the Fascist powers, and their permanence depended solely upon their victory in the coming European struggle for supremacy.

The Awards increased the territory of the Hungarian state to nearly twice its pre-1938 size, and added about 5 million new subjects to its population of whom about 2 million were ethnically non-Hungarian. From the point of view of agriculture — aside from moral and realistic political considerations — the gains proved to be a mixed blessing indeed.

First of all, smallholders possessing less than 142 acres each predominated in all the agricultural areas returned to Hungary. Their farms were under-mechanized, using mostly family labor and, in general, were in financial difficulties. After the Awards, the ratio of ploughland from the arable lands declined by nearly 11%. On the other hand, the ratio of forest lands increased by an equal amount.[76] For the short run, the changes were not necessarily advantageous for Hungary from the point of view of agricultural production. While Axis demands for the delivery of grains and other foodstuff continued to increase, the ratio of lands on which these could be grown decreased relative to the size of Hungary's population. This was also the case with animal husbandry; the ratio of cattle increased by about 20% per capita, but the number of hogs and horses seriously declined.

Before the Awards, the density of Hungary's population was 97 persons per square kilometers. After the Awards, it declined to 83-84. Given the inability of industry in the 1930's to absorb rural surplus labor, this might be considered a favorable change. In fact, the labor market in relation to the country's size became more restricted, contributing to higher wages paid to agricultural laborers. This implied an improvement in agrarian prices and the extension of the internal market for agrarian goods. This was exactly what happened. On the other hand, the peasant proprietors and the large estates had to pay for this process with reduced profits. Underlying the situation was the continuing increase of demand for food by both the growing Hungarian army and the industrial population.

The war stimulated industrial and agricultural production indeed and, as a consequence, more people find employment in the rural sphere. Rural unemployment was reduced to a mere 5% of the agrarian labor force by 1941. Since industry also needed more workers, wages increased. This way an artificial boom was created similar to that of World War I.

In terms of capital accumulation, the agriculture of the returned territories was generally in worse shape than that of pre-1938 Hungary. This was understandable; the Czechoslovak, Rumanian and Yugoslav governments were not anxious to invest their funds in areas inhabited by Hungarians who were considered, in any case, as second class citizens and a potential source of trouble in their states. Roads and transportation facilities were in worse conditions than those in the Hungarian countryside. Thus, in the final count, the Vienna Awards — and World War II — created artificial conditions that were not necessarily advantageous for the Hungarian state in the short run. At the same time, the increased distances on which produce had to be transported, the generally poor rural road system, and the aggregate effect of outdated political and social institutions created bottlenecks in agricultural development. It was during this time that the neglect of agriculture in the first two decades of the interwar years had come home to haunt Hungarian society. When large numbers of young peasants were drafted into the army, there was no machinery to replace them on the fields. This eventually resulted in grave food shortages as the war advanced.

The government accordingly made further efforts to stimulate food production in this period. Improved seeds of alfalfa and other fodder crops were freely distributed in the villages. Experimental stations (really showcases) were set up in the rural sphere to demonstrate the correct treatment of natural fertilizers. The improvement of alkaline lands in the

Great Plain and eastern Hungary began. But all these efforts were conducted on a relatively minor scale and they generally came too late to have a universally beneficial effect. Nor did the government come around to the solution of the real problems, the wasteful production methods followed by the large estates and independent peasant proprietors alike, and the primitive and degrading living conditions of the servants living on the large estates.[79] The slow improvements in the mechanization of production were helped by German deliveries of small tractors and other machinery after 1938, especially on the large estates; chemical fertilizer production and its use, however, continued to remain inadequate.

The unevenness of rural development in the first two decades of the interwar years reflected the general conditions of society as a whole. The revival of interest in the modernization of agriculture in the late 1930's, however, came too late to cause serious structural changes in the rural sphere. The efforts of the government only underlined the fact that, during these decades, Hungary had remained a pre-modern, semi-industrial society whose leaders were unsure of the course that they wanted the nation to follow and who, despite their own propaganda, were lacking in a vision and trust in the future of Hungary.

And yet, it is undeniable that a slow, gradual transformation of the countryside continued during these decades. By 1939, small farms in eastern Hungary were selling 54.9% of their produce on the markets; this ratio was 45.4% in northern Hungary and 59.9 in western Hungary. This was evidence that a gradual capitalist transformation of the rural sphere was taking place. With the outbreak of World War II, however, it also became clear that even with increased governmental support and the centralization and strengthening of the collecting agencies, Hungary could not fulfill all its foreign obligations and feed its own people at the same time.

The war was to end not only with Hungary's defeat once again, but also with the complete devastation of its land, the virtual destruction of its entire economic system, including agriculture. The "newest" Hungary which was to emerge from this devastation in 1945, carried many of the burdens of the "old", although a large part of the former elite fled the country forever.

NOTES

1. For the pattern of land distribution see Magyar Statisztikai Hivatal, *Magyarorszag foldbirtokviszinyai az 1935. evben* (Land Ownership Patterns in Hungary in 1935) (Budapest, 1937).
2. See Bela Kovrig, *Magyar tarsadalompolitika* (Hungarian Social Policies) (New York, 1954), 5-6.
3. Laszlo Gesztelyi-Nagy, "Mezogazdasagi politikank uj utjai es eszkozei," (New Paths and Tools for Our Agricultural Policies) *Kozgazdasagi Szemle* (From now on; *KGSZ*) 97(1934)233.
4. The Italians at the Paris Peace Conference wanted 3 billion gold crowns in reparations; the British asked for between 480-600 million; the French suggested 100 million pound sterlings (2.135 billion gold crowns). See, Orszagos Leveltar, *Kulugyminiszterium, Gazdasagpolitikai Gyujtemeny (*National Archives, Ministry of Foreign Affairs, Economic Policy Collection) (1926), 113, 50263; (113023/1922). See also, Ivan T. Berend, Gyorgy Ranki, *Kozep-Keleteuropa gazdasagi fejlodese a 19.-20. szazadban* (Economic Development of East-Central Europe in the 19th and 20th centuries) (Budapest, 1976), 260-1, and Maria Sz. Ormos, *Az 1924. evi magyar allamkolcson megszerzese* (Acquiring the Hungarian State Loan of 1924) (Budapest, 1964), 20. Direct war losses included the following; 500,000 horses, 1.7 million heads of cattle, 2.4 million swine, 6.3 million sheep, 1.2 million goats. The losses in railroad stock, factory equipment and other goods were never exactly ascertained. Indirect losses included about 50% of all industrial firms, 49% of the industrial labor force, 77.7% of all forests, 42.4% of the food processing industries and 45% of all the chemical firms.

5. See Gyula Hajpal, *Aralakulas a ket vilaghaboru kozott. Mezogazdasagi termekek ara* (The Development of Prices Between the Wars. Prices of Agrarian Goods) (Budapest, 1973), 13.
6. For instance, milk consumption in Hungary was 30% lower per capita than in Germany in the 1920's and a good part of the 1930's; it was lower than in Denmark and much lower than in Great Britain. Similarly, the yearly per capita sugar consumption was 22 lbs. in Hungary, 46 lbs. in Germany, 94.8 lbs. in Great Britain, and 49 lbs. in France. Meat consumption was 56.1 lbs per capita in Hungary, 94.6 lbs in France, 107.8 lbs. in Germany, 141.9 lbs. in Denmark and 154.0 lbs. in Great Britain. Arpa Ujlaki, "Elelmezesi gondok," (Problems of Nutrition) *Magyar Szemle* (Budapest), 44(1943)77.
7. See, for instance, the petition of unemployed seasonal agrarian workers of the village of Kistaly, addressed to the Minister of Agriculture in May, 1923, in *Parasztsors-Parasztgond* (Peasant Fate - Peasant Worries) (Budapest, 1960), 44-5. See also, Peter Hanak, Gyorgy Ranki, Miklos Lacko, "Gazdasag, tarsadalom, tarsadalom-politikai gondolkodas Magyararszagon a kapitalizmus koraban," (Economy, Society, Socio-political Thinking in Hungary during the Age of Capitalism) *Tortenelmi Szemle* (1969) No. 2, 315.
8. For instance, Prince Pal Eszterhazy owned 294,000 acres; Prince Gyorgy Festetics had 97,168 acres of land; Count Alfonz Pallavicini possessed 70,561 acres; the Habsburg family's possessions came close to 100,000 acres of land. The city of Debrecen owned 121,717 acres; Szeged was the owner of 96,866 acres. Nor were the religious denominations bashful when it came to land acquisitions; the Roman Catholic Archbishopric of Esztergom owned 94,155 acres; the Bishopric of Eger owned 53,247 acres of land; that of Veszprem possessed 63,264 acres; the Cathedral chapter of Veszprem was in possession of 66,717 acres of land. The various abbeys did not fall far

behind; the Benedictine abbey of Pannonhalma owned 84,442 acres; the Cistercian abbey at Zirc possessed 69,987 acres. Altogether the Roman Catholic Church of Hungary was the richest single landlord by possessing 1,704,000 acres of landed properties. The Calvinist Reformed Church owned the relatively modest amount of 142,000 acres of land. Berend-Ranki, *Kelet-Kozepeuropa, op. cit.*, 214.

9. *Magyarorszag foldbirtokviszonyai, op. cit.*, 14.
10. Istvan Sajohegyi, "Kulfoldi honos birtokosaink" (Our Foreign-Citizen Landholders) *MSSZ* 1930, 412.
11. For instance, three-fourth of the members of the Upper House and 20% of the Lower House's membership consisted of large estate-owners, many of them of aristrocratic lineage. The cabinet of the Regent consisted almost exclusively of members of the landowning aristocracy throughout the interwar years. See Ferenc Donath, *Reform es Forradalom. A Magyar mezogazdasag strukturalis atalakulasa 1945-1975* (Reform and Revolution. The Structural Transformation of Hungarian Agriculture 1945-1975) (Budapest, 1977), 24. See also: Tibor Toth, *Nagybirtoktol a nagyuzemig. A mernyei uradalom gazdalkodasa a jobbagyfelszabaditastol az elso vilaghaboruig* (From Large Estate to Large Firm. The activities of the Estate of Mernye from the Emancipation of the Serfs to the First World War) (Budapest, 1977), 70-71; Mihaly Kerek, *A magyar foldkerdes* (The Problem of Hungarian Landholdings) (Budapest, 1939), 39-44.
12. See "Hungaria," *MSSZ* (1938), 107-111.
13. See Ferenc Eckhart, *A magyar kozgazdasag szaz eve, 1848-1941* (One-Hundred Years of the Hungarian Economy) (Budapest, 1941), 223.
14. W. Sorbi (sic!) "A mezogazdasag iparositasa es eszerusitese," (Rationalization and Industrialization of Agriculture) *(KGSZ)* 68(1938), 363-5.
15. The comparable rise of tariffs in Eastern Europe was a follows;

(Averages)	1913	1925
Czechoslovakia	18%	29%
Yugoslavia	—	23%
Poland	—	32%
Hungary	—	30%

Kovrig, *op. cit.* 36.

16. Semi-feudal was defined by Eric Molnar as being production relations as well as legal, political and social functions which, originating from the feudal era, survived during the capitalist transformation of the economy. Molnar listed these elements in the Hungarian economic system as 1. entailed properties; 2. wages paid in kind to agrarian workers; 3. aristocracy-owned mammoth estates. Lajos Szentmiklosy (Eric Molnar), "Foldreformilluziok," (Illusions of Land Reform) *Gondolat* (Budapest), 1(1935), 261.
17. The Great Plain consisted of 52,000 square kilometers or 52% of all the areable lands of Hungary. It was part of the great continental steppes. Its sub-regions included flood plains, loess regions and marginal lowlands that were formerly forested, as well as sandy regions. The Little Plain covered 5,500 square kilometers, similar in character to the Great Plain. The West Hungarian marginal region consisted of 7,000 square kilometers including a great deal of swampy and wetlands. The Transdanubian Hilly area included another 7,000 square kilometers of land, rising between 200-350 meters above sea level, interspersed by fertile valleys. The Transdanubian Highlands consisted of 11,500 square kilometers of land rising between 350-1,000 meters above sea level. Finally, the Northern Highlands comprised were a small area similar in character to the Transdanubian Highlands. See Marton Pecsi and Bela Sarfalvi, *Physical and Economic Geo-Graphy of Hungary* (Budapest, 1977), 18-23.
18. Laszlo Gesztelyi-Nagy, "Az Alfold gazdasagi jelentosege," (The Economic Importance of the Great Plain) *KGSZ, 68 (1925) 471.*

19. During the interwar years there were some efforts to improve the quality of alkaline lands and to eliminate the swamps of the Great Plain and eastern Hungary. The former project was under the direction of Samuel Szentannay, director of the agricultural school of Karcag, who worked in cooperation with the Agricultural Institute of the University of Szeged. The latter was to be accomplished by the constrution of a canal system based on three major navigable waterways connecting with the Tisza River. Gesztely-Nagy, Az Alford op.cit., 473-5.
20. The dwarf- and smallholders used a disproportionately large area of their lands for grain production. The four major grain crops — wheat, 33.6%, rye 13.4%, barley 7.7% and oats 4.1% — took up 58.8% of all their ploughlands. In contrast, large estates over 1,420 acres in size each, planted about 50.1% of their lands with grains. Erno Eber, "A foldbirtokmegoszlas jelentosege termelesunkben," (Significance of the Distribution Patterns of Land in Our Production) *KGSZ,* 73(1930) 268-9. See also by the same author, "Mezogazdasagi termelesunk taji vizsgalata," (Examination of Our Agricultural Production by Region) *Ibid.,* 83(1940) 210.
21. Eber, "mezogazdasagi," *op. cit.,* 213. See also, Donath, *op. cit.,* 17.
22. There were, for instance, 2,539 heads of cattle for every 100 square kilometers of farmland in Hungary in 1939; in Austria, the comparable number was 5,399; in Czechoslovakia, 5,129; in Poland, 3,983. Only in Yugoslavia and Rumania were the numbers similar to that in Hungary, being 2,885 and 2,515 respectively. The actual number of cattle in Hungary was 908,383 in 1929. Of these, 757,317 were improved western breeds with an average yearly milk production of 1,600 liters each. Frigyes Fellner, *Csonka Magyarorszag nemzeti jovedelme* (The National Income of Rump Hungary) (Budapest, 1930), 30. According to Fellner, the total income derived from animal husbandry

was relatively low, coming close to 799,805 *pengos* in 1929, not including income received from exports. See also, Laszlo Gesztelyi-Nagy, "A gazdatarsadalom felelossege," (Responsibilities of the Community of Landowners) *KGSZ,* 81 (1938) 935-6; Karoly Ihrig, "A szovetkezeti allatertekesites," (Cooperative Marketing of Animal Products) *KGSZ,* 74(1931) 681.

23. Average crop yields were as follows; [in lbs. per 1.42 acres]

Crop	1901-1910	1911-1920	1921-1930	1931-1937
wheat	2,574	2,464	2,794	2,926
rye	2,442	2,288	2,310	2,442
barley	2,640	2,574	2,618	2,882
oats	2,354	2,288	2,468	2,618
corn	3,212	3,212	3,212	4,004

from Donath, *op. cit.,* 18.

24. The share of various crops in total production in % were;

Year	Grains	Fodder	Corn, potatoes beats	other	fallow lands
1870	53%	2.7%	21.4%	—	22.9%
1895	53.7	7.5	26.3	—	12.9
1914	51.9	10.0	27.1	2.4	8.6
1921-25	51.1	12.8	25.7	2.7	.7
1926-30	54.4	11.8	27.5	2.5	3.8
1931-35	53.4	11.8	28.9	3.7	1.9
1936	53.4	12.0	29.0	3.7	1.9
1937	50.8	12.3	30.0	3.9	3.0

from *MSSZ,* (1938) 107-111.

24. *MSEK* (1928), 94.

25. Hajpal, *op. cit.,* 13, suggests a different periodization based on the changes in agricultural prices. According to him, the various periods would be like this; 1. the period of inflation, 1920-1924; 2. the era of stable currency, 1925-1939; 3. the period of the Second World War. But this method is really insufficient to account for such periods as the depression, and it does not take into account the fact that inflation began long before 1920.
26. Ivan Berend, Miklos Szuhay, *A tokes gazdasag tortenete Magyarorszagon* (A History of the Capitalist Economy in Hungary) (Budapest, 1975), 212. See also, Hajpal *op. cit.,* 14.
27. Ormos, *op. cit.,* 24.
28. The total pre-World War I debt of Hungarian agriculture was 1.5 billion gold crowns. By 1924, this was reduced to 613,000 gold crowns! Most of the remaining debt was owned by medium- and smallholders. See Laszlo Zelovics, "A magyar mezogazdasagi hitelkerdes jelenlegi allapota," (Current Status of Hungarian Agricultural Credit) *KGSZ,* 70(1927), 506.
29. *Ibid.*
30. British banks advanced the most, 7,902,700 pound sterlings; Americans provided 44,415 gold crowns; Italian bankers gave 170 million lira or 36,228,064 gold crowns. Other sums were provided by Swedish, Swiss, Dutch and even Czech lenders. But their terms were generally severe; only 70-80% of the funds were actually paid to the Hungarian treasury, while interests of 7.5% annually were demanded after the total amount of 307,153,851 gold crowns. Furthermore, Hungary had to assume 1.1 billion gold crowns worth of pre-War debts of the Habsburg Empire. See Ormos, *op. cit.,* 135-6.
31. Istvan Varga, "Az aranypengo," (The gold pengo) *KGSZ* 74(1931), 745.
32. Zelovics, *op. cit.,* 509.

33. Fellner, *op. cit.,* 25. See also, Berend-Szuhay, *op. cit.,* 341.
34. Hajpal, *op. cit.,* 20. See also, Jeno Dalnoki-Kovacs and Gyula Bernat, "A megelhetesi koltsegek alakulasa az 1925.evben," (Changes in the Market Basket Prices in 1935) *KGSZ* 69(1926), 50.
35. Gyorgy Ranki, ed. *Magyarorszag tortenete, 1918-1919, 1919-1945* (The History of Hungary 1918-1919 and 1919-1945) (Budapest, 1976), vol. 8 of the series, *Magyarorszag tortenete 10 kotetben,* 768.
36. Kerek, *op. cit.,* 152.
37. Institutional preferences at the land reform were as follows:

Parish priests and teachers received	16,128 acres
Village and county notaries received	2,471 acres
Gandarms received	5,556 acres
Agricultural schools received	2,972 acres
Sport-playing fields and yards received	513 acres
Members of the Order of Heroes received	50,0036 acres
Common grazing lands in 919 villages received	123,130 acres
Cemetaries, clay pits, etc. received	23,489 acres
Medium-landholders received	14,221 acres
Churches, in 12 cases received	8,128 acres
total	246,644 acres

The distribution preferences for individuals were as follows:

Gold- and silver medal winners in World War I	2,690 persons
Disabled veterans	30,082 persons
War widows	25,712 persons
Adult war orphans	1,040 persons
Landless agrarian workers	186,794 persons
Dwarf- and smallholder peasants	114,254 persons
Civil servants	3,791 persons
Professional soldiers and officers	1,117 persons

Craftsmen and former industrial workers	....	40,947 persons
Officials of large estates	....	53 persons
Others	....	4,081 persons
total participants	....	411,561 persons

Source; Kerek, *op. cit.*, 198-9.

38. Istvan Varga, "A magyarorszagi foldbirtokmegoszlas egyenetlensege es a foldbirtokreform," (The Unevenness of the Distribution of Land in Hungary and the Land Reform) *KGSZ*, 69(1926) 27.
39. *Ibid.*, 31-2.
40. Berend-Ranki, *Kozep-Keleteuropa, op. cit.*, 273-9.
41. The land distribution patterns according to counties were as follows; [acres]

County	total land [agricult.]	large estates	% of county's lands	number of owners
Baranya	976,479	263,293	27%	35
Fejer	1,004,140	455,284	45.4	89
Gyor-Moson	580,459	176,138	30.3	29
Pozsony	—	—	—	—
Komarom-Esztergom	482,211	203,771	42.3	22
Somogy	1,628,851	708,684	43.5	108
Sopron	471,892	167,097	35.4	21
tolna	875,959	240,006	27.4	43
Vas	804,554	203,061	25.2	43
Veszprem	964,758	374,257	38.8	58
Zala	1,183,742	383,374	32.4	58
Bacs-Bodrog	456,379	119,119	26.1	16
Bekes	895,521	221,064	24.7	65
Bihar	674,202	193,429	28.7	52
Totals	22,642,820	6,763,268	30.3	1,242

Note; the counties of Csongrad and Pest are not included. Large estates in this statistical survey meant holdings over 142 ares each.

Source; Bajcsy-Zsilinszky, *op. cit.*, 69.

42. Eckhart, op. cit., 229.

43. Magyar Kiralyi Statisztikai Hivatal, *Magyarorszag foldbirtokosai es foldberloi. A 100 kataszteri holdas es ennel nagyobb foldbirtokok az 1925.ev eleji adatok alapjan* (Hungary's Landowners and Land Renters. Landholdings over 100 *holds* (142 acres) according to the Data of Early 1925) (Budapest, 1926), 122. Ten years later, the following patterns still prevailed;

Size	Number of holdings	Holdings in acres	% of areable lands
less than 1.4 acres	775,487	437,364	1.9%
1.4-7.5	664,263	1,620,942	10.0
7.5-70	428,547	5,654,125	34.5
70-142	14,895	1,008,597	7.0
142-700	10,699	2,251,629	14.0
700-1420	1,816	1,272,094	7.9
1420—	1,560	3,962,094	24.7

Source: *Ibid.*, 12. See also, Matyas Matolcsy, *Uj elet a magyar foldon* (New Life in the Land of Hungary) (Budapest, 1938), 67.

44. As one opponent of the land reform put it, "the Hungarians brought with them from their original homeland the grains of noble wheat . . . How could one decide, then, purely on the basis of current demand, to limit wheat production, using only statistical information, when wheat production has been so deeply embeded in the history of the Hungarians?" Erno Eber, "A buzakerdes szempontjai (Questions of Wheat Growing) *KGSZ* 85 (1942), 322.

45. See one of these in Erno Eber, "A foldbirtokmegoszlas jelentosege termelesunkben" (The Significance of Land Ownership Patterns in our Production) *Ibid.*, 73 (1930), 274-5.

46. *Ibid.*, 280-1.

47. Kerek, op. cit. 216.
48. *Ibid.* For various modifications of this law see Jozsef Kanyar, *Elsikkasztott foldreform, megvalosult foldosztas Somogyban, 1920, 1945* (The Land Reform that was Embezzled, and the One that was Completed in Somogy County, 1920, 1945) (Budapest, 1964), 28-32.
49. Erno Eber, "A magyar mezogazdasag jovedelmenek alakulasa," (Development of the Income of Hungarian Agriculture) *KGSZ* 79(1936), 165. See also, Kerek, *op. cit.*, 266.
50. See Antal Eber (sic!) "Jaradekbirtok vagy kisberlet? (Land Ownership or Small Rental Property?) *Ibid.*, 82(1939) 168-9.
51. For instance, by Endre Bajcsy-Zsilinszky. He proposed a thoroughgoing land reform in his *Egyetlen ut- a magyar paraszt* (The Only Way- the Hungarian Peasant) (Budapest, 1938), 81-120. Tibor Eckhart, a member of the leadership of the Smallholders' Party discussed by Bela Kiraly above, also submitted proposals for land reform. See Mihaly Kerek, "A foldreform korul," (Around the Land Reform) *Magyar Szemle* 35(1939), 206.Matyas Matolcsy, among others in the interwar years came to a close, as proposed some sort of land reform. Yet, of course, very little was done.
52. See, for instance the typical complaint addressed to the Minister of Agriculture by the seasonal workers of Fuzesabony in 1924 about the increadibly low wages paid them by the local estate of the Roman Catholic Church, in *Parasztsors op. cit.*, 54-55.
53. Hanak, *op. cit.*, 315; Ranki, ed., *Magyarorszag, op. cit.*, 8:739.
54. This will, naturally, remain a controversial issue which will be discussed later in this essay.
55. See the efforts of Erdei and his failure in Ferenc Erdei, "Szovetkezeti *Naplo* (Diary of a Collective) in *Gondolat* 3 (1937-38) 366.
56. I. Berend- M. Szuhay, *op. cit.*, 342.

57. Lajos Leopold, "Munkaber es nagybirtok" (Wages and Large Estates)
58. *KGSZ,* 77 (1934) 455. The nature of climatic differences also contributed to this. For instance, the growing season was 15% shorter on the Great Plain than it was in Transdanubia, meaning that unemployment for agrarian workers that much longer in the Great Plain than in Transdanubia.
59. This region usually received the brunt of eastern invasions from the time of the Tartars on. It was also here where the fighting of the Revolution of 1848-1849 lasted for the longest time in Europe; it was this same region that was thoroughly looted by the Rumanians in 1919-1920.
60. The towns included Nagyvarad-Oradea, Temesvar-Timisoara, Szatmarnemeti-Satu Mare, Brasso-Brasov, in Transylvania and Kassa-Kosice, Ungvar-Uzhorod, Munkacs-Mukacevo in Czechoslovakia, and, finally, Ujvidek-Novi Sad and Szabadka-Subotica in Yugoslavia. In pre- World War I days the producers of eastern Hungary were able to use the Debrecen-Nyiregyhaza-Mateszalka-Zahony railroad line stretching between 66-124 kilometers to reach their markets; after 1920, they had to ship their goods over 4-600 kilometers. Thus, wheat from Transdanubia paid 97 *pengos* for a railroad wagon-load, while that from eastern Hungary paid 207 *pengos* on its way to the same market. See Kalman Pongracz, "Az agrarvalsag a Tiszantulon," (The Agrarian Crisis in the Left Bank of the Tisza River) *KGSZ,* 80 (1937) 211.
61. See A Tiszantuli Mezogazdasagi Kamara, *A Tiszantul mezogazdasaga* (The Agriculture of the Left Bank of the Tisza) (Debrecen, 1934), 14-5.
62. Tibor Szadecky- Kardos, "Mezogazdasagunk megadoztatasa," (The Taxation of Our Agriculture) *KGSZ,* 86 (1944) 283.
63. On an average, 19% of individual income was taken away by the tax collectors in the form of direct taxes in the 1930's. This was especially hard on smallholders whose

income was mostly in kind, not in cash. See Matolcsy, *Uj elet, op. cit.,* 101-5.

64. Berend-Szuhay, op. cit., 342.
65. *Ibid.,* 343.
66. Lajos Keztyus, *A tiszantuli es eszaki dombosvideki kisgazdak jovedelme es vagyoni helyzete* (The Income and Financial Condition of Smallholders on the Left Bank of the Tisza and the Northern Highlands) (Debrecen, 1935), 3-4.
67. Pongracz, *op. cit.,* 216.
68. Matolcsy, *Us elet, op. cit.,* 106-8.
69. *Ibid.* The reason for this disparity was that tax assessments were not revised since the early part of the 20th century, when they were based on a variety of factors, including the income derived from the respective parcels. At that time the large estates could — and did — easily influence the assessments in their favor.
70. Berend-Szuhay, *op. cit.,* 345.
71. Jozsef Nadujfalvy, Az elso mezo gazdasagi munkabermegallapitas," (The First Regulation of Wages in Agriculture) *Magyar Statisztikai Szemle* 11 (1940) Okt., 114.
72. This had a generally beneficial effect on the income of agriculture.This income developed during the 4 years after the depression as follows:

1933/34	1934/35	1935/36	1936/37
615 million *pengos*	640 million *pengos*	730 million *pengos*	860 million *pengos*

Better prices paid for agricultural goods, the revived export market all contributed to this income, of course. Matolcsy, *Uj elet, op. cit.,* 41.

73. See the petition of the village of Puspokladany, for instance, which stated that over 1,500 agricultural workers in their village alone were still unemployed, and living on soup served in the public kitchens, in*Parasztsors, op. cit.,* 78.

74. In fact, the daily wages of agrarian workers went virtually unchanged between 1933-1935, and only in 1936 was there some improvement. Average daily wages developed as follows;

1933	1934	1935	1936
1.26 *pengos*	1.24 *pengos*	1.28 *pengos*	1.42 *pengos*

For this it must be obvius that even in 1936, the improvements were only slight. When compared with the growth of the income of large estates, the discrepancy becomes even more glaring; [averages in *pengos*]

1932-1934	1935	1936
8.5 per acre	12.1 per acre	35.4 per acre

Matolcsy, *Uj elet, op. cit.*, 42.

75. Deutsches Zentral Archiv, Potsdam, Ausswertiges Amt, Abt. II, 41 288, quoted by Berend-Ranki, *Kozep-Kelet Europa, op. cit.*, 382.
76. Tivadar Suranyi-Unger, "Az orszaggyarapodas gazdasagi hatasai," (Economic consequences of the Enlargement of the Country) *KGSZ* 83 (1940) 685.
77. See Lajos Sarkadi Keztyus, *Jovedelmezosegi kutatasok a tiszantuli es az eszaki dombosvideki kisuzemekben* (Researches of the Profatibility of the Smallholds of the Left Bank of the Tisza and the Northern Highlands), (Debrecen, 1942), 46.

II

TRADITIONAL PEASANTRY: THE LAST PHASE

1. Demographic Conditions

The demographic history of the Hungarian people during the last century reflects the slow process of economic development. If, as one Hungarian observer stated, the rate of urbanization is a reliable indicator of advancing modernity, and a truly advanced stage is reached when 75-80% of the population live in urban areas, work in industry and the service sector,[1] then Hungary was not very far along the road to a modern society during the interwar years. Although the movement of people into urban areas continued in the period under discussion, in 1941, out of a total population of about 9 million, only 3.7 million lived in the cities. Furthermore, a disproportionately large part of this population movement was directed mainly towards one single urban center, the capital city of Budapest.[2]

Hungarian demographers have not yet focused on the interwar demographic development of the peasantry. Only general works dealing with the entire population are available.[3] One major reason for this lacuna has been the uncertain demarcation line between rural and urban areas in interwar Hungary. It was presumed that peasants lived mainly in villages; for a long time in this century, all settlements below a certain number of inhabitants were indeed designated as villages, hence, rural. However, owing to special historical developments,[4] there existed some huge settlements, especially in the Great Plain and eastern Hungary, that were both rural and urban in character. Some of these, such as the large "village" of Oroshaza containing 24,000 inhabitants, and Balmazujvaros with 15,000 people, certainly did not fit neatly into either category strictly on the basis of their inhabitants. On the other hand, towns with large agricultural hinterlands in which a large number of *tanyas* (the detached, isolated dwellings) were scattered, sometimes making up more than half of the town's population, were designated as urban areas. Therefore, a village was not necessarily rural, nor were all towns completely urban in character.[5]

The outstanding single demographic factor in Hungary during the past century was the steady growth of the population as a whole. But statistical data related to this fact must, by the nature of a Hungarian history, be considered with caution. The major problem in dealing with this data is that a comparison of the population of Hungary in the interwar years with that of pre-1914 Hungary (even with extensive qualifications) is unrealistic. Not only was Hungary three times larger in territory and two-and-a-half times larger in population before World War I than after, but the accurate social and ethnic composition of this population was not always reflected by the statistics. For that matter, statistics on populations in Eastern Europe, even in our own time, no matter who produced them, must always be suspect. In fact, statistics served nationalistic aims more often than not, and they cannot be accepted at their face value. Nor are there reliable data available on intra-and inter-state emigration, an important aspect of the pre'1914 demographic history of Hungary.[6]

One fact seems certain, however, namely, that the approximately five million ethnic Hungarians who lived on territories in 1869 which, after 1919 became parts of the land of the independent Hungarian state, grew in the early 1970's to the current population of ten million people. In 1944, this number was slightly above 9.3 million. Average population density increased by about four persons per square kilometer in every decade between 1910 and 1941.[7] However, this did not represent a uniform level of growth. For instance, during the decade of 1910-1920 which, of course, included World War I, population increase came only to 0.48% as opposed to the average 0.8% during the interwar decades as a whole. In fact, population increase by natural growth would probably have been zero in this decade had not nearly 350,000 ethnic Hungarians, fleeing from persecution in the Successor States and Rumania, entered Hungary. On the other hand, Hungary's territory was enlarged twice by the Vienna Awards as discussed above, bringing the number of inhabitants to 14 million in 1940. But this was only a temporary gain.[8]

In the rural districts there was a slow but gradual loss of the population attributable partly to the attraction of the cities and partly to the negative demographic influence of the large estates.[9] The very existence of the large estate was an impediment to demographic growth in interwar Hungary, and its role has not yet been fully explored by historians from this point of view.

Another significant demographic factor of these decades was the gradual aging of the Hungarian population. The reason for this was partly the war, as well as the lengthening of life expectancy, and the simultaneous decrease of live births among the population.[10] In 1941, a demographer noted that the rate of children in the population was reduced by 9% since 1910. At the same time, the ratio of adults between the ages of 40 and 59 increased from 19% to 23%.[11] Less children were born, in general, both in the rural and the urban areas. Spreading knowledge of birth control methods and aspirations for higher living standards (usually associated with the advance of industrial society) were already reaching various peasant layers in Hungary. This factor influenced not only the average age of the population but also the size of the average family.[12]

By the early 1920's, the extended peasant family largely disappeared. Marriages were contracted generally at a later age.[13] The number of divorces increased, although peasants were still reluctant to file for divorce. While in 1910, only .04% of marriage-age adults were divorced, in 1941, this ratio was 1.1%.[14] Simultaneously, the number of illegitimate births also increased slightly; in 1920, 7.4% of all live births were illegitimate; 1941, the ratio was 8.1%.[15] At the same time, the number of live births declined; in 1924, 28-30 live births were recorded for every 1,000 people; in 1941, only 19.[16] As we shall see later, urban areas generally produced fewer children than rural districts; of the latter, the poorest produced the most.

Among the improvements in living conditions in interwar Hungary one must mention the advances in health care in both the rural and urban districts. Infectious disease became less frequent among the urban population. As a result of the longer life span, however, the cases of illnesses of the heart and the circulatory system increased in number. Cancer was reported for the first time as a major illness. But the rural sphere continued to lag behind the cities and towns in medical improvements. Tuberculosis remained a major killer in the villages. In the Great Plain, 55% of all deaths between the ages of 20-30 years resulted from TB and 37% of all those who died between the ages of 31-45 were lost to this illness.[17] Infant mortality was high in some regions. In the environs of Kecskemet, for instance, 40% of all infants who died before reaching their first birthday died of colic, an easily preventable illness. In 1923, 404 such infants made up 19.8% of all deaths in that area, and improvements were slow in coming in later years.[18]

But the mortality rate continued to decline nationwide. In 1913, the rate was the highest in Europe, 22/1,000 people. In 1918, due to the Spanish influenza epidemic, the rate climbed to 26.2/1,000. By 1924, the rate was appreciably lowered to 20/1,00 in 1941 it was down to 15/1,000.[19] By then, the Hungarian mortality rate was similar to the rate in Austria, Italy and Poland, and it was lower than in Rumania and Yugoslavia. However, it was still higher than that of the West European states.[20]

Between the two World Wars, Hungary remained a society whose population was largely agricultural. In 1920, 55.7% of all people lived from agriculture, 30% worked in industry, 6.2% labored in the service sectors, 5.4% were professionals, and 2.5% were pensioners. Only in 1941 was the size of the agricultural population reduced to 48.7% of the total number of people in the country.[21]

The agrarian population consisted of several economic groupings. In 1910, 24% of all wage earners were landless agrarian workers. During the interwar years their ratio grew to 31% of all wage earners in the country.[22] However, the economic stratification of the peasantry was not as important from the point of view of class differences than that of the rest of society. The peasantry remained, despite differences in wealth, very much a single social stratum. As a historian remarked, "the backwardness of village life, the similarity of living conditions and cultural levels . . . and the exclusion from sophisticated society strengthened common peasant characteristics . . . .[23] Or, as another observer noted:

> the internal stratification of peasant society did not resemble bourgeois social stratification . . . . In fact, all peasants lived the same way; the significance of the possession of landed property was only in that one felt one's fate a bit easier when having it than one who did not. The landless peasant was trying to get land . . . . He hoped that insecurity and the interference of outside powers in his life would be lessened if he had land of his own . . . .[24]

Although political and economic antagonism and simmering class-hatred between rich and poor peasants did exist in some areas of the country, there was also a good measure of cooperation between them. This was based on the fact that life styles were not fundamentally different between rich and poor. The rich peasant worked just as hard, often with his own hands and alongside his hired laborers,as poor ones and his attire was also similar. He ate similar food and obeyed the same village customs as his poorer counterparts. The major difference could be observed between village peasants and others who resided in isolated settlements, the *tanyas* or the *pusztas,* the administrative centers of large estates. Sandor Orban observed that:

> . . . during the interwar years, one characteristic of peasant life was the slowing down of the polarization and the dis-

> integration of the peasantry. This was the result of the lack of dynamism and the rigidity of the social organizational structure.[25]

Orban was certainly right when he implied that this was the direct result of general conditions of Hungarian society; in these decades mobility indeed slowed down, although it did not completely disappear.

About 50,000 peasant families possessed between 35 and 142 acres of land each. Together they controlled about 20% of the arable lands of Hungary. Their majority lived on the Great Plain, where the number of large estates was lower than in other parts of the country.[26] Because of their relatively greater economic security, these peasants were looked up to by their fellow villagers. Their methods of cultivating the soil, their practices in rearing their children, and their attitude towards outsiders (usually inherited from traditional society) set the tone of their village communities. They were also often the leaders of peasant movements against the large estates; in some areas, especially in southern Transdanubia, they influenced demographic patterns by their methods of birth control. These people were the most "progressive" elements in the rural sphere, although their "progressivism" usually exhausted itself after they became small capitalist proprietors. But for every one who bought a tractor and/or threshing machine, there were many others who continued to dress in rags and eat only sparingly. Nor were they truly becoming capitalist in the sense that they would be interested in increasing their production for the purpose of gaining higher profits. What they wanted, most of all, was to be able to buy more land.

By 1941, 630,000 peasant families constituted the stratum of the upwardbound. Of these, 330,000 families possessed between 1.4-7.5 acres of land each (barely enough for survival, but a possible beginning towards an independent existence). 180,000 families controlled 7.5-14.2 acres each, and these were the respected members of their villages. Their number was the highest in Transdanubian communities. 120,000 families owned between 14.2-35 acres each, most of them able to make a decent living and using one or two hired hands on their farms. What united all these people despite their differences in wealth was that they all followed common traditions of peasant behavior, and acted according to expectations.

The most important tradition was the drive to acquire more land, not because peasants inherently loved the land, but because it meant independence and freedom. Owning land meant freedom from the vexations of estate supervisors and the other petty tyrants of the rural sphere. Another tradition was the thorough exploitation of family labor; peasants hired help only if it was absolutely necessary, and then tried to pay as little as possible.

The largest single substratum of the peasantry consisted of the agrarian day laborers. The majority of them lived in six administrative districts in Fejer, Gyor, Komarom, Somogy, an Sopron and Veszprem Counties, where a large number of the mammoth estates were located. In addition, 400,000 families of servants worked, partly on the *pusztas,* that is, administrative centers of the large estates, and partly on the farms of better-off peasants. Their existence depended solely upon the whims of their superivisors but, in exchange, they had a greater degree of security. Their contracts usually extended for the entire calendar year, during which they were dismissed only if they committed a serious offense—and were caught. In turn, they received little cash in compensation, most of their salary was paid in kind and they were, for all practical purposes, modern-day serfs.

The number of seasonal workers (the true agrarian proletariat) living from daily wages was around 560,000 people. In contrast to the servants, they lived from day to day and from hand to mouth. Their very survival depended upon the work offered by large estates or rich peasants. This was a stratum of the peasantry that provided the largest number of physically mobile people. Many agrarian proletarians became "guest workers" in the cities and towns, sweeping the streets in summer, shoveling the snow in wintertime, carrying bricks and mortar for skilled masons, or providing women for the cleaning of the houses of the urban bourgeoisie. These people gradually ceased to be peasants, their habits and behavior no longer resembled those of the villagers. Nor were they, as yet, urban proletarians; too many roots continued to connect them with their villages. They became, in fact, declasse elements, standing somewhere between the peasantry and the industrial workers. But work was not always available for them in the rural sphere or in the towns and cities. In 1935, 150,000 were unemployed and, as noted above, in 1938, still more than 100,000 were without jobs.[28]

The lowest stratum of the agrarian proletariat was, understandably, the most prolific. In Szabolcs-Szatmar Counties, one of the poorest regions in interwar Hungary, the ratio of live births was the highest in the country. In 1922, this ratio was 44/1,000 people. Although this ratio decreased as the interwar years progressed, in 1939, the ratio was still the highest in Hungary with 30/1,000. The lowest birth rate was registered (outside Budapest) in the rich southwestern counties of Baranya and Somogy, and the southern parts of Csongrad County on the Great Plain.[29]

Needless to say, the highest infant mortality rate could also be found in the poorest regions, while the lowest were registered in Gyor, Sopron and Vas Counties.[30] In Szabolcs-Szatmar Counties peasant families with five to seven children were the norm.[31] Health care for the poor was minimal and the schooling of their children was sporadic.

Although the number of illiterates was reduced from 15% of the adult population as a whole in 1920, to 7% by 1941, there remained pockets of illiteracy in many rural districts. For instance, in the outskirts of Kiskunfelegyhaza, out of 17,519 people of adult age 8,875 could not read nor write. In Szabolcs-Szatmar Counties, 73.9% and 71% of the adult population respectively were illiterates. In the village of Balkany on the Great Plain, 99% of the peasants fell in this category. In the *tanyas* in the environs of Nyaracsad (an administrative center) 13.6% of the population were illiterates.[32]

The demographic data of the interwar years, therefore, seem to support the assertion that the modernization of Hungarian society was a sluggish and uneven affair at best. More than half of the peasant population continued to live traditional lives. Yet, on the shoulders of this segment rested the major burden of modernization; it was to be achieved at their expense. No wonder that they were reluctant to accept this role voluntarily.

2. Servants of the Puszta and Other Agrarian Laborers.

Puszta in Hungarian denotes the seemingly endless flatlands of eastern and central Hungary with their deceitful mirages, where the roving eye is not obstructed by forests, hills or mountains. Romantic notions have always been attached to the image of the *puszta;* it was admired by generations of writers and other artists, as well as by modern-day travel agents. But there was another, less romantic, meaning to the *puszta;* in the interwar years it usually denoted the administrative centers of the large estates.

Such a center was a self-contained "little rural community," quite different from ordinary peasant villages. Its focus was the manor house (sometimes a small "castle" at other times only a fancy house, preserved for the occasional visit of the landlord or his immediate family). Some of the great aristocratic families maintained palace-like castles on their estates. For instance, the castle of the Esterhazys at Rede consisted of 32 exquisitely decorated and furnished rooms. These castles were surrounded by high, wrought-iron fences, shutting out the undesirable elements from their grounds (namely, the servants and their children). The *puszta* usually had a one-room school building for the children of the servants which was also used for worship during Sundays.[33]

Outside the enclosure of the castle the largest, most imposing building was usually the barn for the oxen. Next came the house of the chief overseer. The houses of the lesser officials were smaller in size, paralleling their occupants' weight in the hierarchy of supervisors.

There were servants who emerged out of the common herd and became the supervisors of other servants. They worked just as hard but they were entrusted with special tasks for which they received special compensation. This ensured a higher place for them in the social hierarchy of servants. The drivers of horses were higher in standing than were foot servants; the herders of sheep, cattle or swine were also in a higher social position. The hierarchical order at work was carried over into everyday life; the son of a carriage driver seldom wed the daughter of a foot servant. Even if their families occupied the same room, the men did not use the familiar in their conversations and the children were sometimes forbidden to speak to one another.[36]

The servants represented the core of the labor force of the large estates; they took care of everyday chores according to their "specialization." But they all started work at three o'clock every morning from St. George's Day (April 24) to St. Michael's Day (September 29), seven days a week. Their workday lasted until sunset (about 8:00 p.m. in the summer). They usually worked in gangs, the gang leader being responsible for the completion of their assignments. Work in early spring usually began with the draining of excess water from the lands. When the weather permitted, spring ploughing began, followed by planting and other jobs necessary to put the seeds in the soil. Then came corn and potato planting, and this was followed by the hoeing and weeding of the various crops. By the end of June, harvesting began, and it continued well into November, concluding with the picking of grapes and the harvesting of turnip for fodder. This last was one of the most difficult jobs since not only had each turnip to be dug up by hand, but it had to be cleaned in the freezing mud. Very few of these processes were mechanized, and then only on some exceptional estates. "There was no need for machines to do the work" explained Peter Veres, "since the poor worked better than machines."[37]

Day after day, the life of the servants was monotonously the same. On Sundays, the animals had to be fed just as on other days, but then the servants had the afternoon off until 5:00 p.m. when the next feeding cycle began. Most of them used this

The servants constituted a separate substratum of peasant society with their own rules, mores and values. They had a hierarchical order of their own.[34]

Servitude was an ancient institution in Hungary, rooted in the feudal past. The liberation of the serfs in the mid-19th century did not eliminate this type of servitude, partly because it was voluntary, and partly since the former landless serfs found it hard to acquire property for themselves. In the interwar years, servitude continued to exist, stimulated by the need of the large estates for a permanent labor force, and the lack of alternative jobs for the servants.

In general, the servants lived apart from the main buildings of the *puszta* in low-ceilinged buildings that were often unhealthy dwellings. Each "apartment" consisted of a single room. The occupants of two, three or sometimes even four rooms shared a common kitchen. The servant families usually doubled up in each room, but often three, or even four families occupied the same "apartment." Since they were usually prolific, this meant that 14-16, or even 20 people shared a common room. Most of them were of different generations, the majority of them children. Next to the servants' house there stood the chicken coops and the pig pens. Most stalls and barns were better built and maintained than were the servants' quarters; this was a perfect reflection of the priorities of the owners of the large estates.[35]

The youngest servants employed were children between the ages of 8-10 years. They advanced progressively from weeding and picking off bugs from plants to goose herding, and finally to the tending of swine and cattle. They were mostly boys; girls were regarded as less valuable as workers by the estates, and they were usually employed for a pittance at weeding or hoeing in the gardens.

When a boy reached the age of 14, he was gradually entrusted with heavier and more responsible work. At the age of 18, he became a full-fledged servant with a full share of compensation. By then, he was expected to have mastered all the necessary skills for work around the estate, including the handling and cleaning of animals.

"free time" to tend their own gardens which were given them as part of their compensation packages. Only on rainy Sundays did the servants relax and sleep through their "free" time.

The only way such a monotonous, back-breaking work could be endured was by slowing down one's movements. This was recognized by everyone, including the overseers. For instance, in Orbopuszta, in Tolna County, when young oxen were broken into the yoke, they received an extra few days of "training." This consisted of beatings by their future drivers the moment the oxen began to move faster than it was deemed desirable. The animals quickly learned to match their caretakers' walking speed. Slow movements also characterized the servants in every moment of their lives. Unless the overseers kept a close watch on them, they stopped working, lay down and even went to sleep. They had no desire or initiative to work faster than was absolutely necessary. Although outwardly most of them looked strong and healthy, they were usually tired. No one ever saw a fat servant at a *puszta*![38]

The servants were, for all practical purposes, tied to their place of work. Generation after generation they labored, usually for the same family, although not always at the same location, since the landlords freely transferred them from one of their estates to another. This did not really matter; conditions were basically the same wherever they went.

The servants usually showed open, almost fawning respect for any kind of authority. At the same time, since they as individuals amounted to very little, they also developed a very high degree of collective feeling. Stealing from a landlord was almost a necessity for survival and was not regarded as a crime. On the other hand, stealing from each other was considered an unforgiveable sin. They valued personal friendship above all else, and were willing to share their last piece of bread with their friends. At the same time, they turned on each other at the least provocation (when, for instance, one's manhood was challenged) with a suddenness that stunned even themselves.

Although the servants were nominally Christian, they lived by a mixture of superstitions and magic. They believed in the existence of demons and all sorts of evil spirits.[39] The behavior of their overseers did not give them much encouragement to develop religious values. For instance, at Orbopuszta, two race horses were stolen from the stables in the mid-1930's. When the investigation of the local gendarmes proved unsuccessful in finding them, the owner, Count Aurel Desevffy, had a Roman Catholic priest brought to the *puszta* the following Sunday. The overseers announced to all servants that everyone from the age of six up would have to go to confession, regardless of the religious denomination to which he or she belonged! Even the sick were carried out to confession. Despite all this the horses were not recovered, mainly, as the servants said, "since none of the overseers went to confession."[40]

The everyday speech of the servants was plain and vulgar; swearing and cursing flew from their mouths as a normal way of conversation. At the same time, all sorts of religious sects flourished among them. The existence of these sects was a sign of the alienation of the servants from peasant society.

Sex was an often indiscriminate affair among the servants. Since the women were entirely at the call of the supervisors, chastity for the sake of purity had little meaning for them. Premarital sex from an early age was considered normal; adultery was not a serious offense.

Besides crowding in their one-room apartments, brutal treatment by the overseers, and an almost complete control over their lives by their employers, one all-important aspect of the servants' life was their isolation from the rest of the peasantry. This was fostered not only by the distances that often separated the *puszta* from the nearest village, but also by the contempt that the rest of the peasantry felt towards the servants. Illyes observed that the servants "had little consciousness of patriotism or nationalism;" they lived so far from villages and towns that the behavior of non-servants appeared to them as obscure and often hostile. The outside world simply terrified them.[41]

The peculiar nature of compensation that the servants received added to their bondage. Compensation was not uniform, minor variations (magnified by the meagerness of the amounts they all received) existed in the various estates. By and large, however, a common characteristic of all compensation packages was their inadequacy to provide for a decent living. In the early 1940's, the government tried to set minimum standards of compensation for all servants, but the enforcement of the law proved very difficult indeed.[42] But during the 1930's, the compensation package was much lower than mandated by the government. According to the chronicler, the value of an average compensation package was 350-400 *pengos* a year.[43] In the case of a servant family of five (rather small for that time) the share of each member came to 0.25 *pengos* a day. Considering the fact that the estimated minimum standard of living was, during the mid-1930's, 480-600 *pengos* a year per person, such an income was less than 20% of the minimum required for a vegetative existence.[44] In comparison, the yearly salary of the manager of the Eszterhazy estate in the village of Rede in Transdanubia, and estate of about 7,000 acres in size, was 24,000 *pengos*. The salaries of overseers and white-collar employes were as follows:

secretary to the manager	12,000 *pengos*
chief accountant	10,800 *pengos*
accountant	5,400 *pengos*
chief overseer of laborers	12,000 *pengos*
typists	2,400 *pengos*
telephone operators	1,800 *pengos*
craftsmen employed by the estate	300 *pengos*

Migrant workers received 20.0 pengos per month in cash, altogether 160.00 *pengos* for the entire agricultural season.[45]

According to Sandor Kozma, the former manager of this estate, the yearly income of the Eszterhazys from the estate (which included several food processing firms within its confines) came to 2.5 million *pengos* during the 1930's. Operating expenses totalled 2.2 million *pengos*, leaving a net profit for the princely family of 300,000 *pengos* a year.

Characteristically, the children of the Eszterhazy family received a yearly allowance of 12,000 *pengos* until they reached the age of 18.

Matyas Matolcsy estimated the total aggregate income of the servants of the large estates in 1936 as having been 123.1 million *pengos*.[46] This was higher than indicated by Illyes, salary schedule, since in the case of a family of five, each member's share would have come to 0.34 *pengos* per day. In any case, both estimates were well below the minimum living standards. Thus, the servants secured their survival the only way they could, by stealing. But they were not alone; the overseers often showed them the way. Out of the servants' need, there developed the peculiar system of lawlessness that characterized servant life on the *puszta*.

Typically, the schooling that the children received on the *puszta* was minimal. In fact, it seemed that they spent more time working in the garden of their poorly-paid teacher than learning the three R's. In any case, they left school early (around their tenth year), since their families badly needed whatever they could contribute to collective survival. Reading was considered, in any case, a dangerous pastime by the overseers, since books could infect the "simple people" with "Communistic" ideas.[47]

The bottled-up feelings and emotions of the servants often erupted into sudden, swift violence. On such occasions they used everything that came to hand to inflict serious injuries on each other. This was the expression not only of their overwrought emotions, but sometimes of mental illness.[48] The beatings of old people by the young was part of their everyday existence.

The overseers who directed the work of such a group of people had to be just as brutal. An observer recorded the case of one who, in the mid-1930's, stumbled over a child in the early morning darkness as the latter squatted on the ground. The overseer kicked the child who died within a few days of the incident because of the injuries he had received. In another case, an overseer denied the use of a wagon to a servant who was then compelled to carry his dead child in his arms to the funeral in the nearest village several miles away.[49] In fact, the job of an overseer *required* a certain measure of brutality. A humane overseer was judged insane by the servants themselves, and he would have had to be taken advantage of quickly before he came to his senses. Thus, under such an overseer, stealing became so rampant that he soon found himself without a job.

Under such conditions the servants had only two choices: either they remained on the *puszta* trying to make the best of their situation, or fled the countryside altogether, attempting to get a job in a city or town. A few made the latter choice and "succeeded." Jozsef Darvas described the poverty into which the former servants entered in the cities which, for them, still represented the better hope for the future.[50] But most servants stayed on the *puszta*. They knew no other way of making a living, and the outside world seemed confusing and terrifyingly strange for most of them. While working on the *puszta,* they knew exactly how much they were going to receive from the estate as long as they refrained from doing something openly against the rules of their employer. Even in their misery they felt secure. Yet, they knew that when they were to become old, they would be told to leave, and that they would receive no compensation whatsoever in their old age. The pension laws of Hungary did not cover servants, and the old could live or die as far as the estate owners were concerned. But the servants had little thought of self-pity, nor did they consider themselves "poor." "A poor man was one who was sick; or the devil was poor, since he had no soul," was their commonly expressed opinion.[51] Living on the *puszta* generation after generation, forced the servants to adopt an attitude of almost Oriental fatalism.

This picture would not be complete without mentioning the exceptional estates where the servants were treated as human beings. For instance, at the estate of Sebestyen E. Kovacs at Gyapa, not only were the servants paid exceptionally well, but the estate maintained 40 milk cows for them. These provided their families not only with sufficient quantities of milk, but also with 12,00 *pengos* as the price of the calves which they sold. On the estate of the Archduke Joseph of Habsburg at Alcsut, the servants received new quarters in the early 1930's, with separate rooms and individual kitchens for each family, the housing being built with well-insulated walls and wooden floors. Counts Gyula Karolyi and Montenuovo spent considerable sums on housing improvements for their servants, providing healthy, pleasant living conditions for their permanent workers.[52] There were other estates where the landlords paid close attention to the health of their servants and their families. According to an observer, one such estate owner on the Great Plain who possessed 8,400 acres of land, spent, on an average, 55 *pengos* a year for health care for every one of his 291 servants and their families in 1933.[53] Others made a beginning in providing either a small pension or "light work" for aged servants when they were no longer able to perform their regular jobs. Unfortunately, the number of such estates was small.

Besides the regular servants, the estates hired seasonal workers to help in harvesting the crops and perform other jobs. There were two kinds of seasonal workers: migrants (called *summasok*) who moved in gangs often on long distances and sharecroppers hired from neighboring villages. In both cases these workers were landless peasants.

The migrant workers were hired and arrived at the *puszta* in early spring. They were lodged in barns from which the cattle had already been driven to the grazing grounds. They spread straw on the floor for their beds. There were no bathing facilities for them, and often minimal comforts were also absent.[54]

Migrant workers usually came from one village per gang, and they followed their own set of rules. Some gangs had loose morals, others were strict. This depended largely upon their leaders who were not only their spokesmen but also their business managers. Illyes observed that there was a sense of doggedness in them akin to the gold diggers or pioneers, and that they rarely disagreed among themselves. They usually worked under their own leaders. Although finding average salary scales for the migrant workers would be very difficult indeed, their compensation was usually minimal.[55]

Since most migrant workers labored only five to eight months a year, and since they were not less prolific than the other poor of the rural sphere, their income was generally even less adequate than that of the permanent servants. Their compensation came to 130-180 *pengos* a year in cash value. Unless they could supplement this income during the late fall or winter months, their families simply starved.[56] Their situation became particularly desperate during the depression. For instance, in the area of Mezokovesd in Nograd County, 3,630 migrant-worker families—their members totalling almost 13,000—resided. Of these, nearly 6,000 laborers migrated each spring to distant estates, but only 3,122 were hired during the season of 1932-1933 and 2,196 souls were without work for more than a year-and-a-half having no income whatsoever. "What they were living on at that time they themselves did not know," reported an observer.[57] Even in "good years" their food was totally inadequate, consisting mainly of bread and soup. Their children had milk only if the school that they attended provided it for them. They lived in dirty hovels with dirt floors and, at least around Mezokovesd, in caves like prehistoric men.

The sharecroppers also worked in gangs under their own leaders. Their compensation was between 1/10th-1/14th of the harvested crops. Darvas examined the income of some sharecroppers in the mid-1930's and came up with some typical cases.[58] Valeria Korek, economist, found that the average daily wage of an agricultural worker during the early 1930's was as follows:[59]

in 1930, 2.68 *pengos*	in 1931, 2.28 *pengos*
in 1932, 1.72 *pengos*	in 1933, 1.38 *pengos*
in 1934, 1.37 *pengos*	in 1935, 1.22 *pengos*

Considering the fact that the average number of workdays hovered around 120-150 a year, the income of such workers was also well below the minimum standard of living.

About 35% of the servants worked on medium-sized holdings, usually for individual peasant proprietors. The major difference between them and the servants of large estates was that the former did not lose their close, personal relations with their employers, and they also remained largely within the village communities.

If a servant of a medium-landholder worked for a good owner, and he, in turn, was considered a good workman, he returned to his service year after year. This went on until the servant was drafted into the army. After his discharge, he usually began working once again for his former employer. The compensation of these servants was never regulated by law. There were, thus, wide divergences in their compensation packages.[60]

Servants on small farms generally felt less dissatisfaction with their lot than their counterparts on the *puszta*. Their everyday contacts with the owner (who usually worked with them) made these relations less impersonal, more intimate. Most of all, there was always the hope that they could make some money if they lived parsimoniously. They dreamed of eventually becoming their own masters by acquiring some land. Although for most of them this remained simply a dream, the few who did succeed provided incentives for the rest. The personal degradation, the constant reminders of servant status, and the incredibly primitive conditions of life of the servants of the *puszta* was certainly not the lot of these servants. Although many of them starved (mostly because they saved on their food), they were still peasants who could look forward to a possibly better future. What was even more important was that they participated in village life, even if they were not the most respected members of the village community.

Let us not be mistaken, however; the life of a servant, no matter who his employer was, was hard. He worked from early morning until late at night, and he had few amusements and rest periods. His compensation was inadequate for the hard work that he performed. Only by starving himself and his family could he hope to save some money which could be wiped out by the least misfortune.

A special problem was presented on the Great Plain and eastern Hungary by the *tanya* system. These dwellings were different than the individual homes of peasants in Austria or Germany, and were certainly not comparable in their functions to the farms of the United States or Canada. They were not *Einzelhofen* of the West European peasants. What made the *tanyas* unique was that not all of them were permanent settlements. The true *tanyas* were miniature agricultural firms used mainly during the agricultural seasons, providing shelter and easy, immediate access to the land. At the same time, they were an organic part of the economic system that had developed around the large market towns of the Great Plain and eastern Hungary, from which most of their population originated.[61] Living on the *tanyas* during the spring and summer and part of the autumn saved a great deal of time and travel, enabling the peasants to work their lands more effectively.

There are conflicting views about the origins of the *tanya* systems in Hungary.[62] Be it as it may, the final form of this type of settlement emerged only during the second half of the 19th century. By then, many of the great market towns were bursting with population, and some of the people found it more convenient to work their lands by moving closer to them during the agricultural season. The *tanyas* were connected with their respective towns by footpaths and dirt roads. By the beginning of this century, a considerable portion of the population of the market towns lived on *tanyas*.[63]

A good example of the development of this system was that which emerged around the market town of Kecskemet. In the early 1830's, only 12 such dwellings existed. By 1845, there were 177. According to the census of 1910, there existed 7,275 *tanyas* around Kecskemet with an aggregate population of 31,583. Around the city of Szeged a similar development took place. By the early 20th century, there existed 9,274 *tanyas* with a population of about 40,000 in the environs of Szeged. Other cities and towns had similar systems developed around them in these regions.[64]

The true *tanyas*, regardless of the distance separating them from their respective towns, did not isolate their owners from city life. Every weekend they went to attend church and see their relatives in town. Many *tanya* owners had a second house in the city to which they returned during the winter months. They had grain storage bins and barns built next to their houses in town where they transported the harvest and their animals every autumn. They participated in the cultural life of their town, attended weddings, baptisms and funerals, and took part in the town's political life. They usually sent their children to school there, and the children then lived with their grandparents or other relatives.[65] There was, therefore, a constant communication between the people of the true *tanyas* and the urban centers from which they had originated. These people had a chance to rise out of traditional peasant roles and move gradually closer in attitudes, as well as in their living standards, to the urban bourgeoisie. "They are no longer peasants," remarked an observer, "although they are not yet bourgeois. But they are well on their way to a higher level of existence, leading towards the elimination of tensions between town and countryside . . . ."[66]

The social stratification of the peasantry, however, had its reflection in the functions of the various *tanyas*. The dwellings of the rich and poor peasants had different functions, and the relations of their owners to the city often differed. The *tanyas* were usually not the permanent abodes of the rich, who went there only to supervise the work of their hired hands. Their families were left in town; if they were not, only the essential furniture was transported to the *tanya*. On the other hand, many of the poor peasants, together with their families, lived on the *tanyas* for a longer time. Some of them even stayed out for the entire year; yet, they, too, visited the town's market and church, their relatives or parents regularly. Even the poor *tanya*-owners considered their stay only temporary, even if it lasted most of their working life. They worked hard to buy a house in the city where they could move in their old age. Their connections with the urban center was, therefore, never completely broken. As the observer noted, "the difference between poor and rich *tanya* dwellers was that the latter stayed out for the agricultural season, while the former remained for the season of one's working life."[67]

Consequently, the social relations of the owners of the *tanyas* centered on their town, "there are circles of *tanya*-dwellers," remarked Erdei,

> where they have special interest groups and they do act together on a few special occasions. However, all their actions have their true base in the urban areas, they all begin and end there, and they are never completely separated from the urban centers . . . .[68]

These tendencies were reinforced by the fact that there existed few special administrative, cultural or religious centers for the various *tanya* systems. The owners of *tanyas* had their churches, markets, specialty shops, their administrative organs and even their cemeteries in town. They simply did not need these in the country.

While the conditions of life for the *tanya*-owners were, by and large, better than one would expect from a cursory acquaintance with their existence, an entirely different picture emerges from the examination of the life of the permanent *tanya*-dwellers. These were peasants who rented their dwelling from municipal corporations, churches or individual owners who no longer needed to work the land by their own hands. Lawyers, doctors, even artists owned *tanyas* which were considered excellent investments during the interwar years.[69] Other *tanyas* were populated by struggling peasants who were too poor to have any connection with their towns. Finally, there was a large number of hired hands living on the *tanyas* all year round, working for wages, usually paid in kind.

Although these people (except the hired hands, of course) did deliver their produce to their town's market during the agricultural season, they were completely cut off from the urban areas during late autumn, winter and early spring. In these seasons the roads were simply impassable; thus, about 700,000 people were excluded from all contact with the outside world for a good part of each year.

The nature of the road systems connecting these settlements prevented their permanent settlers to market their produce in the wrong season. This meant that they were forced into grain growing since the harvest could be promptly delivered to the markets. However, at such times grain prices tended to be the lowest in any given year, and this had an adverse effect on the lives of these people.[70]

Their problems were multiplied by the lack of grazing grounds and forests. Since they, too, lacked heating fuel, they used dried manure or straw to heat their *tanyas* during the winter months, depriving the land of much needed natural fertilizers. Veterinary services were practically nonexistent in the *tanyas;* consequently, animal husbandry was backward. All this meant low living standards, coupled with primitive conditions of life for the permanent *tanya* dwellers.

Those who had to live on the *tanyas* the whole year round were, therefore, exposed to all sorts of health and other hazards. Health care was practically nonexistent. The sick had to be carted by horse-drawn carriages often 15-20 miles to see a doctor, and sometimes they had to wait long hours for the return of the physician who was out making his calls. Pharmacies were all located in the urban centers.[71] Schools were few and far between. Children had to go to school in deep snow and often heavy wind, to badly-heated rooms, undermanned in teachers. Illiteracy, infectious diseases, alcoholism and other social ills were widespread among the permanent dwellers of the *tanya* systems.[72]

Most administrative institutions were located in the urban centers, just as other institutions of a more civilized existence. Although the permanent *tanya*-dwellers paid their taxes as did other peasants, they received practically no services in return. Mail deliveries, telegrams, money transfers were slow, taking weeks to reach these remote areas. For most people in these regions the administrative organs of rural districts were alien institutions, represented mostly by the occasional visit of the gendarmes. But even the vigilant arm of the law went to the *tanyas* only if a crime or other antisocial action was reported. Since churches were seldom built for the *tanyas*,[73] and since the clergy seldom reached the people of the isolated dwellings, sects of all sorts freely flourished among them, offering the most bizarre practices.[74]

With all these problems, however, the *tanyas* did provide an opportunity for all those living on these isolated settlements to improve their lives. Those who could afford a house in nearby towns were well on their way to a semi-bourgeois existence, not looking upon their *tanyas* as a way of life, but as a means of material advancement. Even some of the permanent settlers or hired hands could look forward to a possibly better future and an eventual dwelling place in the city. It was, as Erdei stated,[75] that

> village life was tied to a particular place, it flowed tightly in controlled channels, always moved in small circles. It did not provide room for entrepreneurship, new starts, free and open relations; neither did it permit individual ruin. Thus, productive work and other functions of life were continuously retarded and everything moved very slowly. In contrast, life had a different character on the *tanyas*. Production was open to individual initiative and experimentation. Outside of production, the thread of life led to the towns where it shaped much more advanced forms than did village life. Life in the *tanyas* was, therefore, partly isolated and partly urban existence. In both cases, it was far more advanced than was village life.

3. The Peasant Family and the Village

Ferenc Erdei once remarked that the smallest unit of peasant society was not the individual peasants, but the family. "There is no peasant outside the family," he wrote.[76] Hungarian peasants were no different in this sense than other peasants.

Here, as elsewhere, the family of the agriculturist was not only the basic unit of economic organization and the division of labor, but also a school for life. The division of labor in the family went along age and sex lines. The output of the family was, first of all, consumed by its members and the surplus, if any, was sold to provide cash for the purchase of non-agrarian goods.[77]

Private property was considered to be the possession of the family. The house in which the family lived, the lands which it owned, were all held in common. The head of each family was the eldest male, usually the father. He made all decisions in matters that affected the family. Its authority was concentrated in his hands. Together with the other heads of families in his village, he was the store of traditions of the community.

The grown-up sons were their fathers' helpers even after marriage. They could expect to share in the family's possessions only after the death of their father, when they could form their own separate families if they so desired. The woman of the house was, in turn, responsible for the actions of the female members of the family, for feeding and clothing everyone. She was also usually the transmitter of the family's spiritual and religious customs.

The traditional peasant family was not only a source of authority, the provider of shelter and security for its members, but also a school and center around which the life of the members revolved. The children learned not only proper "peasant ways" in the family circle, but also the mores by which the village community operated, and the customs and relationships by which they were to live for the rest of their lives. They also learned the traditional peasant methods of tilling the soil.

Peasant families were not characterized by warm closeness between husband and wife on the one hand, and parents and children on the other. Mothers were not friends to their daughters, nor were fathers, in general, apt to forget their authority over their sons. Children were usually required by parents to use formal speech when addressing them, and younger children spoke to their older siblings in the same fashion.[78]

The peasants drove themselves and their families hard; since economic survival depended upon eternal diligence, laziness was not tolerated. Most peasant families were suspicious of contacts with "outsiders." Such suspicions extended over a wide range of experiences. For instance a sick peasant would go to see a doctor only when he was already incapacitated. Otherwise, he would use patent medicines. The most widely used medicine was strong palinka, generally used to "cure" all sorts of illnesses. The peasants strengthened this drink with hot and black pepper. If this did not help, or if it were not available, the next most widely used "medicine" was raw onion. "The sick took a head of raw onion," reported the observer, "scooped out its center, filled the hole up with salt and ate it on an empty stomach."[79] This concoction, of course, purged him like no other "medicine" would.

The consequences were often appalling. Coupled with malnutrition, this produced generations of children who were beset by all sorts of health problems. According to Jozsef Soos, a doctor at the school of Monorpuszta near Oroshaza in eastern Hungary, the following problems were discovered in the examination of 75 schoolchildren:[80]

bad teeth	65.8%	pulmonary illnesses	13.2%
eye problems	10.6%	dermatological problems	4.0%
nervous problems	7.9%	low blood count	6.6%
digestive problems	5.3%	malnutrition	55.3%

healthy—25% of all the children!

Nutrition of peasant children was in no better shape in a different area of the country, at the giant village of Mezokovesd in Nograd County. This village had a population of nearly 20,000 peasants. A school physician reported in 1937 that out of 3,540 meals consumed at home by the children who attended his school, only three (!) ate boiled eggs and only two had scrambled eggs. Only 1.35% of the children had milk regularly and bread constituted 41.2% of all meals. Most other meals consisted of soup. Bacon was consumed only in 5.6% of the meals.[81] The same doctor reported that infant mortality in the area was near 25%, mostly due to malnutrition and infectious diseases, especially tuberculosis.[82]

Yet, the attempts at the modernization of peasant life were regarded by the peasants with suspicion. Not only were innovations and suggestions for change coming from people who lived in the "alien" cities, but the peasants generally perceived modernization as a threat, resulting in the dispersal of their families, the scattering of young peasants in distant towns and cities thus alienating them for their parents and their village. They thought that modern ideas bred contempt in young people for the peasant way of life, providing a break in the continuity of generations. Many peasants looked upon all that was related to change in society with disfavor; this was one major reason why even well-to-do peasants were reluctant to have their children educated beyond a few years of elementary schooling. Although the children of village peasants usually remained in school for longer years than those of servants, and richer peasants were slightly less rigid in this than were poorer ones, they, too, were afraid of losing their children to the "outside world." Partly as the result of general educational policies but also because of such peasant attitudes, only 1.3% of male high school students came from peasant families in the 1930's; out of 13,046 girl students in the high schools of the country, only six were from the villages! In the 40 universities and colleges that operated in interwar Hungary, including 18 seminaries for the training of priests and ministers, which altogether enrolled nearly 70,000 students, only 1.5% of the students had a peasant background.[83]

The peasant family, thus, served its members not only as a shelter in hard times, a school for life, and the center of work, but also as the first line of defense against the "outside world." The village, in turn, provided the second line of defense.

There were 3,322 settlements designated as villages in interwar Hungary with an aggregate population of 5,315,000, or 60% of the total population.[84] Not all people living in these settlements were peasants; nor were all the villages purely agricultural settlements. There were villages where the majority of the population was transitory, such as the resorts of Zebegeny and Szentendre along the Danube River. Only a few people lived permanently in these villages and their seasonal population was made up of vacationing urban dwellers. Many of their original inhabitants became renters or commuted to work in Budapest. There were villages that were populated by miners and other craftsmen who had little to do with agriculture. We are not concerned with these settlements.

A truly peasant village was classified according to several characteristics. First of all, most inhabitants made their living from some form of agriculture. Second, the shape of the village (whether it was round, long or random) signified that the population lived mainly by grain-growing or animal husbandry. Another criterion of classification was the size of the village. According to this, there existed typical, small and giant villages. Another method described villages according to their economic functions. Each of these classifications focused on some functions that the settlements fulfilled in the quest of their inhabitants for economic survival. However, it seems that size may have been the most important factor in determining not only the general characteristics of a peasant village, but also its administrative and social structure.

According to Erdei, the population of typical villages consisted of a majority of independent peasant proprietors; it also included a sizable number of agrarian workers as well as such craftsmen as one or two blacksmiths, a tailor and several masons. Its intelligentsia included the teachers, a physician (if available), a pharmacist, and one or more priests and ministers. The administrative organs consisted of a village judge (*biro*), a local gendarmary station, a village notary, perhaps even a lawyer, several watchmen and a drummer. (The latter served as a substitute for newspapers in providing information for the population about the latest laws or ordinances as well as urgent public tasks). The size of the population in a typical village varied between 2,000-2,500. The physical size of such a village was small enough to enable the peasants to reach their lands comfortably, that is, it was composed within the radius of a circle of about five kilometers or, if the lands lay along a rectangle, each side of the rectangle was usually not longer than 10 kilometers. There existed about 1,225 typical villages in Hungary.[85]

A typical peasant village during the interwar years was a small, closed society. It was administered by its own inhabitants, and economically it was nearly self-sufficient. It needed precious little contact with "outsiders" for its survival. Such villages were the bastions of peasant conservatism and a stable way of life.

In contrast to the typical villages, there were about 1,705 small villages with a total population of about 950,000 peasants. Because of their relatively small size (with less than 1,000 inhabitants), the small villages were unable to provide enough work for full-time craftsmen. They were also too small to have an adequate number of teachers and other intellectuals; they usually shared a physician with other small villages and had no resident merchants to supply them with needed industrial goods. They had no veterinarian services, and often lacked a permanent priest or minister. Although a small village needed more outside contacts than larger ones, it was nevertheless a closed society. As Erdei explained, this was the result partly of geographic conditions (which originally limited the growth of the village into a typical size) and partly of the fact that a smaller population acquired a greater sense of interdependence than the people of larger settlements.[86]

In a few exceptional cases, especially when a small village was located close to an urban center, its peasants visited the town or city in question more and more often, in order to obtain their necessities of life. Thus, they came into increasing contact with urban culture. Many such villages developed into garden centers, their peasants supplying the city with fruits and vegetables. Vecses, Dunakeszi, Solymar, Budakeszi, Nagykovacsi and Hidegkut provided examples of such villages, supplying Budapest with parts of its needs in fruits, vegetables and dairy products, and later with commuting workers. The inhabitants of these and other similar villages near other urban centers were usually quite prosperous; they built their houses on urban patterns and bought their clothes in the city's stores. Here, the old peasant way of life gradually disappeared. Entire systems of such villages developed around urban centers such as Szombathely, Baja, Miskolc and Gyor.[87]

There were also peasant villages of giant size. These included 45 settlements whose population reached more than 10,000 each. Of these, 36 villages contained their own *tanya*-systems; their population simply swarmed into their environs while maintaining their residences in their original villages. However, nine giant villages did not have *tanyas;* these were Mor, Dunafoldvar, Paks, Berettyoujfalu, Sarkad, Nagykata, Nyirbator, Tiszafured and Heves. A tenth giant village was Mezokovesd whose situation was, however, somewhat different from that of the others.

All these giant villages were peasant settlements, located in eastern Hungary. Some of them did not have enough room for the development of a healthy, independent peasant population, since their lands were taken up by large estates. Such was the case with Paks, Dunafoldvar and, above all, Mezokovesd. Much of their population, therefore, became migrant agricultural workers, spending their spring, summer and autumn working on large estates, usually in distant regions. Their craftsmen population was small in size, since the poverty of the inhabitants provided proportionately less work for them. Their administrative systems were, on the other hand, better developed than that of a typical or small village; they needed more gendarmes and other administrative officials to maintain law and order. Curiously enough, some of these giant villages had a well-developed intelligentsia. For instance, in Mezokovesd, there was a gymnasium (the Hungarian high school), a theatre and several movie houses.

Yet the large villages were usually less well-supplied with social services than a typical village. Health care was usually in bad shape, veterinarian services were generally neglected, and the population was, on the whole, less well educated. The large villages were often stagnant pools whose social life did not provide for the closeness of a small village, nor were they as well developed communally as were the typical peasant villages.

The giant village of Mezokovesd represented a special case among peasant settlements. It contained a huge population, most of which had no land. Yet there was no industry to speak of in the vicinity to take up the surplus labor from the village. Those who possessed some land were smallholders; few of them had more than 7.5 acres, and their lands were scattered in small strips. But since the village was located in an area rich in folklore and peasant traditions, it became the center of tourist trade during the 1920's and 1930's. Embroidery became an important industry, yet it could not provide enough work for all the peasants. As a consequence, Mezokovesd remained an important supplier of migrant workers during the entire interwar period. While some of its young people were encouraged by entrepreneurs to parade in colorful costumes at the inns and other public places, most of the others had to earn a living by migrating to distant parts of Hungary. The peasants of Mezokovesd and other giant villages continued to live poverty-stricken, backward lives. But as the 1930's began to draw to a close, some of the giant villages began to feel the effects of modernization at a somewhat faster rate than other peasant settlements. Some of the richer of their communities began to send their children to schools away from home, and they started to look upon land as a commodity whose value depended upon the profits it produced. Many of these peasants no longer worked themselves but hired others. On the other hand many of the poor agrarian workers began to seek out industrial jobs in the neighborhood of their villages, if possible, but commuting to long distances, if necessary.[88]

Slow change, minimal levels of culture and education, the almost complete absence of bold, individual initiative for the improvement of rural life, and little hope for real change in existing conditions; these were the factors that characterized life in most villages in interwar Hungary. As an observer remarked:

> there was a feudal, or even pagan view of the world among the peasants, and a corresponding moral view, thus, a backwardness, centuries behind modern life and work techniques. There was animal-like identification with the home, with work; backward views on health care, apathy, lack of understanding of a new way of life . . . . There was only one matter on which all the peasants agreed; namely, they regarded the whole outside world, the world that surrounded and oppressed them for centuries as hostile, alien, and one that could not be understood.[89]

The old peasant way of life had a stubborn hold in the Hungarian countryside. It supported social rigidity and general backwardness to such an extent that only war or a thoroughgoing social revolution could bring it to an end.

NOTES

1. Viktor Kulcsar, *A valtozo falu* (The Changing Village) (Budapest, 1976), 17. According to the author there is a direct relationship between modernization and urbanization and per capita national product. The line of development, he states, levels off at 1,800-2,000 dollars per capita gross national product and 75-80% of urbanization. Hungarian demographers finally defined urban and rural areas according to their political and economic functions, but such definitions were not yet used in the interwar years. For somewhat different analyses, see Cyril E. Black, *The Dynamics of Modernization* (New York, 1966).

2. In 1880, the population of Budapest was 7.5% of all the population of the Hungarian half of the Habsburg Empire. In 1910, it grew to 13%; in 1930, it was already 16.6%. During the same time span the population of all other cities and towns increased only by 0.3%, from 19.6% to 19.9%. See Gyorgy Acsady and Andras Klinger. *Magyarorszag nepesedese a ket vilaghaboru kozott* (The Population of Hungary Between the Two World Wars) (Budapest, 1965), 14.
3. These include: *Magyar Statisztikai Evkonyv* (Hungarian Statistical Yearbook), 1919-1946, yearly; *Magyar Statisztkai Kozlemenyek. Nepmozgalmi Kotetek* (Hungarian Statistical Reports. Volumes on Demography), 1900-1932, 1910, 1920, 1920, 1930; *Magyar Statisztikai Zsebkonyv* (Hungarian Statistical Handbook) 1931-1935; and articles in *Demografia, Statisztikai Szemle,* to be quoted below.
4. These included the depopulation of the central areas of Hungary during the Turkish wars of the 16th-17th centuries, and the anti-Hungarian policies of the Habsburg rulers of the Habsburg Empire in preventing the return of Hungarians to their ancestral lands after the explusion of the Turks.
5. Kulcsar, *op. cit.,* 11-12. Only after 1945 was there a determined effort to correct the confusion attached to this problem. After that, as Kulcsar stated, the designation "city" connoted a settlement not only with a large number of inhabitants, but also a certain level of industrialization, of administrative functions that extended beyond the immediate border of the city line, better developed community activities, health care and cultural institutions. A rural settlement, on the other hand, was characterized by the opposite elements. *Ibid.,* 13. However, during the interwar years, the separation between village and city was unclear. For instance, in Bekes County alone there were four villages with over 4,000 inhabitants each, three with over 5,000 three with 6,000 one each with 10,000, 11,000 and 12,000 respectively, two with 13,000 each, one

with 24,000 and one with more than 24,000 inhabitants! There was also a so-called village whose inhabitants numbered 28,000 people! See Karoly Kaan, *op. cit.*, 175.

6. The forthcoming volume by Julia Puskas on emigration will discuss this issue at length. According to my discussions with the author, she stated that the number of ethnic Hungarians to emigrate to North America was around 500,000. See also, Peter Hanak, "Skizzen Uber die Ungarische Gesellschaft am Anfang des 20. Jahrhunderts," *Acta Historica* 10 (1963) 1-41.
7. Lajos Thirring, "Magyarorszag nepessege 1869-1949 kozott" (The Population of Hungary between 1869-1949) in Jozsef Kovacsics, ed., *Magyarorszag torteneti demografiaja. Magyarorszag nepessege a Honfoglalastol 1949-ig* (Historical Demography of Hungary. The Population of Hungary from the Time of the Conquest to 1949) (Budapest, 1963), 272.
8. Wartime losses included 250,000 young men in 1914-1919. This meant the estimated loss of 400,000 people including the unborn children of the dead. The losses of the Second World War came close to 600,000 people, including civilians and those who left Hungary in 1944 never to return. See Laszlo Buday, "Magyarorszag haborus nepvesztesege" (Hungary's Population Losses in the War) *KGSZ,* 63 (1920) 217. See also, Thirring, *op. cit.*, 236 and 241.
9. Average population density in villages without large estates in their vicinity was close to 79.6 people per square kilometer; in others, with large estates close by, it was only 46.2. See Miklos Moricz, "Nagybirtok, nepszaporodas, nepsuruseg," (Large Estates, Population Increase and Population Density), *MSSZ* (1936) 293-4. See also Thirring, *op. cit.*, 273-3, and note 196 on page 367, and M. Matlcsy, *op. cit.*, 82. The growth of urbanization is illustrated by the following numbers:

Year	Population of Hungary	Population of Budapest	Population of Other Cities Together	Cities total
		In thousands		
1869	5,001	302.1	991.2	1,293.3
1900	6,854	861.4	1,414.6	2,276.0
1920	7,978	1,232.0	1,701.0	2,933.0
1941	9,316	1,712.8	1,987.4	3,700.2

Kulcsar, *op. cit.*, 16.

10. Before 1914, average life expectancy was 40 years in Hungary. In 1930 it increased to 50 years, and by 1941, it was 57 years. Ranki, (ed.) *Magyarorszag, op. cit.*, 768. However, many villages did not share in these improvements. For instance, in the village of Rede in Transdanubia, a village surrounded by the estates of the Princes Eszterhazy, average life expectancy in the 1930's was only 17 years! See Ferenc Poloskei and Ferenc Takacs, *Dunantuli tortenetek* (Stories of Transdanubia), (Budapest, 1976), 14.
11. Acsady-Klinger, *op. cit.*, 11.
12. In 1869, an average household consisted of 4.8 people; in 1930, this was reduced to 3.9. Family size was simultaneously reduced from 4.0 to 3.4 people. Thirring, *op. cit.*, 295.
13. For the extended family see Judit Morvay, "The Joint Family in Hungary," *Europa et Hungaria. Congressus Ethnographicus in Hungaria* (Budapest, 1965), 231-41. See also, Edit Fel, "Nagycsalad es jogszokasai a komarom-megyei Martoson" (The Extended Family and its Legal Customs in Martos, Komarom County), *Kisalfoldi Kozlemenyek,* Series I, No. 2 (1944), 104-18; Berend-Szuhay, *op. cit.*, 333-4.
14. Andras Klinger, "A valas" (The Divorce) (Budapest, 1957). See also, Tivadar Szel, "Az elvalasok ujabb alakulasa" (Latest Trends of Divorces), *MSSZ* (1934), 756-76.
15. Tivadar Szel, "A torvenytelen szuletesek" (Illegitimate Births), *Ibid.* (1941), 71-93. See also, Acsady-Klinger, *op. cit.*, 29.

16. Acsady-Klinger, *op. cit.*, 34.
17. Mihaly Csikos, "A tbc halalozasok alakulasa Magyarorszagon a szazadfordulotol napjainkig" (changes in Mortality in Hungary due to TB from the Turn of the Century until Today), *MSSZ* (1945), 828-33.
18. Gesztelyi-Nagy, "Az Alfold," *op. cit.*, 482-3. See also, Karoly Goldziher, "A csecsemohalandosag ujabb alakulasa" (Latest Developments in Infant Mortality Rates) *MSSZ* (1937), 1035-9.
19. Acsady-Klinger, *op. cit.*, 37.
20. Gyula Barsi-Emil Pallos, "A magyar halandosag a szazadfordulo ota. Az 1935. evi halandosagi tabla" (Hungarian Mortality Rates Since the Turn of the Century. Table of Mortality Rates in 1935) *Demografia* (Budapest, 1958), 239-73. See also, Dudley Kirk, *Europe's Population in the Interwar Years* (Princeton 1946).
21. Thirring, *op. cit.*, 320.
22. Acsady-Klinger, *op. cit.*, 13.
23. Ranki et al, eds., *Magyarorszag, op. cit.*, 791.
24. Ferenc Erdei, *Parasztok* (Peasants) (Budapest, 1973), 2nd ed., 23.
25. *in Ket agrarforradalom Magyarorszagon. Demokratikus es szocialista atalakulas, 1945-1961* (Two Agrarian Revolutions in Hungary, Democratic and Socialist Transformation, 1945-1961) (Budapest, 1972), 16. It is also worth noting that the rule was valid from the point of view of the poor as well. See Szabo, *Cifra, op. cit.*, 607.
26. Ranki, et al, eds, *Magyarorszag, op. cit.*, 789.
27. See the dramatic and often exaggerated reports of Jozsef Darvas, *A legnagyobb magyar falu* (The Largest Hungarian Village) (Budapest, 1937), 16.
28. Ranki, et al., eds., *Magyarorszag, op. cit.*, 793.
29. Acsady-klinger, *op. cit.*, 35. The average birth rate in Hungary in 1941 was 19/1000. Csongrad County was not rich; however, its southern districts were better off than the rest of the county.
30. *Ibid.*, 52.

31. Peter Veres, *Falusi kronika* (Chronicle of a Village) (Budapest, 1941), 165-6.
32. Gesztelyi-Nagy, "Az Alfold," op. cit., 489. According to his research conducted in 1925, there were the following percentages of illiterates in the Great Plain:

35% at Kiskunfelegyhaza	15.3% at Szolnok
14.5% at Szeged	16.3% at Szentas
13.6% at Debrecen	24.3% at Jaszbereny
22.8% at Kecskemet	18.3% at Hajduboszormeny
15.1% at Hodmezovasarhely	20.1% at Nagykoros
13.6% at Mako	14.9% at Bekes
14.0% at Cegled	15.7% at Mezotur
21.2% at Torokszentmiklos	24.6% at Kiskunhalas

33. Gyula Illyes, *Pusztak Nepe* (People of the Pusztas) (Budapest, 1936), 8.
34. Poloskei-Takacs, *op. cit.*, 19.
35. Laws regulating the housing of servants and other agrarian workers were enacted in 1901, 1907, 1936 and 1938. The law of 1907:XLVI provided government support for owners who wanted to build new workers' housing in order to stop congestion. See Janos Szeibert, "A mezogazdasagi s cseledlakasepites kozuleti tamogatasa" (Public Support of the Building of Servants' and Workers' Housing in Agriculture), *KGSZ,* 82 (1939), 49-50. As to the enforcement of these laws, nothing was done. According to Lajos Leopold, an economist who was certainly partial in favor of the large estates, 45-55% of all workers' housing was unhealthy and outright unlawful. *KGSZ,* 77 (1934), 467. Andras Heller reported that the law went universally unobserved in regard to its prohibition of housing more than one family in one room. According to his private survey in Fejer County in Transdanubia in 1935, in only 22.5% of all servants' houses was this law obeyed. In 77.5% of the cases he examined, between 5-15 people were living in one room that also served as a kitchen. Only in

7.7% of the cases did children sleep one to a bed; *Cseledsors. A mezogazdasagi cseledek helyzete 1935-ben* (The Fate of Servants. The Conditions of Agrarian Servants in 1935) (Budapest, 1937), 74.

36. Gyula Illyes described his experienced as a child when the mason of the estate where he grew up forbade his daughter even to speak to children of regular servants, because he was in a "higher" social bracket. And they all lived in the same room! Illyes, *op. cit.,* 16.
37. Veres, *Falusi, op. cit.,* 146.
38. See Ferenc Kunszabo, *Sarkoz. Magyarorszag felfedezese.* (The Discovery of Hungary) (Budapest, 1972), 209.
39. Illyes described this curious mixture when, as a child, he watched his aunt calling for help from St. Joseph while dropping pieces of live coal into a can full of water to see if they settled down in the bottom. If they did—as it invariably happened—then someone put the evil eye on one of her grandchildren who was ill, or cursed the cow that stopped giving milk. Illyes, *op. cit.,* 56.
40. Kunszabo, *op. cit.,* 214.
41. Illyes, this genuine fount of peasant life, described his first visit to a village as a child, where the "multitudes of people" conjured for him the vision of a beehive, with clusters of strange-looking houses and streets whose purpose he simply could not fathom. Illyes, *op. cit.,* 33.
42. According to the decree 168,600 of the Minister of Agriculture issued in 1940, the following minimum standards had to be observed by employers of servants in Hungary in a one-year package:

cash payments	60 *pengos*
grain, of which 3,080 had to be bread grains	3,520 lbs.
a parcel of garden	1,440 square yards
ploughed ploughlands	2,844 square yards
maintenance of one cow or	1 liter milk/day
for every child over three years of age	½ liter milk/day

maintenance of one/two sows
  and her brood.................. 7 swines
poultry .... 6 hens, 1 rooster
firewood .... 3 cords
salt .... 53.3 lbs./year
free housing ....

According to an economist who had a strong bias in favor of large estates, the cash value of this compensation package in 1941 was as follows:

cash .... 60 *pengos*
wheat, 1,760 lbs .... 176 *pengos*
rye, 1,320 lbs. .... 115 *pengos*
barley, 440 lbs. .... 40 *pengos*
rental value of ploughland, 2,844 square
  yards 88*pengos*
(including fertilization, transport, etc.)
garden land rental value, 1,440
square yards ______________________ *15 pengos*
taxes for above .... 12 *pengos*
hay for one cow, green feed, straw ...... 42 *pengos*
cowherd's salary, one share .... 20 *pengos*
maintenance of 7 swine .... 62 *pengos*
swineherd's salary, one share .... 20 *pengos*
maintenance of 7 fowl .... 5 *pengos* (est.)
3 cords of firewood .... 72 *pengos*
housing costs .... 80 *pengos*

Aside from the inflated housing value and the over-estimation of such items as the share of a cowherd's and swineherd's salaries, the total cash value of this package would come to 780 *pengos* a year. The daily share of one person in a family of five would, therefore, be 0.42 *pengos,* less than the price of one kilogram bread in the early 1940's. In contrast, the yearly average income of industrial workers during the same time period was 1,080 *pengos.* Given the fact that the families of such workers tended to be much smaller, this was more than one-third higher than the income of the servants. Although even this income was very low, it certainly provided for a better living than the servant's salary. See Erno Eber, "Mezogazdasagi cseledber-mezogazdasagi cseledkereset," (Wages of Agricultural Servants—Income of Agricultural Servants) *KGSZ*, 84 (1939), 45. See also, Matyas Matolcsy, *Magyarorszag nemzeti jovedelme, 1934-1935* (National Income of Hungary, 1934-1935) (Budapest 1936), 76.

43. Illyes, *op. cit.*, 154-6; he estimated the salary of a servant as follows:

cash payment	12-40 *pengos*
wheat, rye, barley	3,520 lbs.
firewood	2½-3 cords
garden land	600 square yards
ploughed ploughland	3,200 square yards
maintenance of	1-2 sows and brood
poultry	30-35 hens
milk	½ liter/day/family
bacon	44 lbs.
salt	24 lbs.

44. Minimum living standards were based on the "market basket" provisions of the ILO issued in 1933, providing for the minimum amount of food necessary for an adult to survive for a week. On that basis, Matolcsy figured that the living standard of an average Hungarian agricultural worker was less than one-third of his English or German counterpart. (Matolcsy, *op. cit.*, 32). See also, Imre Kovacs, "Az uradlmi cseledek es mezogazdasagi munkasok foglalkozasi, kereseti es megelhetesi viszonyai az Alfoldon," (Conditions of Work, Income and Living of Servants of Large Estates and Agricultural Workers in the Great Plain), *Valasz* (Budapest) 1 (1935), 66-7.

45. Poloskei-Takacs, *op. cit.*, 16.

46. Matyas Matolcsy, "Jovedelemelosztas Magyarorszagon," (Income Distribution in Hungary) *KGSZ* 79 (1936), 9. This

estimate included housing costs, not figured in Illyes, report.

47. Illyes, *op. cit.*, 202.
48. See Kunszabo, *op. cit.*, 211.
49. *Ibid.*, 213. See also, *Parasztsors, op. cit.*, 94, 95.
50. Jozsef Darvas, *Orszaguton, varoson* (On the Highway and in the City). (Budapest, 1960), 180-201, 2nd ed.
51. Lajos Kiss, *A szegeny emberek elete* (Life of the Poor People) (Budapest, 1955), 23. See also the petition of servants Ferenc Nadrai and Jozsef Horvath, who had worked for 43 and 52 years respectively for the same estate in Tapsony, owned by the Capitulum of Esztergom, unceremoniously kicked out by the priests in 1923 when they were no longer able to perform their jobs, in *Parasztsors, op. cit.*, 96-97. Another complaint was registered by a former servant, Jozsef Asboth, who had served for 40 years on the estate owned by Oliver Rupprecht in Sajtoskal, *Ibid.*, 101. But most complaints were not registered, since the old peasants expected no help from the authorities.
52. Lajos Leopold, "Munkaber es nagybirtok" (Wages and Large Estates), *KGSZ*, 77 (1934), 466-7.
53. *Ibid.*, 471.
54. Although the decree of the Minister of Public Welfare stipulated in 1930 that migrant workers must be housed in airy, dry, well-ventilated buildings, and men and women were to live separately, this was largely ignored. So were the provisions that stipulated that each group would have to be provided with rooms for personal hygiene. Leopold, *op. cit.*, 469, and Poloskei-Takacs, *op. cit.*, 28.
55. Illyes, *op. city.*, 236; this package was, naturally, different from that of an average servant:

cash	7-10 *pengos*/month
wheat	264 lbs.
bread flour	44 lbs.
cooking flour	22 lbs.
bacon	7½ lbs.
lard	0.45 lbs.

beans	6½ lbs.
potatoes	25 lbs.
salt	2 lbs.
salted or fresh meat	7½ lbs.
vinegar	1 liter
condiments	0.30 *pengos* worth

56. See the complaint of migrant workers of Hencse, addressed to the Minister of Agriculture, describing their lives and their meager incomes in *Parasztsors, op. cit.,* 55-6. A similar complaint was registered by the people of Erzsebet-major in Gyor County. *Ibid.,* 94-5.
57. Zoltan Szabo, *Cifra nyomorusag. A Cserhat, Matra, Bukk foldje es nepe* (Vanity and Misery. The Land and People of the Cserhat, Matra and Bukk), 106.
58. These cases included: 1. Ferenc Benko, 37 years old with a wife and two children. From January to April 24, he made 32 *pengos* from daily wages by doing odd jobs. From April 24 to harvesttime, he was unemployed. His share of the harvest was 906.4 lbs. of wheat, 303 lbs. of barley. In September, he worked at the local brick works and received 78 *pengos* in cash. In October-November, he made 78.80 *pengos* by doing odd jobs. He worked 216 days in 1935, and his total income came to 275 *pengos,* or 0.75 *pengos* a day for each one of his family members. From this he had to pay for his housing as well as for all necessities of life. 2. Mihaly Horvath was another of Darvas' samples. He was 40 years old, with a wife and three children. He worked 100 days doing odd jobs. At the harvest his share came to 781 lbs. of wheat and 242 lbs. of barley. His wife sewed clothes for clients and made 70 *pengos* for the year. His eleven year-old son served as a swineherd and received 20 *pengos.* The total daily income of this family also came to 0.75 *pengos* for 1935. Jozsef Darvas, *A legnagyobb magyar falu* (The Largest Hungarian Village) (Budapest, 1937), 61, 62.

59. Valeria Korek, "A magyar mezogazdasag jovedelmezosege," (Profitability of Hungarian Agriculture) *KGSZ* 80 (1937), 643.
60. For instance, one servant whose son served with him as an assistant swineherd, received for both of them the following yearly compensation:

cash	150 *pengos*
wheat	6,600 lbs.
harvested corn	from 2 acres of land
maintenance of	1 cow
poultry	unlimited number
eggs	as many as needed
boots	2 pairs

Another servant working in the same village for a different owner received the following compensation:

wheat	1,100 lbs.
bacon	84 lbs.
porridge	22 lbs.
beans	12½ lbs.
salt	25½ lbs.

2 petticoats and 2 scarves for his wife.

One more illustration of the wide disparity between compensation packages was given by Darvas. "His" servant received in 1935 the following:

cash	10-20 *pengos*
wheat and rye	1,980-2,200 lbs.
one complete suit	
one pair of boots	
straw	1-2 wagon loads
One small swine (6 weeks old)	
free room and board	

Kiss, *op. cit.*, 80, and Darvas, *op. cit.* 48.
61. Ferenc Erdei, *Magyar Tanyak* (Hungarian tanyas) 2nd. ed. (Budapest, 1976), 12. See also, Istvan Gyorffy, "A magyar tanya," (The Hungarian tanya) *Foldrajzi Kozlemenyek* (Budapest) 14 (1937) Nos. 4-5; Kalman Szabo,

Kecskemeti tanyak (The Tanyas of Kecskemet) (Kecs kemet, 1926); Jeno Czettler, "A tanyai kerdes" (The Problem of Tanyas) *Magyar Gazdak Szemleje* (Budapest) 1 (1921), 7-8.

62. Istvan Szabo, "A debreceni tanyarendszer kialakulasa" (The Evolution of the Tanya-system of Debrecen) *Fold es Ember 8* (1929), 38-41. See also, Marta Belenyesy, *Adatok a tanyakialakulas kerdesehez* (Data for the Evolution of Tanyas) (Budapest, 1948).
63. Between 1.2-1.5 million people or 14-19% of the entire population of Hungary. See Berend, Szuhay, *op. cit.*, 72, and Laszlo Gesztely-Nagy, *A magyar tanyakerdes* (The Problem of Hungarian Tanyas) (Kecskemet, 1927) 1.
64. Karoly Kaan. *A magyar alfold. Gazdasagpolitikai tanulmany* (The Hungarian Great Plain. A Study in Economic Politic) (Budapest, 1927), 171. According to Gesztelyi-Nagy, 52.3% of the population of Kiskunfelegyhaza, and 41.1% of Mako lived on *tanyas. Op. cit.*, 1. For the *tanya* population of other towns and cities in eastern Hungary and the Great Plain see *MSSZ*, 1 (1921), 308-11.
65. See Erdei, *Magyar tanyak, op. cit.*, 20-21.
66. *Ibid.*, 244-5.
67. *Ibid.*, 21.
68. *Ibid.*, 124.
69. Interestingly enough, while the owners of rented *tanyas* lived usually in urban areas and their life-style resembled that of the bourgeoisie, the rent agreements that they concluded with their renters were in the form of the old feudal relations. For instance, a typical rental arrangement in 1921 was the following: A *tanya* of 28.4 acres of land was rented out for 660 lbs. of rye and barley, 1 fattened hog of 330 lbs., 400 eggs. It also included support for one old woman, 880 lbs. of wheat, 400 lbs. of potatoes, 110 lbs. of shelled corn, 12,000 paper crowns (inflationary), 15 pairs of chickens, 7 ducks and 6 turkeys, 50 cartloads of sand or other building material as desired, 90% of all taxes 5,000 paper crowns for fees for signing the agreement and

support for the owner and his horses when visiting his *tanya*. Another agreement included the following: for a *tanya* with 179 acres of land, the renter paid 440 lbs. of wheat, one fattened hog, 100 chickens, 20 geese, 20 ducks and 20 turkeys, 600 eggs, 66 lbs. of cheese, 61 lbs. of cottage cheese, 30 liters of sour cream, 2 cartloads of straw, one load of hay and one load of clay, the maintenance of the buildings, the cost of insurance and all fees for signing the contract. Lajos Domotor, "Kecskemeti tanya telepulesek es Kecskemet varos foldbirtokpolitikaja" (*Tanya* Settlements of Kecskemet and the City's Agrarian Policies) *Magyar Gazdak Szemleje* 1 (1921) 436 and 456. See also, Gyula Sinko, Nyiregyhaza es tanyainak telepulese (Nyiregyhaza and the Settlement of its *Tanyas*) (Budapest, 1909.)

70. Laszlo Aczel, "A tanyai kozlekedes problemaja" (The Problem of Transportation on the *Tanyas*) *Neptanitok Lapja* 6 (1926), Nos. 7-8, 41-4.
71. Gesztelyi-Nagy, *op. cit.*, 15.
72. *Ibid.* See also, Jozsef Hubner, "A tanya kulturajaert"(For the Culture of the *Tanya*) *Neptanitok Lapja* 5 (1925), Nos. 17-18, 210-17; Laszlo Csikesz, "A tanya egeszsegugye" (The Health Issue on the *Tanyas*) *Magyar Rona* (1926), No. No. 1, 10-12.
73. Gesztelyi-Nagy, *op. cit.*, 29. In the huge hinterlands of Kecskemet, for instance, there were only five church buildings serving over 30,000 Roman Catholic and Calvinist believers. For the taxes paid by the *tanya* dwellers, see *Ibid.*, 112-116. See also, Lajos Szuts, "A tanya-vilag kozigazgatasa (Administration of the *Tanya-*World) *Kozsegi Kozlony* June 10 (1926), 92.
74. An excellent description of the causes of the emergence of the sects and their *modus operandi* can be found in Imre Kovacs, *A nema forradalom* (Silent Revolution) (Budapest, 1941), 18, 19 and 217-27.
75. Erdei, *Magyar tanyak, op. cit., 244-5.*
76. *Erdei, Parasztok, op. cit.,* 25.

77. See George Rosen, *Peasant Society in a Changing Society. Comparative Developments in Southeast Asia and India* (Urbana-Chicago-London, 1975), 6.
78. Darvas, *A lagnagyobb, op. cit.*, 73.
79. Veres, *Falusi, op. cit.*, 122.
80. Darvas, *A legnagyobb, op. cit.*, 76.
81. Szabo, *Cifra, op. cit.*, 69, 70.
82. *Ibid.*, 71-2.
83. Ferenc Voldes, *A munkassag es a parasztsag kulturalis helyzete Magyarorszagon* (Cultural Conditions of the Workers and Peasants in Hungary) (Budapest, 1941), 13. See also, Artur Benisch, "elemi nepoktatasunk kulturpoliticai problemai" (Culture-political Problems of Our Elementary People's Education), *KGSZ*, 78 (1935), 78-88.
84. Ferenc Erdei, *A magyar falu* (The Hungarian Village) (Budapest, 1976), 2nd ed., 132. See also, Istvan Gyorffy, *Magyar falu, magyar haz* (Hungarian Village, Hungarian House) (Budapest, 1943), 97-109.
85. Erdei, *A magyar falu, op. cit.*
86. *Ibid.*, 95-6.
87. *Ibid.*, 97.
88. Szabo, *Cifra, op. cit.*, 72. Also, Erdei, *op. cit.*, 99-106.
89. Kunszabo, *op. cit.*, 223.

III.

MODERNIZATION OF AGRICULTURE: A MISSED OPPORTUNITY

1. Introduction

No social organism can escape the influence of that intangible factor, the atmosphere, which seems so dominant in a particular age. In turn, the atmosphere undoubtedly influences events that determine the fate of the respective society. It was not different in Hungary after World War I; society was deeply influenced by the dies that accompanied the rebuilding of the nation, the recreation of the shattered economic, social and political systems. Thus, the atmosphere was pessimistic. "Each and every social stratum had its particular reasons for pessimism," remarked an acute observer:

> The high lords who were accustomed to look to Vienna for guidance now preferred to retire into their castles and watch the efforts of the *homo novus* with bemused condescension . . . . the capitalist urban middle class worried about spreading anti-Liberalism and anti-Semitism . . . . The industrial proletariat fell to the greatest depth, after the Communist dictatorship proclaimed it the ruling class of the nation . . . . All these grudges were amalgamated into a general pessimism created by /the peace treaty of/ Trianon. Hungarians became the bitterest people of Europe. . . .[1]

It was obvious to the best minds of the country (if not to all the political leaders), especially during the early 1930's, that economic, social and political reforms were essential if the atmosphere of general pessimism was to change. But there was no agreement on just how to bring the necessary reforms about or even on what sort of changes were absolutely necessary. However, it seemed to many a would-be reformer as self-evident that, since misery affected the greatest number of people in the countryside, reform (above all the redistribution of land) ought to begin in the rural sphere.

There were three issues in this debate. The first of these was the question of leadership in the pending reforms of rural society, especially in the modernization of agricultural production. The other disputes explored the projected costs and potential contributors to rural transformation, and the model to be followed by the Hungarians.

2. Who Was To Lead?

It will be recalled that during the interwar decades large estates controlled about one-third of the arable lands of Hungary, and that their owners had a disproportionately large influence over governmental affairs. One would expect that leadership for agricultural modernization would have come from the owners of these estates. But the major concern of most owners of large estates was to fend off any efforts for a more equitable distribution of land in society.

The controversial argument that the large estates were, on the whole, more productive acre for acre than were small landholds and, therefore, their continued existence was in the national interest, was rejected by some economists. Average yields of crops were indeed higher on large estates than on small plots. Furthermore, some large estates did pioneer a slow mechanization process in agriculture. But the higher productivity of large estates was achieved through extensive cultivation of grain crops (for which but a limited number of machines was available). It was also the result of extraneous factors.

In general, the mechanization of production was not a primary concern of the large estates; in 1938, only 19% of their crops were cultivated by machines, the rest were produced by manual labor. Furthermore, higher average yields of grain did not necessarily mean higher incomes for the owners. The competition of Canadian, U. S. and Soviet Russian grains lowered the prices of these commodities on the world markets to such an extent that the Hungarians were no longer competitive. Higher income was achieved by a large estate through a combination of factors, including bank loans, state subsidies—and lower wages paid to agrarian workers.[2] If the modernization of agriculture included improvements in the living conditions of the peasantry, then most large estates were actually impeding the process of modernization. Under such circumstances leadership for rural reforms—both social and agricultural—could not come from owners of large estates. Even if a few individuals among them would have been willing to assume such a role their efforts would not have been supported by the majority of large landowners.

The relations between the peasantry and the large estates were ambivalent. Most frequently, peasants and owners hardly knew each other. The owners were usually absent from their estates for the larger part of the year, except if their "castle" happened to be located at a particular estate. They usually conducted their business through hired officials who then bore the brunt of unpopular decisions.[3] But most such owners sensed that they were fighting a rear-guard battle against the break-up of their properties. For many of them, the champions of rural reform were "dangerous Communist agitators" who were out ot incite the peasantry against private property rights.[4] In sum, the owners of large estates were unwilling to lead the process of rural reform in Hungary.

There was an equally small chance that owners of medium-sized estates (each owning between 750-1,420 acres) would assume leadership in agricultural modernization. In spite of the fact that many of these owners regarded themselves as "progressive" in that they readily and haphazardly experimented with new methods and products, they were not really conscious modernizers, the pioneers of production for profit. A typical example of such an estate owner was the Gaal-

Kropf family, possessing large properties at Pusztamiske in Veszprem County in Transdanubia.[5] When analyzing the reasons for maintaining the estate which was working at a deficit, the son of the last owner provided the following explanation:

> First of all, family traditions demandeed the maintenance of the estate however unprofitable. . . . Secondly, there was a feeling of security in knowing that the family possessed a place where the old folks could retire and spend their old age in comfort. Thirdly, owning the estate meant belonging to a higher social class . . . . Fourthly, the owner had to deal with landowners in his regular job (he was the director of the *Tattersaal,* the state's racing center in Budapest, J. H.) and it was appreciated that he was one of them. Finally, the estate provided a place for the entire family and its friends to spend long, carefree summer vacations there . . . .[6]

None of these reasons speak about profit-making or about attempts to produce goods more efficiently. If anything, they reflect the desire of the typical medium-landowner of Hungary to live the life of leisure so much appreciated by the aristocrats, even if only for part of the year.

The possibility of self-help through village-peasant leadership was equally remote. If the paradigm of George M. Foster concerning peasant cognition as representing the "Image of Limited Good"[7] was valid for the Hungarian peasants,[8] then no individual peasant in a village could assume leadership in agrarian modernization without arousing the suspicions—and opposition—of his fellow peasants. It was true that in the Hungarian peasant communities "one worked in order to eat, not to create wealth"[9] (as Foster maintained for the South American agriculturists) and reform would necessarily mean the opening of opportunities for individual initiative. In the Hungarian situation, this could have happened only if the peasantry as a whole could be convinced *from the outside* that individual gain or the advancement of individual families were not depriving the community of the "Limited Good" which had hitherto obtained.[10]

In addition, conditions for agrarian modernization were not uniform throughout Hungary. In the wheat-growing regions of the Great Plain, the peasants could have changed from extensive to intensive methods of production only through substantial governmental help. The primary handicap in this case was—and not only on the Great Plain—the existing system of large estates. These estates exerted an oppressive influence that could have been removed only through land reform. For instance, in the large east Hungarian village of Balmazujvaros, whose inhabitants numbered close to 15,000 people, only 3,500 acres were available for individual peasant cultivators, while 63,000 acres were possessed by large estates. Aggravating this situation was the lack of a paved road system, storage facilities for perishable goods, and marketing services.[11] In the lands of Transdanubia where the road system was better developed, the peasants were similarly prevented from changing over to intensive methods of production. In general, as Peter Veres aptly remarked, "there was no market, capital and knowledge for intensive agriculture in Hungary."[12]

Most peasant communities included rich and poor peasants; yet, the rich were careful to dress, eat and behave the same way as the poor, in order to preserve their place in the village community. Jozsef Darvas described several rich peasants in the village of Oroshaza who lived almost like beggars.[13] The children of the village rich remained mostly peasants. Whether they sent their sons and daughters to live on *tanyas* (as was the case in many Bekes and Csongrad County villages[14]) or kept them at home to work under their own supervision, these children were intended to live according to peasant traditions.

In general, the greatest ambition of these peasants—as that of all peasants in interwar Hungary—was to acquire more land. But "they wanted land not because they loved it, but because it meant a certain freedom of control by others."[15] It was, as John Duncan Powell found in other peasant communities, that "the basic pattern of social relations were, in general, anxiety-reduction behaviors, by which the peasants attempted to build some security in the face of the perceived environmental threat, or at least to make life more tolerable within a basically threatening context."[16]

Regardless of wealth, most Hungarian peasants remained suspicious of changes proposed by "outsiders." Many of them considered proposed reforms (except the redistribution of land) as a threat to their very survival. A primary example of this sort of attitude was the response of the villagers at Bujak, in Nograd County, where the local notary wanted to organize a dairy cooperative in 1937. The peasants simply refused to join the cooperative, despite the fact that it would have secured higher prices for their milk. But, as the notary complained, the peasants were so suspicious of any suggested improvement in their conditions "coming from the lords," that they simply refused to accept them.[17] This was a vicious circle; no reforms were acceptable from "outside" yet, in order to have reforms, they would have had to come from outside of peasant society. In some cases reforms were unacceptable even if they would have immediately improved living conditions.[18]

The extended use of agricultural machinery and chemical fertilizers, ideas for better methods of cultivation, proposals for a more frequent recourse to scientific medicine, were ideas usually propagated by educated persons who, even if they originally came from peasant stock, had already been judged to have been "infected" by the alien outside world, and were "out to destroy the equilibrium of the community." The village institutions, the peasant family were, in the final reckoning, regarded by peasants as more important instruments of their survival than reforms. After all, most of these instruments were sanctioned by time and practice! The common saying that "what was good for my father will be good for my son" must be viewed as an expression of the defensive mechanism of the "little community" in the face of apparent threats of disruption coming from outside. The contempt of the rich peasants towards the poor, regarding them as lazy thieves who could only blame themselves for their plight, was also an expression of the defensive mechanism of the community. It was the other side of the explanation that the life of the community would *not* be disrupted if the rich were permitted to hold on to their wealth without making substantial contributions to the welfare of the community. In other words, it was the "fault" of the poor that they were not rich. In turn, the peasants were considered uncultured, cunning, but stupid brutes by the "outsiders," that is, the urban inhabitants, and this made them turn even more inward.[19]

This did not mean that peasant society was simple or static. Quite the contrary: the peasants did adapt methods of better production, new techniques of cultivation, *when and where they discovered these themselves.* But even when they did so, this did not mean that their motives were to increase productivity or to obtain greater profits by doing so. What they really wanted was to achieve greater security of existence and a larger measure of freedom from control by others. They had been disappointed so many times in the past that they were reluctant to accept advice.

It was true that the invisible walls that confined peasant communities to the hothouse of traditional existence began gradually to crumble in the late 1930's. Darvas observed that a few of the rich peasants in his village broke out of their isolation and began to orient themselves politically towards the reformists.[20] They started to send their children to schools away from home (into the cities) and favored their marriages with the children of the urban bourgeoisie. New furniture appeared in their homes, and their dress gradually changed to resemble that of city people. They became managers, not co-workers, of their employees. Yet, even these rich peasants were reluctant to take the final step and become the leaders of rural change; they were, first of all, too preoccupied with discovering the new world of the bourgeoisie which they entered, and were still too fearful of the reaction of the peasant community which they were about to leave.

If the rich peasants were reluctant to assume leadership in agrarian modernization, even less could be expected from other peasant strata. As noted above, 21% of all peasants—about 1.8 million people—were landless agricultural workers (peasants in name only). Another 1.2 million possessed such meager amounts of land that they could not provide a decent living for their families solely from their landholdings. The major concern of these peasants was to keep body and soul together. Most of them starved year in and year out, desperately trying to save some money in order to buy a piece of land. Even if they did succeed after great deprivation and did fulfill their ambitions, this did not mean that they could relax and enjoy their success. Now they were expected to begin saving for another piece of land and this went on *ad infinitum.* A bad year, a sickness or other misfortune could set them back for years to come, but hope was eternal that their luck might change, and then they would move up among the more secure members of their community.[21]

Individual peasant families who possessed enough land for a relatively secure existence—between 20-75 acres—were just as reluctant to support rural change as were richer peasants. Most of them continued to work their lands with tools and techniques handed down from previous generations, exploiting the labor of their families to the utmost.[22]

There were few possibilities for the opening up of the closed peasant communities. Every move in this direction was suspect; most peasants believed that the transformation of rural life, if it ever came about, would be accomplished at their expense—as it indeed eventually proved to be the case, and they could hardly be expected to contribute voluntarily to the process. This was, of course, unfortunate, because, by the late 1930's, when industrialization in Hungary began to accelerate and when its consequences were increasingly being felt in the rural sphere, the villages were left without indigenous leadership.[23]

Among the political institutions, the government itself could have done the most to alleviate the crisis of rural life. It would be erroneous to say that the Hungarian government was unconcerned, or that it made no effort to change the conditions of life in the countryside. But its major efforts were directed at change through the agency of the large estate owners.[24] In all other respects, the government attempted only piecemeal solutions to general problems and was not willing to advance thorough-going, fundamental reforms.[25]

Thus there was no massive governmental effort in interwar Hungary to change the conditions of rural life. No one should be surprised at this, however, when one considers the nature of the governing institutions. The government was called syncratic,[26] meaning it was created by the fusion of the aristocracy, the army and the gentry-controlled state bureaucracy, in alliance with some leading industrialists. Some credit is indeed due to this government for its success in creating a functioning economic and social system after World War I. But in doing so, its leaders relied on the political and economic power of the "historical classes" and the instruments of chauvinistic-jingoistic nationalism and militarism, and had little time left for policies aimed at rural modernization.

But given the general atmosphere in Hungarian society during these years, it is doubtful that the government could have done a great deal more, even if it had wanted to, without a fundamental change in its personnel and political orientation. The peasants, on their part, were rightfully suspicious of every move made by the government. They would have been difficult to convince of its good intentions. No wonder! "For the peasants, Hungary was indeed the promised land," remarked an observer, "so much had been promised to the peasants in the past . . . that if all the promises were fulfilled every village footpath would have been turned into metalled roads by now!"[27]

Of the other insitutions, the Roman Catholic Church was equally ambivalent towards rural change. The bishops and prelates considered the interests of their institution to be so closely intertwined with those of the ruling circles that there was little likelihood of bold action on their part. Not only was the Roman Catholic Church the single richest landlord of Hungary, but the traumatic experiences of its priesthood during the revolutions of 1918-19 made their attitude towards rural reform almost preordained.

At the same time, the hierarchy of the church regarded itself as the guardian of "right" morals, and the major spiritual force for the preservation of traditions, the alleged basis of national life. The prelates demanded, in turn, that the state provide political protection and even coercive force to secure the interests of the church.[28] In exchange, the bishops regarded the protection of state interests, identified with conservatism, as their moral obligation. The Roman Catholic Church was, therefore, more than an institution of the *status quo*. It was a truly reactionary social force in interwar Hungary. This did not necessarily mean opposition to the perceived interests of individual peasant communities. Since social stability and the preservation of the *status quo* was also an underlying premise of peasant existence, the peasants and the church could meet on this ground.

However, the priesthood as a whole was not homogeneous in promoting the *status quo* in the rural sphere. Many priests worried about what they considered the decline of the spiritual influence of the church in the villages.[29] This feeling seems also to have persisted among some of the regular clergy, who have been traditionally interested in missionary work among the people. As we shall see in the next part of this work, these concerned clergy tried to help the peasants.

But the leaders of the Roman Church remained largely indifferent to rural modernization in Hungary throughout the interwar years.

Leadership in rural modernization could hardly be expected from the social stratum whose counterparts had performed such tasks in Western European societies, namely, the middle class. Most Hungarian bourgeois cared little for the peasantry and were not interested in land as an object of profit-making. Working mostly in governmental office or industrial enterprise, the Hungarian bourgeois acquired many of the habits of his workplace. He carried into his everyday life the discipline and methods of rational problem-solving experiences. His thinking ran along the lines of what Karl Mannheim called "functional rationalism," meaning that he was, first of all, an employee whose thinking was shaped by the strict rationality of the shop in which he worked. His attitude towards the peasantry and rural life in general was shaped by his urban-industrial existence. He was a man of a practical mind to whom the peasantry appeared as a group of backward, often cunning, but basically unimaginative primitives. If the peasants wanted to remain in their present condition, the bourgeoisie reasoned, so be it. After all, it was their own fault if they did not move into the city and live like "decent human beings."[30]

Many educated bourgeois, compelled to pursue a profession in the rural sphere, were hardly less prejudiced against the peasants. To have to accept a rural assignment was regarded as a personal disaster: it was a sign of low regard for one's abilities, possibly the consequence of low grades and failed examinations. The bourgeois living in the rural sphere formed small enclaves in which they would congregate, speaking mostly among themselves. Some of them regarded the peasants with benevolent condescension: many of them were more concerned about the disappearance of folk-costumes than about the miserable conditions of the poor in the villages. But the peasant communities remained closed for most of them and they continued to be "outsiders" in the villages in which "bad luck" or lack of family connections had landed them. Their desire was to get away as soon as possible, preferably to Budapest, where the amenities of urban life beckoned to them. There was, therefore, little chance that the bourgeoisie would assume the leadership in the transformation of the rural sphere in Hungary.

And yet, the very expansion of the cities, and urban life in general, could not but leave their imprint on the peasantry even if only in an indirect way. Although urban influences diminished in direct relation to the distances that separated villages from the respective urban centers, these influences were there to stay. Not only were the growing cities drawing the landless peasants unto themselves, but their products penetrated every rural settlement. The railroads, pioneer instruments of capitalist development, carried the goods of the cities into the countryside and vice versa. Spreading advertisements in the form of the catalogues of department stores and newspaper ads reached most peasant families, introducing them to often strange but desirable goods. Travelling merchants sold cheap industrial goods, such as clothes, tools and other necessities of life to peasant households, slowly starting to change peasant cognition of the perimeters of existence. New plans and methods of house-building, mass-produced furniture, and an occasional radio set changed not only the outward appearance of peasant households but also the thinking of the peasant population. This was a common fate of all the rural people of Eastern Europe and the Hungarians were no exception.[31] Yet, one must remember that these were the organic inroads of urbanism and industrialization into the rural sphere, the byproducts of a strange yet enticing world which nevertheless continued to remain alien to most peasants.

3. Interlude: Who Was To Pay?

Before the early 1930's there was little dispute as to who should pay for whatever changes were to take place in Hungarian society. The "historical classes," especially the aristocrats, now safely ensconced in their commanding social and political positions claimed that, by right of their nation-sustaining efforts through past centuries, they deserved special consideration in the social and political processes.[32] This included relief from heavy taxation and the preservation of their estates against land reform. The government quite agreed; no matter which faction dominated this government during the interwar years, they were all for the preservation of the *latifundia*. Governmental policies, therefore, indirectly contributed to the maintenance of huge surplus labor forces in the countryside that were essential for the operations of the large estates.

On the other hand, the industrial workers, although suspect in the eyes of the ruling elite for their role in the revolution of 1918-19, found support against the most blatant exploitation in their trade unions and the Social Democratic Party of Hungary. The Social Democrats agreed with the government early in the 1920's not to recruit peasants into their organization, concentrating instead on the defense of the interests of urban industrial workers.[33] The government was cautious in its treatment of workers; its major concern was their political neutralization. This in itself prevented the introduction of policies that would have strained their relations.

The middle class was even better protected against demands to contribute its share to rural modernization not only by the numerous threads connecting its members to the state bureaucracy, but also by its very existence as the major representative of the urban-industrial culture. This left the peasant population as the most vulnerable stratum of society, one that was not organized for concerted political action and, therefore, the only candidate to pay for rural transformation.

The argument that agriculture was indeed in the position to support rural modernization was not without some validity. The value of agrarian wealth after World War I came close to 60% of the total national wealth (about 9.4 billion gold crowns), excluding the value of buildings. While in 1913, the total debt of agrarian holdings came to 1,180 billion gold crowns, by 1924 the debt was reduced to the paltry sum of 630,000 gold crowns. We have already described the process in a previous chapter by which most landholders were able to pay off their pre-war debts in the debased currency. However, by 1927, agrarian debt grew once again to continue rising throughout the interwar years. By 1932, this debt already reached 2 billion pengos—400 million dollars—paying higher interest rates than before 1914.[34] After the depression, agriculture could certainly not sustain the expenses of reforms in the rural sphere, despite rising prices.

The major means of the exploitation of the peasants was the so-called agrarian scissor. This meant that agricultural prices were maintained on an artifically low level (simply by denying them protection). Industrial prices, on the other hand, were protected by high tariffs averaging about 30% during the mid-1920's and 1930's. Thus, the peasant population was forced to pay comparatively higher prices for industrial goods such as clothing, tools, chemical fertilizers, and machinery than did the rest of the population for agrarian goods. This way the peasants indirectly subsidized the slow industrial progress that was taking place in the Hungarian economy. The large estates were able to transfer the burden to the independent smallholders and agrarian workers. The means by which this was achieved included payments from the government in the form of bonuses for large-scale grain production, preferential treatment by the banks, and, above all, low wages paid to agricultural laborers.

Not every stratum of the peasantry was affected the same way. Although the agrarian scissor was generally exploitative, it was the greatest burden on those who had to buy a large part of their provisions and other everyday necessities on the market, namely, the poorest strata of the peasantry. The burden was especially heavy on those who became smallholders for the first time in 1920, following the land reforms. Many of these peasants, burdened as they were with the redemption payments, were unable to pay for seeds, fertilizers and draft animals and soon went into bankruptcy.

One might argue that the Hungarian government, lacking adequate funds for the simultaneous support of industry and agriculture, made the logical choice. Using funds derived from agriculture to subsidize industrial progress could be justified on the grounds that once industry was sufficiently developed, overall improvements in the economy and the living standards of the population would follow. The government could insist that it was simply following the example set by the advanced industrial nations of the West. But such an argument would have been valid only if available funds were used mostly for productive investments. We have seen that this was not the case even when the Hungarian government obtained large loans the mid-1920's. Furthermore, the banks usually favored the large estates when dispensing funds for the rural sphere. When they lent money to smallholders, they demanded the unharvested crops as security (green loans). When the weather did not cooperate or some other disaster struck, the independent peasant smallholder was unable to pay and lost all that he possessed.

In short, there was only one social group in Hungary to pay for rural modernization, namely, the peasants.

4. By Way of a Conclusion: Who Was a Typical Peasant in Interwar Hungary?

From the foregoing discussion it would appear difficult indeed to describe a typical peasant who lived in the Hungarian countryside between the two World Wars. Changes in rural life and the advanced stratification of the peasantry had already reached a stage by then so that enumerating allegedly common peasant characteristics would be met by justified general skepticism. The "outside world" still discussed the various peasant strata under the generic term "peasant," but most such discussions in fact regarded the landowning stratum as their archetype. But differences in behavior, attitudes, and motivations among the various layers of the peasantry made such generalizations obsolete.

The image of a "typical" Hungarian peasant as a sturdy, staid specimen, bravely standing up to the vagaries of nature while preserving the essential "Hungarianness" of his character, was already unrealistic by the mid-19th century, and its reemergence in the early 20th century was due to a neo-romantic revival, furthered by poets and writers. Yet a "typical" Hungarian peasant would have been somewhat easier to describe in the 1850's, since rural changes were still slow at that time. By the early 20th century, however, several types of peasants existed, their characteristics determined partly by their economic conditions, their education and, among other factors, by the location of their settlements in terms of distances that separated them from the nearest urban centers.

They were undoubtedly still peasants; at least they all made their living from agriculture, although not all who so made their living were peasants. Their major distinguishing characteristics were supplied by the "outside world" which lumped them all together as standing outside "civilized society." On the whole, their life did have a greater degree of stability than that of non-peasants; they also had greater physical endurance due to constant hard work, partly justifying the belief of urban dwellers that peasants were "natural men," for whom the land was nature itself. But beyond that, each substratum had characteristics that distinguished it from the others.

The majority of peasants were landholders, although the size of their possessions varied widely. They were the least mobile elements of the peasantry. However small or large the parcel of land that they held, by their very stability they were the guardians of peasant traditions.

These traditions centered on two institutions, the family and the village community. The family was, first of all, the place for raising and schooling children in peasant life and traditions. Secondly, it was a means for the organization of work. As Erdei stated, "it certainly was not a place for harmonious cooperation or the personal fulfillment of two persons." It was strictly a means of survival, closely controlled by the father, for whom the children were both an aim and a means of material advancement. The life of the family unit revolved around agricultural production; no single individual counted in this context except as he or she could contribute to the survival of the whole. For the landholder peasants the inhabitants of the cities, no matter what their social positions or occupations were, were "aliens." "They all looked alike," said Erdei.[35]

Thus, the peasant family encouraged obedience; since the survival of the family depended upon the close cooperation of its members, it was enforced by the father through a series of strictly observed rules. Disobedience received harsh punishment from an early age on; fathers often beat their children who, in turn, disciplined their younger siblings. Disrespect towards older family members was not tolerated; nor was any leeway given to those who were unwilling to shoulder the common burdens. This instilled in landholding peasants a sense of humility and tolerance, and a willingness to work whether one liked to or not. At the same time, the upbringing of these peasants taught them to respect outside authority, religious as well as secular. But the religion which they followed was not based on "optimistic belief in the eternal laws of nature or in an infinitely merciful God; rather it was a faith in a mysterious force, all-powerful, capricious and undependable."[36] It was always lurking in the background, ready to punish the peasant for even minor deviations from the rules of his life.

Land for the peasant family who possessed it was the embodiment of the fundamental rule of life; it sustained its members and, however unpredictable the crops that it provided, it meant freedom from control by others. But the possession of land did not free the peasant from work. On the contrary, it always demanded more in exertion and toil than it returned in produce. But it provided the means of survival, in good times and bad, in the midst of an alien world, security in insecurity, without which life was miserable.

The other institution, the village community, was both a simple conglomeration of individual peasant families living side by side, and a complex unit of kinship groups in which peasant morals and traditions were played out on a somewhat larger stage. Its activities included the Sunday church services, where a little gossip was exchanged each time, and where holy day clothes could be paraded. It also provided the stage for courtship and other rituals that were essential for the establishment of new families. The other important aspects of village community life included the kinship networks which, in times of trouble, helped individual families to survive. Other than that, the village had no special role to play in peasant life; it certainly did not encourage cooperative ventures for the improvement of life for individuals or for the community as a whole.

Thus, the horizons of landholding peasants seldom expanded beyond the confines of their village where their land was located, and the influence of the urban centers reached them only indirectly. At the same time, they belonged to the respected, leading stratum of their village communities. As such, they had an important influence in maintaining village traditions.

Few landholders had higher aspirations than to increase their family's holdings. As Erdei remarked, "the highest height was represented to them by the steeple of the village church, and the deepest depth was that of the village's wells."[37] Narrow in their outlook, suspicious of innovations not initiated by them, the landowning peasants were the most secure, conservative, and stagnant stratum of the interwar peasantry in Hungary.

In contrast, the landless peasant was a great deal more mobile and less tradition-bound than the landowner. But he received even less support and encouragement from the "outside world." Having no land of his own meant that he was completely at the mercy of others for his living, yet he was not a proletarian, even if he lived off his wages. Unlike the urban industrial worker, he had no trade union or political party that he trusted, and which would have protected his interests. He lived from agriculture, no matter how meager a living it provided, subject to the double control of landowners and the uncertainties of nature. Although he desired land no less strongly than other peasants, the possession of it was often such a remote possibility for him that he considered it as almost against the rules of his existence.

The life of the landless peasant was necessarily passive and humble; he constantly humbled himself in front of other peasants and the "outsiders." At the same time, he burned with feverish hatred towards those who, in his judgment, prevented him from becoming a secure, landowning peasant. Yet, he was no less fatalistic for that; he was long accustomed to the yoke almost to the point that he no longer needed to be reminded that he was "under orders." He was also puritanical, his life revolving around the crises of everyday life which came with regularity. Providing everyday necessities in food, clothing and shelter for himself and his family required the exertion of all his physical and mental abilities. Thus, every one of his actions, every one of his thoughts, had been forced into the mold of physical survival. He could not move faster, he could not take one single unnecessary step when working for others than was absolutely essential. He could never eat as much as to feel satiated, he could not burn more oil in his lamp at home than was absolutely necessary. Education was, for him, an unnecessary luxury; health care was mainly for the "rich." Yet there was escape if life became intolerable. While the landowner would rather die than leave his land and rural life, the landless peasant often moved into an urban center. If he could not or would not move, release was often found in drunken stupor that often ended in bloody violence.

The servants of large estates represented a special case among the landless rural folk. Their security was somewhat greater than that of other agrarian workers. At least their food, even if often inadequate, was assured by their contract with the landlord. But they were more humbled by their condition, more tied to the estate in question, than were others. Since they were at the constant call of overseers, body and soul, they were passive and deeply fatalistic in facing life's crises. In contrast to other landless peasants, they valued life but little; there was in them an indifference towards suffering, a resignation to mental and physical pain that hardly existed outside their circles. They were truly the tools of those who lorded over them and crippled them in body and soul.

The migrating landless peasants had greater mobility but even less security than other peasants. Their collective sense was, however, greater; fostered, no doubt, by the fact that they had to rely on each other for survival more than others. Their families were not as closed as were those of the landowners; the able-bodied members spent at least half the year away from home, working at distant estates. They had few peasant traditions to observe and to maintain; they were well on their way to becoming proletarians.

The fifth category of the peasantry included people living around the market towns and cities in eastern Hungary and the Great Plain in the *tanya*-system. Some of these were the most advanced members of the Hungarian peasantry. They eagerly pursued the amenities of modern urban culture. Having a constant contact with their respective towns, conducting their official business with the authorities on the footing of citizenship, these people often resembled the free peasantry of West European nations. To be sure, there were as many peasants who lived isolated lives in the *tanyas* as there were those who did not; the former seldom went to town, being as badly off economically as were other landless peasants. But it was also true that most of those who were not permanent *tanya*-dwellers acquired industrial goods, built their houses on an urban pattern, and aspired to higher living standards and status in society. They were, strictly speaking, no longer peasants, nor were they as yet members of the urban bourgeoisie. They closely resembled the Dutch or Scandinavian peasants whose integration into society was at an advanced stage.

Peasant society as a whole was in transition in interwar Hungary. The modernization of agriculture had not yet advanced very far, and it had not yet swept the old ways of life completely away. Most peasants were still backward, not yet full members of the community of the nation. By and large, however, their integration into society began by the end of the interwar period, and it was a painful and sometimes destructive process that was becoming increasingly difficult to avoid.

NOTES

1. Kovrig, *op. cit.*, 135.
2. In the vicinity of the market towns of Cegled and Kiskunfelegyhaza on the Great Plain, for example, there were practically no large estates. The lands in the area of these towns were owned mostly by smallholders (65% and 70% respectively). The average yearly income of the inhabitants of Cegled in the late 1920's and early 1930's

was altogether 19.9 million *pengos,* while that of Kiskunfelegyhaza was 16.1 million *pengos.* In contrast, a town of similar size, Sovenyhaza, located between the two market towns, had one large estate in its neighborhood, controlling 51,800 acres of land. Only 5% of the town's lands was owned by smallholders. The yearly average income of the population of this town was only 2.7 million *pengos.* All three towns had about the same amount of land within their borders; the number of inhabitants in each case was also similar. Comparable results were obtained by Matyas Matolcsy in other regions of the country. See *Uj elet a magyar foldon* (New Life in the Hungarian Lands) (Budapest, Cserepfalvi, 1938), 76-81. At the same time, some large estates did pioneer agricultural modernization, even if this was not shown in their large-scale use of machinery. But the process was reflected in the general use of fertilizers as recorded by the statistical survey of 1927:

regularly fertilized by natural manure—	
on landholds less than 28 acres	25%
on landholds between 28-142 acres	21.5%
on landholds between 142-1420 acres	19.5%
on landholds over 1420 acres	19.7%

regularly fertilized by chemical fertilizers—	
on landholds less than 28 acres	1.5%
on landholds between 28-142 acres	4.1%
on landholds between 142-1420 acres	13.7%
on landholds over 1420 acres	19.7%

Magyar Statisztikai Evkonyv, Budapest, 1928, 63.

3. The huge Bakony estate of the Csesznek branch of the Eszterhazy family provides the best example of these methods. Here the family itself was surrounded by a certain aura of respect by the peasants who seldom met them face to face. The people of the region saw the personification of their exploitation in the manager of the estate, Gyula Elekes. See Poloskei-Takacs, *op. cit.,* 16.

4. Illyes, *op. cit.*, 52.
5. This estate consisted of 971.6 acres of land mostly poor in quality. Despite this handicap, the owners consistently produced grain crops. Only potatoes were successful when they experimented with new crops. Animal husbandry — what there was on the estate — served mainly the needs of the kitchen of the owners who lived in Budapest most of the year and spent only their summers at Pusztamiske. The machines were mostly second-hand; innovations included the building of a wind-mill which collapsed after the first storm hit the estate. The last owners spent a considerable amount of their own personal income just to keep the estate going. See Laszlo Gaal-Kropf, "A Gaal-Kropf csalad pusztamiskei gazdasaga," (The Pusztamiske-estate of the Gaal-Kropf Family) *Agrartorteneti Szemle* 19(1977), 219-34.
6. *Ibid.*, 233.
7. Foster, *op. cit.*
8. Hungarian peasant communities were never as isolated from society and were, consequently, never as "backward" as the Latin American villages from which Foster derived his paradigm. In this sense, it may be somewhat misleading to speak of peasantry as if it were a commonly accepted term, generally valid for rural folk the world over. But this is a subject that would need a separate volume to discuss.
9. Foster, *op. cit.*, 298.
10. Ferenc Erdei in *Parasztok, op. cit.*, had discussed the resilence of peasant communities in terms very similar to Foster's, and Zoltan Szabo in *Cifra, op. cit.*, 54, also spoke in similar terms.
11. Szabo, *Cifra, op. cit.*, 55.
12. Veres, *Falusi, op. cit.*, 179.
13. Darvas, *A legnagyobb, op. cit.*, 46. One such man, called the "greasy Baranyai," was especially noteworthy. He possessed more than 100 acres of the best lands of the village, had a house that looked like a palace—which he rented out—yet he wore boots whose soles were fastened

on by wire, his clothes were ragged, and his hat was so greasy that, as the saying went, it could have been used for soapmaking.

14. See Marietta Boros, "Totkomlos mezogazdasagi fejlodesenek vazlata," (The Outline of the Agrarian Development of the Village of Totkomlos) *A Bekes Megyei Muzeumok Kozlemenyei* (Bekes) 2(1974), 218.
15. Erdei, *Parasztok, op. cit.*, 22, 23.
16. John Duncan Powell, "Peasant Society and Clientist Politics," *The American Political Science Review* 64 (1979), No. 2, 411.
17. Szabo, Cifra, op. cit., 57-8.
18. Darvas, *A legnagyobb, op. cit.*, 44-5.
19. *Ibid.*, 46.
20. *Ibid.*, 47. See also, Ranki et al, *Magyarorszag, op. cit.*, 8:790-1.
21. Veres, *Falusi, op, cit.*, 180, and the comments by Imre Somogyi in Szarszo. Az 1943. evi balatonszarszoi Magyar Elet Tabor eloadasai es megbeszelessorozata (Szarszo. The Series of Discussions and Lectures of the Magyar Elet Camp in 1943) (Budapest, Magyar Elet Kiado, 1943), 77.
22. *Ibid.*
23. *Ibid.*
24. A good example of such policies was noted by Szabo in *Cifra, op. cit.*, 102, in the building of a railroad station two kilometers from the village of Dejtar in Nograd County, in open fields. The reason for this was that the local owner of a large estate raised a large number of turnips in the fields, and it was at the end of his fields where the station was established. In general, the bond between the large estate owners and the government was just too strong. Policies, however rational and beneficial they appeared to be for the peasantry, were never enacted if they were opposed by large landed interests.
25. A perfect example of this approach was provided by Minister of Welfare, Jozsef Vass, in the late 1920's. In trying to alleviate at least some of the problems of the unemployed rural poor, Vass placed the children of some

poor rural family into state care as "orphans." As such, the children were transferred to the care of their parents and the latter received government payments to maintain their "wards." But the scheme was stopped in 1930 when the Minister of Finance discovered it. A similar approach was evident in the establishment of the National Fund for the Defense of Families (*Orszagos Nemzeti Csaladvedelmi Alap* or ONCSA) by public law 1940:XXIII. Although 100 million pengos ($20 million) were provided for the fund in 1942, most of which was spent in the rural sphere, the operations were never fully successful and were cut short by the war. Such actions, laudable as they were, were certainly not substitutes for thoroughgoing social reforms.

26. Gati, *op. cit.*, 62.
27. Veres, *Falusi, op. cit.*, 194.
28. Somogyi in *Szarszo, op. cit.*, 77.
29. According to a report, between 1937-1943, 40-50% of church members stopped attending Catholic services in the villages. Exceptions were areas where the peasantry were the least touched by modern life. The situation was even worse in areas dominated by the Protestant religions, especially Calvinism and Lutheranism. In their churches, absenteeism came close to 50-70% of adult membership. The same observer reported that in some regions of Hungary the entire adult population simply stopped attending church services, regardless of the denominations to which they belonged. Somogyi, *Szarszo, op. cit.*, 76. It seems that in most advanced societies the leading elements that initiated the modernization process were members of some Protestant religious denominations. Where this was not the case, religion was altogether replaced by some sort of secular ideology performing a quasi-religious function. For the modernization of Hungarian agriculture to be successful, it was necessary (1) to break the bonds between the ruling elite of the nation and the Roman Catholic Church which stifled any effort at modernization, and (2) eliminate the influence of the

church over everyday rural life. Neither of these steps could be undertaken during the interwar years.

30. Szabo, *Cifra, op. cit.*, 59.
31. See Wolfgang Jacobeit, "Az iparositas tarsadalmi-kulturalis es tarsadalmi-gazdasagi hatasa Kozepeuropa-parasztsagara," (The Social-Cultural and Social- Economic Effects of Industrialization on the Peasantry of Central Europe) *Agrartorteneti Szemle* 19 (1977), Nos. 3-4, 318-34.
32. See Gyula Szekfu, *Harom nemzedek es ami utana kovetkezik* (Three Generations and What Comes After Them) (Budapest, 1935).
33. Dezso Farkas, *A magyarorszagi Szocialdemokrata Part es az agrarkerdes* (The Social Democratic Party of Hungary and the Agrarian Question) (Budapest, Akademiai Kiado, 1974).
34. *Magyar Gazdasagkutato Intezet, 9. Jelentes* (Report No. 9), 85.
35. Erdei, *Parasztok, op. cit.*, 15.
36. *Ibid.*, 21.
37. Ferenc Erdei, *Magyar falu* (Hungarian Village) (Budapest, 1974), 2nd ed., 61.

PART VI

PEASANT MOVEMENTS IN THE TWENTIETH CENTURY*

1. The Smallholders' Party of Istvan Nagyatadi Szabo

The founder of the Smallholders' Party, Istvan Nagyatadi Szabo,[1] was the descendant of an *inquilinus* (zseller) family; he was of the humblest cottar origin.[2] He could not have been more different from Andras L. Achim, the *Viharsarok* peasant leader who was a rich farmer of lesser noble descent. Achim was born well-to-do and independent; he became radical and arrogant, and he defied his enemies. Nagyatadi Szabo was born a poor farmhand in Transdanubia; he was meek by nature, preferred gradual change by peaceful means and avoided

*The following part of this essay was published as part of Professor Kiraly's study entitled "Democratic Peasant Movements in Hungary in the 20th Century," in *Europaische Bauerparteien im 20. Jahrhundert* (Stuttgart-New York, von H. Gollwitzer, 1977) in *Quellen u. Forschungen zur Agrargeschichte,* Band 29, reproduced here with the kind permission of the publisher.

controversy. Yet, both were honest and tried sincerely to improve the lot of the peasantry, and "both were swept away by the blind selfishness of Hungarian feudalism."[3] The difference between their personalities was reflected in their careers. By 1908, Nagyatadi Szabo had become sufficiently well-off to afford the time to go into national politics. At the interim elections of that year he was elected to Parliament, and was continually reelected until his death.[4]

In 1909, Nagyatadi Szabo founded his own party, the *Orszagos Fuggetlensegi es 48-as Kisgazdapart* (National Independence and Smallholders' Party of (18)48), whose official journal was *Magyar Lobo* (Hungarian Standard). The constituent convention held on November 21 in Szentgal, Veszprem county, adopted the "Szentgal Program" which remained the party's official platform until its end. This program demanded political democracy with universal suffrage and the secret ballot. Its economic stance was less clear but included "improvement of the lot of rural laborers" and "advancement of smallholders and small shopkeepers." Other demands were more definite; the program demanded the exemption of basic foodstuffs from taxes and of incomes below the annual subsistence level of 88 crowns. On land reform the program sounded radical but was in fact moderate; the owners of entailed estates were to be obliged to carry out intensive, modern cultivation, and the *latifundia* and church lands were to be nationalized. But since nothing was stated about what would happen after nationalization, it was obvious that these planks were radical in tone only. The program in fact made no provision for distributing land to the peasantry and fell far short of Achim's Whitsun Program of the previous year. Its welfare measures were more progressive: free medical services for the rural poor; cheaper insurance for the smallholders, and nationalization of the insurance business.[5] A comparison between Achim's and Nagyatadi Szabo's program reflects the wide gulf between the radical *Viharsarok* projects and programs developed by the peasants movements of the Transdanubian area.

When the newly elected Parliament of 1910 assembled, Nagyatadi Szabo told the house: "We do not demand leadership for ourselves. We readily acknowledge that others are better suited for it and they have the right to lead."[6] Little wonder that Nagyatadi Szabo was gladly accepted by the Hungarian ruling class at a time when they were already determined to crush Achim.

The party gradually spread its organization through the Great Hungarian Plain during 1910-1911, causing inevitable competition with Mezofi's party. Relations with Achim and his party, however, were friendly. Before the general elections of 1910, indeed, Nagyatadi Szabo had even contemplated fusing the two parties and the two leaders twice met to discuss the possibility. But the idea was abandoned since Achim was simply too radical for Nagyatadi Szabo.[7] After Achim's death. Nagyatadi Szabo had some success in absorbing into his own party the wealthy smallholders who had formerly backed Achim. During 1911-1913, his party extended its activities into northern Hungary (Slovakia) and moved its headquarters to Budapest. However, the party was not yet a truly mass organization before World War I; a considerable number of the landed peasantry remained loyal to the traditional parties. Now that the Smallholders' Party was established in the capital city, it developed closer connections with the Social Democratic Party. Istvan Nagyatadi Szabo endorsed the Social Democrats' struggle for democracy and the freedom of the individual, but he was scandalized by their internationalism, atheism and intention to socialize landed properties. He and his party feared the Socialists more than they trusted them. They disapproved of their mass-movement approach. Gradually, therefore, the Smallholders' Party drifted towards the conservatives.[8] Part of the cause of this drift was a decline in rural discontent as the result of prewar-industrial growth, urbanization, and increased overseas emigration.[9]

All through World War I Istvan Nagyatadi Szabo and two colleagues, Janos Meyer and Janos Novak, represented the

Smallholders' Party in Parliament. A fourth, Sandor Herczeg, was elected at the 1914 interim elections. The Smallholders, thus, had four legislators on a fairly permanent basis. The party was still far from sharing power with the ruling circles, but at least it had representatives where the fate of the nation was decided upon, even though they were not much more than eyewitnesses on the legislative scene. It is beyond the scope of this study to deal with the misery caused by the war or the details of the revolutions that originated in those miseries. Suffice it to say that the men of the old regime reached out for the Smallholders' Party and offered its leaders a share of the executive power only when the regime was in mortal danger. The very last administration of the old regime under the premiership of Janos Hadik offered the Ministry of Agriculture to Nagyatadi Szabo on October 29, 1918. This offer was in no way an acknowledgment that the Smallholders' representative was entitled to share power. It was simply an attempt to counterbalance the climactic influence of Count Mihaly Karolyi.

The attempt failed. The administration was swept away, before even it took office, by Karolyi's bourgeois democratic revolution of October 31, 1918. Karolyi's two ministries also included Nagyatadi Szabo as Minister of Agriculture. The revolutionary ministries genuinely intended to carry through a sweeping land reform, and Nagyatadi would have been an excellent man to execute it. However, when Karolyi was replaced by Bela Kun's regime, Nagyatadi Szabo adopted a stance of passive resistance.

After the fall of Bela Kun's Soviet Republic of Hungary, the "Trade Union" cabinet of Gyula Peidl administered the country and undid the changes introduced by the Soviet Republic. On August 7, 1919, the administration was ousted by a coup d'etat and succeeded by the Istvan Friedrich government which, on August 15, again offered the Ministry of Agriculture to Nagyatadi Szabo. The new administration included two other representatives of the Smallholders' Party, Janos Meyer and Istvan Sokoropatkai Szabo. At least, it seemed, the peasantry was home and safe as a partner in the exercise of political power in Hungary.

On November 17, 1919, the government issued Ministerial Decree No. 5987/ME-1919 which established universal suffrage with the secret ballot and equal, direct and obligatory voting by men and women. The permanent, basic goal of the peasant movements, political democracy, appeared to have been achieved.

The new government formed on November 23, 1919, under Karoly Huszar, however, relieved Nagyatadi Szabo of the agricultural portfolio and moved him to the controversial Ministry of Public Supply. The Ministry of Agriculture went to a man of the old regime, Gyula Rubinek, and Istvan Sokoropatkai Szabo was named Minister of Smallholders with no specific field of authority. The changes were portentous. The revolutionary wave was nearly over and the representatives of the old regime had no interest in a vigorous land reform such as Istvan Nagyatadi Szabo so earnestly desired.[10]

New elections were held between January 25 and February 13, 1920. Since thousands were being kept in concentration camps for alleged crimes committed during the Bela Kun regime, the Social Democrats abstained in protest. The largest single party to emerge was Istvan Nagyatadi's Smallholders' Party, winning 71 seats, while an additional 7 seats went to smallholders with no party affiliation. This was the core of the political left, which was joined by three liberals and three independents. The Christian Party won 68 seats and with nine independent conservatives made up the right wing which could, thus, muster 77 votes to the left's 87. On March 14, 1920, a coalition government of reconstruction representing both left and right was formed under the premiership of Sandor Simonyi-Semadam.[11] Supplementary elections were held in June, 1920, after the Rumanians evacuated the left bank of the Tisza River. The parliamentary representation of the Smallholders' Party was increased. Of the 203 seats Parliament now contained, 91 belonged to the Smallholders and 59 to the Christians. The Smallholders were, however, internally divided. Nineteen of them, headed by County Kuno Klebelsberg, were dissident Christian Party members for personal rather than political reasons, and soon 17 of them declared themselves Independents. Many others joined the Smallholders not out of interest in the party's prime objective, land reform, but because it was fashionable to be "progressive." Others joined because Nagyatadi's anti-Habsburg stance attracted them. Nagyatadi's majority in Parliament were not actually peasants. Many were aristocrats like Margrave Gyorgy Pallavicini, Baron Frigyes Koranyi, Count Gedeon Raday. Not more than about a dozen of the parliamentarians of the Smallholders' Party were genuine peasants.[12]

The parliamentary membership of the Smallholders' Party simply was not leaning towards radical and badly needed land reform. It was, however, true that most of its legislators were in favor of moderate social reforms. But before the 1922 elections the party was to be purged of its radical members. In the coming Bethlen era, named after Prime Minister Count Istvan Bethlen, himself a large landowner, those who would be elected "were easily dealt with and, for their salaries as MPs and the patronage which went with the position, despite their hobnails, were obediently at Bethlen's disposal."[13]

Nagyatadi Szabo and his Smallholders, with a parliamentary majority and holding three portfolios in the government, were in a position to formulate policy. Had Andras L. Achim been in the same position, it is hard to think that he would not have extracted the maximum benefit for the peasants from the representatives of the old regime. Nagyatadi Szabo, however, was a fundamentally different man. He knew that the men of the old regime still held too much power to collide with them, for his party was too divided to make an effective stand. He decided to bargain with them in good faith. The question was how the men of the old regime would respect the bargain they struck after the revolutionary dangers had passed away.

Nagyatadi Szabo's primary goal was the creation of a thoroughgoing land reform. This he was promised by Bethlen, the new *eminence grise* of Hungary, if he would consent to the repeal of the Friedrich government's decree on universal suffrage and the secret ballot. Nagyatadi Szabo concurred; a new ministerial decree was issued annulling universal suffrage and the secret ballot except in a few districts. (The elections of 1922 would be held under this restricted franchise.)

A further condition of the compromise between the two statesmen was realized on July 12, 1920, when the Smallholders' Party and the Christian Party merged into a unitary government party. As the *quid pro quo,* Nagyatadi Szabo was made Minister of Agriculture once again on August 17. The New Unitary Party assumed the name of *Kereszteny Kisgazda, Foldmunkas es Polgari Part* (Christian Smallholders, Farmworkers and Bourgeois Party).

Early in February, 1921, however, the two components separated once more. Nagyatadi Szabo's party still held 90 seats in Parliament and was still the largest party. On April 14, 1921, Count Bethlen formed his first cabinet. His second he formed on December 3. Neither included Nagyatadi Szabo. Bethlen was concentrating on normalizing relations with the Social Democrats. On December 21, 1921, he concluded with them the so-called Bethlen-Payer pact. The government made considerable concessions: the inmates of concentration camps were to be freed; the Social Democratic Party and the trade unions were to enjoy freedom of association, of assembly, speech, and of the press. Both were to have their properties restored, and extensive general amnesty for political prisoners was to be decreed. In return, the Social Democrats agreed that the trade unions would refrain from political activities, would restrict their organizing activities to industrial laborers, and would in no way seek to organize public employees, railwaymen or postal workers. The Social Democrats agreed not to agitate against the regime abroad and to sever their ties with exiles. Above all, they agreed not to undertake any activities among the rural population. The real political gain for the Social Democrats was the chance for parliamentary representation, and for this purpose in industrial and urban areas only, the ballot was made secret.[14]

Bethlen's next goal was a settlement with Nagyatadi Szabo and the Smallholders' Party. On January 5, 1922, Bethlen and a score of his immediate followers attended a meeting of the Smallholders' Party and were admitted into membership. From now on, the Unitary Party (*Egyseges Part*), officially still called the *Kereszteny, Kisgazda, Foldmunkas es Polgari Part*, became a permanent feature of Hungarian politics. The chairman remained Nagyatadi Szabo but control over political strategy was given to Count Bethlen, who received the title of *partvezeto* (party leader), while the internal affairs of the party fell to Gyula Gombos, who had the title of executive chairman.

Like a lamb led to the slaughter, Istvan Nagyatadi Szabo voluntarily laid his head and that of his followers on the block. Under the new franchise decree new elections were held in May, 1922, at which 144 seats were won by the Unitary Party, an absolute majority. The labor movement was pacified, the peasant movement was absorbed. In all but the name the old regime had been reestablished. All this had been achieved at the price of Nagyatadi Szabo's surrender on all issues; he had consented to the abolition of universal suffrage and the secret ballot in the countryside, had agreed to the fusion of the forces of the old regime with his majority Smallholders' Party, he had even yielded predominance in the new party to the representatives old regime—in return for the single undertaking that a program of broad land reform would be carried out. Would Bethlen and his associates honor the agreement? Would they use the Unitary Party to quash such a program or promote it? Was it even possible to carry out serious land reform without democracy? In other words, had Nagyatadi Szabo lost the chance for radical land reform when he sold out democracy?

The land reform that Bethlen permitted was a miserable pittance of what Nagyatadi Szabo wanted and what was needed to solve Hungary's greatest ill, the problem of its "three million beggars." (For the details of this reform, see the pertinent chapter in Joseph Held's essay in this volume.) When it finally became clear to Nagyatadi Szabo late in 1922, he threatened Bethlen that he would split the Unitary Party again and reestablish the Smallholders' Party in opposition. So in 1923 and 1924, some piecemeal improvements were made but they were merely tactical, to mollify Nagyatadi Szabo, rather than really solve the problem. The basic fact remained; Bethlen and his associates had sabotaged the land reform they were committed to. For every concession, Nagyatadi Szabo had to fight tooth and nail.

In August, 1924, Nagyatadi Szabo delivered a 16 point ultimatum to Bethlen and threatened to resign if it were rejected. His main demands were vigorous prosecution of land reform, amelioration of the intolerable conditions of the poor peasantry, and minimal advance toward a democratic form of government.[15] The showdown bore bitter fruit. Bethlen, the master tactician, was willing to yield on all unimportant points but was adamant on anything of significance. Belatedly, Nagyatadi Szabo realized that his policies had led him into a blind alley; his statesmanship had been proven a dismal failure. He resigned his portfolio and retired to his farm in Erdokocsonya, Somogy county, where he spent the last three months of his life in mental agony until November 1, 1924, when his heart failed and he died at the age of 60.

> "He went to his grave a broken man, aware that he had come nowhere near fulfilling his life's goal . . . His death was met with apathy and disappointment and lack of sympathy, even amidst his own villagers . . . The feudal forces that were dragging the country down wove a web around him, a web that was his undoing."[16]

2. The Independent Smallholders' Party

The political and economic consolidation of Hungary under Istvan Bethlen reached its peak in 1929. (for the actual process see the relevant chapter in Joseph Hold's essay in this volume). Then the world depression struck and Hungary could not escape its effects. The security of the farmers, the foundation stone of the precarious economic balance, was destroyed and the entire fabric of Hungary's economy fell to pieces. The collapse of the price of grain, Hungary's principal export, illustrates the extent of the disaster. Wholesale wheat prices (in gold crown per quintal) fell from 21.86 in 1929, to 18.83 in 1932, and 7.76 in 1933. Simultaneously, industrial production fell and unemployment grew by leaps and bounds. Misery activized the peasantry in the field of politics.

The peasantry's renewed political activity was first manifested, as in the past, in local clubs. In 1930, two centers began to acquire the trappings of potential nuclei for future national peasant movements, one in Transdanubia revolving around a Calvanist minister, Zoltan Tildy, and a young farmer, Ferenc Nagy, and the other in the *Viharsarok* revolving around a school teacher, Lajos Nagy. Interestingly, the old pattern repeated itself with the Transdanubian group moderate and the *Viharsarok* radical. The *Viharsarok* group issued the first manifesto, the Mezobereny program, which was to form the basis of the nascent Smallholders' Party's official platform.[17] The significance of the Mezobereny program is less in its content than the syndrome it represented. An organized peasant movement was again in the making, the first since the Smallholders' Party of Nagyatadi Szabo had merged with the forces of the old regime in 1922. In January, 1930, the leaders of the *Viharsarok* and the Transdanubian groups met in Felsonyek, Tolna County. The extended the Mezobereny Program further. This was the major step out of which the new party was to emerge.[18] The three basic tenets of the new party's eventual program were crystallized here: nationalism, an antisocialist bias, and a lack of interest in radical land reform. Only during World War II were these characteristics to change.

The Smallholders were nationalists to be sure, but nationalism was rife all over East Central Europe during the interwar years. The difference was that Hungary's neighbors' nationalsim was satisfied, while the Hungarians' was frustrated. Only 74% of all Hungarians lived in post-World War I Hungary. The rest were under the rule of neighboring foreign states. Rump Hungary was a uninational state. All the neighboring Little Entente states were multinational. Only 72% of the population of Rumania were Rumanians, 79% of Yugoslavia Serbs, Croats or Slovenes, and 62% of Czechoslovakia Czechs or Slovaks. This disposition was in flagrant violation of the Wilsonian principle of national self-determination.[19]

No politician or political organization could escape these facts or disregard the burning, unsatisfied nationalism of the Hungarians. There was no one in Hungary without relatives who were either under foreign rule or refugees from the place of their birth, for the new regimes expelled a great number of Hungarians, mostly professionals and intellectuals. The masses demanded redress of this injustice. Support for this sentiment was not opportunism on the part of the Smallholders' leaders; they shared the understandable state of mind of the masses.

Antisocialist bias was another part and parcel of the Smallholders' ideology, which was opposed to socialist internationalism. In the last years of the Bethlen regime the Social Democrats were allowed to start organizing in the countryside in the expectation that this would provoke a confrontation between the Social Democrats and the emerging new smallholder forces. That is exactly what happened. Lajos Nagy, the smallholder leader in the *Viharsarok,* denounced the appearance of Social Democratic organizers in the rural areas. "If no specific laws are passed against those Red bastards, we shall use our fists against them," he wrote.[20] Ferenc Nagy, the Transdanubian leader, likewise demanded "administrative" measures against the Social Democrats and the Communists.[21] The smallholder leaders easily forgot that democracy exists only when it assures freedom for all, not just for some. More dangerous and irritating was for the smallholders the Social Democratic Party's resolution at its 22nd Congress in 1930 that demanded the expropriation of all land greater than 282 acres in the hands of a single owner, and their redistribution to those who would till them.[22] This was a complete turnaround to the Social Democrats' agrarian policy. They had abandoned the idea of socialization of the land. The new policy was in fact anti-Marxist, and rather bourgeois. No wonder the smallholder leaders were fearful that the Social Democrats would take the wind out of their sails. Anna Kethly, the Social Democratic leader and member of Parliament, stressed the Social Democratic intention of penetrating rural Hungary when she declared in Parliament in February, 1932, that the Bethlen-Peyer pact that banned Social Democratic activities in the villages was null and void.[23] By early 1930, the Social Democratic Party, the strongest democratic opposition party, and the up and coming Independent Smallholders' Party were locked in no-holds barred combat. Only in the spring of 1943, under the duress of the war, did they sink their differences and conclude a political alliance.[24]

The new party's founding convention was held in October 12, 1930, in Bekes in the *Viharsarok*. Balint Szijj, a life-member of the Upper House, was elected party chairman, Zoltan Tildy executive vice-chairman, and Ferenc Nagy secretary general. The party's organ was *A Magyar Fold* (Hungarian Soil).[25] The convention adopted as the party's platform the Bekes Program, and took much from Nagyatadi Szabo's Szentgal Program. Its full title was "The Program of the Independent Smallholders', Farmworkers' and Bourgeois Party (*A Fuggetlen Kisgazda, Foldmunkas es Polgari Part Programmja*). It is an impressive work of 48 paragraphs with an introduction, provisions for a period that would elapse before it could be implemented, and a peroration.[26]

The program came short of demanding universal suffrage. It called for "the broadest popular representation," but elsewhere spoke of the "protection of the clearly popular representation of the (existing) legislature," indicating that the new party was not interested in radical expansion of the restricted electorate. What was fundamental was the proposal for the introduction of secret balloting in rural areas, which would at least have given sense to the rich peasants' right to vote, because the hustings corrupted and distorted the political process. Freedom of association, of assembly and of the press, trial by jury for political offenders, and the secret ballot in rural constituencies were not demands that would have secured democracy to be sure, but they would have been a definite improvement of the system, and universal conscription for one year's military service. In foreign policy the platform stood for peace in international relations, but since lasting peace could be built only on justice, it demanded revision of the "terror peace treaty" of Trianon and institutional protection for Hungarians living under foreign rule, that is, the territories annexed to Rumania, Czechoslovakia, Yugoslavia and Austria. To this end, a modern, efficient, less costly, incorruptible and much smaller central bureaucracy was proposed, with autonomous local and regional government under community control. As a move towards the democratization of government, the *virilista* system was to be abolished.

The Bekes Program referred to a new "national land policy" without even using the term, "land reform." This extremely moderate policy would do away with entailments and other restrictions on landed property. The state was to be given the right to buy land for division into lots of a size to support a family, and expropriate land that blocked the expansion of village communities. Excessive prices paid by the beneficiaries of earlier land distributions were to be revised, and the credit system was to be reformed so that smallholders could obtain cheap long term loans and big capital could be brought under effective control. Farmers' groups were to be organized, and the legal status of farmhands regulated. Unemployment would be eliminated in the rural areas by "correct land policies" and in the industrial sector through the "increasing purchasing power of the consumers."

The program's economic policies were contradictory. On the one hand, they were *laissez faire,* advocating no interference by the state in the economic process, and on the other, they sought judicious adjustment of the economy to Hungary's agrarian nature to serve the development of agriculture. Industries were to be developed that could use agricultural raw materials. Trusts were to be restricted and subjected to state control. Progressive taxation was proposed with double taxes for those who lived abroad and exemption for those with minimal subsistence incomes and for basic foodstuffs.

The program urged debureaucratization of the welfare system, and expansion of the eligibility requirements. A nationwide social security system was to be set up for the orphaned and the aged, and free medical care was to be available for the poor. The state was to help finance a village health system and regulate doctors' and hospitals' fees. A better school system was demanded to raise the cultural level of the many who lived in scattered cottages on the Great Hungarian Plain far from cultural and educational centers. Higher national cultural standards were to be achieved not through an oversized system of higher education but by the expansion and strengthening of elementary education. Foreign influences were to be eliminated from the school system which was to have a sounder national basis. The program proposed greater state support for elementary schools.

The Bekes Program was, then, for the rich peasantry. The poor peasants barely figured in it. In some respects it was even a retreat from Nagyatadi Szabo's Szentgal Program. It made no demand for universal, direct and compulsory suffrage; while in 1919, Nagyatadi Szabo referred to the necessity of promoting the welfare of industrial workers, the program promulgated eleven years later turned its back on them completely. It resembled Nagyatadi Szabo's policy of neutralizing the rural proletariat rather than mobilizing them for action, but it nevertheless belongs among the progressive political programs of Hungary in the early 1930's.

After the Bekes congress, Gaszton Gaal, the owner of a 1,000 *hold* estate in Somogy County, was invited at Zoltan Tildy's suggestion to become party leader. He brought in with him seeral legitimist landlords and such notorious extreme right-wing radicals as Dr. Tibor Eckhardt. Shortly after the party had been organized, the genuine peasant founders of it found themselves eased into the second rank of leadership. Gaszton Gaal himself was not to blame. According to Ferenc Nagy:

> In the political life of the era, the figure of Gaszton Gaal stood out as a man of stern principles, respected by everyone .... We invited him to become the political leader of our party. We laid our plans and platform before him, and Gaszton Gaal accepted.[27]

Indeed, Gaal was opposed to the alliance of big capital and the large estates. But besides this attitude and his personal integrity, he had little qualification to be the leader of the only peasant party of the time.

After Gaal's untimely death in 1932, the party committed the monstrous blunder of inviting Eckhardt to lead it. Tibor Eckhardt began his political career after World War I as a militant, anti-Semitic, illiberal anti-socialist. With Gyula Gombos, he in 1920 founded the protofascist Party of Racial Defense (Fajvedo Part). Since 1923, he had also been president of the Association of Awakening Hungarians (Ebredo Magyarok Egyesulete), a protofascist terror organization. Eckhardt changed color all to easily. Macartney, an objective foreign observer states:

> He was not even genuinely radical on the question of land reform, for although when definitely in opposition Eckhardt produced a fairly far-reaching plan for land reform, yet when there was a chance of his wishes carrying weight, he never seriously pressed for anything more than fulfillment of the far less extensive proposals (of the regime).[28]

With such a man directing the fortunes of the Independent Smallholders' Party, it is no surprise that it failed miserably at the polls. The cumulative effects of internal blunders and external harassment of the party was to give it 10 seats in 1931 and 14 in 1939. If these results are compared with those of Nagyatadi Szabo's Smallholders' Party, which won 57 seats in

1920 and in June of the same year increased them to 91, the extent of the failure of the Independent Smallholders' Party becomes obvious.

In the atmosphere created by Eckhardt, the Bekes Program was completely forgotten. Only after the elections of 1939 did the genuinely peasant wing headed by Ferenc Nagy and Zoltan Tildy regain a say in the party's affairs. Their control was fully reestablished in March, 1941, when Eckhardt left Hungary for good. Miklos Kallay, the former prime minister claimed that with the departure of Eckhardt the party "lost its importance and quality."[29] In fact, the truth seems to be diametrically the opposite. The Independent Smallholders' Party started to breathe freely once its affairs were being conducted by its own men, and not by outsiders. The Bekes Program was revived and remained the party platform all during the war, but only in principle, it was forgotten in practice. After World War II, when in the spring of 1947 a definitive platform was needed by the party, the leadership decided to study and adjust the Bekes Program to the prevailing circumstances. But for several weeks no copies of the program could even be found, according to one of the radical members of the party, Istvan Dobi.[30] This despite the fact that the party chairman, Zoltan Tildy, immediately after the war, stated that the Bekes Program had stood the test of time and the time had now come for it to be realized.[31]

After Ferenc Nagy finally left Hungary in 1947, circumstances put the entire issue of the Bekes Program outside the realm of reality. In 1930, when it had been drafted, the party itself let it be set aside. It was too modest anyway to be the basis of a mass radical peasant movement of defiance, and yet it was too much for the regime, so it did not stand a chance. After World War II, factors outside the framework of Hungary's own political forces created a situation in which, at least temporarily, the wildest dreams of the peasants became a reality. So again the Bekes Program lost any practical meaning. Both it and its authors were simply overtaken by events.

3. The National Peasant Party and Hungarian Populism

The last democratic peasant movement in pre-People's Democratic Hungary was a paradox. It was the first movement that addressed itself almost exclusively to the problems of the rural proletariat and dwarfholders, who were the poorest and least educated stratum of Hungarian society. Yet those who now championed them were the most literate men any peasant movement ever produced in Hungary. The movement was bifocal. Its political side was the National Peasant Party; its intellectual side was literary populism. Several figures were leaders of both.[32]

Populism was a radical movement of intellectuals who rejected the Horthy regime and deplored Hungary's lack of modernization. The populists were under the influence of the most varied Western thinkers. They were affected by social positivism, Marxism, Scandinavian and German socialist revisionism, nationalism, romanticism, the social pessimism of men like Ortega y Gasset, and, of course, democracy. Individual populists showed these various influences in differing manners and degrees. Without becoming *narodniki,* they envisaged Hungary's peasantry as a class upon whose virtues, wisdom and energies a modern Hungary could and should be built. They disdained only the existing peasant party, the Independent Smallholders', because it neglected the rural proletariat and had never produced a program that would satisfy or attract it.[33] Many populists were "village explorers" (falukatatok), a back-to-the-land movement begun by Mihaly Kerek in the early 1930's after prolonged research and observations in Germany.[34] Gyula Illyes also urged educated people to go into the countryside, and many heeded him.[35] Their purpose was to shed light on conditions in the rural areas. These "village explorers" were guided and inspired by the example and success of Bela Bartok and Zoltan Kodaly, who had collected Hungarian folk tunes and turned them into very modern and sophisticated symphonic music which "was a tremendous source of enthusiasm for the young."[36] The result of the "village explorers" investigations was the publication of a series of extremely interesting and radical studies. It was the most genuinely native Hungarian and original of any of the movements of the time and encouraged many others.[37] The prime value of the "village explorers" work wrote Kerek, was that "it did not deal with the land problem exclusively from a party-political point of view, which is changeable and transitory; its approach was literary and intellectual with deep sociological convictions. For these reasons its effect was all the greater."[38]

An eminent and original view of the Hungarian "village explorers" was that of Professor Hugh Seton-Watson:

> Curious though it may seem, I would argue that these four quite different groups—Russian Narodniks, Serbian Leninists, Rumanian Fascists and Hungarian village explorers—had in common a basic social attitude and moral political mentality which is at least as important as the difference in the doctrine they professed. This I would describe as the "Populist mentality"—the idea of service to the people, the belief that it was their duty, as they had risen from the people and had achieved a material and cultural level that was inaccessible to the people, to use the skills and knowledge they had acquired in order to free the people from its oppressors and raise it up out of its poverty.[39]

The populists formulated a doctrine of international relations that amounted to a Hungarian brand of "third way." The most comprehensive statement of it was Istvan Bibo's book, *Harmadik ut: Politikai es torteneti tanulmanyok.*[40] He advocated the cooperation of industrial and rural labor, in contrast to the antisocialist policies of the Independent Smallholders' Party. At the heart of the populist movement lay a demand for a radical land reform and the establishment of peasant democracy.[41] In 1937 an inner circle of the populists decided that more politically oriented activities were necessary than had so far been engaged in. Out of this decision emerged the March Front. On March 15, 1937, the anniversary of the Revolution of 1848, the front was formed and promulgated its Twelve Points Program.[42] This program demanded political democracy through universal and equal suffrage and the secret ballot void of any impediment, and freedom of conscience, speech, the press, assembly and association. Radical land reform was to be implemented by expropriating all single holdings of land in excess of 500 *hold* (700 acres) for distribution among the peasants. The power of the house of magnates was to be eliminated; progressive taxation was to be introduced; job opportunities were to be created for all those willing and able to work; minimum wage levels were to be established; and all workers' associations were to be free of restrictions. Education costs would be on a sliding scale with college entrance open to the best talents. National self-determination was urged for the Danubian peoples with their consolidation into a Danubian Confederation. This platform topped everything that had gone on before as a clear and progressive plea for democracy and social and political equality for all the peasantry, and indeed for the whole nation. It was imbued with the intellectual power and radicalism of its creators, the populist intellectuals.

As the populist intellectuals became more involved in political activity and the March Front developed, they decided that their program required refinement. So in the fall of 1937 at Mako, a town in the Viharsarok, the Mako Manifesto was issued.[43] It left untouched the basic demands of the Twelve Point Program since they were still valid. What needed clarification was the March Front's relationship to Marxism and the Social Democratic Party.

Marxism as the exclusive recipe for the liberation of oppressed classes was rejected. The manifesto, a true expression of populism, considered the Hungarian people capable of creating a democratic form of government and society without resorting to foreign patterns or cliches. It also rejected the Leninist thesis of the primacy of the industrial laborers' revolutionary movement. Instead, it advocated intimate cooperation between industrial and rural laborers in a partnership of equals.[44]

On May 28-30, 1939, Hungary's last prewar election was held in accordance with an amendment of the electoral law that introduced virtual political democracy with universal suffrage and the secret ballot. It was the most democratic general election in Hungary since 1920, free enough to reflect the political power balance of the moment. The results showed that democracy, so long frustrated by the Horthy regime, was incapable of overcoming the obstacles the regime had created and was now in sharp decline. It had simply lost its appeal. The Independent Smallholders' Party's prestige had been damaged by the policies of Tibor Eckhardt. Many democrats were offended by his monarchist utterances and even more of them had realized that he conspired against democracy rather than upheld it. Despite the benevolence of Prime Minister Pal Teleki towards the Smallholders, of the 161 candidates they put up only 14 were returned and of them only one won in a direct personal contest. The other 13 came in on list votes.[45]

The defeat of democracy and the resounding victory of right-wing radicalism tipped the balance in the prolonged debate within the March Front. It was decided that a new peasant party had to be formed to replace the discredited Independent Smallholders' Party. On June 29, 1939, in Mako, the founding convention of the National Peasant Party was held. The new party's platform was an extended version of the March Front's Twelve Points Program and the Mako Manifesto. It stood for an independent Hungary with its government exclusively run by Hungarians. Universal and equal suffrage and the secret ballot, and all the other stipulations of the two previous programs were there. Its innovations included social security for disabled workers, the old and the unemployed; the establishment of cooperatives; the industrialization of the country; and universal free popular education. This program was then both the continuation of the platforms of all earlier peasant democratic movements and the climax of them, the clearest and most precise and most radical of them all. Politically its aim was the most modern form of democratic government: the welfare state. It included all the advantages a free political system could offer by involving all its citizens in the process of government. It basically maintained the capitalist system, but not laissez-faire capitalism, for the program would curb the excesses of it by an effort to eliminate extreme poverty at the expense of extreme wealth. It drew on the most modern European political thought, adapting it to Hungary's particular circumstances. The program, in short, embodied all that populism offered for the creation of a modern Hungary, with a free peasantry in a free state.

On August 20, 1939, the party held its first leadership conference, which made decisions on matters of organization and elected a permanent leadership.[46] The official organ of the party was *Szabad Szo* (Free Word) which had originally been founded a generation earlier as the journal of the Reorganized Social Democratic Party of Vilmos Mezofi. Imre Kovacs edited it for the National Peasant Party.

Early in January, 1945, the National Peasant Party instructed its members to organize the landless peasants and dwarfholders in the villages. Farmhands as well as progressive intellectuals of popular origin were to be considered potential party members. Peter Veres and Gyula Illyes, distinguished populist writers of peasant origin, issued manifestoes in Transdanubia on the organization of farm-hands and poor peasants. The party was indeed addressing itself to Hungary's "three million beggars," and by mid-1945, it was estimated to have had 200,000 members.[47]

4. Non-Party Peasant Mass Organizations

Two peasant mass organizations still need to be mentioned: the Peasant Union or Alliance (Parasztszovetseg) and KALOT or State Secretariat of Young Catholic Farmworkers, Organizations (Katholikus Agrarifjusagi Legenyegyletek Orszagos Titkarsaga). Their juxtaposition here is not meant to suggest that there was any connection or similarity between the two for there was none.

On September 1, 1941, the Ministry of the Interior issued a permit for the organization of a peasant-interest organization. The regime encouraged the work of the new Peasant Alliance because it hoped it would develop into a means of curbing rather than encouraging the peasants' democratic and land reform demands. It also saw it as a shield against fascist penetration of the peasants and hoped it would unite them into a reserve of support rather than of opposition.[48]

The founders, Ferenc Nagy above all, saw the organization in a very different light. Nagy wrote: "Through a new, strong peasant organization, I felt an old dream come true. It would not only serve the economic, cultural and social interests of the peasantry, but enlighten, inform and train it for the future task of reshaping society along democratic lines."[49] Truly, at the outset he did not envision the alliance as a political organization. At the founding congress he stated, "The Hungarian Peasant Alliance is not a political organization, it is not a party ready to wage a class struggle. It intends to become a permanent assurance of the balance of national life by uniting the entire peasantry, modernizing its economic structure, and elevating it to a higher sphere in cultural life."[50]

It was hoped that the Peasant Alliance would become a link between the Independent Smallholders' Party which dominated it,[51] and the National Peasant Party, which did not want it to be an organization representing the interests exclusively of the rich peasants. Accordingly, at an editorial meeting of *Szabad Szo* in March, 1942, it was decided to promote the cause of the new organization and urge all levels of the peasantry to join it. It was also proposed that a special section for the rural proletariat should be organized within it, a proposal warmly supported by the underground Communist Party. Membership grew rapidly and by the summer of 1942, there were 213 operating branches in 14 counties with a total membership of 30,000.[52]

An article published by *Szabad Szo* on March 13, 1943, appealed to the rural proletariat and the rich peasantry to cooperate against the regime instead of their being in opposite camps as was usually the case. The same article continued:

> In our view, the farm laborers' section and the rural proletariat that is united in it should fulfill the role for which its social position has destined it: to be a bridge of its own building between the Hungarian peasantry and the industrial workers.

Here again was the populist view of the independent role of the peasantry subordinate to no other group and of the need of cooperation between industrial and rural labor, a view that colored all the policies of the farm laborers' section of the Peasant Alliance.

The other organization was KALOT. Under the devoted leadership of a Jesuit, Jeno Kerkai

> a political, economic, social and moral organization was formed to offer specific training for rural youth in specialized schools with the intention of generating a young peasant leadership elite.[53]

The center of the movement was in the city of Szeged. Its inspiration was Roman Catholic but its basic goals were not sectarian but sociopolitical. It did not wish to separate young peasants from each other along denominational lines but rather to unite them all. The organization's published program, entitled *Magyar Cel* (Hungarian Purpose), listed as its goals: national independence free from any foreign domination; a state spiritually, defensively and economically strong; an administration that would make government serve the public interest rather than vice versa; government that would preserve the balance between the authority of the state and the freedom of the individual; assurance of the right to live, earn and own property on the basis of social justice; self-governing organizations for all classes of workers; workers' boards to regulate wages not by upheaval but in accordance with the law; protection of the family and family supplements for children; protection of motherhood; and "organic" settlement campaign (telepites) that would offer a home plot for each family and cheap mortgage loans; "the prime foundation of the nation and the source of its strength is the economically independent smallholder farming class which should be expanded at the expense of the great estates, primarily land-leasing cooperatives;" capital made subordinate to national interests; protection of Christianity; and peace in the Danube basin between the Hungarians and other local ethnic groups.[54]

Two Papal encyclicals were issued endorsing and encouraging the movement. The movement began in 1934; by 1936, its monthly magazine already had 5,000 subscribers and in 1938, 17,000 copies a month were being published. KALOT reached its peak during the war years and immediately after. At the 1947 general elections KALOT handled all the publicity and organizational work for the Democratic Peoples' Party or Christian Democratic Party (*Demokrata Neppart*), and even administered the finances for its election campaign. The result was a resounding success: 61 members of parliament were returned on the party's ticket, 30of them born peasants.[55] As a democratic movement KALOT was of extraordinary significance, but like all similar organizations it fell victim to the Communist regime.

5. Conclusions

A final assessment of the Hungarian democratic peasant movements must take account of three elements: the movements' relationship to political democracy; their theories and practice on the issue of land ownership; and how much political power they shared in.

1. Democracy was a basic goal of all the peasants' movements in Hungary. A short-lived Fascist experiment of Zoltan Boszormeny's Scythe-Cross movement scarcely rates a footnote. In fact, while a considerable number of industrial workers went fascist and voted so in 1939, the peasant masses

remained aloof. The same was true with the other totalitarian ideology, Communism. During the Bela Kun regime, the peasants remained either sullenly passive or became outright counterrevolutionaries. As Dezso Sulyok points out, while not one aristocrat fell victim to the red terror, there are 240 known cases of peasants who were executed for counterrevolutionary activities.[56] So the mainstream of the peasants' movements was democratic. There were, however, two notable instances when this conscious adherence to democracy was of vital importance but faltered. In one case in 1920, indeed, democracy was within the grasp of peasants, but their leaders not only let it slip but Istvan Nagyatadi Szabo also traded the democratic transformation of Hungary for Count Istvan Bethlen's promise of land reform, which was dependent upon a democratic form of government, and by so doing forfeited the chance for both. The other instance was the Independent Smallholders' Party's Bekes Program of 1930, which omitted the demand for democracy, partly because the party spoke for the rich peasants who were already enfranchised, and party as a matter of realpolitik because the party leaders did not wish to see their organization nipped in the bud by a reactionary regime. It is somehow pathetic that when univesal suffrage was introduced in 1939, both democracy and the Independent Smallholders' Party lost out to fascism. Only in the brief spell of democracy that followed World War II did the Independent Smallholders' Party at last get its majority in Parliament.

The electoral ordinance of September, 1945, provided for members of Parliament to be elected by universal suffrage and secret ballotting on the basis of proportional representation. There was a seat in Parliament for every 12,000 votes cast. This ordinance doubled the electorate of Hungary, enfranchising 59.7% of the population. The results of general elections (November 4, 1945)[57] were:

	Votes	Percent of Ballot	Number of Seats
Independent Smallholders	2,691,384	57.0%	245
Social Democrats	822,666	17.4%	70
Communists	801,341	17.0%	69
National Peasant Party	323,571	6.9%	23
Civic Democrats	76,331	1.6%	2
Hungarian Radicals	5,762	0.1%	—
Total —	4,721,055	100%	409

The Independent Smallholders' Party had an absolute majority in Parliament. But the plain fact that universal suffrage does not alone make democracy was soon demonstrated. Real power lay not with the electorate but with the Soviet occupation forces who took pains to undo the embryonic democratic experiment, and two years later Hungary witnessed the year of the Turning of the Tide, during which totalitarian Communism was installed and democracy was laid to an early rest.

2. Peasant movement theories and practice on land ownership varied widely. Since democracy did not exist and the regime was ready to crush any attempt at radical alteration of land ownership, the movements faced two alternatives. They either had to follow their theories through and change the status quo, which was really impossible other than by revolution, or else they had to accept the prevailing circumstances and adjust their theories to them. Those who conscientiously adhered to their theories demanding radical change of the land ownership system and tried to change conditions by radical land reform included most notably Varkonyi and his Independent Social Democratic Party, Achim and his Peasant Party, Nagyatadi Szabo and his Smallholders' Party until 1920, the Populist Movement and the

National Peasant Party. Above all those who made their ideas conform to circumstances was the Social Democratic Party, which began by demanding socialization of the land but showed that its social radicalism was superficial by its failure to organize the peasantry for radical agrarian socialist action. It abandoned the plan for socialization and its demand for genuine land reform at the time of the Great Depression was simply another adjustment of ideas to circumstances. This latter adjustment was tantamount to doing a favor to the regime, which looked on with great sympathy in the hope that a confrontation between the Social Democrats and the emergent Independent Smallholders would bring both major opposition parties down in internecine feuding.

3. Lastly, the answer to how big a share the peasant movements had in political power must be given. True, during the Karolyi regime they took part in power, but the regime's brevity and the chaos that succeeded it make that share little more than symbolic. The Bela Kun regime was more against than for the peasants, and the peasants' leaders went into passive resistance. When in 1920 the majority of seats in Parliament went to the Smallholders, for reasons already stated, power slipped out of their hands. Not until the end of World War II did they have a second chance as a majority in Parliament, but it was worthless. Afte World War I, the extremely skilled tacticians of the gentry outmaneuvered them; after World War II, they were forced out by ruthless Soviet policy. In fact, never in the history of Hungary have the peasants really shared power, definitely never to the degree warranted by their numbers. It is, then, fair to consider the entire period from the emancipation act to the seizure of power by communists as a gradual evolution from "second serfdom" into the "third serfdom" of Communist collective society.[58]

NOTES

1. There were two members of Parliament with the same name: Istvan Szabo. To distinguish between them, the house stenographers attached to their names the name of the constituency that returned them. These epithets have stuck so they have come down in history as Istvan Nagyatadi Szabo and Istvan Sokoropatkai Szabo. Sulyok, *op. cit.*, 415; Bodrogkozy, *op. cit.*, 108.
2. For the status of the *inquilinus* see Bela Kiraly, *op. cit.*, 263. Szabo completed eight grades of grammar school and afterwards continued to educate himself. Bodrogkozy, *op. cit.*, 106.
3. Sulyok, *op. cit.*, 412. Nagyatadi Szabo was elected to the Somogy County Assembly in 1904. Bodrogkozy, *op. cit.*, 105.
4. Bodrogkozy, *op. cit.*, 107.
5. *Ibid.*, 109-11.
6. *Pester Lloyd,* November 3, 1924; Bodrogkozy, *op. cit.*, 111.
7. Kiraly, *op. cit.*, 62.
8. Poloskei and Szakacs, *op. cit.*, I: 459, 681.
9. Farm labor force declined from 1,459,681 in 1900 to 1,278,263 in 1910. *Ibid.*, 438.
10. For details of the reactionary strategy see "land Reform, the Organic Settlement and Cooperative Efforts."
11. Macartney, *op. cit.*, I: 23-24.
12. *Ibid.*, I:27, note 1.
13. Sulyok, *op. cit.*, 417. Count Istvan Bethlen, a Transylvanian aristocrat, was the most characteristic tactician of the time. His Prime Ministry between 1921 and 1931 is called with justification the "Bethlen era," a period of progresive conservatism.
14. *Nyugat Magyarorszag* (Western Hungary), October, 1950. See also Macartney, *op. cit.*, 1:44 and 266.
15. Sulyok, *op. cit.*, 417.
16. *Ibid.*
17. Istvan Vida, "A Fuggetlen Kisgazda Part 1930. evi bekesi programja" (The 1930 program of the Independent Small-

holders' Party at Bekes) *Tortenelmi Szemle* 10 (1967) No. 1, 78.

18. Ferenc Nagy, *The Struggle Behind the Iron Curtain* (New York, 1948), 22-3.
19. Stephen J. Kertesz, *Diplomacy in a Whirlpool; Hungary* Between Nazi *Germany and Soviet Russia* (Notre Dame, Ind., 1953), 198, note 14. See also, Pal Teleki, *The Evolution of Hungary and its Place in European History* (New York, 1923), 93-7, and C. A. Macartney and A. W. Palmer, *Independent Eastern Europe; A History* (London, 1966), 125-30.
20. *Magyarfold,* June 22, 1930. Quoted by Vida, *op. cit.,* 78.
21. *Ibid.,* March 30 and June 8, 1930, quoted by *Ibid.,* 83.
22. *Nepszava,* September 12, 1930.
23. Vida, *op. cit.,* 84, note 33.
24. Ferenc Nagy, *op. cit.,* 39.
25. *Ibid.,* 24.
26. The entire text is reprinted in Vida, *op. cit.,* 93-100.
27. Ferenc Nagy, *op. cit.,* 24.
28. Macartney, *op. cit.,* I:122.
29. Miklos Kallay, *Hungarian Premier: A Personal Account of a Nation's Struggle in the Second World War* (New York, 1954), 34.
30. Istvan Dobi, *Vallomas es tortenelem* (Confessions and History) (Budapest, 1961), II:21.
31. Address given in Debrecen, March 8, 1945, quoted by Vida, *op. cit.,* 92.
32. On Hungarian populism in general see Charles Gati, *The Populist Current in Hungarian Politics, 1935-1955.* Unpublished MA thesis, Indiana University, 1965; Rudolf L. Tokes, *The Hungarian Populists' 'Third Road' Ideology.* Unpublished Ph.D. thesis, Columbia University, 1961. See also, Paul Ignotus, "Radical Writers in Hungary," *Journal of Contemporary History* 1 (1966), No. 2, 149-67; George Gomori, "Social Conflict in Hungarian Literature," *Journal of International Affairs* 20 (1966), No. 1, 151-64; Hugh Seton-Watson, "East European Intellectuals and the Populist Spirit," *The New Leader* 41 (1958), No. 1, 6-8; Paul

Zinner, *Revolution in Hungary* (New York, 1962). "In fact, the mainstream of the populist intellectuals gave rise to the National Peasant Party, without including all the populists, or compromising their literary reputation;" Imre Kovacs to Bela K. Kiraly, December 4, 1972. See also, Gyula Borbandi, *Der ungarische Populismus* (Mainz, 1976).

33. The leading representatives of the populists were Gyula Illyes, Aron Tamasi, Janos Kodolanyi, Peter Veres, Jozsef Erdelyi, Laszlo Nemeth, Pal Szabo, Zoltan Szabo, Ferenc Erdei, Jozsef Darvas, Geza Feja, Sandor Kazinczy, Gyorgy Sarkozi, Gyorgy Budai, Viola Tomori, Imre Kovacs and others. Imre Kovacs, "Populism," unpublished MSS made available to me by the author.
34. Mihaly Kerek spent eight months doing research at the *Deutsches Forschungs-Institut fur Agrar und Siedlungswesen,* in Berlin, under the direction of Professor Sering. Afterwards he made on-the-spot studies at German state-assisted resettlement projects in Brandenberg, Silesia, Pomerania, the Grenzmark, East Prussia, Hanover, Brunswick and Mecklenburg. Their experience is what Kerek wanted to put to use in Hungary. See his book, *A telepites felevszazada: A mezogazdasagi telepites rendszere es eredmenyei Nemetorszagban, 1886-1935-ig* (Half a Century of Resettlement: The System and Results of Agrarian Resettlement in Germany from 1886 to 1935) (Budapest, 1935).
35. Imre Kovacs, *op. cit.,* Unpublished MS.
36. *Ibid.*
37. Macartney, *op. cit.,* 1:156.
38. Mihaly Kerek, *op. cit.,* 248.
39. Seton-Watson, *op. cit.,* 7. See also, Gyula Rezler, *Falukutatok es szociografusok: A magyar tarsadalom onvizsgalata az elmult evtizedben* (Village Explorers and Sociographers: Hungarian Society's Search for Self during the Last Decade) (Budapest, 1943).
40. *The Third Road: Political and Historical Essays* (London, 1960).

41. Istvan Toth, *A Nemzeti Parasztpart tortenete 1944-1948* (A History of the National Peasant Party, 1944-1948) (Budapest, 1972), 8.
42. The entire text in Imre Kovacs, *op. cit.*, and in Toth, *op. cit.*, 8. See also, Macartney, *op. cit.*, I:184.
43. Kovacs, *op. cit.*, and Toth, *op. cit.*, 8.
44. Kovacs, *op. cit.*, and Poloskei and Szakacs, *op. cit.*, II: 970-1.
45. 45. The results of the general elections of 1939 (in parentheses is the number of seats held in the previous Parliament) were the following: Smallholders 14 (23), Christians 8 (14), Liberals 5 (7), Social Democrats 5 (11), a total of 32 for the democratic left, Arrow Cross Party 31 (0), Mesko Party 3 (0), Marothy Party 2 (0), National Will 1 (0), Szollosi Independents 1 (0), total of right-wing radical, 49; government party (Party of Hungarian Life or Magyar Elet Partja) 179; representatives of the recently returned Northern Highlands (Felvidek), supporting the government party, 26; representatives from Ruthenia, supporting the government party, 10; total of the government block, 215. Macartney, *op. cit.*, I:351.
46. The chairman was Pal Szabo. The members of the executive committee were Lajos Hajdu-Nemeth, Ferenc Ilias, Vince Voros, Mihaly Guba, Laszlo Nanasi, Gyorgy Horvath, Ferenc Varga, Imre Rozsa, Pal Kocsi, Bertalan Szabo, Jozsef Sellyei, Ferenc Erdei, Imre Kovacs and Peter Veres. Toth, *op. cit.*, 11-12.
47. *Ibid.*, 29.
48. Poloskei and Szakacs, *op. cit.*, II:988.
49. Ferenc Nagy, *op. cit.*, 34.
50. *Parasztnaptar, 1946* (Peasant Calendar) (Budapest, 1946), 19 and 30. See also, Poloskei and Szakacs, *op. cit.*, II:988-89.
51. Two key officials were party members: Ferenc Nagy, the chairman, and Bela Kovacs, the secretary general. Ferenc Nagy, *op. cit.*, 36.
52. Poloskei and Szakacs, *op. cit.*, II:989.
53. Istvan Barankovics, former secretary general of the Hungarian Democratic Peoples' Party, to Bela K. Kiraly,

November, 1972. KALOT, in fact, like the Democratic Peoples' Party, based its theory on the Papal encyclicals *De rerum novarum* and *Quadragesimo anno*. Jeno Gergely, "Keresztenydemokracia vagy nepi demokracia," (Christian Democracy of People's Democracy:) *Vilagossag*, February, 1972, 72-80.

54. Laszlo Tiry, "EMSzO es KALOT" (EMSzO: Catholic Youth Labor Movement and KALOT) *Magyar Szemle* 34 (1938), 174-6.
55. Istvan Barankovics to Bela K. Kiraly, November, 1972.
56. Sulyok, *op. cit.*, 243, 246 and 276.
57. Kertesz, *op. cit.*, 140-1.
58. The first term is Friedrich Engles', the second is mine.

*Research for this portion of the volume was undertaken with the support of a Fullbright-Hays and an American Council of Learned Societies—IREX—Grant to the author who gratefully acknowledges this assistance.

PART VII

DYNAMIC CHANGE: RURAL TRANSFORMATION, 1945-1975.

Ivan Volgyes

I

THE IMPACT OF COMMUNISM ON THE RURAL SPHERE

1. Introduction

The history of rural transformation in post-World War II Hungary is the story of misperception and misplaced convictions. The Communists, as well as their opponents (and all those in Hungary who were concerned with agrarian reform) have regarded the pattern of the ownership structure of land as the independent variable of the modernization of rural society. Changing that structure to correspond to the socialist mode of production was viewed as the key ingredient of the process of rural modernization. Without changing the pattern of land ownership, the Communists reasoned, there could not be meaningful progress, while changing it to reflect the socialist production was supposed to guarantee that expected alteration and progress. In the end, the country discovered that Marxist theory was dead wrong, that production improvements, modernization and agrarian progress did not solely depend upon man's relationship to the means of production, that there can be poor, average and excellent farms all characterized by the same relationships. The discovery had been made that other variables also entered into the general transformation process, factors that had nothing to do with the structure of ownership. Eventually it became clear that attitudes toward production, political participation, citizen-integration, were not dependent upon the relationship to the means of production at all—as the Marxist theory claimed—but were a function of a more generalized process of modernization in which the relationship to the land was merely one variable. The discovery of this reality is the story of rural change in Hungary during the last thirty years, with which the seventh part of this volume is concerned.

At the end of the devastating war that swept over Europe, the rural sphere of Hungary stood barren. Fields had been turned into minefields, bomb craters gaped along the ruined roads. Burned out hectares and uprooted earth gaped side by side, forcing the onlooker to wonder if there were ever a chance for these lands to produce again. The pantries of the peasant houses, the store-rooms of the large estates stood empty in living testimony to the requisitioning activities of the various armies that had criss-crossed the land. In villages, towns, and cities food distribution stood at a standstill, but food—scarce as it was—became the medium of exchange resulting in widespread starvation, especially during the first half of 1945. The nearly 250,000 men who disappeared from the villages and from agricultural production in the steppes of the USSR never returned. Long after the war was over, an additional 100,000 young peasants were forcibly taken away to the USSR to work in reparation-payments, rebuilding the damaged industries of the Soviet Union. The bitter winter, the hard snows, and the frozen land gave way to a muddy spring in which the isolation of the villages seemed greater than ever, and the peasants of the land asked the question over and over: "Will there ever be a real transformation of the countryside, and will our lives be worth living again?"

As one looks at the Hungarian countryside at the end of the 1970's, it seems inconceivable that the changes that have occurred really took place during the last three decades, during the lifetime of a single generation. The young men and women in today's villages, strolling in their American-made jeans, driving American or Soviet-built modern tractors and combines, getting in and out of their own cars or off their motorcycles, dancing to blaring rock music, watching the ever-present television screen or visiting far-away cities in their own country and in Europe, can hardly be the children of the generation which tilled their own and others' land by hand, eking out a hand-to-mouth existence. And yet, this remarkable transformation—the only real revolutionary modernization—did take place in Hungary during the last three decades, and the process of change we shall describe in this part of our study remains the most dynamic accomplishment of the Hungarian Communist system.

Paradoxically, the process of the transformation of the Hungarian countryside has been the most complex part of policies that were frequently helter-skelter, confused, contradictory, but which consistently aimed at the modernization of Hungarian agriculture. The bases of the transformation have been the alteration of the existing relationship between the people and the land on the one hand, and the general modernization of the socio-economic structure of Hungary on the other. The changes that have taken place can, therefore, be characterized as follows:

1. changes directly related to the structure of land ownership;
2. changes partly attributable to the structure of land ownership;
3. changes that resulted from the general process of modernization.

Land ownership, land hunger and land use have become mythologized in much of the literature dealing with the peasantry in general and the Hungarian peasantry in particular. And yet, for social scientists to accept such a highly idealized picture as presented by those who argue the extreme importance of land ownership, would be indeed a serious error. In studying the concept of land ownership in an objective manner, one can come to accept the fact that the ownership of land has been one of the most significant aspects of peasant demands throughout centuries of Hungarian history. Yet, we must not be content to stop there; we must ask the question, is it ownership, *per se,* that the peasants were after?

Historically, land ownership and the redistribution of the land of the large estates had been one of the basic demands of many non-communist peasant movements, as described in Bela Kiraly's study in a previous section of this volume. These were demanded as the peasants perceived land ownership to be the only concrete way to survival and material advancement, and they regarded the land as the only certain, comprehensible and visible form of wealth. Their experience with history taught them that survival depended upon food, and it was the land that provided them with food. Regimes and rulers came and went, money changed shape and color, size and national origin, but the land and *what benefit it could give them* remained permanent; the land, and it alone, insured their survival. Consequently, their relationship to the structure of ownership-*and to the benefits perceived and expected from that ownership structure*—remains the key to our understanding of the transformation process.

In this sense, the changing structure of land ownership is the independent variable of a large portion of the transformation process. This, and this alone, helps to explain the two most significant dependent variables of rural transformation in Hungary: the changes in the number of people living in a rural locality, and the changes in the number of people employed in agriculture.

These two dependent variables, indeed, have shown significant alterations during the last three decades. Table I shows the distribution of people living in the rural sphere in selected years during the process of transformation.

TABLE I. Total Agrarian Population in Hungary, 1941-1976.

	1941	1976
Total population	9,317,000	10,572,000
Agrarian population as % of total population	62%	49.3%

The number of people living in the rural sphere, thus, decreased from 5,777,000 in 1941 to 5,190,000 in 1976. This means that in spite of the enormous losses of rural people in the war and the emigration resulting from the post-war uncertainties, nearly 10% of the entire Hungarian population, or almost one million people, had left the rural sphere and had become urban residents during the last three decades.

The pattern of occupational changes, however, show far greater divergencies. Table II describes the occupational changes in the Hungarian population for selected years.

TABLE II. Occupational and Employment Changes in Hungary, 1941-1976.

	1941	1976
Total number of people employed	3,815,000	4,085,000
Number of people employed in agriculture	1,984,000	1,169,000
Percentage of people employed in agriculture	52%	23%

Here we also must note the shift away from agricultural occupations. The number of people employed in agriculture decreased by more than 800,000, while the number working in other sectors grew by 1.3 million. As we mentioned above, the two changes can directly be explained by the alterations of the structure of land ownership. As the peasants perceived that collectivization took away their land, and gave them no opportunity to work for their own benefit in accordance with their expectations, they left the land and the rural community and tried to fit into the urban-industrial pattern of production and existence.

The peasants' perception of man-land relations, however, was also partially responsible for two other factors: the structure of agricultural employment and the benefits derived from the existing system. One of the most significant changes that has taken place relates to the employment structure in agriculture. The figures presented above show that over five million people live in the rural sphere, of whom only one million are actively involved with earning a living from agriculture. An interesting development seems to have taken place during the last three decades; nearly one million rural citizens have chosen urban and industrial jobs, working in towns and cities, while maintaining their residences in the villages. They became commuters, leaving their families for a working day, a working week, or, frequently, for months at a time. Most of these commuters are workers who were either attracted to the better opportunities provided by urban industry, or were convinced that the new agrarian ownership structure of the collectives would not provide the opportunities commensurate with the expected benefits. They left their wives as members of collectives to work on the farm. It should be clear, however, that the general modernization and urbanization of the country, the attraction of greater urban opportunity for work and recreation, higher wages, more "elegant" jobs, the advanced educational and administrative opportunities that accompany the general modernization process, were just as responsible for their move as the lack of faith or disappointment in the changed ownership structure of the land.

Another important change was in the expectations of the rural population of the benefits that can be extended by the system. Today, the peasants expect the cooperatives to offer them free social security benefits, medical costs, educational opportunities and recreational possibilities in addition to the customary retirement pensions that are due to other members of society. Such benefits were unheard of for peasants a mere two decades before. For a peasant to demand the right to take a vacation was an unimaginable idea in the past; to demand that he work a 44 hour week and no more is another new concept. But here, too, the changed ownership structure can only be used as a partially explanatory variable, for other variables—such as the general process of modernization—also affected the peasants' style of living.

The variable of the general modernization of the country, far more than the land ownership structure or the political system itself, seems to have been responsible fcr a new attitude towards culture, the city, society as a whole and the "system" in general. For the first time in history, the Hungarian peasants are beginning to live well, spending rather than saving their money, and their expectations for the continuation of this existence is the keystone of the stability of the regime. The peasants now realize that they hold the regime "at bay"—if they do not produce what is needed and in the quantity needed, the cities will go hungry. Their productivity depends now on the benefits derived from the system, and they are convinced that the system "can't change." The new spending pattern so clearly evident to the observers of Hungarian villages reflects this attitude and the knowledge that the *modus vivendi* they worked out with the regime works to the advantage of both. The peasants realize that to disturb this *modus vivendi* (as the regime tried to do in 1972-1974) would be more detrimental to the regime than to the peasants.

Thus, the peasants enjoy the benefits of the modernization process. Now they build their houses with indoor bathrooms and with garages instead of stalls. They buy durable goods and useless gadgets with unprecedented abandon. And if the "good life" affects their attitude towards land and the ownership of land, if they desire to give up their household plots as many have done in the latter part of the 1970's, this simply means that many of them ceased being traditional peasants, no longer possessing the "traditional peasant mentality." For the first time in history, the agricultural population (the agricultural worker) has become integrated into the system. This accomplished the goals the regime set for itself in the early exuberance of its existence, when Marxism was considered a theory that provided answers to all problems of society.

The trouble with Marxist theory was its very anti-peasant nature. Conceived in the middle of the 19th century and refined through the machinations of successive "theoreticians" to fit ideology to political realities (vastly different from the early doctrinal base), Marxism was anti-peasant by its very proletarian-urban orientation. Decrying the "idiocy of village life," Marx had probably envisioned a society where the villages would become miniature cities, distinctive only by the agrarian character of their productive activities.[1] Marxist ideas were spelled out in the *Communist Manifesto* in which three points directly relate to agrarian problems:

7. Extension of factories and instruments of production owned by the state; cultivation of wastelands; and improvement of the soil, generally in accordance with a common plan.
8. Creation of industrial armies especially for agriculture.
9. Combination of agriculture with manufacturing industries; and the gradual abolition of distinctions between town and country by a more equitable distribution of the population over the territory of the country.[2]

Naturally, one can never be sure as to what exactly Marx, who knew little or nothing of rural life in general, or East European, non-Russian rural life specifically, had in mind. Living in London at a time when the concentration of land in the hands of a few appeared to be the most widespread, he took the English process to reflect a "universal" law which, of course, it did not. In his broadest outlook, he probably envisioned the creation of large state farms, owned by the state and worked with machinery, rendering the population merely agricultural workers. He clearly envisioned the turning of the villages into modern sub-urban centers with all the urban conveniences available to rural people. Certainly, a very positive bias towards creating regional equalities by the lessening role of primate cities and primate production centers was characteristic of Marx's thought.

The trouble with all this was not that the points raised were anti-peasant *per se*. In fact, these points were admirable as goal-orientations. But the underlying theoretical considerations were altered by two major perspectives: first, the anti-peasant attitude that developed among Marxists after Marx's death, and secondly, Soviet Russian practices as they developed after 1917. The anti-peasant bias, while understandable, was based on misconceptions and did not stem from malice; after all Marx viewed the peasants as human beings undertaking superhuman labor in order to maintain a subhuman existence.[3] The trouble was that to Marx and his followers the proletarian was the "hero in history" and, as Marxist ideology became simplified and was made more crudely political rather than philosophical, this attitude became sloganized. Thus, Marxists equated the process of building socialism in the USSR with urban regimentation, exploitation, and the exhaustion of the rural sphere. The urban proletariat—in whose name the Communists were later to rule—insisted on the superiority of large-scale rural production units and fought against peasant "stupidity" that stuck to the concept of the private ownership of land and justified a separate rural existence. The fact that the establishment of larger units of production did not necessarily mean more efficient production—especially in Eastern Europe—and that the consolidation toward larger size was frequently achieved by disregarding economic necessities, did not bother Marxist thinkers. Their gigantomania extended to the rural sphere as well. The important point for us to remember is that the greatest damage of Marxist theory lay not in the long-range goals of socialism described by Marx, but in the Marxist image of the peasant as inferior when compared to industrial workers. An added factor was blind acceptance of the alleged superiority of a centrally developed—and hence urban, and *ipso facto* anti-rural—plan aimed at the transformation of the countryside.

The development of the "Soviet example" further distorted the Marxist interpretation of reality. This is not the place to relate the waxing and waning of the Soviet line on land policies; David Mitrany has undertaken that task far better than we could do it here. Suffice it to say, that after some initial hesitation, Lenin came out in favor of the Land Socialization Act of 1918, giving land to the peasants to ensure their loyalty to his system and fostering their ties to the industrial proletariat.[4]

Throughout the 1920's, Soviet experience indicated a "go easy" policy toward the peasants. However, in 1929, the large-scale collectivization of agriculture began in earnest, forcing the peasants to join the collectives, establishing state farms and employing the crudest forms of coercion. The result of the brutal collectivization policies are well known; millions were killed or shipped to Siberia and other locations, and millions of uprooted peasants became the pool of labor on whose shoulders the industrialization of Russia rested. The key words to Soviet policy were: force, compulsion, excess labor for the cities through tightly-controlled collectives and state productive organizations. The legacies of collectivization were clear; they included a lasting antagonism between the peasants and the party; the reluctance of peasants to produce; inefficiency and lack of personal incentives to produce; and 100 million backward *muzhiks* living in a modern industrial state. In spite of the zig-zags of Soviet policies, it was these legacies that characterized the Soviet bases of agrarian planning.

In Hungary, one must also remember the events that occurred during the brief rule of Bela Kun in 1919.[5] Kun's agrarian policy, as mentioned briefly in Part IV of this volume, was not as flexible and successful as Lenin's. Kun wanted to go one up on Lenin by directly establishing collective farms, by nationalizing the land, and by creating commonly-owned farms on a large scale. For the Hungarian peasants who had begun to receive land for the first time in Hungarian history a few months prior to the establishment of the Hungarian Soviet Republic, such a policy was clearly unacceptable. The force used by Kun while mild when compared to the brutality later employed by the Soviet Union, was enough for the peasantry to withdraw its support from Kun and his comrades. Hence, the memory of 1919, stamped the Communists in peasant minds as inexorable enemies whose desire was to collectivize the land and take it away from the peasants. The Hungarian Communists who returned from Moscow at the end of the Second World War, therefore, inherited an attitude on the part of the peasants that they really did not know how to overcome.

The problem of the Communists in 1945 was made even more difficult by the traitional antagonism that existed between the rural and urban sectors and the general uncertainties of the post-war era. The first of these factors related to the historically contrasts between the urban and rural spheres in Eastern Europe in general, and in Hungary in particular.

It is a seemingly tautological statement that the peasants of Eastern Europe live in rural environments, but this statement must still be made to reiterate two elements of our analysis: (1) due to increased mobility (fostered by long-range industrialization attempts of the Eastern European states), a large number of peasants were forced to leave their rural environment. Some of them were assimilated into the working class, others continued to live as peasant urbanites. (2) Rural life has been for centuries fundamentally different in Eastern Europe than urban life. Peasant attitudes toward the city have been shifting in close correlation with the (a) altered perceptions of the city as a source of benefits; (b) closer communication with and greater attractions of the city and (c) the perception of attractiveness of rural life itself.[6]

Urban development has historically been different in Eastern Europe than in the West. Unlike in the West, where urban developments were associated with certain rights, e.g., coinage, market, defense, autonomous courts of law, in Eastern

Europe urban development was always associated with administrative-legal-military functions, frequently aimed against the peasantry. In the West, the rise of the cities was always associated with "native" activities and viewed as positive developments by most members of the polity. In Eastern Europe, as a result of the relatively short rule of native dynasties, foreign princes were "invited" to ascend the throne. Jagiellonians and Anjous, and assorted German princes began to rule the administrative centers, bringing with them their own native traditions, religious and secular advisors, and native languages. A chasm was opened between the language of the country, including the peasantry on the one hand, and the city, the court, the church on the other. Magyar became increasingly the language of peasants, while Latin was the language of the Church and the native language of the imported dynasty, and those of other imported "accomplices" became the languages of the cities.

In most of East Europe's cities the development of a native bourgeoisie was lagging behind that of Western Europe, and there was, thus, no agency that could unite the complex social fabric of society against exogenous forces. The greatest chasm was not one between classes that were hostile to one another, but between the city folks and the peasantry. The former affected Western ways of life, spoke French, German or Latin—or later a refined, "unaccented" city language that had little in common with the language of the peasantry—and despised the "stupid peasant" regarding him as primitive in his attitudes and "funny" in his peasant folk costume. Even the peasants' language was highly suspicious as it was inflected and reeked of ancient storms not used in the cities. The peasants in turn also viewed the city-folk as hostile, incomprehensible and equally funny in their manner, and feared them because the cities possessed coercive power over the life of the peasantry. Only during the rise of populist nationalism in the 19th and 20th centuries do we begin to see an amalgamation of conflicting attitudes toward non-native, hostile invaders, but the chasm remains very wide even to date.

The distrust of the cities by the peasants was reciprocated by the people in the urban sector. The urban population, which suffered perhaps the most from the wars and the economic crises of the 1920's-1930's, regarded the peasants with suspicion. They were seen as a stratum which has always had some possibilities of earning at least enough food for survival and gaining "wealth" at the expense of the urban population. The "cunning peasant" was viewed as "backward" and "stupid," "traditional" rather than "modern," and the contempt expressed by the very connotation of the word *"paraszt"* referred less to productive employment than to class distinction. It was this mutual distrust that was partially responsible for the fragmented and unintegrated society that existed after the Second World War, which had presented formidable obstacles to the creation of a permanent and mutually acceptable policy for the regime and the agrarian population.

2. Land Reform

Given such a confusing background of the problem, one can hardly blame the Communist leadership for vacillating in its desire to develop an acceptable agrarian policy in the immediate post-war years. The roots of the Communist policies of these years will be found in the early debates within the Communist hierarchy after the failure of the first Hungarian Soviet Republic.[7] In highly factionalized debates between Kun and the followers of Jeno Landler after the demise of the Kun regime, the one point on which everyone, including Lenin, could agree was that the agrarian policy of immediate nationalization and collectivization was disastrous. We do not know what the long-range intentions of the leaders of the Hungarian Communist Party were when they returned to Hungary in 1945; we do know that already in 1944, the Communists adopted the tactic of offering land to the peasants. On December 30, 1944, in Debrecen, under Soviet auspices, the declaration of the Hungarian Communists included a demand for widespread land reform, "the distribution of land among those desiring it, and the division of all landed estates belonging to those who were regarded as traitors or who served the German cause."[8]

In addition, perhaps one more reason can be established which influenced the Communist decision to introduce land reform, namely, their uncertainty as to the length of time during which a coalition regime would rule in Hungary. As the newly opened British Foreign Office Archives show, there can be no doubt that the Soviet leadership planned to bring the entire region under its rule, and that Hungary's fate was already sealed on October 11, 1944, at the time of the Eden-Molotov discussions in Moscow.[9] The Soviet leadership, and consequently the Moscow-based elite of the Hungarian Communist Party, expected the Western allies to put up considerably greater resistance than they did to Soviet demands or to the Sovietization of the region, and thus expected that the period of coalition politics would be considerably longer.[10] Under these circumstances, regardless of the Hungarian Communist leadership's desire to please the Soviet leaders by emulating their agrarian policies to the "tee," it seemed considerably wiser not to alienate the peasantry. This leadership was anxious to erase the unfortunate memories of 1919 by coming out strongly on the side of forces that wanted to give land to the peasants. The very insistence of the Communists to place the Communist Imre Nagy as the first Minister of Agriculture in the Temporary National Government between December 22, 1944 and November 12, 1945, had shown the interest of the Communists in land reform.

The biggest question for the Communists was not whether there was need for a land reform, but what type of reform should be introduced. Here the Communists came into sharp conflict with the Hungarian Peasant Party. For the Communists, the lesson of 1919 and that of the Russian policies of 1929 were clear; the land had to be given to the agrarian poor who had no land at all, and not to the middle-or productive small peasants who could till it most efficiently and with the greatest productivity for the state and for themselves. This was also proposed by Bela Kovacs, the Smallholder, and some of the influential members of the Peasant Party.[11] In other words, giving land to the peasants was not supposed to enhance the development of agriculture, the development of greater productivity, but was intended instead as a means for the establishment of bases of support for the Communist Party among the poor peasantry, among the agrarian proletariat, and among those who had no land or only a tiny plot of land! Therefore, it is clear today that this tactic was intended to become the basis for making political inroads and it is equally clear that it was successful. By the time the land reform was largely completed (approximately May 1, 1945) the Communist Party had accomplished its task; it gave land to the former agrarian poor, set them against the richer, better trained, better equipped and more productive stratum of the village, and became dubbed as the "champion of the agrarian poor." It no longer mattered that the Communist Party's role *vis a vis* the peasantry had been relegated to the backburners in the new coalition government, where the Smallholders' Party dominated; the political task had already been accomplished.

The doctrinal bases of Jozsef Revai's views were not free of bias; the tactical considerations were very heavily influenced by the Soviet experience. To Revai and the orthodox Communists, conditions in the Hungarian countryside were basically the same as in the USSR. Hence, just like in Russia in the 1920's, the party viewed the peasants as sharply divided into strata, pitting the poor against the middle-and the rich peasants.[12] But in Hungary, such a neat division did not fit existing conditions. The Communist Party's leadership expected the "sharpening of the class conflict" between the three peasant strata and came out in favor, doctrinally and tactically, of the agrarian poor.

Giving land to the peasants was easier in theory than in practice, but it was accomplished, nonetheless, with considerable speed. By the end of 1945, 34.6% of all arable land was divided up, comprising 5,764,414 acres. Altogether, 75,505 estates that were larger than 142 acres each were divided.[13] Of all these lands, 58.2% or 3,528,212 acres were given to individuals, 24.3% or 1,453,520 acres were nationalized, and the rest was put aside for various forms of public use. Indirectly, the peasantry also utilized an additional 15% of the divided lands through housing plots, common grazing fields and the like, but the fact remains that the divided lands used for private plots were still only 20.1% of the areable lands of the country.[14]

The beneficiaries of the land reform were clearly delineated. Altogether 643,342 persons were given land; on the average, 5.9 acres were given to each individual. Ninety-three percent of all lands that were redistributed were given to the poorest peasants, to the former agrarian proletariat who possessed little or no land previously. Table III below lists the beneficiaries of the land reform.

TABLE III. Beneficiaries of Land Reform

Stratum of Peasants	Number Receiving land	Amount distributed-%		Average amount distributed in hectares*
Servants of large estates	109,875	525,685	18.3%	4.79
Agricultural laborers	261,088	734,642	39.5%	2.79
Dwarfholders	213,930	472,802	25.5%	2.22
Smallholders	32,865	81,585	4.4%	2.51
Village craftsmen	22,164	30,703	1.7%	1.37
Certified, trained smallholders	1,256	8,292	0.7%	6.61
Employees of Forestry Service	1,164	3,989	0.2%	3.42
Total	642,342	1,857,698*	100.%	2.89

*Figure slightly different from the one listed on preceding pages because of computational difficulties from *hold* to acres. Computational error is 0.01%. One hectare equals 1.9 acres.
Adapted from Orbar, p. 89 and Mezogazdasag: Adatck, I. pp. 12,14.

But even such a radical alteration of the number of people owning land failed to alleviate the agrarian problem. In the rural sphere there remained roughly two million people, including active earners and dependents, who had little or no land at all. And while nearly one million people were affected by the land reform, there remained more people in agricultural occupations who had no land at all or possessed insufficient amounts to make a living. Even after the land reform, there were 506,500 people among the agrarian workers who had no land at all, 164,200 owning less than one-half of one hectare, and 1,376,300 possessing between one-half and 2.5 hectares of land.[16]

Despite these shortcomings, Hungary's structure of land ownership was fundamentally altered.[17] After the land reform, holdings of less than 11 acres of land continued to predominate the pattern of agricultural production. Their number had increased from 1,389,254 to 1,794,504, and the percentage of the total area they occupied grew from 19.2% to 39%. Secondly, the number of estates above 284 acres showed a slight decrease from 6,272 estates in 1935 to 4,629 in 1949, while the acreage held by these estates decreased significantly from 43.1% of all arable land in 1935 to 16.5% in 1949. Thirdly, the middle peasantry registered little or no changes in their landholdings or their numbers. Although the number of their estates increased from 238,881 to 266,921, and the amount of land they held grew from 6,259,325 acres to 7,174,123 acres, the percentage held by them did not show significant change; while in 1935 they held 38% of all arable lands, this ratio increased in 1949 only to 45%. In short, the clear winners were the poor peasants and dwarfholders and the clear losers were the large estate owners. But the vast majority of the peasants could not claim a qualitative improvement as a result of the land reform. Agricultural poverty remained a very real problem and poor and landless peasants still made up nearly 50% of the agrarian population. It was no wonder that severe dissatisfaction prevailed during the post-reform years among those who were given no land at all. In addition, many new landowners remained dissatisfied.

3. Collectivization

The Communist Party expected that the new landowners would support its agrarian policies. But to the surprise of the Communist leaders, the new landowners voted in 1945 and in 1947 for "those parties that based their position on the sanctity of private ownership" withdrawing their allegiance from the Communists, who claimed to have given them what they wanted.[18] Paradoxically, thus, the party had destroyed much of its own base of support among the agrarian poor; by giving them land, they were turned into champions of private property ownership. They proved once again the dictum that nothing fails like success.[19]

The new landowners' dissatisfaction was caused by the lack of credit, the unavailability of small-scale machinery and tools, a shortage of draft animals and the inefficiency of the new land distribution patterns. Many peasants received a small strip of land here, another small strip there, sometimes a considerable distance from one another. The Communist rhetoric, often imitated by other parties, gave the peasants unrealistic expectations concerning credits in coming years, when agriculture as a whole only received 16% of all credits extended to the industry.[20] These problems were compounded by the stagnation of the agrarian middle class, and the subdivision of the sometimes highly productive large estates. These had resulted in decreased agrarian productivity when compared to 1938, the last pre-war year for which we have adequate statistical data.[21] Compared to that year, the total productivity of agriculture was 15% less, while its commodity index was fully 28% below that of 1938.[22]

These failures coincided with the capture of power by the Communist Party in 1948. Soon it became very clear that the leadership of the Communist Party viewed the land reform as only a tactical step; these leaders expected to base agriculture on collectivized production methods, on the establishment of cooperative and collective farms.

The Communists were not the only ones who preached the necessity of establishing cooperatives in Hungary. The populist writers and even some important members of the Peasant and Smallholders' Parties regarded cooperative movements as the only form capable of replacing the productive organization of the large estates.

TABLE IV

Distribution of Persons Given Land During the 1945 Land Reform.

Stratum of Peasants	Number Re-Receiving Land	Amount of Land Distributed in Hectares	%	Average Amount of Distributed Land in Hectares
Servants on large estates	109,875	525,685	28.3%	4.79
Agricultural laborers	261,088	734,642	39.5	2.79
Dwarfholders	213,930	472,802	25.5	2.22
Smallholders	32,865	81,585	4.4	2.51
Handicraftsmen in village	22,164	30,703	1.7	1.37
Certified trained smallholders	1,256	8,292	0.7	6.61
Employees of Forestry firms	1,164	3,989	0.2	3.42
TOTAL	642,342	1,857.698*	100.0%	2.89

*Figure slightly different from the one listed on preceding pages because of computational difficulties from *hold* to hectares. Computational error is .01&.

TABLE V.

Changes in Private Ownership of Land 1949-1953

Year	Total area State	Collective	Private	Total employment in State	Collective	Private	Total %
	in percent			sectors in percent			
1949	25.4%	0.6%	74.0%	3.4%	0.5%	96.1%	100
1950	27.4%	3.2%	69.8%	4.5%	1.6%	93.9%	100
1951	31.2%	9.4%	49.4%	5.6%	5.7%	88.7%	100
1952	34.4%	13.4%	52.3%	10.2%	15.2%	74.6%	100
1953	36.6%	18.3%	45.3%	13.2%	19.1%	67.7%	100

Adopted from O., p. 89, MA, I, pp. 12, 15., II, 4.

At the same time, the Communist Party was far from united in the matter of collectivization. The Party's Committee on Agriarian Policy, and its secretariat's Department of Rural Affairs (*Falusi Osztaly*), led by Imre Nagy, throughout the first period of 1948 advocated the encouragement of both the private and collective sectors.[23] This policy continued to be applied. The Cominform break with Yugoslavia in June, 1948, however, brought about a fundamentally different situation. Today we know that Stalin had suggested the collectivization of agriculture much earlier; in March, 1948, he and Molotov sent a note to the Hungarian party leaders suggesting that the collectivization of the rural sphere be speeded up. Until June 30, 1948, however, the party leadership seems to have been deadlocked by the different positions held by Matyas Rakosi and Imre Nagy. On that date, using the Yugoslav "heresy" as an excuse, Rakosi appeared to have won the upper hand. By July 2, 1948, Rakosi's policy line was accepted in the Central Committee.[24] The policy officially accepted by the Politburo on July 13, 1949, was based upon the desire to follow the Soviet model,[25] and to reject the "Yugoslav heresy."[26] It pitted the small and the middle-peasants against the rich (the so-called "kukaks") and expected that by stripping the "kulak" of his land by adding it to that of the local collective, would give the incentive to small and middle-peasants to join the "commons: By the beginning of January, 1949, over the sole dissenting voice of Nagy, the party Politburo went on record to liquidate the "kulaks" and collectivize the peasantry.[27]

The problem was with the definition of the term Kulak. Who were these people in the Hungarian circumstances? Traditionally, Hungarians defined the rich peasant as a person who owned more than 25 *holds* (14.5 hectares or 35.5 acres) of land or received a net imcome of 35 gold crowns from one *hold* of land. But the classification of rich peasants based on the 1949 census regarded all those who had possessed wealth based upon either definition, or a combination of both regardless of the source of income, as "kulaks." Many independent craftsmen, village store owners, teachers, rural physicians, traders, et al, were included. Moreover, in some parts of the country where large tracts of land were located, these farms frequently produced income that equalled those of less than five hectares elsewhere. The law passed by the government did not differentiate. Desiring to "sharpen the class struggle among the peasantry," it included in the "kulak list" nearly 70,000 persons, among them more than 50,000 peasants, 10,000 shopkeepers, butchers, millers, bar-keepers, more than 4,000 physicians, lawyers, clerical employees and more than 1,600 tradesmen.[28] By the decision of 1949, the government practically ordered the expropriation and redistribution of approximately 130,000 hectares of land taken from the "kulaks" to those who had no land at all.

At the same time, however, the government also ordered the intensification of pressures to organize collective farms.[29] In regard to the collectivization, however, this process in Hungary took a different form than in other socialist states. The collective farms in Hungary were not created on the large estates—some of which were previously nationalized rather than subdivided—instead, they were expected to come into being by the pooling of the small landholdings of the peasants. One consequence of this was that the large number of peasant smallholders who most desired to join the collectives did so without having any land, animals, implements or even the know-how to contribute. Force, coercion, brutality, have all been used to collectivize the land. Compulsory delivery figures were given to every individual household at prices that produced continuous losses for the peasants; "parity" considerations were never used. If delivery were not made, land and property confiscations followed. Cows, pigs, chickens, livestock, draft animals were herded away, and if the hapless peasant met his delivery quota by luck or incredible effort, his quotas were immediately raised. Interrogators pressed the peasants—preferably after midnight—to reveal their "anti-government activities," and if they fell asleep in their own fields during the day, they were charged with "sabotage." We do not wish to dwell here on the brutality with which the collectivization drive was handled in the period of 1949-1953. It should suffice to say that it was there. And while it is also true that it did not match the brutality of the Soviet collectivization drive of the 1930's (especially during the years 1950-1952), it certainly came close to it.[30]

What was remarkable, however, was how unsuccessful the collectivization drive had proved to be, even with the utilization of *force majeure* by the state. Table VI indicates the change in the percentage of agrarian active earners and the proportion of privately owned lands between 1949 and 1953:

TABLE VI. Changes in the Private Ownership of Land, 1949-1953.[31]

Year	Total Area State, Collective, Private in %			Total	total Employment in State, Collective, Private Sectors in %			total
1949	25.4%	0.6%	74.0%	100	3.4%	0.5%	96.1%	100
1950	27.4%	3.2%	69.8	100	4.5%	1.6%	93.9%	100
1951	31.2%	9.4%	49.4	100	5.7%	5.7%	88.7%	100
1952	34.4%	13.4%	52.3	100	10.2%	15.2%	74.6%	100
1953	36.6%	18.3%	45.3	100	13.2%	19.1%	67.7%	100

Adopted from Orbar, p. 89 and Mezogazdasag: Adatob, I. pp. 12, 15, II. 4.

In short, in spite of all pressures, coercion and terror, only one-third of the peasantry joined the collectives, two-thirds simply refused to buckle down under the power of the authorities. At the same time, it is instructive to note the type of people who joined the collectives. The number of collectives grew from roughly 500 in 1949 to 5,224 in 1953 and the land area, either expropriated outright or "voluntarily pledged" for collective use, increased from 54,912 hectares to 1,706,025 hectares.[32] It is less known though not unexpected, that the membership of the collectives also changed drastically through these five years. While between 1949 and 1951, only about 3-5% of the collectives' membership came from among the middle-and small peasantry who had owned land before the land reform, and 38% came from among those who had been given land in 1945, fully 57% of those who joined had absolutely no land at all. It was no wonder that these collectives had no tools, few machines or draft animals, their members had little knowledge of modern production methods and were doomed to failure![33] The character of the membership changed drastically by 1952; by then, the vast majority of members (nearly 77%) were made up of peasants who had been owners of land either before or after the reform.[34] Most of these peasants were tired of harassment and the terror; they slaughtered their animals and "pledged" their land, except for a small household plot, to the collective. The slaughtering of animals before joining the collectives was shown in the decrease of the number of animals per acre between 1949 and 1953; from 23.8% in 1949, the number dropped to 21.4% in 1950, and to 20.6% in 1951.[35]

The terror resulted in other developments as well—and some of them were not exactly undesirable from the perspective of the regime. Between 1949 and 1953, a large number of those who "pledged" their lands left the agricultural sector altogether. Some of them found employment within the state farm system and became simply hired agrarian workers. The number of people employed by the state farms during these years rose from 80,000 to 316,000, and most of them were former agrarian proletarians. Compared to the approximately 50,000 landless peasants who had joined the collective farms between 1949 and 1953, at least twice as many found employment during these years in the urban industries of the state.[36]

As expected, productivity dropped disastrously. Between 1949 and 1953, agricultural growth remained at an annual average of 2.4%. Instead of climbing by 50% as predicted during these years, it merely managed to rise by 12%.[37] It is not surprising that in 1952, the private peasant households produced 20% more per hectare of land (and in 1953 by 38% more!) than the collective farms of the state.[38] The sharp drop in yield of every conceivable produce during these years was equally shocking. These policies and the bad harvest of 1952 resulted in hunger and scarcities in the cities, demoralizing the entire population. They were a mute testimony to the failure and horror of the party's handling of the collectivization process.

4. De-Collectivization

The merciful death of Stalin in March, 1953, and the subsequent June, 1953 decision of the Hungarian Communist leadership had put an end to the forcible collectivization and resulted in *laissez-faire* guidelines for the future. Imre Nagy's coming to power and the adoption of a "go slow" policy during the Third Party Congress (held between May 24-30, 1954) resulted in the formulation of plans to strengthen the existing cooperatives, and to allow people to leave them if they so desired. As a result of these policies, nearly 200,000 peasants "voted with their feet" and left the collectives between 1954 and 1955, once again establishing a private farm-based existence. In fact, some 500 collective farms were dissolved during these two years.[39] The largest number of those who left the collectives were people who were forced during the previous years to enter, people who had been landowners before the terror coerced them to enter the collectives! As a result, the number of those who had brought more than four hectares of their own land to the collectives had fallen from 38.8% in 1952 to 28% in 1954.[40]

The intraparty struggle and Rakosi's return to power in February, 1955, did not result in a return to the typical, urban-oriented, traditional Soviet-type anti-peasant policy.[41] The government realized the importance of adopting a new and strongly agrarian-oriented investment plan. Giving incentives to the peasants by allowing them to sell, after the compulsory deliveries had been made to the state, at nearly "market" prices, their produce, succeeded not only in reaching 100% of the delivery goals, but even to exceed them by 8%. During these years average yields in the collectives exceeded, for the first time, those on private plots, bringing the question of private ownership of land into serious question. But Rakosi and his clique were not content with resting on their success. At a meeting of the Politburo on May 26, 1955, he had outlined (and the Politburo accepted) a plan for the forced collectivization of a further one-half million private peasant holdings.

Instead of being content with the fact that 15-16,000 peasant families voluntarily joined the collectives every year, Rakosi wanted to raise their number in August, 1955, to 70-80,000 annually.[42] Once again, the most draconic measures were to be utilized to force the peasants into the collectives. And terror once again did the trick; the peasants "voluntarily" gave up their land rather than try to fight the coercion. In a large percentage of the 450 collectives started by force in 1955, the work never began; many of the newly recruited members simply left and the following demoralization resulted in a disastrous situation in the villages.[43] Force achieved the exact opposite of what it was intended to achieve; the members simply left in droves, most of them seldom showed up for work, and they eventually thumbed their noses at the terror. One can only be killed once, so they reasoned, and the extreme force utilized earlier was now of no use. The peasant struck back as he could; he withheld his production and refused to deliver foods for the cities. Indirectly, although aided considerably by the secret speech of N. S. Khrushchev delivered at the February, 1956 XXth Congress of the CPSU, the peasants made the decision by themselves to dissolve the cooperatives. There was now no way to stop those who desired to leave and to take with them what they rightfully claimed was theirs. The regime's authority had no more power that could be effectively used against those who desired to leave. The local police forces were of no use; the pitch-fork rebellion ended Rakosi's reign of terror in the villages as much as the October Revolution in 1956 ended his power in the cities and within the Communist Party of Hungary itself.

The role played by the peasantry during the 1956 October Revolution is a controversial one.[44] The only peasants who really trusted the regime were the ones who gained both from the land reform and the collectivization drives. These included some of the peasants who were given earlier small plots of land, and who joined the collectives during the early years of collectivization upon discovering that they were unable to make an adequate living on their small private plots. Even if the party leadership realized the need for change, they could no longer implement it as events overtook them. The effect of the revolution in the political sphere took place almost entirely in the cities. The rural population did not trust either leadership; it rejected Rakosi's, Gero's or Nagy's rule with about the same intensity. Even Nagy's sympathy for the peasantry made little difference—time was too short to penetrate the cognition of the peasants and the reputation of a *Communist* Nagy could not be perceived differently from the reputation of a *Communist gero.* For the peasants, the city remained the domain of the distrusted "them" and their alienation from city rule was was manifest in their withholding of support from all the rulers. The occaisonal acts of sympathy—such as the shipment of foodstuffs to Budapest at the very beginning of November—remained isolated and largely meaningless. At the same time, the revolution did not fall because of the lack of support by the peasantry; it would have been destroyed by Soviet tanks anyway.

Early claims of the Communists that former owners of large estates wanted to retake their estates notwithstanding, the land ownership structure was hardly altered during the revolution. Only in a very few places did the owners or their descendants tender claims to large estates and even the owners of land above 28 acres refrained by and large from reclaiming their former lands. The antagonism between the various strata of the peasantry and especially the antagonism between the poor and formerly landless peasants on the one hand and the better off peasants on the other continued and even sharpened during the October Revolution. The elementary destructive power against some functionaries—usually imposed upon the villages from outside—and against the primitive local little tyrants, did result in a few mini-*jacqueries,* in burnings and even the murder of a few people. The disappearance of the former party fuctionaries, hacks, collective-farm chairmen, helped to prevent more trouble. The bitterness with which they were regarded by the peasants was perhaps the strongest in places where the village had been populated by smallholders and medium-holders of land in the past, and weakest in areas that had been dominated by large estates.

5. In Limbo

Structurally, the greatest difference in the agricultural sector came from a reduction in the number of peasants who had worked until 1956 on the lands of cooperatives and small farms. The number of cooperatives dropped from 4,863 in October, 1956, to 3,457 in June, 1957. The percentage of collective farm members decreased from 14.7% of the agrarian labor force to 6.1% during the same period.[45] Specifically, the former middle-and large-landholders left the collectives in droves. Given the roughly 18,000 agrarian workers who, during this time, left the state farms and machine-tractor stations, and the 180,000 peasants who left the collective sector, one can clearly appreciate the peasants' attitude towards the state and its perceived "benefits." These events, however, cannot solely be attributed to the revolution; most frequently, they occurred after November 4, 1956, and were rarely the result of "kulak" or "Fascist" agitation. The main reason for the division of collective lands, the taking apart of collective goods and products, and the desire to leave the collectitate farms seems to have been localized grievances that were attributed to the structure of ownership, to the force utilized in the defense and enhancement of Socialist ownership, and to the nature of the leadership of the collective and state farms.

The Kadar government made its shrewdest move by not insisting on recollectivization at that time, and by trying to mollify the peasantry by letting them keep the land. The government did not force the peasantry immediately to pay for the goods, products and land values they had retaken from the collectives from which they had withdrawn. It even tolerated the tensions that emerged between the small-and middle-landholders that resulted from the poor peasants' view that the middle-landholders left the collectives with greater wealth than they brought with them. The Kadar government refused to intervene on their behalf, since it did not want to create a situation in which the villages would become a center of anti-government activities.

This policy held some danger from the regime's point of view. First, it truly jeopardized the support of the peasants who stayed in the collective farms. They were left largely without animals, agricultural implements and know-how, forcing a large number of them to start working as day-laborers for the richer and middle peasants. The only other alternative for the regime was to accept an inoperable, weak or poor collective farm-system from which only minimal benefits could be expected. As a result, the percentage of poor or landless peasants among the collective farm members rose from 20% in June, 1956 to 55% in June, 1957.[46] And the nearly 20,000 poor peasants who were forced to leave the poor collectives—due to the withdrawal of the large-and middle-landholders—could only seek jobs in industrial or urban enterprises.

Government policy and the subsequent control of agricultural development had to be carried out without a trusted agrarian cadre. The collective and party leadership practically disappeared by January, 1957. Seventy to eighty percent of the district and county administrative leadership and 80% of the former collective farm presidents were forced out, left voluntarily, or emigrated to the West in a period of less than two months.[47] Coupled with the fact that there were practically no agronomists, and that most of the local agrarian leadership had little or no higher education of any sort, the crisis of agriculture was serious indeed. In 1957, for example, only 2% of the collective farm chairmen had a degree from a college of any sort, and even among the accountants, 22% had no accounting training whatsoever. There were counties where the vast majority of collective farm presidents—in Bacs County, 91%!—did not even have an eighth grade education! While the training and experience of most of the new and old collective farm presidents were perhaps sufficient to work a small plot of land, the task of organizing production and managing a large-scale estate was well beyond the grasp of these individuals.

The conflict between the collective and the private sector in agriculture, thus, remained real. Structurally, the private peasants made great advances. The number of private landholds grew from 1,445,000 in 1956 to 1,634,100 in 1958; their holdings increased from 4.3 million hectares to 4.9 million during the same period.[48] But the average *size* of private landholds remained approximately three hectares each. Their freedom of marketing their produce (which had increased from 32.8% of all produced articles in 1955 to 69.8% in 1958) provided great incentives for production.[49] Most of them made between 10-35,000 forints annually, representing a standard of living equal to or better than that attained by the industrial workers, and considerably more than that of the members of most collective farms.

It is important to realize, however, that the party never gave up the idea that eventually the collective farms had to dominate agriculture. The conviction that collectivized agriculture was "superior" was not merely ideological or patterned after the Soviet experience. Indeed, given the bases of Hungarian agriculture, the view that large-scale extensive production is "more profitable" was not a revolutionary idea. The regime realized that small plots produced well through large labor demand, that productivity per hectare was quite high on the small plots even without mechanization. At the same time, the economists of the regime also knew that, especially in the case of certain products such as grains, large-scale mechanized production was far more productive from the perspective of labor-efficiency. They understood that large farms operated with minimal energy demands per hectare and the collective farms in general produced far more for the general market than the small-scale peasant farms. Although the party leadership had beaten a hasty tactical retreat from outright collectivization in 1956-1957, by April, 1958, the Central Committee decided to extend significant support to the collectives; after all, aside from *force majeure,* the only way to gain the support of the peasantry for the collectives was by making them attractive.[50] Thus, through various instruments and price-support measures, the number of animals kept by the collectives had been increased, a large number of tractors was given to them and the increased fertilizer output began to show its results in production yields.

But the reluctance of the private landholding peasants to reenter the collectives remained obvious. They argued that had they received the subsidies given to the collectives they could have produced a great deal more. In spite of the massive support given to them, many collectives continued to show poor results. For the government to claim that socialist agriculture was superior, that its collectives would eventually attract the peasants by producing and earning more, was still a matter of promise whose fulfillment was, perhaps, far in the future. The private peasants' argument found additional support in the productivity of Hungary's neighbors, notably nonsocialist Austria. While in 1958, Hungary produced more in terms of gross agricultural product than in 1938, in Austria the rate of growth for the same years was twice as much.[51] Thus, the reluctance of the peasants to join the collectives had to be conquered not merely by countering these arguments but by providing positive alternatives and incentives. Economic success had to be the supplementary incentive (added to the use of "persuasive force") if the regime wished to recollectivize the land.

The desire of the regime to accomplish recollectivization was enhanced by the Moscow meeting of December, 1957 of the representatives of the Communist Parties, where a common strategy for the collectivization of agriculture had been worked out. After that meeting, the tempo of collectivization increased in all the Communist states with the exception of Poland and Yugoslavia. As a result, collective farm properties extended to 92% of the land in Bulgaria, 75% in Czechoslovakia, 63% in East Germany, and 55% in Rumania.[52] Furthermore, the regime's desire to collectivize has been hastened by the fact that it needed new labor reserves for its expanding industries, and by the concern that the agrarian population was growing rapidly older. Since the new labor reserves could only come from agriculture, and since agriculture had to be made more productive, the Moscow decision only reinforced the Hungarian party's own interpretation of what was needed to be done.[53]

We can pinpoint three basic dates of decision-making regarding the recollectivization of agriculture. The first date is April 25, 1958, when the Central Committee of the HSWP adopted a decision for the improvement of political work in the countryside. The second is July 7, 1958, when a recommendation to further develop the collectives was made by the Agricultural Department of the Central Committee. The third date is December 7, 1958, when the Central Committee of the party made the final decision to collectivize. The question was: how to accomplish these goals?

Two different methods had been suggested; the first tried to advance collectivization by extending further assistance to the collectives. Those who supported this method expected that the incentives given to the collectives, the employment of highly trained specialist leadership, and the natural attractiveness of highly productive and highly remunerative collectives would be sufficient to entice the private landholding peasants to join. The second method suggested the utilization of coercive force once again—though not on the scale of the previous regimes, and the use of such "administrative pressures" on the private landowners that they would feel compelled to give up their lands. The party leaders who supported the latter method tended to show antipeasant attitudes and their demagoguery was striking.

Since both of these views were strongly held by various members of the leadership, during the summer of 1958, a special Party Preparatory Commission was created which made its recommendation to the Politburo on November 18, 1958. The recommendations combined the two methods, supporting both the policy of providing incentives and improvements for the collectives and the administrative pressure to be exerted on the private landholders. It was a "carrot and stick" policy and it was adopted on December 7, 1958, by the Central Committee of the HSWP.[54]

There were positive sides to recollectivization: unlike a decade earlier, the newly joined members were allowed to keep their livestock, the disparate lands were still worked by those who used to own them, the newly joined members were given cash payments for their lands, and provided with a nice and "adequate" household plot. But there were negative sides as well:

> In addition to the continuous harassment of calling people to be interviewed by the local council, private peasants were threatened by fines, forced to take unpaid vacations, or were sent without pay to certain places. There was a threat of removal from high school and college of their children; older peasants, people who had dual residences as industrial workers, were forced to give up their jobs.[55]

There were places where excessive force was used: outsiders beat up reluctant peasants, industrial workers were brought in from urban centers and even teams of thugs were utilized. While the regime intended to use minimal force, it was bent upon accomplishing its goal, the recollectivization of the land, by simply wearing down peasant opposition.

The first efforts of recollectivization were aimed at the most vulnerable stratum of the peasantry. These were the least successful middle-and small landholders and those who were older. These efforts were concentrated in those areas of the country where private farming had been the least successful, in the most backward parts of Hungary such as certain areas of the Great Plain. By mid-1959, the first phase was completed. Aided by an unusually excellent growing season, the peasants observed that the collective farms had been far more profitable indeed than even in the best previous years.[56]

The second phase of recollectivization started roughly in the middle of 1959. Its intention was the creation of collective farms in areas that were more difficult to organize. The regime encountered greater resistance and used more force. The physical aspects of coercion in 45 villages—beatings, the terrorizing of peasants, and the confiscation of their lands and animals—became well known.[57] The peasants did join the collectives, but they repaid the regime with less work.[58]

The two phases of the recollectivization process accomplished the objectives of the regime; they virtually ended private farming and completed the massive "expulsion" of the peasantry from the villages, channeling them into the work force of the cities.[59] The changes in land ownership structure are well illustrated in the following table:

TABLE VII. Changes in Land Ownership and Employment Structure[60]

Year	% of Active Agrarian Earners Employed in		% of Land Held by	
	Collective	Private	Collective	Private
	Sector		Sector	
1958	7.4%	79.1%	8.5%	51.1%
1959	8.5%	77.1%	21.6%	40.5%
1960	37.1%	54.2%	45.0%	18.1%
1961	61.6%	20.0%	57.0%	3.7%
1962	75.1%	6.5%	58.0%	3.3%

Source: Mezogazdasag. Adattar, I., pp. 12, 15; II. p. 4.

The departure of non-joiners from the villages was especially fast during these years. In 1959, for example, 61,500; in 1960, 47,800; in 1961, 25,600 people left agriculture for other sectors of the economy.[61] And while those who left were not all peasants unwilling to join the cooperatives, a large number of them were certainly former landholders. Among those who left, however, one could also find members of the collectives. They were convinced that the collective members' average income was eventually bound to become lower. Indeed, fears of lower income were born out in these years. While in 1958, the average income of a member after his/her share in the common lands was 11,956 forints, and 10,510 forints in 1959, it had dropped to 7,572 forints in 1969, and 7,098 in 1961.[62] It is also significant that those who left were generally men, young men, most of all.

The collectivization drive was completed by the beginning of 1961, but the regime inherited a peasantry whose work intensity in the collectives was low. Since the regime's efforts were aimed at creating "true collective farms" where all production activities were carried out in common, at least 300-400 poor cooperatives were created.[63] There was no logical reason for their existence. Statistics show that the increased territory of the collectives reflected no comparable increase in productivity. It seemed doubtful that the pressures utilized in creating the collective farms would ever induce the peasantry voluntarily to produce unselfishly for the common good.

Other "contradictions" were also created by the collectivization process. The labor force left in the villages was of inferior quality consisting, in many instances, mainly of women, older people and untrained personnel. The young and older men who commuted to work in the cities and to industries tended only their own gardens at home, and cherished their total social security benefits, medical insurance and old age pensions. Moreover, inside the collective farms, increasing numbers of peasants brought local class-conflicts once more into focus. The leadership of the poor peasants was frequently questioned by the more successful newcomers: "he could not even make it on two hectares, how can we expect him to make it as president of a 1,000 hectare collective farm?" was a commonly raised question. On the other hand, the poor peasants also resented working with and sometimes under the direction of peasants for whom they used to work as day laborers or servants before and who, because of their expertise and kowtowing to the regime, became their masters again.

6. The Doldrums

The years between 1961 and 1968, were years of doldrums; they were of slow rates of growth, but growth nonetheless. In all categories of indicators, yields slowly increased, collective production flourished, but no radical improvements took place. Although the peasant had been allowed to keep his small household plot, incentives to produce mostly for the market were not provided until 1968. The production of the collective farms, however, did increase during these years because of other factors. The regime's efforts had been notable in places where it really mattered; they raised a sound, technically capable, well trained agrarian leadership, increased assistance for the collectives enabling them to acquire new and highly productive machinery and supported the widespread uses of land improvement and fertilizing techniques. These methods resulted in quantitative changes and created the bases for the important accomplishments of the New Economic Mechanism (NEM) introduced in 1968.

In retrospect, it seems correct to state that the Hungarian Communist regimes between 1949 and 1968 were bent upon the exploitation of the peasantry, making capital out of their hide and turning them into cannon fodder in the "war" to industrialize the country. It would also be correct to observe that the anti-peasant, worker-centered demagoguery of the various post-war Communist regimes regarded the peasants with contempt, hatred and suspicion. We would be remiss, however, if we failed to point out at the same time that in the treatment of the countryside one additional perspective influenced the attitudes and behavior of the Communist leadership. This was the conviction that in the modern, industrial age, society could advance rapidly only by rapid industrialization. Looking at the diverse economic patterns of development facing them (whether in the U.S., where the government had to pay parity support to keep up farm prices at the subsistence level for farmers, or in the USSR, where the peasant population barely grew enough to satisfy the basic needs of the Soviety citizenry), the Hungarian leadership saw its only hope in a drive for all-out industrialization. Moreover, the Soviet example of keeping 50% of the population second-class citizens (*muzhiks* in a modern age) offered one acceptable, and to some of the Hungarian leaders, an even admirable way of treating the Hungarian peasantry. Such treatment seemed to insure an adequate labor supply for the ever-hungry urban industries.

The importance ofthe 1968 reforms lies in the fact that they changed all of these premises. These reforms evolved slowly since the beginning of the decade. They were part of the general economic reforms created through the adoption of the New Economic Mechanism. They enunciated two radically different, new goals *vis a vis* the peasantry: (1)to make agriculture profitable for both the state and the peasants; and (2) to integrate the peasantry into the citizenry of the state.

The regime could not tamper with the ownership-structure of land *per se,* that would have been ideologically unacceptable. Moreover, the leaders were still convinced that social and community ownership was a far more advanced form—and, hence, hopefully, eventually more profitable—than private ownership. But both the members of the preparatory commission of the reform and the leadership in charge of its implementation (such as, Politburo member Lajos Feher) were convinced that incentives for production could be provided within the existing system of ownership. The cautious steps towards this end began by the discrading of the Soviet theory of ownership structure.

Between 1965 and 1968, the regime began to downgrade the ideological differentiation between state and collective farm properties, the Soviet view being that state property was a "higher form." The reform of 1968 codified the equality of the two forms of socialist ownership, making it a principal part of agrarian policy.[64]

7. Reform and Reconstruction

Subsequently, further reforms were enacted. In 1965, the obligatory plan-targets for agriculture were abolished and supply quotas disappeared in 1966. In 1967, the cooperatives were freed from the supervision of the non-administrative organs of the state—owned firms; and, between 1968 and 1971 the cooperatives gained independence in the sense that their members could cast votes in secret ballot for all their officers including the president of their collective farm. Since the introduction of the reform, the cooperatives could also purchase and own their own large machinery, sign direct contracts with state enterprises, and, in some cases, could even contract with Western firms for the delivery of goods produced under their own supervision and on their own farms. They could now decide what they whished to produce, wheel and deal, and distribute their profits as they saw fit.

The peasants gained many new benefits as the result of these reforms. In 1968, the work hours on the state farms were officially reduced to a 48-hour work week. At the same time, financial incentives were given to productive peasants which in effect lengthened the collective farmers' work hours by allowing them to earn practically unlimited amounts of money from work accomplished after the work hours were completed in the collective.

Other incentives were also provided for the collective peasantry. These included substantially higher earning possibilities on the collective farms themselves. This was the result of the removal of centralized control. Consequently, the collectives began to produce more goods. Most farm prices were freed of centralized regulations. They were allowed to follow the supply-demand of the market to fluctuate relatively freely. This had resulted in higher agricultural prices and also considerably higher incomes for the peasantry as a whole. The real income of the peasantry, thus, increased by 41% between 1966 and 1970, and the peasants' income continued to exceed that of industrial workers by 2% on the average, even in 1971.[65] The combination of household-plot production and production on the collective farms, the adoption of the so-called Nadudvar share-cropping method, the encouragement and assistance given to peasants who raised poultry, hogs or cattle on the household plots for both the collective and the free market, and the extension of social security pensions and medical insurance to the villages, all combined to create a hitherto unknown and unequalled prosperity in the life of the peasantry.

It was precisely this unequalled prosperity of the villages that began to endanger the very success of the reforms. Between 1970 and 1974, anti-peasant rhetorics emerged anew, together with pro-industrial worker demagoguery. Orthodox party-ideologues claimed that the peasants gained disproportionately higher incomes than industrial workers, that they spent practically nothing on food or transportation, and that they made enormous profits on the free market. The alleged amassing of wealth by the peasants was a convenient excuse for the demagogic left-wing worker and trade-union leadership to hide their own desire to turn the tide to reform away from the embattled shores of "working class" rule.[66] Worker dissatisfaction with the rapidly growing income differentiation during these years had led to the 1974 debates. As a result of these debates, a temporary reversal of the reforms of agriculture was initiated. The state began to tax small-scale production heavily, and raised the prices of industrial goods used in farming. The demagogues basked in the sunshine of their success in "showing to the peasants" that the "working class" remained in control.

The peasants' response—both on the cooperative farms and on the private household plots—was swift and predictable. As the price of animal products declined on the free market and as their profits dwindled, so did their desire to produce. By 1975, the number of cattle sold dropped by 200,000 heads, the number of pigs marketed decreased by a whopping 1,600,000 animals. A milk shortage replaced the previous glut in dairy products; meat, fruit and vegetables became scarce. The peasants' reasoning was simple: "Why should I work more in my free time, after fulfilling my workhours in the collective, why should I slave for an extra three to five hours a day, if I am unable to make a healthy profit? I have all the food I need, let the cities, the regime and the industrial workers buy elsewhere what they need."[67]

Faced now with real worker dissatisfaction over the lack of food in the stores and on the free market, the government reversed itself in February, 1975, returning to the policies in force until the previous year. Since then, the assistance was given to small units of production based on family labor; the market was opened for their produce once again; unreasonable taxes were removed and the peasants who amassed large incomes through their own hard labor are now at least tolerated.

With these decisions, the privatization of Hungarian agriculture (like the privatization of a great part of the Hungarian economy), continued in full swing. But the Hungary of the late 1970's is far more different than was the Hungary of the late 1940's. The 1350 giant collective farms are now a real part of daily existence, accepted, used, exploited, exploiting, trusted and mistrusted; they are a melange of good and bad characteristics, the sources of conflict and benefits. Private farming in various forms also continues to exist. Some are successful, some are not, some exist out of habit, others out of greed. Such farming coexist side by side with the large-scale production of the collective farms far more integrally than the small private plots coexisted with the large estates before the war. The peasants themselves have been changed; from backwardness and poverty, peasant life has been transformed to include modern citizens as well as traditionals, rich peasants as well as poor. It is still a peasantry, one that has been finally integrated into the fabric of the nation. And that has been the greatest accomplishment of the regime.

NOTES

1. David Mitrany, *Marx Against the Peasant* (New York,) 25. Mitrany's original essay under the title of "Marx versus the Peasant" was written in 1927.
2. Karl Marx and Freidrich Engels, "Manifesto of the Communist Party" in Robert C. Tucker, ed., *The Marx-Engels Reader* (New York, 1972), 352.

3. This oft-repeated term was first used in its original form by J.C. Eccarius, *Eines Arbeiters Widerlegung der National-oekonomischen Lehren John Stuart Mills* (Zurich 1968), Quoted by Mitrany, *op. cit.*, 218.
4. V. I. Lenin, March 8, 1921, in *Polnoe Sobranie Sochinenii* (Moscow, 1927), v. 8 pp. 216-7. Quoted by Mitrany, *op. cit.* 233.
5. For the most objective and comprehensive treatment of the agrarian question during the Soviet Republic of 1919 see Tibor Hajdu, *A magyaroszagi tanacskoztarsasag* (The Soviet Republic of Hungary((Budapest, 1969), 377-87, and Frank Eckelt, "The Internal Policies of the Hungarian Societ Republic" In Ivan volgyes, ed., *Hungary in Revolution, 1918-1919* (Lincoln, Nebraska 1971), 81-187. *1918-1919* (Lincoln, Nebraska 1971), 81-187.
6. The systematic study of the cleavages between urban and rural communities of course, is more developed in regard to Western Europe. See Stein Rokkan's excellent article, "Geography, Religion and Social Class" in Seymour M. Lipset and Stein Rokkan (eds.), *Party Systems and Voter Alignment: Cross-National Perspectives* (New York, 1967), 367-444 and Sidney Tarrow, "The Urban-Rural Cleavage in Political Involvement: The Case of France," *The American Political Science Review,* June, 1967, 341-357.
7. For some of the more vituperous charges and counter-charges cf. Ernst Bettelheim, *Zur Krise der Kommunistischen Partei Ungarns* (Vienna, 1922) and *Die Taktik der Kommunistischen Internationale gegen die Offensive des Kapitals* (Hamburg, 1922).
8. "Magyarorszag demokratikus ujjaepitesenek es felemelkedesenek programmja (The Program for the Democratic Rebuilding and Development of Hungary), *Neplap* (Debrecen), November 30, 1944, 1.
9. Recently declassified documents in the British Public Archives suggest that Anthony Eden in discussions with V. M. Molotov had already agreed on allowing the USSR to maintain 75% influence in Hungary and retaining only the symbolic 25% for the rest of the wartime Allies.

10. *A szocializmus utjan* (On the Road Toward Socialism) (Budapest: 1970), 379.
11. Jozsef Revai, *Marxizmus, nepiesseg, magyarsag* (Marxism,, Populism, *Hungarianism* (Budapest, 1949), 222. The manuscript, originally written in 1938, became the key to Communist agrarian policy.
12. From the minutes of the Central Executive Committee of the Hungarian Communist Party, taken on March 22, 1945, the expectation that there would be sharpened class-conflict in the villages becomes very clear. Quoted in Sandor Orban, *Ket agrarforradalom Magyarorszagon* (Two Agrarian Revolutions in Hungary) (Budapest, 1972), 37, 104.
13. *Mezogazdasagi Adattar* (compendium of Agricultural Data) (Budapest, 1965), v. 1, p. 45. In the future *Adattar.*
14. *Adattar,* I, 46.
15. Table adopted from data in Orban, *op. cit.,* 42.
16. *Ibid.,* 45.
17. Ferenc Donath, in his excellent *Reform es forradalom* (Reform and Revolution) (Budapest, 1977), gives the best data on the altered ownership structure. Although Donath argues that the socialist transformation should have taken place without intermediate steps, his volume should still be perused by all researchers interested in the problem for the thought-provoking manner in which he handles his examination.
18. Orban, *Ket agrarforradalom . . . op. cit.,* 63.
19. *Ibid.,* 51 and 158.
20. Gyorgy Ranki, *Magyarorszag gazdasaga az elso 3 eves terv idoszakaban* (The Economy of Hungary during the Period of the First Three-Year Plan) (Budapest, 1963), 214.
21. *Adattar,* I:160.
22. Bela Fekete, *Parasztprogram, agrarprogram* (Peasant Program, Agrarian Program) (Budapest, n.d.); see also, "A Magyar Kommunista part szovetkezeti iranyelvei," (The Guiding Principles of the Hungarian Communist Party concerning Cooperatives) *A Magyar Kommunista Part es*

a Szocialdemokrata Part Hatarozatai (The Decisions of the Hungarian Communist Party and the Social Democratic Party) (Budapest, 1951), 567.

23. Imre Nagy, *Egy evitized* (One Decade) (Budapest, 1954), vol. I, 438, 449 and vol. 2, 44, 113-4.
24. Orban, *Ket agrarforradalom,* op. cit., 71 fn. 29, contains the only known reference to the Stalin-Molotov letter.
25. Matyas Rakosi, *Epitjuk a nep orszagat* (We Are Building the Country for the People) (Budapest, 1949), 55.
26. Matyas Rakosi, *Valogatott beszedek es cikkek* (Selected Speeches and Articles) (Budapest, 1950), 378-80. See also, Erno Gero, *Harcban a szocialista nepgazdasagert* (In Battle for the Socialist People's Economy) (Budapest, 1950), 410-1.
27. Orban, *Ket agrarforradalom, op. cit.,* 73, cites as proof the documents contained in the Film Archives of the Institute of Party History (Budapest), PB/384.

29. The reader may quarrel with the somewhat value-laden term "Collective farm" as used in this volume. The early forms of the "agricultural cooperatives"(mezogazdasagi termeloszovetkezetek), however, were clearly based on the Soviet *kolkhoz* example. While later, specifically in the 1960's, real and significant differences developed and deviated from the Soviet pattern, for the sake of continuity and usage we will retain the use of the term "collective farm" for agricultural cooperative in this part of our volume.
30. Orban, *Ket agrarforradalom* . . . . , 92-101.
31. Adopted from *Adattar,* I, 12, 15, and II, 4.
32. *Ibid.,* I, 8-9, 12-15, II, 22.
33. *Ibid.,* II, 13.
34. *Ibid.*
35. *Ibid.,* 161-162.
36. *Ibid.,* 6, 13, and Peter Kovacs, "A munkas-paraszt szovetseg kerdesehez." (Additions to the Question of Worker-Peasant Alliance), *Tarsadalmi Szemle* I (1951), pp. 112-114.

37. *Adattar,* II, 399.
38. Orban, *Ket agrarforradalom* . . . . , 123.
39. *Adattar,* I, 8, 15, and II, 11.
40. *Ibid.* II, 13.
41. Minutes of the Politburo, May 26, 1955, PB/2005, in Orban, *Ket agrarforradolom* . . . ., 147, fn. 441.
42. These decisions were made at the June 23, 1955 meeting of the Politburo. *Ibid.,* 149, fn. 453.
43. Two interesting articles in which the leaderships' recognition that past policies were correct were Andras Sandor, 'Uj szerepet a termeloszovetkezeteknek" (New Roles for the Collective Farms) *Szabad Fold,* September 30, 1956, p. 3 and Istvan Markus, "Somogyi osszegzes" (Somogy Accounting) *Csillag* 9 (1956), 525-540.
44. Istvan Pinter, "Az 1956. evi ellenforradalom falun (The 1956 Counter-revolution in the Villages), *Szazadok,* 5-6 (1960), 863-864.
45. *Adattar,* II, 11.
46. *Ibid.,* 12-13.
47. Orban, *Ket agrarforradalom* . . . . , 169, fns. 54-55.
48. *Mezogazdasagi Statisztikai Zsebkonyv* (Agricultural Statistical Pocket Book) (Budapest, 1959), 16-17.
49. Orban, *Ket agrarforradalom* . . . . , 184.
50. Quoted in *Az MSzMP hatarozatai es kokumentumai* (The Decisions and Documents of the HSWP) (Budapest, 1959), 182-189. The final decisions were made at the December 7, 1958 meeting of the Central Committee of the HSWP. Quoted in *ibid.,* 267 ff.
51. *Osterreichs Wirtschaftsstruktur gestern-heute-morgen* (Berlin, 1961), II, 678. Although quoted widely by Hungarian sources, among others by Orban, the findings in this volume do give rise to some concern because of the methodological and statistical problems of this huge volume.
52. The central direction of collectivization can be clearly seen by the articles published about Bulgaria on September 9, East Germany, on October 7, Poland, on September 10,

and Rumania on December 3, 1958 in the Moscow editions of *Pravda.*

53. Even Kadar admitted the strong "influence" of the Moscow decisions in his *A szocializmus teljes gyozelmeert* (For the Complete Victory of Socialism) (Budapest, 1962), 278.
54. *Az MSzMP hatarozatai es dokumentumai,* 188-189.
55. Orban, *Ket agrarforradalom* .... 220 clearly states that the terror was not the result of peasant activities aimed at the destruction of the collective farm system; even during the height of collectivization only 131 peasants were charged by the state police forces with such activities.
56. Bela Fazekas, *A mezogazdasagi termeloszovetkezeti mozgalom Magyarorszagon* (The Agricultural Cooperative Movement in Hungary) (Budapest: 1976), 115.
57. Quoted in Orban, *Ket agrarforradalom* . . . , 228, fn. 314.
58. For example, in 1969 7% of the entire membership did not work on the common holding a single workday, while the new members worked only 251 work units on the average compared to that of 339 units worked by the old members in 1959. According to Ferenc Donath during the years 1961-1964 2-25% of the peasantry did not work on the common lands at all! Ferenc Donath, *Reform es forradalom* (Reform and Revolution) (Budapest: 1977), 200.
59. Fazekas, *A mezogazdasagi* . . . . , 127-128.
60. Table based on sources from *Adattar,* I, 12, 15 and II, 4.
61. *Ibid.,* II, 5.
62. *Ibid.,* 38.
63. Orban, *Ket agrarforradalom* . . . . , 235, quoting a note reporting the problems to the Politburo, dated February 3, 1961. See fn. 352.
64. The Xth Congress of the HSWP (1971), the XIth Congress (1975) and Section 34 of the III/1971 Act on the Cooperatives were all emphatic in making clear that both state and collective farm ownerships are of the same standing and character and that neither is "more advanced" than the other.

65. Data based upon the Statistical Pocket Books of the relevant years.
66. For the most extreme attacks on the "pro-peasant policies" see *Nepszava,* October 3, 6, 1970 and *Nepszebadsag,* November 3, 1970.
67. Istvan Lazar, "The Collective Farm and the Private Plot," *New Hungarian Quarterly,* Autumn, (1976), p. 72.

II

RURAL TRANSFORMATION: AN ECONOMIC ANALYSIS

1. The Organization of the Rural Sphere

The contribution of agriculture to economic prosperity is so significant that even a cursory economic survey—necesitated by the limited length of this study—reveals its enormous importance. While in 1938, agriculture contributed around 50% to the gross national income of Hungary, in 1975 that contribution decreased to only 10%. In spite of the decrease, the agricultural production volume in 1975 was nearly twice as much (1938-100, 1976-185) as in 1938. The average rate of growth for the years 1950-1975 was 3.2%. It is significant to point out, however, that the average rate of growth is misleading since the rate during these years differed from year to year. In contrast with the 5.5% annual rate of growth during 1971-75, the 1951-61 decade yielded only 1.5%, 1962-65 only 1.8% and 1966-70 only 2.8% growth rates respectively. On the other hand, productivity had increased in all fields of agriculture, tripling the volume of all major products except wheat, corn and industrial crops. The importance of agriculture today to the economy and to the legitimacy of the regime is even greater than before; alone among the COMECON states, Hungary is able to satisfy *all* the major food demands of its population. Moreover, agricultural products account for around 20% of all exports of Hungary and, most significantly, this represents around 40% of all hard currency trade with the West.

With all these successes of the agricultural sphere, it would be tempting to say that the fundamental transformation of the economic sphere brought about an equalization of the villages with the cities. Such a generalization can only be made, however, in regard to the administrative organization of the village economy. Like the cities, the villages have become closely organized, integrated units of economics production.

The organization of the agrarian system can be separated into two distinct spheres: the administrative organization and the economic organization. Until 1968, the administrative superstructure acted as the overlord over the village economy and was technically responsible for setting individual production targets for the cooperatives. Since that date, however local councils have been required merely to assist the cooperatives, and the latter were given carte blanche in terms of productive organization and activities.

The administrative functions of the rural sphere are carried out primarily by the local councils. They control the supplementary agrarian activities, maintain liaison between district (jaras) authorities, deal with transport problems and organize cooperation in regard to the sale and purchase of agrarian goods.[1] In addition to these functions, relating largely to collective farms, far more important for their effect on the entire rural sphere are the traditional concerns of the local administrative apparatus. These concerns are generally broken down into two major areas: those that are directly handled by representatives of the central authorities and those that are handled locally by elected or appointed individuals. The most significant centrally directed activities are: police, health and education, and general state administration of employees directly employed by the state (e.g., teachers, veterinarians, nurses, etc.). The most significant local functions concern financial problems, industrial development and location, commerce, issues related to agrarian development and administration, construction, health, labor and matters of justice leading to trials of the first instance.[2]

The local administrative set-up is therefore complicated with organization charts that would make the U. S. Department of HEW proud of its simplicity. The Socialist state directly exercise control over local activities from the seat of the district council not merely by the appointment of police-authorities, teachers, doctors, veterinarians, but also by the establishment of frequently arbitrary standards regarding the allocation of state-support. The council—whose president is answerable to the local population as well as the higher authorities—must justify the collection of taxes for unpopular projects from the local population.[3] The classic and not very Communist dilemma facing the population of supporting often not very popular teachers, policemen, or not very courteous doctors or administrators of all sorts foisted on them by a higher administrative decision, makes the work of local administrative bodies often difficult.[4]

The organization of the economic sphere, with which most of this chapter will be concerned, is equally complex, but at the same time, somewhat more clearly delineated. In Hungary, the economic activities of the rural sphere are characterized by the three basic types of production units: state farms, collective farms and private farms.

2. Productive Units

State farms were created largely on the former large estates, which were not divided up at the time of the various land reforms but were expropriated from their owners and kept intact. Some of these large estates had already been in the hands of the state, and have been maintained as the mainstay of modernization in the backward rural sphere. The Babolna State Farm, for example, was founded as a state stud-farm by Joseph II in 1789 and since then it has been the breeding ground of some of the finest racing and walking horses of Europe.[5]

The function of the state farms has remained largely the same as those of the best large estates of the past, namely, to introduce new production methods, to offer examples to the rest of agriculture on its way to modernization (and to assist the collective farms as much as possible). With the reform of the economic mechanism introduced in 1968, however, the state farms suddenly found that they had to meet one additional criterion: profitability. The managers of the economic reforms rightly reasoned that it was indeed very nice of the Hungarian government to provide capital, bring in additional tech nologies, and offer all the inducements available to the state-farms, but they also realized that it was time for the latter to "reciprocate" and to start being really productive units. As a result, since 1968, while the right of the state-farms to engage in direct agrarian foreign trade was expanded and financial assistance to them was greatly increased, the new requirement of profitability has also come into the fore.

The number and size of the state farms have fluctuated in Hungary. In 1960, there were 333 state farms; the number had dwindled to 147 by 1976. At the same time, the territory occupied by the state farms has grown from 1,843,687 acres in 1960 to 1,939,746 acres in 1976, accounting for about 8% of the total usable land area. The average size of a state farm has increased from 5,536 acres to 13,066 acres in 1976.[6] However, while there are some very large state farms, there are also some whose territory barely reaches 950 acres. In 1976, the state farm sector employed 147,500 people and accounted for only 15% of the total number of agrarian workers.[7] The relatively minor economic importance of the state farm sector is reflected in a comparison with the collective sector. In 1976, there were ten times as many collective farms than state farms in operation, accounting for slightly over 63.7% of the usable lands, employing 61% of the total number of agrarian employees. However, the numerical weight of the state farms is not quite comparable to their weight in agricultural production. In 1976, for example, the state sector produced 17.4% of all agrarian goods while the collective farms produced only 55%. In certain commodities, such as the production of corn, or in poultry farming, the state-sector has produced far more than the number of state farms would indicate.

The state-farms are excellent examples of the ability of large, centralized organizations to compete on even terms with large national and multinational enterprises. They have been able to adopt imported techniques and obtain foreign licenses in areas that can be used by Hungarian agriculture as a whole. The best example of the successful state farm-operation is the famous Babolna state farm, although the Sarvar, Barcs, or Szekszard state farms are almost equally well-managed and well-organized concerns.[8]

It would be tempting to describe the Babolna state-farm as a "typical" agrarian state combine.[9] But it is not typical at all, rather it is a prototype of a highly developed and specialized state-farm, one of Hungary's showpieces of agricultural success. It is a living proof of many things—the modernization, and industrialization of agricultural production among others—but more than that, it is also the living testimony of the abilities, energy and personal charisma of one of the most colorful personalities of Hungarian agriculture, Dr. Robert Burgert, its President. By sheer energy, great organizational talent, and relative freedom for his initiatives during the last two decades, Burgert has transformed Babolna from a small stud-farm to an international agrarian concern. The sheer size and variety of production activities recall a Western conglomerate; this state-farm breeds and exports poultry, breeds studs, produces fertilizers and fodder, breeds sheep on a large scale. The farm also has its own construction firms, its own architectural planners, possesses a computer center complete with the most up-to-date hardware and software. Babolna even owns a publishing house and an export-import firm, the Agraria Foreign Trade Office, which is responsible for the entire export-import business of the farm.

Babolna is amazing for its sheer, bustling energy. It was the first Hungarian firm to break into the tough international export-import competition among the large multinational concerns. Today, Babolna exports entire production systems (among them several million broilers to the Arab world annually), operating from a mere hundred million selection-bases as compared to the 500 million selection-bases used by its

Western competitors. With an export business that utilizes 460 charter aircrafts and thousands of truck-loads a year to ship produce to Iraq, Jordan, Kuwait, Iran, Austria, Yugoslavia, East Germany, Czechoslovakia, West Germany, France, Italy and Spain, Babolna in 1976 produced 664,954 forints gross agricultural products and 43,511 forints net profits per capita-employee. In 1976, it was ranked fourth among the broiler and egg-exporting international firms, and was battling to gain an even higher position with the export of complex broiler production systems to the developing countries. Its salesmen utilize high-pressure techniques; its competitive pricing abroad makes the farm a tough customer to beat at negotiations.

Burgert, President of the Babolna farm, is a phenomenon that occurs rarely. He kept tabs on the operation of the farm at all times and has even been granted permission by the state authorities to establish Babolna's own short-wave sender and receiver radio system. The top leaders of the firm are never more than a bleep away from one another and from Burgert. His insistence on using the most modern methods of production resulted in the adoption of the Chicago Corn Production System (CPS). This system was subsequently adopted to the Hungarian circumstances by the Babolna State Farm and by the Nadudvar organization for the complex production of corn; it has resulted in Hungary's ability to produce more feed and leguminous plants per hectare than any other nation in the world, except the U.S., since 1975.[10]

Burgert has been given all the honors the state can bestow upon one man, including membership in the prestigious Central Committee of the party. But he remains an explosive individual. His energy explodes equally against bureaucratic red tape and stupidity. On a television program called "Forum," for example, he has argued vehemently against needless control by the state, exemplified by the bureaucrats' insistence that his salesmen abroad, particularly his agents in the Arab world, use only Russian-made autos. Noting the grave difficulties in servicing these automobiles in a nonCommunist state, he asked why there was any need for such regimentation.[11] He explodes regularly at stupidities in credit allocation; since he runs a *state* farm, he must get credit for each of his ventures from the Hungarian National Bank. But Burgert is lucky; because of his success, his prestige, his connections, and his vitality, he usually succeeds where others fail.

Burgert is never satisfied. He notes that the Babolna farm pays the same salary as other state-farms, which is frequently less than the income one could gain from a good collective farm. He points out that while in 1975 the average salary of all of the workers at Babolna was 3854 forints, or slightly higher than at the nearby collective, the household plot and the various benefits offered by the collective farm had resulted in about 30% higher earnings for the collective farm membership than state farm employment.[12] He realized the importance of highly trained manpower and it is to his credit that he continues to upgrade the skills of personnel. Of the 4266 individuals employed directly by Babolna, for example, 162 have university education and 610 employees had completed secondary schools. Fully 2900 or 68% of all employees are skilled workers and all of them are required to work six days a week. They must never slack off and are not permitted to drink on the job.

In spite of all this, Burgert notes the enormous tension that exists within this successful system between the young men and women working on the farm whose average age is 32 and 29 respectively and the older middle and top-level leadership. He is trying to deal with the daily problems arising from the constant and, for him incomprehensible thievery from the farm, and the tension between the efficiency demanded by a modern space-age management system, and the backwardness which sometimes surrounds the state-farms. He resents domestic provincialism and bureaucratic wrangling that stifles adaptation and progress.[13] He is an angry but successful man who would have become a highly paid manager or a millionaire anywhere in the West, but who chooses to work himself literally to death, believing in measuring his and his state-farm's success not against the past but against the potentialities of the future. His is not a typical state-farm, but an example of what other state-farms could accomplish and what should be emulated by his colleagues.

The example of Babolna shows what a good state-farm can accomplish, but most of the managers are not Burgerts and most of the farms of Hungary are collective farms, with far greater problems and far more difficult production activities. As briefly described in the previous chapter, the term "collective farm" is misleading in its English usage. In Hungary, collective farms or cooperative farms have existed in various forms since the latter part of the 19th century; Public Law No. XXXVII (1875), for example, had already contained paragraphs for the protection of agrarian cooperation and cooperatives (*szovetkezes*). The upper stratum of the peasantry was especially interested in cooperation and in 1898, the National Central Credit Cooperative (*Orszagos Kozponti Hitelszovetkezet,* or OKH), was founded. Several other similar cooperatives were founded in Hungary, but most of these were the results of voluntary specialized types of cooperation among the more prosperous peasants. In the inter-war period there were some cooperatives indeed that were established by poor peasants—such as the Melykut, Medgyesegyhaza and Mako Cooperatives—but most peasants rejected this form of common activity and instead tried to attain private ownership of land.[14]

The Communist Party's doctrinal position found adequate support among some who believed in the creation of cooperatives early in 1945. The 137 collectives that were created between January and May, 1945, were living examples of this position. Although the freshly established cooperatives had not wielded much influence, their very existence signified the shape of future agrarian developments.[15] Executive order No. 131,000/1945 of the Ministry of Agriculture, dated September 18, 1945, aimed at legalizing and supporting the collectives. In fact, the decree became the seedbed for the future force that was to be utilized a mere two years later, the germ of the mandatory establishment of collective farms in every village.[16] Aided by the passage of a law in 1947 (XI/1974), the cooperative form of ownership and production registered significant gains and it appeared clear that it was here to stay.

Between 1945 and 1948, the number of collective farms grew from 270 to 2,584 and their workers increased from approximately 10,000 people in 1945 to 426,000 in 1948. Forcible collectivization between 1949 and 1953 raised the percentage of the total agrarian employees working in the collective sectors from 0.5% in 1949 to 19.1% in 1953.[17] However, this ratio dropped to 15.4% during the doldrums of 1956. Between 1959 and 1961, the complete collectivization of the country resulted in the steep rise in the percentage of agrarian employees working on collective farms; their percentage grew from 37.5% in 1960 to 94% of all agrarian employees not employed by the state sector in 1962.[18] Although the number of cooperatives decreased through mergers between 1972 and 1976, the predominant position of collective agriculture in Hungary has not been challenged.

3. Mechanization, Regionalization, Consolidation

Currently there are three basic forms of collective or cooperative farming in Hungary. The agricultural collective farm (*mezogazdasagi termeloszovetkezet*) is defined as a

> "large-scale productive activity which takes place as a result of the voluntary pooling of common implements ... whose aim is collective work, the division of goods based on socialist principles ... the creation, growth, and profitability of large-scale socialist agrarian production, the raising of the social, living and work conditions of its members."[19]

In addition to the collective farm, there are two less complex, less completely integrated types of cooperatives: the collective crafts groups *(szakszovetkezetek)* and the specialized collective enterprises. They do not pool their implements and their private property. The former usually restrict their common work to grain and sometimes livestock production on a large scale and allow their members to work on their own in other agricultural occupations.[20] The specialized collectives do possess common tools. Their members are engaged in specialized production activities that are more profitably done in common rather than individually.[21] They work in vini-and viticulture, fruit-growing, raising of fur, of rabbits, or are involved in bee-keeping, and although they own their own tools—such as vats, fermentation barrels, etc.—in common, most of the work is done individually. The profits are shared according to agreements that vary from farm to farm. Although, until 1968, there existed some other similar semi-private farms, such as cooperative mountain villages or nursery tree-growing cooperatives, since 1968, these specialized farms have been subsumed under the general rubric of specialized collectives.[22]

In Hungary, the most complex and hence most integrated form of collective farms have dominated the collective production activities.[23] The simpler forms of cooperation have rarely amounted to more than a fraction of the more complex form, although their contribution to the national economy has consistently ranged around 10% of gross agricultural production.[24]

At the height of the collectivization drive in 1960-1961, there were 4,507 collective farms; as a result of the consolidation of a large number of collectives between 1970 and 1977, their number has dwindled to 1,300. Similarly, the average size of the collective farms increased from 1,628 acres in 1960 to 7,030 acres in 1977.[25] The distribution of collective farm size in 1975 shows that while there were 282 farms ranging between 0-2,800 acres, and 606 collectives ranging between 2,800 and 5,700 acres, 501 collective farms possessed between 3,801.9 and 9,500 acres each and 209 farms had giant landholdings encompassing more than 9,500 acres of land each.[26]

Why such a tendency to gigantism? For one, the Hungarian government has realized that large-scale farming still provides the best possible source for marketable production-systems. The large farms' ability to invest, organize and produce more efficiently is noted by the Hungarians in Soviet and U.S. practice. But gigantism is not necessarily a blessing.

The former principle of collective farm organization—one village, one or more than one collective—was based on the notion that local peasants tended to be familiar with their surroundings, with the land they worked and therefore were able to produce according to the productive circumstances.[27] The new principle of organization—one collective farm encompassing many villages—negated this idea. Now the peasant or collective farm member tends to be less familiar with conditions of production. In spite of this and in spite of the "alienation" of the peasant from a well-known land area, gigantism seems to be preferred because of the scarcity of investment funds and their better utilization by the large farms. Although Hungarian policy-makers are quite emphatic in asserting that collective farm consolidation had come to an end by 1975, it seems to us that the consolidation process ended less because of the desire of the leaders than because they had already reached the "critical size." Many of the agricultural leaders of the country have recognized that mergers were not always the most efficient way to insure the further growth of agrarian production. Frequently, in order to make use of the full potential of a large farm—often about 19,000 acres—enormous investments have to be made in buildings, machinery and well-trained staff, and the large farms have run into obstacles in obtaining these necessities for increased productivity. Thus, the peculiar requirement of Hungarian investment policies, developed since 1968, stating that investment credits be returned within three years—although the turn-around time in agriculture is generally five years—limited the funds for such purposes. Moreover, the personnel needed to run large-scale farming operations efficiently has been missing from many of these enterprises and as a result many faulty decisions have been taken.[28] Consequently, local resentment, the distances that the members had to travel to reach their place of work, and the fact that the further growth of the collective farms would be both impractical and financially unprofitable, were equally important factors in limiting the growth of the size of collective farms.

As mentioned earlier, the simpler forms of collective organization account for only a fraction of the land and a fraction of agrarian production. In 1970, there were 243 such groupings, but by 1976, their numbers had dwindled to 108. In terms of the gross production of agricultural goods they accounted for around 14% in 1970. However, as a result of the disbanding of the least profitable specialized collectives, their contribution to agricultural gross production had dwindled to less than six percent in 1976.[29] In addition to the 108 simpler agricultural groupings, there were 20 fishing and a number of bee and fur-producing cooperative ventures. In general, however, the less complex forms of cooperation seem to be slowly disappearing.

How good are the cooperative farms? Have they been able to attain what was expected of them and transform agricultural production from backward, simple production farms to efficient, well-producing farms? These are questions that are difficult to answer from the perspective of the "average" farm or from the perspective of a single criterion. In productive capacity, the collective farms are the mainstays of agricultural production. In 1975, for example, the collective farms accounted for 64.7% of all agricultural gross production, slightly exceeding their proportion of all agricultural lands.[30] Since the years of the doldrums, in every single area production efficiency has considerably increased. Thus, for example, wheat yield per hectare has grown from 17.1 quintals (1 quintal-220 lbs.) per hectare in 1959—a better than average year prior to the full-fledged collectivization effort—to 42.8 quintals per hectare in 1976. Corn production, mostly as a result of the adoption of the Chicago-Babolna Corn Production System, has also increased dramatically from 26.2 quintals per hectare in 1959 to above 50 quintals per hectare in 1977.[31] Similar gains were registered in all aspects of collective production activities.

Much of these successes can be attributed to the speedy mechanization of agriculture and the expanded use of various chemical fertilizers. For example, in 1960, only 50.2% of the total amount of draft power came from mechanical sources; by 1975, this figure had risen to 92%. Similarly, the degree of mechanization of harvesting has greatly increased. Only in sugar beet and potato harvesting does the percent of mechanization fall below 90%.[32] All additional indices point to the radical mechanization of agriculture during the last few years, and the collective farms have been the major beneficiaries of this growth.

Radical improvements could be observed in the application of fertilizers as well, especially during the period of 1958-1975. In 1958, the national average utilization of fertilizers was merely 85.7 kilogram per hectare; this figure more than tripled to 276 kilograms per hectare in 1975.[33] While these figures are still not comparable to the amount of fertilizers used by farmers in the advanced Western countries—in 1975, for example, Holland used 757 kilograms per hectare and Belgium 570 kilograms per hectare—the advances are still notable and obviously contribute to the rapid growth of agricultural production in the collective farm.[34]

Problems, however, also continue to plague the collective farms, and these problems frequently stem from the very areas of development we mentioned above. Thus, for example, the quality of manpower and leadership of the collective farms is frequently not the best; even though there are more than 200,000 people below 30 years of age working on the collective farms, there remain at least 40% of all members who are already above or approaching retirement age.[35] In addition, as the bureaucratization of the system proceeded, by 1975 only 72% of the members were actually involved in productive work; the rest were either on pension or worked as office employees.[36] Bureaucracy has plagued reporting and planning activities; in five years, just the *number* of general state directives regulating collective farm activities amounted to more than one hundred! And we must take into account that every collective venture must write up a quarterly balance sheet and report it to *every* authority above it in duplicate; must send (that report) also to the Hungarian National Bank as well as to the Central Statistical Office.[37] With the myriad other mandated reports, complete bureaucratization has finally reached the collective farms.

Moreover the education and specialization required for the successful running of a large organization are more difficult to attain. Although the educational and specialization level of leaders has increased since 1958, it is still far from being adequate from the perspective of the goal-orientation of the regime. Compared to 1970, when 28.1% of all collective farm chairmen had a college or university degree and 73.1% had finished at least secondary school, by 1974, these percentages had risen to 40.6% and 81.7% respectively.[38] When compared to the level of education in the state farms, however (in 1974, 80% and 91.7%, respectively), it becomes obvious that the collective farms still have a long way to go.

The educational achievement of the leaders, of course, is not commensurate with their abilities, and very frequently even the most educated chairmen fail in their tasks. Leadership and management training is still lacking. Qualities that make a leader humanly acceptable to a rapidly changing society are very hard to fathom.[39] The skill of dealing with workers, the willingness to experiment, to take risks at good odds, to venture forth and see new roads to development, frequently push even the successful leaders outside the letters of the law. Their "experiments" may become disguised private—or even communal—profiteering that occurs at the expense of the state.[40]

The labor problems of collectives extend to levels below the managers of the farms. The gradual decrease in the pensionable age (from 65 to 60 and from 60 to 55 for men and women respectively), by 1980 is expected to result in further losses of approximately 20-25% of all active members. Already the ratio of those who are either on pension or are on the collective farm's assistance program to those who are active wage earning members is 479,000 to 456,000.[41] The high average age of active members (41 years of age for men and 42 years of age for women) remains a source of real concern.[42] Problems also become apparent when the actual amount of members' work-days in collective farm work is examined; out of a possible 311 work-days yearly, the men worked 290 days, but the women only worked 193 work-days in 1974.[43] While the average 78.5% of all work-days spent on the collective farm compares favorably to 1963, when only 53% of all work-days were spent, the regime would like to raise these figures to 85-90% within the next decade.[44]

The problems with mechanization also continue to plague the collectivized sector in spite of enormous progress.[45] While an ever-increasing number of Western-produced tractors are available (including John Deere, Hesston, Claas, Rau, Akkord and the Raba-Steiger products), Hungarian farming still heavily relies on machinery purchased from Comecon countries. The result is a continuous parts-shortage. Replacement of parts can often take months. The Czechoslovak-made Zetor 12,045-Crystal, and the Soviet K-700 and M TZ tractors (the most widely used machines) are so difficult to service with spare parts that work stoppages seriously affect the economic performance of the entire agricultural sector in Hungary. At specifically designated tractor service stations charged with the repair of these machines, the delays can last up to 3-4 months! And in this shortage "not even the thriving domestic spare-parts industry can be of adequate assistance."[46] Accordin source (the Somogy County representative of the *Agrotroszt* enterprise in charge of export-import activities for agriculture) in the first quarter of 1977 the company ordered over 36 million forints worth of spare-parts but received only 21 million forints worth.[47]

Nor is the problem caused by the lack of spare-parts restricted to Comecon-produced machinery. While the majority of the GDR, Czechoslovak and Soviet tractors are lacking in spare-parts because of the simple unavailability of these items, the repair of Western tractors or machinery is hindered by the fact that spare parts for these machines have to be paid for in convertible currency. Although some currency is available for the collectives' use, their administration is unwieldy and frequently so bureaucratic that the paper shuffling takes more time than the delivery of the spare parts. It is for this reason that both collective and state farm enterprises tried to look for the "back door" (*kiskapu*) legally or semi-legally available to them by maintaining direct relations with Western firms. As a favor, the representatives of many Western firms will be glad to do some "shopping" in Vienna and bring the spare-parts back in their own automobiles directly to the respective farms. In 1975, for example, such a representative had purchased $12,500 worth of agricultural machinery parts in Vienna, delivered them always within 48 hours. His firm was then paid in an excessive number of textile items manufactured by the auxiliary enterprise of the farm.

The delivery and availability of tractors as total productive units, however, cannot be dealt with so simply and in this respect material shortages continue to plague Hungarian farming. Delivery from socialist countries is slow, usually behind schedule, and their administration is cumbersome. In 1977, for example, only 21 out of 200 Zetor-tractors arrived and deliveries from the GDR and the USSR are not much better.[48] Nonetheless, between 1976 and 1980, the mainstays of the agricultural machinery will remain the tractors and combines imported from socialist countries: 52% of new machinery will be purchased from them as compared to 40% purchased from the West.[49] At the same time, there is a growing realization in Hungary that especially the large output wheat combines cannot be purchased, nor could delivery be expected on time from Socialist states, since their production and delivery capacities are limited. Consequently, more and more of these machines (if planned machinery expansion-targets are to be met) must be purchased from the West, notably from the U.S.

and West Germany, and this will involve large-scale expenditure of hard currency. Although a fine start had been made in 1976 by the purchase of several hundred Western tractors— and by the allocation of 100 million forints worth of hard currency credit for further purchases—the cost of the large output machineries will be a very great burden for Hungarian agricultural investment policies.[50] On the other hand, cooperative arrangements within Hungary, such as the Babolna Agricultural Combine-led 200 member Joint Enterprise for the Industrial Production of Maize and Industrial Plants, do help in the pooling of resources and allocation of machinery. Similarly, international cooperative agreements such as the American-Hungarian Corn Production System—a joint enterprise headquartered in Vienna and Zurich—the Australian-Hungarian Cooperative Agreements, the joint Belgar-Hungarian agricultural ventures and Dutch-Hungarian agricultural cooperation make it easier for Hungarian enterprises to market their products on the Western markets and at the same time receive advanced Western technology.

The problem of fertilizers is equally difficult and it has plagued Hungarian agriculture production for several decades. In spite of a ten-fold increase in fertilizer—from 29 kilogram per hectare in 1960 to 276 kilogram per hectare in 1975, Hungary still lags behind Czechoslovakia and East Germany as well as behind all the Western countries in the use of fertilizers.[51] The problem appears to stem from two sources: financial hardship and the uneven application of available fertilizers. In regard to the financial hardship, one must realize that only 55% of Hungary's fertilizer needs are met from domestic sources; 30% has to be imported from rubel and 15% from hard currency economies. This imbalance has resulted in shortage of funds to purchase the needed fertilizers for some of the farms; while the May and August, 1977, reforms lowering fertilizer prices by 15% and allowing far more liberal credits for the purchase of fertilizers helped the situation, they could not be expected completely to alleviate it. Fertilizers remain quite expensive and their uneven application is largely due to the purchase costs. For poorer collectives, the cost is not retrieved by immediate, *significantly* higher yields. Shortsightedness or lack of knowledge on the part of the leadership often results in inadequate application. As some of the collective farm presidents pointed out, the difference in yields on *their* lands, between the use of less than 100 kilograms per hectare and 300 kilograms per hectare active fertilizer substance, does not jusify the added expense. The new chemical technology has not yet filtered down to all farm leaders. The imbalance of chemical fertilizer production created a glut on the domestic market of certain types of fertilizer.[52] As a result, there is a real paradox in the fact that Hungary now is both a fertilizer exporting and importing state.[53]

In addition to the enormous successes and obvious problems of the state and collective farms we would be remiss if we failed to mention an area where Hungarian agriculture has shown remarkable innovation and progress, namely, in the creation of new forms of agricultural activities that go far beyond the traditional breakdown of agricultural units into collective and state farms. There are four such new forms: agricultural associations (*mezogazdasagi tarsulasok*), agricultural combinates (*mezogazdasagi kombinatok*), agro-industrial associations (*agraripari egyesulesek*) and agro-industrial collectives (*mezogazdasagi-ipari szovetkezetek*). The first three of these innovations are new integrative forms and their activities are the most significant from the perspective or our examination.

Generally, the agricultural associations are horizontal forms of integration. Several collectives or some collectives and some state farms and other agricultural organizations pool their capital and their resources to accomplish certain tasks. Thus, for example, in southern Hungary, in the City of Baja, three collective farms, a state farm and the State Meat Trust have pooled their capital and their labor resources to build a large slaughterhouse. This new firm is owned as a joint stock company and the participants in the venture receive their stocks in the company according to the amount of investment and work they contributed to the new firm. In turn, the new firm will slaughter and package the animals produced by the stockholders and market them, disbursing the profits according to the agreed-upon shares of the share holders.

Unlike the agricultural associations, the agricultural combinate is a vertical organization, highly specialized for the planting, production, marketing and distribution of a single produce. Hence, these combinates contain elements of the typical agrobusiness found in other states. Such combinates as the Babolna Poultry Farm, the Tokaj Wine Combinate are the best examples of these new forms.

The agro-industrial associations are also a new form. They are the results of mergers in the production function between the state and collective farms. Essentially, these associations serve territorial functions uniting separate units in the same regions; here the character of the production and not the character of the ownership function is the determinant factor.

The agro-industrial collectives are beginning to be the bases of ever greater rural industrialization functions. Although, originally, these collectives largely utilized construction brigades hiring them out for industrial work, they are now becoming the bases of attracting industry into the rural sphere. Their activities are especially noteworthy for the future of rural industrialization. Together with the collective and state farms as separate productive units, these new forms are the backbone of the organization of Hungarian agrarian production.

4. Agricultural Production in the 1970's: An Evaluation

With all these problems facing the collective sector, can there be an objective evaluation of the successes and failures of the Hungarian collective farm system? How good is it, how good are the farms, in light of the problems and successes?

The evaluation of agricultural production in the collective and state sectors, of course, cannot be separated from our appraisal of the general modernization of the Hungarian agricultural sphere. As has been noted by Gyorgy Enyedi, there are generally three steps from the traditional to the modern agricultural production. The first is the mechanization of production. Notable accomplishments, in general, have included those of the near total mechanization of almost all large-scale maize, cereal and industrial crop-production and the near total replacement of draft animals by machinery. The second step includes the biological improvements that bring mass production methods to unified and similar products. The replacement of the traditional multi-purpose cattle by the introduction of separate meat and dairy cattle, the new strain of poultry used in the industrial mass-produced systems and the interoduction of new high-yield wheat crops from the U.S.S.R. and the U.S. and the excellent domestically produced hybrid corn crops, fall in this second step. Finally, the third step, the integration of agriculture with agro-business, creates the organization necessary for the large-scale production/distribution systems that characterize modern agricultural units.

These steps of modernization are prevalent in the overall agricultural progress of Hungary in the 1970's. Within the rural sphere, however, the collective farm system remains paramount, as the largest percentage of production activities takes place within or alongside the collective farms. It is, therefore, necessary now to turn our attention to the evaluation of the collective farm system as it affects the life of the peasantry.

To this observer it seems that the existing collective farm system has made its greatest successes in three areas: (1) the development of some excellent highly productive collective farms and their differentiation from the rest of the collective agrarian economy; (2) the overall utilization of non-agricultural production in the life of the collective economy; and (3) the semi-privatization of auxiliary agrarian productive activities through extending support to and integrating the household plots and small private plots into the framework of the national economy. The remainder of this chapter shall be devoted to the examination of these issues.

One of the lasting achievements of the system was the creation of some excellent, highly productive collective farms. The system of collective ownership and the economic regulators of collective production have been altered during the years of the NEM to reflect the goal of the regime to allow differentiated production activities to be rewarded on a differentiated scale. Unlike in the state-farms—where only 5% of the salary of workers and 10-15% of the salary of the management is influenced by the productivity of the enterprise—in the collective sector, success or failure directly contributes to the fiscal health of the members.[54] Aside from a relatively small, though growing number of employees hired by the collective farms for other than direct agricultural production activity—between 1965 and 1975 their number increased from 47,000 to 110,000 compared to 935,067 active producers—the members, the retirees and the management are directly affected by the productivity and income of the collective farm.[55] However, it is hard to know exactly the extent to which collective incomes are affected by the volume of production since, as a result of several cautious changes between 1970 and 1975, pre-fixed and guaranteed minimum wages—2000 forints monthly in 1970, 2400 in 1977, have somewhat altered the previous full-risk program. Nonetheless, it can be estimated that a member's income is influenced at least 50% by the productivity of the farm, and this fact alone accounts for the deliberate differentiation between collective farms according to their efficiency.[56] As the result of the purposive policies of the Hungarian government—in regard to the extension of credits, and development an investment funds, to the profitable collectives—as well as of natural circumstances, there still exist three types of collective farms in Hungary: weak, average and good. Thus, contrary to the decisions and policy statements by the VIIIth, IXth, and XIth Congresses of the HSWP, a deliberate developmental and productive differentiation has characterized Hungarian agricultural economic policies during the years since 1968.[57]

On what basis can we talk about "better" or "poorer" collective farms? One way of looking at these collective farms would be according to the value of their lands. Based on the old "gold crown" value of the land, approximately 60% of the collectives possess poor lands, defined as worth less than 20 gold crowns per hectare; 30% possess land valued between 20-25 gold crowns/hectare and around 10% operate on lands that are worth more than 25 gold crowns/hectare.[58] But the old gold crown value no longer accounts for production or efficiency; as Enyedi has shown in his dissertation and subsequent study,[59] land values account for only 34.8% of production differentiation.

A more important correlation can be found when we compare the collectives according to the value of fixed assets, accumulated production value, and the total amount of available development funds. On this basis, collective farms encompass four major groups. As of 1973 (the last date for which we have official breakdowns calculated by the Central Statistical Office of Hungary) there were 214 poor, 1138 average, 650 better-than-average and 312 excellent collective farms.[60] Even if the mergers since 1973 reduced the number of collective farms from 2314 to around 1500, the ratio of poor-average-better-than-average and excellent farms has not really changed.

The result of state policy to support the best collectives has shown up in various areas. For instance, the amount of new state investments per hectare was more than five times higher in the case of excellent cooperatives than poor ones. During the same years, the annual growth rate of production in the 214 poor collectives was only 0.6% compared to 17% in the 312 excellent collectives.[61] Even identical expenditures for the poor or excellent farms result in better yields in the highly productive farms. The state, therefore, has tended to invest in more farms that are likely to be more productive per unit than others which are not.

The favors extended to excellent collective farms can also be observed in their wage and income structure. Contrary to the results noted by Enyedi in 1969, between 1968 and 1973, income differentiation accelerated as a result of the NEM; during those years incomes were 40-70% higher in the above average collectives than in the poor and average collectives.[62] Although income differentiation is somewhat mitigated by the financial support extended to all collectives by the state, the income differentiation among the rich and the poor remains significant[63] even with state-support amounting to 5-600 annual forints per member for poor collectives, the income of members in the excellent collectives is 150-200% higher.[64]

The excellent and better-than-average collectives, in short, are rapidly becoming showcases into which the regime pours its resources, whose success is assured and which, in turn, provide the state with the most efficient utilization of available agricultural resources. The policy undertaken by the leadership seems to be to support the best farms, maintain the average ones and expect that the poor ones will wither away. It is a long-range goal and an apparent cornerstone of the success of the regime's agrarian goals.

The second area of success in the collective policy of the regime has been the deliberate expansion of non-agrarian activities into the agrarian sphere. In fact, this is a rural industrialization policy, a utilization of the available manpower of the countryside for industrial purposes. In 1975, fully 34% of all production activity of the collectives came from what is referred to as auxiliary production activities (*kiegeszito termeles*). Such activities showed the fastest rate of growth (336.7%). Consequently, the ratio of basic to auxiliary production activities changed from 79:21 in 1967 to 66:34 in 1967 and 1975.[65] The auxiliary industrial activities are most significantly related to the production of the collective; 25% of all industrial units operated by the collective farms are related to the food industry, food preparation, canning, freezing, slaughtering, tanning, etc. In 1975, there were approximately 10,000 auxiliary enterpise units, among which 2500 dealt with food preparation, 1000 concentrated ontimber, woodand forest management, 1000 on the production of construction materials, and 5000 on the extension of industrial services, 1500 units sold goods produced by the collectives to the general public and 800 units operated restaurants.[66]

The breadth of rural industrialization of the collectives is truly amazing. Food processing, small parts manufacturing, forestry, gravel yard activities, are of primary importance. Construction brigades from the collectives roam the nation, building houses, bridges and factories all the way from Budapest to the smallest villages. Repair teams of collectives operate service and automobile stations, though the gentle reader is forewarned not to trust his newly obtained automobile to unsophisticated though eager hands. Shoe factories employing more than 1000 workers are operated by the collective farms at Endrod and Rakamaz.

The greatest expansion, however, has taken place in the establishment and operation of several types of light industries, notably textile knitwear and home manufacturing industries, that operate almost exclusively in the collective farm sphere. Since 1970, several firms from Budapest began feeling the pinch of labor shortage and started to establish "satellite plants" located in the villages. Utilizing mostly female labor, unskilled or semi-skilled workers who could easily be taught assembly line work, these firms established small workshops in the collectives all over the nation, literally "farming out" foreign and domestic orders. The spinning, weaving, handicrafts and folklore industries rapidly followed suit. Taking advantage of the revival of folk art—and of the rapidly increasing demands created by enormous growth of tourism in Hungary—the collective farms in addition to some specialized folklore cooperatives, also began to organize their own workshops, where women painted ceramics with traditional folk-motifs, embroidered pillows, or wove bed-spreads.

The rationale for the farms was the considerable income these enterprises produced and the ability to utilize the ancient bases of cottage industry: unharnessed female labor. Only 35.2% of all rural women were employed in the collective sector and more women could still be utilized.[67] The peasant woman who reared children, worked mostly on the household plot, did not mind the work that could be done at home, while cooking dinner or watching the kids. Many of them could arrange a half-day work schedule. Since the workshops are always within easy walking distance in the village, one could run home for a few minutes. The pay is relatively good. The cleanliness of non-farm work, the relative ease with which the work could be accomplished, and the nature of the work—mostly such "women work" as sewing, embroidering or painting ceramics—appealed to them. Unlike the heavier type of construction or manufacturing, the food processing, milling, or sugar refinery work employed mostly manpower—the extension of the light industry into the collectives used mostly idle, semi-idle or less than the most productive workers. This has been the most successful advance in combining industrial or non-agricultural productive activities with the traditional employment practices of the collective farms.[68]

By far the greatest success of the entire Hungarian agricultural policy, however, has been the incorporation of the private activities of the population in the collective sphere and its integration in the national productive effort. Basically, there are two types of "non-state" farming in Hungary: the household plots, farming, sharecropping on the one hand, and small-scale truly private production activities on the other. The most dramatic successes of the regime are in the area of the integration of household plot production with the cooperative effort.

The household plot is a permanently leased piece—or pieces—of land assigned to a person or a family for permanent production activities. The land is assigned from the commons of the collective farm by a "household plot committee" (*haztaji bizottsag*). The size of the household plot varies between 3000 and 6000 square meters, except the size of a vineyard which cannot be larger than 3000 square meters within the limits of the household plot.[69]

The household plot consists of two parts: part of it is enclosed as a garden immediately surrounding the house of the collective farm member, and the auxiliary land assigned by the collective. The garden area is the member's personal property; he/she must pay all the taxes on the entire household plot. The auxiliary part of the household plot may be assigned anywhere by the collective farm leadership in accordance with the decision of the general meeting, but—most frequently—it is within easy walking distance from the residence of the member.

The original reason for the assignment of household lands had been simply to "ease" the transition from the privately owned farms to the collectives and collective production methods. These activities were originally regarded as separate from those on the collective farm, and were largely characterized by a non-market oriented self-sufficiency. However, throughout the last two decades the character of household plot production changed and today it is an integral part of collective farming activities.[70]

The negative view by which the government and the leaders of collective farms originally evaluated the idea of household plots found expression between 1961 and 1967 in several dysfunctional activities. Thus, for example, collective members rarely received feed and fodder for their privately held animals or means of transportation for their privately produced goods; no provisions were made to allow the grazing of animals raised on the household plots, and auxiliary lands were frequently the worst, unusable acreages located at great distances from the house of the members. The sale of products derived from the household plot was sometimes prohibited, the official purchase price of goods was lower than those produced by the collectives and no technical or mechanical improvement could be made in the household plots.

Only since the introduction of public law No. III/1967 has there been a recognition that the household plot is an important and exceedingly productive part of the agrarian economy. The provisions of the law strengthened the popularity of the household plots.

According to the law, as of January 1, 1968, every collective farm member is entitled to a household plot; hence, if there is more than one member within a single family each one of them is entitled to his or her separate household plot. Recognizing the importance of the household plot, the law—and subsequent regulations— (1) allowed the raising of an unlimited number of animals on the plot; (2) raised the amount of contribution to those who raised fattened calves from 5000 to 8000 forints per calf; (3) supported the raising of young pigs and young calves by household farmers, guaranteeing them repurchase rights at advantageous prices; (4) gave them a certain number of workdays for their household plot and animal husbandry activities: (5) paid them percentages for selling the goods they produced through the collective; (6) assisted them with feed, credit, and expert advice, and (7) gave them needed seeds, fertilizers and feed.[71]

As a result of this legislation, during the last decade household plot farming has undegone a transformation process. The direction of household production changed from that of economic self-sufficiency to that of a distinct market orientation. Although even today the majority of items produced on these plots are consumed by the producers, more and more collective farmers produce specialized highly labor-intensive products, whose prices are worth the value of their labor. As a result, consumption trends have changed in the villages; most items needed and used in daily existence by a typical peasant household are now being purchased in the local grocery store usually maintained by the local cooperative. Such activities as, for example, the baking of bread, so typical of an earlier era, are gone forever. The store-bought bread may not be as good or as fresh, but it is certainly easier to purchase than to bake.

The traditional type of household plot activities still hold the attraction of primarily the older generation who are mostly pensioners today. Younger people tend to specialize in such activities as hog raising and fruit or vegetable production. Taking advantage of the mechanization of the collective farms, they have their lands tilled, seeded, and even harvested by the machines available through the collective.

The notion of allowing the household plot to remain as a transitory measure has shifted to its maintenance as a permanent institution as a result of the state's recognition of two factors: (1) that the production of the farm population is essential to the economic legitimacy and health of the regime and (2) that the regime, relatively inexpensively, is able to use some underutilized manpower. The first of these considerations led to the deliberate policy of the regime to improve the economic well-being of the entire population. The depoliticization of the population required that the people should be allowed and even encouraged to turn inward and work toward their own enrichment. The health and stability of the regime depended upon the ability of the people to attain an acceptable standard of living, that there be no bread riots, that is, the stores be always adequately stocked. In short, the ideological bases of agrarian production demanding that it be organized totally through the collective farm, had to be changed. It was recognized by the party leaders that

> while reservations concerning small-scale agricultural production were formulated mainly in the defense of the (presumed) interest of the working class, it was suddenly discovered that, if supply was reduced on the free market and in the state shops, this would be felt primarily by workers and their families. Thus, the workers would not blame the peasants but the regime for their plight.[72]

The most recent approval of these activities came from the March 15, 1978, plenum of the Central Committee of the Hungarian Socialist Workers Party. In its resolution the plenum evaluated the successes of the household plots and declared them officially to be "organic parts of our socialist economic system."[73] It went on to state that

> The party resolutely supports household farming which is based on an individual's own work or that of his family. It takes a stand against the underestimation of these activities, the occurrence of erroneous practices which in some cases weaken the security of production hurts the interests of the production and the people's economy alike.

The second consideration was the utilization of manpower that was not completely used up in agrarian productive activities within the framework of the collective and state farms. Thus, for example, nearly 700,000 pensioners and the families of collective farm members, could be and have been utilized in work on the household plot. Especially, the previously underutilized female labor is used in such activities.[74] According to one source the vast majority of work on the household plots is carried on by family members. Pensioners and fully one-third of male members of the collectives in 1975 no longer carried on any work on the household plot at all.[75] In 1975, there were 713,000 household plots each with an average of slightly less than one-half hectare of land under some form of cultivation.[76] Approximately 1,200,000 people are engaged in some type of household plot activity out of nearly 2.0 million people employed in the agrarian work force. Although the aggregate size of the plots accounts for only 5.9% of the total land area of the state, the household plots produce 16.6% of gross agricultural production. Furthermore, the plots produced 29.6% of the gross agricultural produce of all the collective farms in 1975, and in some cases—poultry, eggs, swine, etc.—they accounted for the lion's share of production.[77]

It is important to recall that the collectives—as a result of clearly stated state policies—are themselves partly responsible for the success of the household plots. For instance, the collective assigns monthly a number of ten-hour workdays in favor of any member who raises animals on his own household plot. For each cow three, for each fattening calf one and a half, for each sow one additional ten-hour workday is counted in favor of the collective farm member. Moreover, for those who contract to sell these animals to the State Meat Trust (*Allatforgalmi es Husipari Troszt*), 800 forint additional support per animal is given, substantially raising his income.[78]

One other rational calculation has been undertaken by the state, namely, that the household plots are remarkably well equipped with buildings and fixed assets. For example, in 1972 of the 782,000 household plots with fixed assets, 314,000 had cattle or horsebarns. Nearly two-thirds of these buildings had electricity and 40% were built since the end of World War II. In 99% of all household plots there were pigstys and 69% were built since 1945. In 25% of all household plots there was some kind of building connected with viticulture or viniculture and the number of other stable buildings, such as poultry hatcheries and garages was nearly two million.[79]

While it would have been perhaps more "efficient" to produce these animals on large-scale assembly lines in the collective farms, the infrastructural investment alone would have been staggering. The state certainly was not willing or able to provide such investments merely to "kill" household plot production. Moreover, it was mercifully also recognized by the economic reformers that "a pigsty in the backyard in all its simplicity flies in the face of the holy writ of economics that it is cheaper to fatten a thousand pigs together than ten or three."[80]

Naturally, not all elements of the household plot production show these advantages. The small acreages are dreadfully under-mechanized and small-scale mechanical tools are almost totally absent. Only in four out of every 1000 household plots can one find some machines—such as garden tractors, or machines used for forage preparation—that cost more than 5000 forints (current official exchange rate: 20.0 forints=$1.00). Price is one of the prohibitive factors in the purchase of this equipment: a 14 horsepower garden tractor costs close to 130,000 forints. Moreover, these machines, some of which can cost up to 300,000 forints even with hefty state subsidies, have to be imported largely from the West. The state's allocation of more than four million dollars worth of such machinery in 1977 somewhat eased the problem, but only to a minimal extent.[81] A new approach has also been promised by Pal Romany, the Minister of Agriculture and Food; in December 1976 he suggested a new policy of renting or leasing cultivators, fodder driers and automatic feeders to household plot and private plot owners for reasonable fees.[82] Private artisans are now permitted to provide service for such machinery and hence, they, too, are now permitted to purchase these machines with significant state support.[83]

All in all, the household plots are proof that the state can integrate the socialist form of land ownership with the private sector in Hungarian agriculture. Such innovation is based on the conviction of the leadership that it is reasonable to permit the enrichment of the hardworking population and that the socialist order is stable enough to allow the luxury of that enrichment if the needs of the entire population are also met. As stated by a collective farm chairman:

> a person who accepts the condition that he will not spend his vacation at some seashore, but will guard his melons, should be allowed to do so. If a person is willing to put his family to work as melon guards, well, let him do so. If not two or three of us will take melons to the market in the city, but if fifty or sixty of us do so, the price of the melon will drop from 12 forints a kilo to 4 or 5 forints. And what this country needs is an abundance of vegetables and cheap fruit prices.[84]

Hence, the recognition that, on the one hand, work on the household plot means hard and excessive labor and the denial of freedom, of leisure time for those who are willing to do it, and on the other hand, that the entire country will benefit from such work has been the bases of the regime's beneficial policy toward household plot activities.

In addition to the household plot, another "semi-private" agricultural activity ("socialist in form—private in content") has been developed and utilized in Hungary, namely, sharecropping. The sharecropping system was an ancient peasant tradition and it has survived well into the twentieth century, especially on the estates of large land owners (see part VI above). It was, of course, unacceptable for the rigid ideologues who directed Hungary's agriculture during the collectivization era. Only in the early 1960's was there a slightly more favorable attitude toward this form of agricultural activity. Sharecropping was first utilized as a part of the collective economy under the innovative leadership of Istvan Szabo, the President of the Nadudvar Collective Farm; he contrcted with some of the peasants to have them sharecrop essentially their own lands in exchange for a part of the final product. The operation of the Nadudvar sharecropping system was extremely simple: "The mechanical work was to be done by the cooperative. But everything else was to be done by members on land allotted to them individually by families or by groups. A share of the crop was their reward. They could feed it to their animals, kept on the household plot, or sell (it) if they so wished."[85] It is ironic that sharecropping, regarded by many peasants as a form of exploitation by the old landlords, is now incorporated among the activities of the new landlords, the directors of collective farms. But the arrangement proved successful, even if critics could charge that it lowered the "true spirit" of collectivized agriculture. The development of the closed production system in the 1970's, and the highly mechanized nature of modern production technologies employed on a large scale, pushed the sharecropping system into the background. It seemed that technology had won a decisive victory over labor intensive agriculture in Hungary and in the process the sharecropping system also seemed to have been doomed. However, during the spring of 1977, major decisions were made by the government to extend the rate of agricultural growth both for the domestic economy and for export. Accordingly, the volume of all domestic agricultural goods had to be increased, especially intensive crops, such as fruits, vegetables and tobacco. The cost of imported machinery was prohibitive; therefore, the government accepted the idea that the easiest way of increasing production was the reintroduction of the system of sharecropping. Since the Nadudvar system had introduced it in March, 1977, and it had proved successful, it was a convenient tool to "sanctify" sharecropping. The harvests of 1977 had shown the success of the new policy.

The government officially came out in favor of sharecropping in November, 1977, with a decree announcing official government support for the system.[86] In areas that were isolated from the main crop lands and in produce that must be cultivated by hand, sharecropping was especially to be encouraged and supported.[87] Such items as fruits and vegetables produced in scattered vineyards, orchards or vegetable plots, paprika or radishes, raspberries or grapes, were to be produced by the sharecroppers.[88]

The sharecropping system has been especially important for the rural pensioners, for whom it is an excellent means to supplement their pensions. In 1977 alone, 110,000 or more than 25% of all rural pensioners had worked as sharecroppes, specifically producing fruits and vegetables.[89] The system has proved to be so successful that even the internal labor balance of the collectives has been affected, and labor shortages on the collective properties showed up during the harvest season. Consequently, the November 1977 regulations, issued by the Ministry of Agriculture and Food, also were intended to systematize and organize the sharecropping system.

The basic provisions of the regulations allow sharecropping on any land not suitable for large-scale mechanized farming. Production of labor intensive crops such as vegetables and fruits will be supported. Furthermore, sharecropping is no longer restricted to agricultural workers; anyone, including industrial workers and employees, even if they live in areas other than those covered by the respective collective farmlands, can sign sharecropping arrangements with the collectives. Income from sharecropping or employment in sharecropping does not count as a "secondary employment" and hence is not covered by restrictions that relate to this type of work. The sharecropper can work the land only by himself or with his family, without subcontractors of any kind, and is allowed to be paid either in kind or in money. The only restriction is that the sharecropper's income cannot exceed 15% of the income received for the same work undertaken in the collective or state farm. In this aspect, too, however, there is an exception, namely, that work in vineyards or isolated orchards is not covered by this restriction.

It is too early, of course, to see the direction in which sharecropping will continue to develop; but around the capital and other large cities there are already signs that large numbers of industrial and office workers are attracted by this arrangement. In any case, many of them are merely a generation removed from work on the land. They see in sharecropping a lucrative way to maintain or reinforce ties that were cut by rapid industrialization. For others it is an escape from the daily frustrations of the regular work-place and a preferable hobby.

The private sector in Hungarian agriculture must also be scrutinized in this portion of our study. The question is frequently posed as to what constitutes the "private" sector. There are basically two aspects of this problem. First, there is still strictly private agricultural property in existence in Hungary. In 1976, there were some 101,400 individuals who undertook private activities on their own small plots of land.[90] On roughly 5.8% of the agricultural lands these small farmers in 1975 produced 1.3% of the gross volume of agricultural goods.[91] Most of the small private farms are located in mountainous regions and on the isolated farmsteads, the *tanyas* of Hungary, especially in Bacs, Bekes, Csongrad, Hajdu, Pest, Szabolcs and Szolnok Counties.

Opposition to private plot farming and the isolated *tanyas* had stemmed both from ideological sources and practical reasons. Ideologically, the *tanyas* and private farming both resisted the "communal" and "socialist" forms of agrarian organization; they showed to other peasants, especially during the early years of collectivization, that one could remain independent and still expect to survive. During the decade of the 1970's, however, two developments changed the fundamentally incompatible ideological hostility. The first was the unheard of progress of the collectives. During this decade, collective agrarian income has equalled that of the industrial workers and with income from the household plots, it has even exceeded the latter. This forced the private peasants to reevaluate their own goals and perspectives. They frequently complained of their inability to join already closed collectives that were now desirous of protecting the new-found wealth of their members.

The second development occurred as a result of the state's own recognition that, for the maintenance of economic legitimacy, they needed all the agrarian production they could get. Consequently, in 1976, the Politburo and the Council of Ministers made the decision to support small scale, and hence also, private farming activities.[92]

During 1976 and 1977, several measures were introduced to assist the private farmers. These included the requirements that collectives support private farming with their machines, supply them with seeds, assist them with the harvest and even provide agricultural and technical advice.[93] Moreover, it was recognized that in the production of livestock, especially pigs, cows and poultry, these private farms were of especially great importance and the collective farms were expected to sell them adequate feed to support these productive activities. The small farms were to be assisted by the sale of their products to the state purchase organization.[94] The resulting improvement has shown up not merely in the increased wealth of the private farmers, but also in the increased availability of food products for the citizens of the state.

Another way of looking at the "private" sector is to apply a less rigid definition to the word "private." If we are to view all non-state and non-collective farm work, the work on the household plots, that of the sharecroppers and the privae farmers, and include in the definition the important work of small gardeners all over Hungary, we can get a better and more objective appraisal of the health, and wealth, derived from small-scale agricultural activity. By evaluating production that is undertaken on a small scale "privately," in contrast to the large-scale collective production activities, we gain a better view of Hungarian agriculture today, one that is more reflective of current realities.

In 1976, 15% of the arable land, or 1.15 million hectares, was farmed by small-scale production methods. Fifty-two percent of this area was farmed as part of the household-farm production component of the collective farms
household-farm production component of the collective farms

and the remainder was worked by people in a variety of occupations. These were full-time farmers, sharecroppers, workers living in towns, bureaucrats and people from many other walks of life. Nearly 1.8 million families, or almost one-half of the entire Hungarian population, have conducted some type of small-scale agrarian productive activities.[95] Small-scale production activities accounted for 36% of all agrarian output, twice as much as the output of the state farms (17%) and only slightly less than that of the collective farms (49%).[96]

The importance of small-scale production has been touched on briefly earlier in this chapter. Let us reiterate, however, that small scale productive activities, totalling 230-240 million workdays in 1975, utilizing 1,178,000 acres, 750,000 units involving about 9,000,000 individuals engaged in some form of agrarian production activities on merely 15% of arable land, account for 36% of all agricultural output.[97] In some areas this average is clearly misleading: in animal husbandry the proportion is higher, for example, than in large-scale maize production. Thus the small plots produced in 1976 more than 50% of beef cattle, 58% of potatoes, 90% of small animals, 70-80% of all berries, 40% of wine and more than 50% of all grapes and other fruit crops.[98]

In the vital sector of animal husbandry and in production sectors where manual labor has not or cannot be replaced by machinery, the importance of small-scale production is great. In 1977, for example, the small-scale farms produced more than 60,000 million pengos worth of goods in the sector of animal husbandry alone, accounting for more than 40% of all animal husbandry gross production activities in Hungary.[99] Within the general sector of animal husbandry, hog breeding and fattening is of special importance since in Hungary pork means meat for many people. 59% of the total meat consumption of Hungary is made up of pork and Hungarians in 1975 consumed 92 lbs. of pork per capita![100] Moreover, pork and pork products alone accounted for 14% of the agricultural and food industry exports in 1977, earning a large amount of much needed foreign currency for the state.[101] In this sector alone, in 1976, more than 53% of all hog breeding and fattening takes place on small-scale units and it is expected that the importance of these small-scale production methods will continue to grow within the next five years with the deliberate and strong financial assistance of the state.[102]

Nor is this strong financial and especially political support given only to hog breeding or meat production alone.[103]

It has become clear that the government was expected to support the small-scale production activities within the agricultural sphere to a greater extent than it was prepared originally in its very liberal support of the private non-agricultural sectoral activities![104] The government recognized that if it expected to attain significant export growths and simultaneous domestic satisfaction with the level of food supplies, such growths had to come from the small-scale sector.[105]

The people who are engaged in small-scale farming, come from all walks of life: the lure of large profits and additional income is clearly irresistible. Of the more than five million people involved in some small-scale farming activity around three million are permanently employed in the agricultural sphere, but an additional two million are part-time farmers whose main occupations are in another sector.[106] The varieties of occupational background are truly amazing, especially in light of the fact that the pure peasant family, where all the members of the family are employed in the agrarian sphere, is gradually reflecting an outmoded way of life. While the father may be employed in a factory, or work as a construction worker, other members of the family may fatten geese, cows, calves, and derive a larger income from these activities than the father with his industrial work. Or an entire industrial community, for example, the miners at Kisterenye, may engage in keeping and fattening hogs in their free time.[107] Still another example is that of the retired tractor driver who, in 1977 alone, received an additional income of 27,000 forints from the raising of export rabbits.[108]

Nor do the collective farms look at small-scale farming with disapproval. Indeed, the general directives issued to the collectives emphasize that they must support small-scale farming activities within their territories.[109] They must increase the supply of seeds, assist with vine grafts, fertilizers, vegetable plants, help with agronomic advice and lend to and repair tools for the small-scale producers. In some cases the collectives have defied the directives and shown a great deal of reluctance to support small-scale farms.[110] In some instances, however, the collectives have gone beyond the required level of support and assisted the small-scale producer with cultivation, fertilizer and even the harvesting of some of the products. In one village in Hungary, for example, the support to small-scale agriculture took a rather unique form: here, young married couples were encouraged to contract for the raising of poultry. The local agricultural collective lent them the sheds that were large enough to keep 1,000 laying hens, assisted them with the initial purchase of hens, gave them feed at reduced prices, helped them market their eggs, and gave free veterinary advice. The couples contract for three years only, and if at the end of that time they have reached their own target—such as a net profit of 100,000 forints—they are free to cancel additional activities; the collective repossesses the used shed and offers it to another young couple willing to sign a contract.[111]

All of these activities in the support of small-scale private activities are, of course, not taken because the Communist ideology likes and accepts small-scale farming and privateering as congruent with its vision of a socialist way of life. Rather, the leadership made some exceedingly pragmatic choices. It recognized that the only way of increasing agricultural productivity would be through the harnessing of the unused labor of the agrarian sphere. Instead of the average eight-hour workday, those laboring in the agrarian sphere still work 10, 12 or 14 hours a day, and, willy-nilly, if the government expects to reap the benefits from those traditional work-hours, it must pay for them. With the exhaustion of surplus labor in the rural sphere, the government had to utilize the labor of those who were under-utilized, such as the unemployed family members, or those who, after their regular work hours, were willing to work on their own plots. Since, however, the people whose labor was to be utilized in the production of much needed agricultural goods, could not be forced to undertake this work, the government had to come up with adequate incentives and desirable financial rewards. It was the decision to do exactly that which is directly responsible for the growing wealth of the Hungarian countryside and the permanently high level of satisfaction of the average Hungarian with the supply of food in both the cities and the villages.

The debate over "efficiency" of production has long been over. It is obvious from the perspective of economic planners that large-scale production is more efficient when there is a large amount of capital and machinery available but only a small amount of labor. The small-scale farms, similarly, are most efficient if they utilize labor in the homestead, commensurately with the size of the land available, and the minimal amount of mechanization needed to accomplish the work. The "efficiency" of large-scale production methods for certain products had to be weighted vis-a-vis the necessary amount of investment required of the state. The Hungarian decision-makers ralized that exclusive and increasing reliance on large-scale methods of production was impractical and unprofitable for a long time to come.

The debate over "ownership" and the mythical "attachment of the peasant to the land" has also ended. Today, the small-scale farmers produce adequately, well or excellently, not because they *own* the land, but because they get enormous profits from it. In many cases, however, the government to its surprise found out that even if the state allows the accumulation of wealth, once "adequate" amounts are garnered, the peasant no longer wants to produce, no longer wishes to engage in the brutal, never-ending, dawn-to-dusk work that farming requires.[112]

> Today there are already numerous examples that those who struggled with all their strength in the beginning—until they acquired a house, a car, the goods needed for a more modern way of life—started to lead another, richer, fuller, more dignified life, once they possessed these basic

> goods. They no longer drive their children, they themselves too find time and opportunity to relax, travel, study, enjoy themselves. They are able to change gears. Their life is divided into two stages: the first is the accumulative stage, the second the consuming one.[113]

Today, the economic activity of the peasantry represents a far smaller numerical importance and far greater economic-political importance than it did when the Communists took over. The various regimes skimmed off all the excess manpower—and income—from the agrarian sphere to the extent that the peasantry as such today consists of less than 20% of all Hungary's population. But economically throughout the last decade a great change has taken place, one that has had its effect on the political sphere. The regime's changed policies, in connection with the adoption of the New Economic Mechanism in 1968, resulted in the making of the agricultural sector not merely a weak sister, but avalued partner in the national economy. The production activities of the agricultural sector not merely a weak sister, but a valued partner in the purposes, and it is the importance of the latter that must be continuously emphasized. The regime's desire to base its legitimacy primarily on economic grounds placed it at the mercy of the peasantry; it needs, and therefore must devise adequate means to insure, the adequate production of the agrarian sector for its survival and continued success.

On the other hand, both the large-scale and the small-scale sectors have irrevocably tied themselves to the very success of the regime itself. Any reversal within the hitherto successful policies of the regime will mean a lessening of profits, of well-being, and hence wealth, in the rural-agrarian sector. And today it is this mutual recognition of dependence upon and support of one another that marks so clearly the economic activities of the rural sphere.

NOTES

1. Gyula Fenyo, *Kozsegi igazgatas* (Village Administration) (Budapest, 1979), 143.
2. Jozsef Varga, "A tanacsi szakigazgatasi szervek nehany alapkerdese," (Some Fundamental Questions of the Specialized Administration of the Councils) in *Allam es igazgatas* (State and Administration) 8 (1968) 702.
3. Lajos Kolozsvari, "A kozsegi tanacs vegrehajto bizottsaga elnokenek feladatairol," (Concerning the Tasks of the Village Council Executive Committee) in *Allam es Igazgatas* 12 (1968), 1120-1, and Zoltan Katona, "A kozsegi VB elnok es az egyseges szakigazgatasi szerv," (The President of the Village Executive Committee and the Principles of Unified Specialized Administration) *Ibid.*, 6 (1968), 540.
4. Fenyo, *op. cit.*, 147.
5. Bulcsu Bertha, "Babilonia," *Elet es Irodalom,* Pt. 2, November 12, 1977, 16.
6. *Magyar Statisztikai Zsebkonyv, 1977* (Hungarian Statistical Pocketbook, 1977) (Budapest, 1977), 96, 99. In the following cited as *Zsebkonyv.*
7. *Ibid.*, 96.
8. Zoltan Bardy, "Sorson innen sorson tul," (On Both Sides of Fate) *Elet es Irodalom,* August 30, 1977, 16.
9. For Babolna, see Bertha, op. cit., II, and Pt. I in *Elet es Irodalom,* November 5, 1977, 16.
10. Ferenc Kunszabo, "termelo es termeles" (Producer and Product), *Valosag* 7 (1975), 48. On the CPS, see *Nepszabadsag,* February 23, 1977; *Magyar Hirlap,* June 21, 1977 and *Magyar Nemzet,* September 21 and October 2, 1977.
11. Istvan Lazar, "Vilagpiac," (World Market) *Elet es Irodalom,* June 16, 1977, 3.
12. In 1975, the average income of state farm employees was 2,940 forints monthly, versus 2,740 for collective farm members. *Mezogazdasagi Adatok,* 1976, 2 (Budapest,

1976), 39. These figures do not include the income from household or auxiliary farm earnings.

13. Lazar, *op. cit.,* 3.
14. Ferenc Erdei, *Szovetkezetek* (Cooperatives) (Budapest, 1945), 32-3.
15. Emil Bors, "A szocialista mezogazdasagi szovetkezeti mozgalom magyarorszagi Kialakulasanak elo-tortenetehez" (Data for the Prehistory of the Development of the Socialist Agrarian Cooperative Movement in Hungary) *Parttorteneti Kozlemenyek* 4 (1968), 38-9, 16.
16. For the decree see *Magyar Kozlony,* 129 (1945), 2.
17. *Adattar, op. cit.* 11:12, 11:4.
18. *Ibid.,* 11:4.
19. *Allamigazgatas a-tol z-ig* (State Administration from A to Z) (Budapest, 1973), 667.
20. *Ibid.,* 451.
21. *Ibid.,* 591.
22. For the order streamlining the simpler forms of cooperation see 50/1968 December 3, 1968, *Magyar Kozlony,* 108 (1968) 1061-72.
23. Bela Fazekas, *Mezogazdasagunk a felszabadulas utan* (Our Agriculture after the Liberation) (Budapest, 1967), 178 and following.
24. *Zsebkonyv, 1977,* 97.
25. *Ibid.,* 96.
26. Fazekas, *op. cit.,* 232.
27. On the problems of the collectives and the relationship of size to social development, see Istvan Markus, "Mezogazdasagfejlesztes es helyi eroviszonyok" (the Development of Agriculture and Local Power Relationships) *Valosag,* 3 (1968) and Ferenc Erdei, "A mezogazdasagi termeloszovetkezetek nehany gazdasagi kerdese" (Several Economic Questions of the Agricultural Productive Cooperatives), *Ibid.,* 2 (1968) 74-89.
28. *Veszprem Megyei Naplo,* November 12, 1976.
29. *Zsebkonyv, 1977,* 97. Figure disaggregated to exclude nonagricultural goods of the agricultural collective sector.

30. *Ibid.*, 97, 99.
31. *Fejer Megyei Hirlap,* December 4, 1977.
32. *Zsebkonyv, 1977,* 106.
33. *Statisztikai Evkonyv, 1976* (Statistical Yearbook, 1976) (Budapest, 1977), 215. In the following cited as *Evkonyv.*
34. *Zsebkonyv, 1977,* 229.
35. *Nepszabadsag,* April 6, 1977.
36. *Evkonyv, 1976,* 11.
37. Bela Szabo, "Vezetes, gazdalkodas erdekeltseg" (Leadership, Management, Interest) *Valosag* (1974) 43.
38. *Mezogazdasagi Adatok, 1973, 1975. Idoszaki Kozlemenyek,* I. (Agricultural Data).
39. Istvan Szabo, "Demokracia es torvenyesseg a szovetkezetekben" (Democarcy and Legality in the Producer Cooperatives) *Tarsadalmi Szemle* 2 (1973) 41.
40. Antal Vegh, "Nyomtato lo" (Treading Horse) in his *Okorsirato* (In Remembrance of Oxen) (Budapest, 1975), 145-63, for a bitter caricature of these leaders.
41. *Evkonyv, 1976,* 336.
42. *Mezogazdasagi Statisztikai Zsebkonyv* (Agricultural Statistical Pocketbook), 129.
43. Fazekas, *op. cit.*, 240.
44. Bela Ivanyi Toth, "Uton, doccenokkel . . . ." (On the Road with Bumps) *Elet es Irodalom,* May 14, 1977, 16.
45. Imre Dimeny, *Mezogazdasagunk es a muszaki fejlesztes* (Agriculture and Technical Development) (Budapest, 1973) is the most comprehensive volume.
46. *Magyar Hirlap,* May 22, 1977.
47. *Somogyi Neplap,* May 4, 1977.
48. *Radio Free Europe/Situation Report,* May 31, 1977, 13.
49. *Nepszabadsag,* August 13, 1977.
50. *Magyar Nemzet,* October 21, 22 and 26, 1977.
51. *Zsebkonyv, 1977,* 103.
52. Sandor Gor Nagy, "A mezogazdasag kemizalasa mint szolgaltatas" (The Chemicalization of Agriculture as a Service Activity) *Valosag,* 5 (1977) 22-8.
53. *Vilaggazdasag,* July 29, 1977.

54. How important the leadership function in the differentiation of the productive activities is evident from the two excellent works by Ferenc Laszlo and Gyula Nagy, *A mezogazdasagi termeloszovetkezetek korszeru vezetese* (Modern Management of the Agricultural Cooperatives) (Budapest, 1974), and Lajos Nagy, *Munka, termelekenyseg es szemelyi jovedelmek a magyar mezogazdasagban* (Work, Productivity and Personal Income in Hungarian Agriculture) (Budapest, 1976).
55. *Mezogazdasagi Adatok, 1976,* 106. See also, *Dolgozok Lapja,* September 22, 1976.
56. *Magyar Kozlony,* November 4, 1977.
57. Emese Egeto, *Felhalmozas es jovedelmezoseg a termeloszovetkezetekben* (Accumulation and Profitability in the Agricultural Cooperatives) (Budapest, 1976).
58. *Mezogazdasagi Adatok, 1975, Idoszaki Kozlemenyek,* 3, 1975.
59. Gyorgy Enyedi, "A magyar mezogazdasagi terfelosztasa" (The Delineation of the Agricultural Sphere of Hungary) *Foldrajzi Ertesito,* vol. 1, 340 For the complete study in an up-to-date version, see Tivadar Bernat and Gyorgy Enyedi, *A magyar mezogazdasagi terulet problemai* (Regional Problems of Hungarian Agriculture) (Budapest, 1977), 56-68.
60. Ferenc Donath, "Gazdasagi novekedes es socialista mezogazdasag" (Economic Growth and Socialist Agriculture) *Valosag,* 9 (1976), 21.
61. *Ibid.*
62. *Enyedi, op. cit.,* 41, and Donath, *op. cit.* 23.
63. In 1975, the amount of state subsidies was fully 300 million florins. See Fazekas, *op. cit.,* 277.
64. *Ibid.,* 290.
65. *Ibid.,* 260.
66. *Ibid.,* 275.
67. *Evkonyu,1976,* 11.
68. Zoltan Tatai, "The Growth of Rural Industry" in Gyorgy Enyedi, *Rural Transformation in Hungary* (Budapest, 1976), 71-88.

69. *Allamigazgatas, op. cit.*, 697.
70. Imre Molnar, ed. *A termeloszovetkezeti kozos es haztaji gazdasagok kapcsolata* (The Relations Between Common and Household Economies of the Collectives) Budapest, 1971), 9.
71. *Ibid.*, 10-11.
72. Lazar, *op. cit.*, 7203.
73. *Nepszabadsag,* March 18, 1978.
74. Donath, *op. cit.*, 30.
75. Fazekas, *op. cit.*, 258.
76. *Zsebkonyv, 1977,* 96.
77. Fazekas, *op. cit.*, 263.
78. *Allamigazgatas, op. cit.*, 698.
79. Fazekas, *op. cit.*, 257.
80. Lazar, *op. cit.*, 75.
81. *Nepszava,* March 25, 1977.
82. *RFE/SR,* June 7, 1977, 8.
83. *Magyar Mezogazdasagi Informaciok* (Hungarian Agricultural Information) April 13, 1977.
84. Tibor Zam, "Egyenes beszed a haztajirol" (Straight Talk About the Household Plots) *Elet es Irodalom,* April 16, 1977, 3.
85. Lazar, *op. cit.*, 66.
86. *Magyar Kozlony,* November 5, 1977.
87. *Magyar Hirlap,* November 26, 1977.
88. Lazar, *op. cit.*, 74.
89. *Magyar Nemzet,* November 25, 1977.
90. *Evkonyv, 1976,* 201.
91. *Zsebkonyv, 1977,* 97.
92. *Magyar Hirlap,* February 26, 1976.
93. *Nepszabadsag,* April 22, 1977.
94. Istvan Gyorvary, *A mezogazdasagi termekek forgalmazasa* (The Marketing of Agricultural Products) (Budapest, 1977), 31-3.
95. Lazar, *op. cit.*, 70-1.
96. Gyorgy Enyedi, "Transformation of the Hungarian Village," *The New Hungarian Quarterly* (Autumn, 1977), 78.

97. *Ibid.*, 78.
98. *Ibid.*, 78.
99. *Nepszabadsag,* January 6, 1978.
100. *Evkonyv,* 1976, 318, and *Nepszabadsag,* August 11, 1977.
101. *Vilaggazdasag,* August 11, 1977.
102. *Magyar Mezogazdasagi Informaciok,* August 17, 199.
103. *Szabad Fold,* January 1, 1978.
104. *Dunantuli Naplo,* October 4, 1977.
105. *Nepszabadsag,* October 29, 1975, and *Magyar Nemzet,* October 7, 1975.
106. *Nepszabadsag,* January 12, 1978.
107. *Ibid.*, January 6, 1978.
108. *Ibid.*, December 2, 1977.
109. *RFE/SR,* January 24, 1978, 3.
110. *Nepszabadsag,* April 21, 1977.
111. Mihaly Gulyas, "Utszeli report," (Report from the Roadside) *Elet es Irodalom,* October 29, 1977, 9.
112. *Hajdu-Birhari Naplo,* January 23, 1975.
113. Lazar, *op. cit.*, 76.

III

THE CHANGED HUNGARIAN VILLAGE

1. Changes in Rural Settlement Structures

The first two parts of our study examined the changes in the ownership structure of land and the economic sector of the rural sphere of Hungary since 1945. In this part we will concentrate our attention on the social changes that have taken place in rural society. We will try to examine continuity and change in settlement structure, and the demographic and occupational distribution of the population and other changes that have altered peasant society as a whole.

No study dealing with the life of the peasantry in Hungary can ignore the general structural changes that have taken place in the rural sphere during the last decades. These changes may be considered in four categories: (a) a decrease of population living in villages and isolated settlements; (b) a decrease in the number of rural settlements; (c) a shift away from the purely agricultural character of the rural environment; and (d) alterations in the function and size of the population living in the isolated settlements, the *tanyas* of Hungary.

In 1949, 60.3% of the entire Hungarian population, or 5,454,800 people lived in non-urban settlements, mostly in villages and unincorporated, isolated *tanyas*. This percentage decreased slowly but steadily; it dipped below 50% in 1976, and reached an all-time low of 49.2% in 1977.[1] This slow decrease, however, did not result in a massive, sudden depopulation of the rural sphere; the absolute number of the people living in non-urban areas had decreased only by 231,000 during the past three decades, reaching its nadir of 5,233,700 people in 1977.[2] The flight to the cities, caused by several collectivization drives, industrialization, and urbanization has created 33 new towns. It also upgraded villages into administrative centers designated as towns. All this resulted in 1,751,000 new urban residents of whom close to one million people were said to have come directly from the rural sphere. The demographic erosion and the natural migration into urban areas left an increasingly aging rural population in the villages, especially in more isolated areas of Hungary. There are numerous settlements where the registry bears no witness to new births and marriages for the last decade. The depopulation caused by the escape of the young people is a depressing sign of this natural erosion.[3]

The flight to the cities and to industries had many causes, among which collectivization must rank as the most significant. Between 1949 and 1953, 365,500 peasants, former landowners as well as landless ones, left the villages and moved to urban locations.[4] A further 109,300 people left the villages during the second spurt of collectivization in 1959-61[5] Altogether during these six years, more than 50% of the internal migration of rural people had taken place!

There were other reasons for the urban migration as well. The seemingly insatiable appetite of the newly built industries, the end to some clearly rural jobs that had been forcibly abolished—such as the closing of 32 coal mines between 1965 and 1972, the disappearance of mills, distilleries caused by more centralized functions exercized by the collectives—the consolidation of administrative units, and most significantly the general decrease of the active agricultural population from 50-55% to less than 20% of the total labor force, have been the most frequently mentioned.[6] But one could certainly include the attraction of better paying industrial jobs, the availability of retirement pay in the urban areas, and the displacement of labor by machines; these were also important causes for the decrease in village population.

The depopulation of the village, of course, has not affected all villages the same way. Settlements with less than 500 inhabitants suffered the most; the loss in their population was

12.8% between 1960 and 1970, as compared to 8.1% of villages having 500-1,000 inhabitants. At the same time, the population loss was minimal for villages which had between 3,000-5,000 inhabitants.[7] It was in these small hamlets, most of them hidden snugly in the hills and valleys of Transdanubia, where agriculture has been the most backward, where the road structure was hardly improved, dooming the population to continued isolation, and where no new modern functions have been added where the population decrease has been the most visible.

The age of the people who left and continue to leave the villages has been an important determinant of the changes that affected the countryside. As mentioned earlier in this volume, in Hungary as well as everywhere in industrializing countries, it is mostly rural male youth, in their teens and twenties, who abandon life in the rural environment; in other words, people whom the dynamic growth of the rural countryside can least afford to lose. The process has not been radically different, for example, in Beale's, Hathaway's or Tarver's studies.[8]

However, some villages have grown enormously during these years. Specifically, these were villages close to large industrial agglomerations. Villages with good bus, train or road facilities served as attractive alternatives to people working on nearby industries. These helped people in preserving a peasant way of life and environment coupling it with industrial activities in the nearby towns. Villages with more than 5,000 inhabitants generally have received a greater share of infrastructural improvements and as the housing shortage was more acute in the industrial-urban centers than elsewhere, living in large villages and commuting to work became the accepted *modus operandi* for a large percentage of the rural population.

There also developed different types of villages. In these, agricultural activity was no longer the only source of income for the population. The major types of settlements that have developed in Hungary during the last three decades are as follows: (1) agricultural villages, (2) industrial villages, (3) villages possessing special functions, and (4) villages of mixed character.[9]

One word of warning should be included here: in these categories the occupational structure of these villages doesn't necessarily match their functional category. Because of the large number of commuters—about whom more will be said later—the residents of the villages, specifically around and in the vicinity of large manufacturing areas and urban centers, may have a non-agrarian occupation, while the village where the may have an agrarian function.

In Hungary, villages with mostly agrarian functions still continue to predominate in the rural sphere; they account for around 54% of the approximately 3,100 settlements. Even if a large number of the residents work in the cities, their agrarian production continues to be the most significant, and it accounts for more than 61% of all productive activities in these villages. Industrial villages, i.e., villages where industrial activities are the primary function of the population, account for only 7.7% of all villages. The industrial village as a type has only become accepted phenomenon recently.

Most of the remaining villages can properly be classified as mixed. They are settlements in which no single activity is overwhelmingly imortant and reach beyond a "threshold" level. One of the most visible measures of change in rural society in 1975 was that there were more than one-third of all villages that could be classified as "mixed" in contrast to the pre-war levels when such classification was prevalent in no more than around 15% of all village settlements.

Mixed villages also contain several sub-categories of which the "villages with special functions" category is one of the most significant. These are villages that have some special attraction, such as tourist, recreation or health-resort areas, where the population makes its service activities the primary function of the village. Around Lake Balaton, or the area at the Great Bend of the Danube River, where the population makes a living by renting rooms, beds or other recreational facilities to tourists or overnight guests, are primary examples of this category.

Another imortant phenomenon has been the rapid development of residential villages during the last decade. Not only the commuters, but full-time urban residents who have built their weekend cottages in these settlements have contributed to the growth of this category. Socialist Hungary's relatively liberal laws on the possession of weekend places have made this type of village a reality. Today, scores of such villages stretch on both shores of Lake Balaton and on the banks of the Danube north of Budapest. Although there is no exact data on how many villages have become largely residential during the last decade, our estimate of this number is 5% of the total number of villages today.

In 1949, fully 31% of all people involved in full-time agricultural work lived in isolated houses, the *tanyas.* In 1949, the government began a process aimed at abolishing these *tanyas.*[10] But these efforts, which included attempts to move people into model-villages, failed: the few people who submitted to the force utilized by the regime, simply gave up their agrarian occupation and went to work in the cities. Thus, there remained, in 1970, close to 900,000 people still living on the *tanyas.*[11] Most of these people had no place else to move, and the building of housing and infrastructural units for the *tanyas'* population would be an economically unfeasible and staggeringly expensive operation. But the *tanyas'* population continued to contribute enormously to agricultural production. Thus, at the urging of Pal Romany, Hungary's current Minister for Agriculture, the authorities began to reconsider their earlier policies. They began systematically to support the *tanyas;* this has been a crucial factor in the slow improvement of conditions in these isolated settlements. The progress resulting from their continuing economic viability as small farms made the life of the inhabitants much more pleasant.[12] Today, four different types of *tanyas* exist: the "farm-*tanyas,*" household *tanyas,* subsistence *tanyas,* and garden *tanyas.*[13] Farm-*tanyas* are privately owned, their owners take advantage of the government's support of the remaining private, small-scale farming, whole household *tanyas* are inhabited by collective farm members who undertake auxiliary household plot farming activities. Subsistence *tanyas* contain people who are generally no longer employed in agriculture but work in the industrial or service sectors, although they continue to produce most of their food on the *tanyas*. Garden *tanyas* are a recent development where people use plots to supplement their income from gardening "for fun and profit."[14]

2. Changes in the Occupational Structure

Significant changes have also taken place in the occupational structure of the rural inhabitants. The increase in the number of commuters and the emergence of the practice of moonlighting have resulted in the basic alteration of the traditional occupational structure of the village.

The main cause of this change has been a strong tendency toward rural industrialization and commuting, practiced by more than a million Hungarians. The process of rural industrialization took place in two phases, the first marked by constriction, the second by expansion.[15] In the 1950's, employees engaged in private industrial activities, specifically those in handicrafts, food-processing activities and the artisans providing rural services were squeezed out of the rural economy by discriminative fiscal policies.[16] The second phase of industrialization policy was marked by the deliberate spread of industries into the rural sphere and has taken place at a rapid rate, especially since the mid-1960's. Most of the secondary sector that has located in the rural sphere is affiliated with chemical and building industries, mining, metallurgy, building, light and electric industries, timber and forestry, knitwear, shoe-production and food processing, although the traditional rural industrial activities, such as folk-art, embroidering and handicraft industries of various sorts also remain important.[17]

The reason for the rapid industrialization of the rural sphere lies in the exhaustion of available manpower in urban industrial centers. Consequently, many of the large, centrally located enterprises established "satellite" centers, using available local labor, mostly women, pensioneers and the young who do not necessarily wish to continue earning their main source of income from agricultural activities. But other reasons also exist for the rapid rise of rural industries. The expansion of the horizontal, auxiliary and highly profitable industrial activities undertaken by collective and state-farms, and the demands for local services created by the rapidly expanding purchase power of the local inhabitants, were also contributing factors. It is clear that many

> "enterprises often shift to the country their facilities with outdated production lines and obsolete, written-off equipment.... However, it would be a mistake to believe... that antiquated 'sweat'shops' are typical of rural industry. Many modern small and medium factories are located in villages—and Hungary has a great need of them. On the average, rural industry hardly lags behind urban industry. Rural industry employs 21.8% of the industrial labor force of Hungary, with 23% of the power used, 20.4% of fixed assets and 20.6% of equipment value."[18]

There are also many problems connected with rural industrialization. Frequently, such industrialization is haphazardly undertaken. The organizers aim at quick returns, they often produce goods for which little demand exists or that are too highly technical, lack support activities or are doomed to failure simply for lack of an infrastructural investment. But sometimes these activities are so successful that they tend to replace the primary activity of a collective. This causes not merely raised eyebrows among the "higher administrative authorities," but threatens the reclassification of a so-called "agricultural" collective as an industrial cooperative with the loss of agricultural subsidies. Problems are also created by the pollution of water sources by industrial or just the destruction of a sometimes fragile local ecological balance.[19]

Other problems that are endemic to rapid change can also be noted. Frequently, the new rural industries are left alone to fend for the needs of their affiliates without the support of the local community. Social necessities, such as new bathrooms, increased demands for scarce food-supplies such as meat, educational and other demands generated by the very modernization of the rural sphere, cannot be met by the rural industry. Nor can the local or district council or the state-apparatus as a whole meet them. Consequently, more dissatisfaction is generated, more social conflict arises than was expected or is acceptable for the smooth running of the social system. The development or rural industry also affects people who "yesterday were occupied by harvesting and planting, pasturing and planting trees . . . families, whose members now have to travel and who have to be fed." According to a local council president, in whose area there are four industrial plants, "We are very happy about that. But how could we miraculously provide the suddenly needed nurseries, kindergartens, canteens and buses for them?"[20] The task of creating the support activities, of providing the needed infrastructure, becomes nearly impossible: the village, the central headquarters of the new firm, the county-authorities, each in turn wash their hands and the people working in the rural industries suffer as the consequence.

A second reason for the altered occupational structure of the village is the increase in the number of commuters in Hungary. In the 1970's there were more than one million commuters, accounting for more than 20% of the entire labor force, compared to merely 141,000 commuters in 1930.[21]

In the beginning of the 1950's, most of the commuters were middle-aged men; in the 1970's they are mostly people in their 20's and 30's. They are men who have not yet settled down, have not yet built their homes, and are spending their youth on crowded buses and filthy trains.

About 700,000 people commute daily from their villages to industries; probably a quarter of a million people travel to the Budapest region alone. The remaining 450,000 people commute home either weekly, monthly or fortnightly, on the "black trains," frequently drunk, waiting for hours at a time for the poor railway or bus connections at such miserable train stations as, for example, Mateszalka. Mateszalka's railroad station is the same today as it was fifty years ago. One does not need statistical indices to observe the manifold growth of passenger traffic at this station; it is visible to the naked eye:

> "From six directions, trains continue to arrive; not a few hundred but thousands and thousands of people are waiting here for connections and these are not simple passengers who rarely take a trip by train, but workers by the tens of thousands. They leave from here to work and it is to this place that they return, to be with their families. They have to wait for hours, for half of their nights . . . . But where? Out on the street, on the platform, during the winter and the summer, day and night, in rain and mud. The waiting room of the station can hardly accommodate a tenth of the transit-traffic . . . . Drunks vomit on the floor of the waiting-room; the smoke is choking. Travelling mothers with their babies, with their children, are waiting here as well . . . . Immediately next to the waiting room is the restroom; it has no door, the passengers stand in line. There are so many drunks that the cops and the station-attendants have no desire to keep law and order . . . . The commuters are coming home. How many tortured, grim faced, used-up, tired men . . . . After a tiring work-week, exhausted, sleepy, drunk, they are returning home to their families."[22]

It would be safe to say that what characterizes an individual and determines his class as well as his perceptions are the needs he has and pursues, though not necessarily fulfills. The aspirations of an individual are, therefore, far more important than the work he undertakes, the locus of his residence or the place of his work. A commuter who happens to demand activities to enhance his peasantness, therefore, can safely be assumed to remain a peasant, but as his demands are altered so is his status.[23] Even if the situation of the commuters is bleak (especially that of the young whose horizons are broadened and whose demands are most quickly raised), they already live outside the influence of the rural community and are perceptibly losing their peasantness.[24] In fact, the demands of the younger commuters who stay away from the village, not just for days, but for weeks at a time, living in dormitories in the cities and villages, are distinctly urban demands. These young people are rapidly becoming peasant urbanites in the best cases as adaptation becomes desired and possible. In the worst cases, however, as tradition retains its hold over them in the urban setting, they remain peasants in an urban environment, "urban peasants." Though they have already lost their ties to the land, their life will remain characterized by universal demands, they will retain their peasantness even in their urban locations. As Adam Wazyk[25] so beautifully characterized them, they are the

> "Distristful souls, torn out of the village soil, half awakened and already half mad . . . They crowd the barracks and hostels with three floors of swear words, a feather pillow, a gallon of vodka and a lust for girls. The commuters are the ties between a brutal rural past and an equally brutal industrializing present that seems to offer the hope of a better future. They are the ones who pay the highest price for progress with their weary bodies and half awakened goals."

Perhaps the picture of commuters is not as bleak and sad everywhere. Many of the stations are better kept and more and more workers try to find additional and different means of getting home at the end of the workweek. But the industrial labor problem affected by commuting on Friday afternoons and Monday mornings, especially in the construction field, is very serious. The commuters, half-urban in their work and their attitudes, keep their home in the village for various reasons. Some do so because housing in the city is simply not available, or because their hard-earned and saved money could probably merely get them a shack at the outskirts of the city. A simple peasant family, that of Lajos Kiss, for example, moved to the city of Szolnok and found abode in such an outlying urban district, jocularly called "gossip village" by the local inhabitants. For 100,000 forints they brought a "miraculously" bad adobe hut, whose walls continue to buckle because they were not properly placed on brick foundations to begin with. And along the walls, the doors also continue to sink further and further below the floor level. Every year since they moved in they have had to plane the doors at the bottom, otherwise one could not even open them.[26]

Some of the commuters also retain their rural residence because when one moves away with one's family, one also loses one's roots. For people who were born in the village and grew up there, living in the city is a harsh, impersonal existence. Thus, many of them, even if they could afford to find housing, still would rather choose the village and accept the necessity and hardship of commuting. The village way of life, the tranquility, the closeness of the community and its accepted mores, remain attractive and make the choice of moving to the city a terrible choice indeed.[27]

It should also be pointed out that recently a different type of commuter emerged. In 1970 14.5% of all commuters were employed in agriculture, and since then this number increased substantially.[28] But most of these commuters are management personnel or white collar workers who live in the administrative centers, the cities, and commute by public conveyances. For them, the agrarian occupation, that of agronomist, accountant, manager of the plant or the chief repair mechanic of the collective farm, is merely a weekly activity. One can escape from this to the "warmth of culture" and the urban environment. For these people reverse commuting is paradoxically far more preferable than moving out to the "uncivilized" countryside.

3. Educational and Social Change

Economic and structural changes in the countryside have been accompanied by sweeping alterations in rural society. A practically new society has been created; vast improvements in rural education and health-systems were introduced; modern media radio and television have become the general means of entertainment, and improvements in the road and transportation systems that had previously doomed the rural citizenry to isolation and separation from the cities were introduced. These changes also contributed to the emergence of a new social stratification that was the unintended result of the modernization process.[29]

The educational system of Hungary, in comparison with the systems of the neighboring states of Eastern Europe, has been relatively advanced. At the end of the 17th century there were operating schools—even though they were administered solely by the churches—in about one-half of all the villages.[30] As a result of demographic growth since the middle of the 19th century, rural education suffered from overcrowding and the lack of adequate educational facilities. For instance, in Jarokszallas, one of the fairly typical villages of the Great Plain, only 75% of school-age children in 1900 could be educated because of the lack of schoolroom space. "The situation was especially deplorable in the *tanyas,* where generations grew up without even the most minimal education . . . . The percentage of illiterates in the village and its environment, consequently, was very high: they amounted to 69.7% of the total population in 1881, 40.6% in 1910 and 28.3% in 1920."[31]

The post-World War II governments were all equally determined to improve the educational system: first of all for political reasons (e.g., the creation of a loyal, politically socialized citizenry) and because of their conviction that a backward and uneducated rural citizenry was more dangerous to the regime and to its goals than an educated, upwardly mobile peasantry. As a result, in 1970, the rate of illiteracy among the rural population amounted to only 2.6% of all those above seven years of age. More than 40% of the population over 15 years of age had finished the eighth grade of school. About 8% of the rural population over the age of 18 received a high school education.[32] These data reflect national averages. Consequently, in some counties, such as Pest, Komarom and Gyor-Sopron, the ratio of educated people in the rural districts is considerably higher, while in the more backward counties—such as Szabolcs-Szatmar, Hajdu-Bihar and Bacs-Kiskun—the ratio of educational achievement is considerably lower. Moreover, educational achievements are, in general, considerably lower in villages than in cities; for example, there are four times as many people with high school matriculation living in Budapest alone than in all the villages.[33]

Rural education suffers from ills that are endemic to the rural sphere: the aging population, the flight to the cities and larger villages made rural education, especially among the rapidly declining smaller villages a losing proposition. The schools that were built to accommodate the children of the early 1950's—a period named after the Minister of Health Anna Ratko who introduced draconic measures prohibiting birth-control and abortion—have slowly begun to lose their clientele. In the Orseg, for example, the only gymnasium of the region was built in 1963 at Oriszentpeter. The number of its students had dropped from 47 in 1963 to 21 by 1966, and 19 in the following year for the entering freshman class. Such a small number of students, according to the principal of the school,

> "is already intolerable since this has a negative effect on the level of learning. Further decreases are unacceptable; we cannot expel or flunk anyone. Consequently, the below average students do not try very hard, while the brighter ones must accommodate to the level of instruction aimed at the average . . . . The school will wither away through

attrition; those who have started are allowed to finish, but no new classes are being introduced today."[34]

In Hegyhatszentalja, a small village within the same region, the decline has affected the elementary schools, just as the decline of the school-age population has affected other small villages all over Hungary.[35] In the Perecse region, in the northeast, the regional school serving an entire district is withering away. While the school had two classes for first and second grades, and one each for the third and fourth grades, by 1976, the school had been forced to close its doors the same as the neighboring district school of Keresztes was compelled to do.[36] The school closings place enormous burdens on school administrators. Gyorgy Timar, the principal of the Ibafa regional school commented with sadness on his fate:

> "I have been here for sixteen years, and so far I have had to liquidate three schools. And during this coming fall I'll have to undertake this last executioner's task as well . . . because there are simply no children of school age. There are only nine school-age children! And how can we expect to see more of them when the adults of child-bearing age leave the village. . . . And since there are an ever decreasing number of children in the schools, the teachers are also leaving. All of a sudden six of our teachers just up and left . . . ."[37]

The fate of these small communities is doomed by the outmigration, but other factors also complicate the educational activities of the villages. As the importance and number of small schools decreases it becomes more and more difficult to find able and enthusiastic teachers and principals. The teacher shortage is especially acute as little or no provisons for the housing of teachers can be made in many of the villages and the teachers' salaries are very low. In Vaja, in eastern Hungary, for example, in a school that is otherwise regarded as far above the average, the monthly salaries of the teachers in 1970 were, on an average, between 1,230 and 2,000 forints while the average wage of an unskilled laborer in the collective was around 3,000 forints.[38] The housing situation has had its most severe effect on young couples, who try to teach in the same school. The case of Mr. & Mrs. Antal Banyai in the school at Vaja can be regarded as typical of the plight of many teachers. They came to the Vaja school system in 1968 and the only housing they could find consisted of one room which they sublet. In 1970, after two moves to similar rooms, they found a 7′ x 9′ long room rented to them for a fourth of their combined salaries.

> "Their clothes are in a suitcase, because they do not fit in the small wardrobe that is full of dishes and books; they also have to keep their bread in there, the bread that they will eat for their supper. The room cannot be heated and they have already lived there when it was cold and it should have been heated. Edit (Mrs. Banyai) has been sick throughout the entire winter . . . . Edit does not complain, does not cry, does not make the situation more dramatic than it is, she merely comments: 'We'll be able to survive until the spring; at the beginning of the summer we are leaving and we have already asked for our transfer.' The principal of the Vaja school comments uncaringly: 'Well, if they'll go,' but repeats over and over again that the young couple are excellent teachers."[39]

It seems, therefore, that the principals are responsible for the deterioration of the schools and the demoralization of the faculty. In fact, in some cases their activities border on the criminal. Their lack of interest in education is frightening beyond words. The director of the No. 4 school of Ujfeherto, a budding and quite rich community of the northeast, is considered typical by our merciless chronicler of the changes in rural life of Hungary:

> . . . This school has received the greatest amount of assistance from the state, from the village, during the last few years. Aside from two schoolrooms, here everything was new . . . . . Now in the courtyard earth lies in mounds,

bricks are strewn around, garbage, filth, dirty walls, unkempt conditions exist.... In the schoolrooms the stoves have not been cleaned for years. The mud lies in such large lumps under the desks that one could take it out by the shovelfuls .... In the halls the doors to the lockers are broken. Three years ago they were brand new .... In the restrooms, doors are off their hinges, the locks are broken. The walls? They defy description. Do children do such a damage? Why are they allowed to do it? The council built a fence around the courtyard with cement posts. The posts are broken out of their holes, the fence lies trampled into the mud .... the principal here is not a true 'owner' here. He commutes from Debrecen to 'act as a principal.' What does he care that everything is a mess! He is waiting to get a job in the city. But until he gets one he comes out here to be a 'principal.' Until he gets one he cannot be fired because he has a 'responsible post.'"[40]

We are not suggesting that similar conditions are typical of the rural schools. Antal Vegh's description is deliberately sharply drawn, but the conditions occur all too frequently in the rural educational sphere to be ignored. It is important to contrast this picture with a much more positive one, that of the Nagyvasad school, where everything is spic-and-span. Mr. & Mrs. Geza Ganzler have taught in this school for the last thirty years, teaching 30-40 students each year.

"Who cleans up here?"
"The children ...."
One group of students is preparing to go home, but on the floor one cannot even find a trace of mud or dirt .... Outside the door, small wooden knives lie on a rack, crafted by the students themselves. Before anyone enters the school, he clears the mud off his shoes with the wooden knives. "What is the purpose of this rubber-ball nailed to the doorframe?" So that if the door gets slammed or thrown against the doorframe, it should not be destroyed." The benches in the room are 14 years old. "I dare anyone to

> show me a single scratch, carving or graffiti on them! The chalkboard has been here since 1963. It is still in nearly perfect shape. The teacher made an iron frame for it, and placed a small aluminum trough at the bottom to prevent the chalk dust from falling on the floor . . . . Outward appearances alone are not enough. But as others say in this village, the students are taught by excellent teachers, who for years have turned out the best students."[41]

The educational services of the rural sphere vary from region to region, village to village, and school to school. The larger the village, the greater the chances are that one can get a good education. It is true that the current regime has tried to improve conditions even in school districts where the students face declining services; since 1965, unified regional schools have operated in central villages, combining dormitory arrangements with the educational institutions. The declining number of students in entire areas, however, also affected the "college" regional centers, and by 1976, there was the necessity even some of these institutions.

The best hope that one has to obtain a good education now lies in going to school in one of the nearby towns, and a growing number of students from the villages commute to the city for a day or for a week, living in ever-growing numbers in city dormitories. The amount that the regime spends on rural education has grown from year to year, but the best future, unfortunately, still lies with obtaining an education in the urban or metropolitan schools.[42]

One of the greatest tasks of the current regime has been the establishment of social services, including free health care for the citizenry. Compared to only 31% in 1941, by the 1970's, all were covered by health insurance.[43]

The new Hungary had inherited a sick rural population in 1945. Infant mortality was high and tuberculosis was omnipresent. Annually, around 10,000 people died of tuberculosis, comprising 16.4% of all deaths; more than two-thirds of all of these deaths occurred in the rural sphere.[44] The number of doctors per 10,000 population was 11 in 1950.[45]

Since the end of World War II, Hungarian rural medical services have been considerably improved. In 1976 only 1,522 people died of tuberculosis and of these only 42 people were below thirty years of age.[46] Infant mortality dropped to 4.6% of all deaths, and is now distributed about evenly among the urban and rural populations.[47] Nationwide, the number of doctors per 10,000 people grew to 26.2 in 1976, although their number is still small in the villages, roughly about 13 for every 10,000 people.[48] Today, around 67% or 73,740 of the 90,848 of all hospital beds are located away from Budapest.

The maintenance of the rural health-delivery systems rests on the shoulders of the district physicians and the general practitioners. On the average a doctor is responsible for treating about 2,500 patients in his district. In the rural sphere, where many of the villages have less than 1,000 inhabitants, a large number of villages exist without the services of a doctor. The shortage of physicians is, however, a national phenomenon: according to the most recent studies of the 4,100 district physicians' posts, 242 were unfilled in 1976; the percentage of unoccupied posts was 6.5% nationally and 7.2% in the rural areas.[50] The situation was most acute in Borsod-Abauj-Zemplen and Szabolcs-Szatmar Counties where the rate of unoccupied posts in 1976 was 13% and 11.4% respectively.[51]

The task of the district physicians in the villages is so complex and so difficult that one wonders what, besides dedication, keeps them going. In Hungary, the rural physician must be a general practitioner who can take care of all ills, of all health problems, without relying on intensive consultations, telephone contacts, frequently even without the medical supplies that should be provided for him. Because, since 1968, most physicians' posts are filled voluntarily and not by compulsion on the part of the state, it is to be expected that only the most dedicated or those who could not find a job elsewhere will accept a rural post. There are, of course, some attractive fringe benefits for the new doctor. Most frequently, he will be given a brand new apartment by the local council; sometimes a house, a garden and other assistance. But his basic salary—slightly above the average Hungarian wages—would not even be enough to begin saving for the car he needs to service a district where he has anywhere between 2,600-3,200 patients distributed over large and isolated tracts. But there are other benefits: the occasional chicken, the meat, the fruit, the vegetables and most frequently, the semi-legal, but always accepted and even expected, "tip" or "honorarium" from his patients. This is viewed by the doctor as the necessary income supplement for his unsatisfactory wages. Still, there are problems for the young doctors who have to furnish the house, buy acceptable clothes and attempt to live in a manner no longer befitting to starving medical student.[52]

There is no leisure time for rural physicians. Unlike his American—or urban—counterpart, he or she cannot ask a "partner" to take calls, to see patients, or to prescribe medication while he or she "plays golf" on the local cow pasture. Depending upon the size of the district, the doctor sees between 50-120 patients a day, visits the bed-ridden, gives lectures on various health topics at least once a week, takes care of pregnant women, treats the children during specifically defined time periods when all other patients are excluded from his office, prescribes and frequently even prepares medication. In general, the workday for the rural doctor is 12-16 hours long. But most importantly, he is on constant call. Only during the evening hours does he have time to be with his family, to be informed of the political events of the day, to try to update his knowledge, or at least to look through the professional journals. It is during these hours that he can listen to music or watch the tube—if he has the strength and inclination to do so. And at night? One of the doctors described the problem of night-calls this way:

> "I usually get to bed very late. I fall asleep immediately and I sleep so deeply that I don't even hear the first ring of our door bell. My husband, who is not a physician, opens the door and if I have to go visit someone who is ill, gets the car started. When he is ready to leave he wakes me up. I get dressed in a matter of seconds. Meanwhile, he

dresses our son who of course has been awakened by the bell. We take him along . . . we just cannot leave a three year old, crying baby at home. We get back and try once again to go to sleep. But in a couple of hours the door bell rings once again. It is extremely rare that a night passes without someone calling for help—And the nearest doctor is 5-10 miles away."[53]

Another problem that influences heavily the health-delivery system of the rural sphere is the structure of the medical professional. While 35% of all physicians are women, only 19% are female in all rural districts.[54] In the villages, traditional distrust of the peasantry toward women doctors remains a real that must be considered as a cause for the shortage of rural physicians. We find that most of the women physicians starting their practice in the villages are also relatively young and, therefore, considerably less "respected" than the older, retired village doctor whom they replace. These factors create social barriers that are very difficult to break.[55] Women physicians in the rural sphere find it considerably more difficult to meet male companions who are their professional equals. This is part of the unattractiveness of the rural physician's post. The rural health-delivery system is thus handicapped by these factors.

One specific feature of the health delivery system that has received a lot of attention concerns the activities of the district nurses who combine medical and paramedical functions and the functions of the social worker. Although this profession started in 1915, it grew very slowly and by 1941 there were only 1,044 such nurses in Hungary. Their number rose to 4,691 by 1976.[56] Although prescribed as a mandatory service in countless regulations, low salaries and difficult working conditions make this profession unattractive for young people. The duties assigned to the welfare nurse are many-sided: assisting the district physician, checking up on pregnant women, teaching the young mothers to take care of their newborn babies; these are only some of their duties. In districts where a large number of people live on isolated *tanyas,* the daily duties of the district nurse are nearly impossible to accomplish. On her low salary, she cannot afford to buy a car; she hitches rides on wagons, trucks or automobiles driven by someone else; at worst, she rides through the eternal spring and autumn mud on borrowed bicycles or walks through untravelled roads.

"Unfortunately, I cannot change the circumstances" one of the district nurses relates. "Mrs. Nagy, for example, is four and a half months pregnant. She began to bleed and I took her to the hospital. She literally escaped the following day. And other women escape as well. They say that they cannot leave the rest of the children and the animals alone at home. The only thing I can do is try to visit them once a week, take their blood pressure, check their urine and give them medicine . . . ." Three women work in a village grocery shop. Two older women and a young girl about fifteen years of age. We go over to the corner where the girl is working. Even before the district nurse has a chance to say anything, the girl defiantly snaps out the words:

"I'm two months along."

"Have you felt any movement yet?"

"How could it move when it's only two months old, like I told you?"

"When did it move the first time?" The district nurse ignores her response.

"About a month ago," sighs the little girl.

"Come into my office on Wednesday and we'll take a look at you."

Silence.

"Don't forget if you don't come you won't get a voucher for a free layette."

"I'll be there!" snaps the girl and goes back behind the counter. We bid her goodbye. She turns away without responding. "And who is the father?" I ask the nurse.

"Aren't you interested in that?

The nurse blurts out angrily: "That is a woman, a wife, not a little girl anymore. A wife of two months. But they only go to the doctor when they can be legally pregnant according to the paper. By that time some of them are seriously anaemic, their legs are swollen, and they have bladder infections. When I was transferred here, eight out of every ten pregnant women brought premature babies into the world. I got angry. That's how I got to know the way they behave."[57]

The Hungarian name for welfare nurse is *"vedono"*. It is a strictly feminine term, referring only to women. They are the unsung heroines and practitioners of preventive and remedial medicine in the rural sphere, whose salary is 30% below the national average and who frequently stand alone between life and death, battling to save new-born and unborn infants from ignorance, maltreatment and disease. They do their jobs the most conscientiously of any medical professional, so conscientiously, in fact, that they often break down in the process, both physically and emotionally.

In spite of all these problems, the health care of the countryside has greatly improved as a result of the determined efforts by the regime. From practically medieval darkness in the interwar years, the medical services and medical enlightenment has spread all over the territory of the state. Today, there are no incorporated settlements in Hungary where some type of medical service is not available for the population. The problem is frequently not so much the unavailability of the medical delivery system or of medicine, as the low health-education standards of the rural population. This is especially the case in the most backward villages and isolated settlements, where the neglect of centuries cannot be overcome in the life of a single generation. Peneszlek, in northeastern Hungary, is a primary example of these problems. This village received a great deal of attention after an excellent report written by one of the best observers of the Hungarian rural scene. In this small village fully one-third of the families were still plagued by lice in 1970. As the observer noted:

> The hydienic conditions of the population are below the minimum. Bathing is practically unknown in the village. There are only nine bathrooms for the 2554 residents—approximately ten percent of the dwelling units have enclosed toilets and 25% have no toilet facilities whatsoever on their premises. The village does have a doctor. This gives a certain 'rank' to Peneszlek, since most of the nearby villages have no local physician at all . . . . One would expect the young doctor to be full of ambition, of a desire to do something, ideas to save the world. But quite to the contrary, he makes a living and since the village council maintains a fully furnished, large apartment for him with all the comforts of the city and with a built-in bathroom and toilet . . . the doctor also has adopted the view of that of the other leaders of the village: everything is okay here. The doctor justifies every misery, every problem, every tragic fact and explains that the children are undeveloped here because the stock is originally small . . . and that denatured alcohol is not really harmful to the body. It is just like other alcohols . . . and that the wild new wine does not destroy the body . . . bringing up examples of people who drank it for years and still reach ripe old age.

The doctor keeps on talking but the facts point in different directions. The percentage of those with tuberculosis is the highest here. Food consumption is unhealthy, vitamin consumption is minimal and meals are lacking in essential proteins. Bat eating habits are the result not merely of poverty but of ignorance. Food is monotonous, the people do not know how to save, how to budget their money.

In this village the concept of family planning is unknown. According to the district nurse, the women here refuse to hear anything connected with sexual information, especially reluctant to hear about this topic are those who would need it the most. Sexual hygiene is unknown, or at best incomplete and primitive. Nearly all members of a family live in the same room. Consequently, sexual activities among husband and wife can only take place when the children are asleep. Thus, during the evening the children are given enough alcohol to get them drunk, so that they will not wake up unexpectedly. Clothes and undergarments are changed at best once a week, but there are many children and adults who have practically no undergarments at all![58]

Peneszlek is an extreme case, but it illustrates the point that the education of the rural population in matters of health should be as much the task of the regime as the supply of medical practitioners. The determined efforts of the current regime in trying to change this situation must be recognized. But there is a long road ahead and success will be costly and difficult.

4. The Role of Communications in Rural Change

Perhaps no single agent of transformation has been more responsible for altered attitudes in the rural sphere than the media of communication. The media in an organized and centralized state is expected to carry the messages of the system and is therefore a direct agent of the political socialization process of the regime.[59] The slightly more than four million Hungarian families in 1976 owned 2,477,000 television sets and 2,559,000 radios, not counting the probably more than half a million portable radio sets that have become widely available in the last few years.[60] Nearly 62% of all Hungarian families owned television sets, and 64% had radios. About the same number of daily papers reached the people as a whole. Therefore, over 60% of the population is brought into the mainstream of the news services and are receptors of some form of official communication.

The distribution of the receptors is uneven. Once again the cities are in a dominant position and such undeveloped counties as Szabolcs-Szatmar or Zala lag far behind.[61] It is interesting to note, however, that the number of television sets in the villages has been stadily rising and in 1976, for the first time, it has exceeded the number of sets in the cities![62] The prominence of television as an instrument of communication goes beyond that of its entertainment value. It is also the instrument of the government for shaping social values. Television provides information that the regime wants to be disseminated or allows to be projected. By excluding information not obtainable elsewhere, the regime is able to shape the information base on which attitudes and values are based. Television also projects images that are concommitant with the values of the regime regarding the future development of the rural sphere. Finally, it projects a "model" for the rural family in terms of behavior and values, a model that they are more ready to accept than if they had not seen it on the television set.

One can understand the enormous popularity of television. Modern life creeps into the backwardness of the village sphere; the unpaved streets contrast sharply with the asphalt-covered streets of the city shown on the screen and bring a desire for less mud and more cement. People depicted on the television set, wearing modern instead of traditional clothes, jeans instead of multi-layered skirts, provide attraction and desire for emulation. Modern habits of hygiene, such as the regular brushing of teeth, taking of baths and showers, indirectly and subtly extolling the advantages of cleanliness and soap, provide visual examples for changes in habits, changes that the peasantry would have been unwilling to accept from the preaching of the local teacher, priest or party-secretary.

The use of electricity, radio and, of late, the television media, also has altered patterns of living that had been ingrained for centuries. People stay up late to watch Kojak or Columbo instead of going to bed at nightfall; the 10:00 p.m. news broadcasts are watched religiously, even in rural communities. The world is brought closer to those who observe it through these means and the process of integration is beginning to show its effects. But television-watching also has brought changes in the social life of the community. While earlier, when only a few sets were available in the village, people congregated in a living room—the clean room as it was commonly called—with the increasing availability of sets, a gradual social isolation of rural families has taken place. The local pub, long a center of evening activities, has lost some of its attraction. People now are staying home *alone* with their families to watch the shows on *their* sets. Perhaps it is an unexpected development, leading to the fragmentation of society. But it is nonetheless a real and not altogether welcome development.

However, the extension of communication to the village is not a homogeneous development. All the indices, such as the readership of newspapers, journals, books, the number of people watching film and theater productions, show that the percentage of those taking advantage of cultural opportunities falls far below comparable ratios among the urban population. This fact is not surprising; after all, there are far more cultural opportunities available in the cities and towns than in the villages. The ratio, however, is troublesome and the continued boredom of rural life—not withstanding the availability of the television—leads to serious drinking problems.[63] In the smaller hamlets modern cultural life is practically nonexistent. In Szaknyer, for example, since the school closed in 1963, an observer noted that

> no other cultural institution or culturally oriented grouping exists, even though before the war frequently 30-40 smallholder peasants took part in the events organized by the Farmers, Circle (Gazdakor). Only the commuters read any books at all; aside from a few exceptional cases those who live here don't even buy the specialized books they could well use for their work.[64]

Rural youth continue to leave the villages in droves and they leave, at least partly, because they are unable to fulfill their cultural and recreational needs. They also depart because they reject the low status, symbols and fate of being a "peasant." Although there are no exact national statistics that we could use for the entire country, since 1945, in one largely model village, the restructuring of the village became very clear: 62% of all children who finished the eighth grade went to work in industry; 28% went away to study at institutions of higher learning, and only one percent continued to work as collective farm members. In Jaszapati district, similar results show that 70% of the young people have moved away into industrial occupations.[65]

Young people leave because they reject their ties to the land, to the village, to the dirt and lack of cultural and recreational opportunities. For many of them, the village remains merely a place of residence at best, or a place where one occasionally visits. As F. Erdei noted:

> "The ideals of rural youth are taken today from the world of technology, of the city, and village life can only attract them insofar as . . . according to the same scale of values—the latter is capable of keeping in competition with industry and the city."[66]

This large-scale population movement has been easier in recent years—and certainly since the last decade—because of the extension of road and transportation networks, both public and private. The "shortening of the distances" served not merely to make the labor force residing in the villages available for industrial production, but also to lessen the traditional "social and psychological" distance between the rural and urban spheres of life.

The delineation of the two worlds—the urban and the rural—has notbeen the result of merely social, economic or psychological delimitations. The two worlds were separated by wide distances; travelling five, twenty or a hundred miles took a long time when it was done on foot. The road networks were particularly undeveloped in Hungary. The railroad lines, introduced in the 19th century, connected mostly the cities. It is significant to note that few railroad centers developed into cities if they were not already urban centers before the railroads came. The railroads were not even expected to open up the rural sphere.

In contrast, between 1950 and 1970, significant advances were made in the development of road and transportation networks. New bus and railroad lines and at least 3,000 miles of new roads were built; many unpaved roads were paved.[67] The primary purpose of this construction has been to insure and to ease the citizen-integration process and, besides, developing the economy to assist commuters in their daily or weekly travel.

By the beginning of the 1970's, however, the Hungarian State Railway System (MAV) began to court trouble. Old passenger lines became less and less profitable to run as the result of the declining number of rural inhabitants. By the beginning of the decade, the decision was made to:

> "divert the unprofitable, minimally-used spur lines to the public road transportation system .... According to the plan, 2,240 kilometers of railroad lines will be terminated; out of this desired number 586 kilometer operational tracks have already been terminated by December 31, 1971."[68]

The results have been mixed. Much of the transportation needs of society have been diverted to long distance bus systems. But the latter have not always been prepared to operate their vehicles to correspond to former railroad timetables. This caused countless problems with work-time schedules and transportation realignments. The bus lines were content with setting up a sign at stops; no waiting rooms, rest rooms, and other facilities had been installed. On the other hand, the shipment of personal goods could no longer be handled easily on the buses where room was limited; scarce items from the cities could not be carried home on the buses.

As a result of these developments, private transports, especially privately-owned automobiles, greatly increased in numbers. The number of privately owned motorcycles (above 125 ccm.) has also grown (from 61,453 in 1960 to 294,489 in 1976). The increase, however, was truly dramatic in the number of privately owned automobiles: they increased from 18,499 to 615,881 in 1976.[69] Much of the increase came through the importation of 141,808 Zhigulis and Ladas from the Soviet Union since 1972—a process that is very likely to continue. There were also imports of 119,075 East German Trabants and 94,563 Czechoslovak Skodas.[70] Although originally restricted to the urban sphere, the privatization of transportation has affected the rural environment as well: in 1977, about 40% of all cars and 60% of all motorcycles were found in the villages.

This process has not yet ended in the villages; it is just beginning to take a real hold in the countryside as a result of the increased wealth of the rural population. The lack of a satisfactory public railroad network, however, will have to be overcome by hard-surfacing the secondary and tertiary roads, specifically those that connect villages and homesteads. Cars, deeply embedded in knee-deep mud, are still a common sight in the rural districts, and the population of the countryside feels that significant improvements in the road system are absolutely necessary. The costs of such improvements, however are enormous. Nonetheless, most transportation specialists are convinced that the improvement of the rural road network will be less expensive than the creation of any other transportation system would be.

We must identify one more element of change, one that has contributed greatly to the lessening of the spiritual and physical distances between the peasants and the rest of society. That element has been provided by the exodus of the young, mostly male and mostly adventurous segment of society, to regions beyond the national borders of Hungary. Mothers and fathers, brothers and sisters have "lost" loved ones to this migration before World War I, after World War II and in 1956. There is scarcely a family in Hungary today which does not have close relatives living in Austria, West Germany, England or in such far away places as Australia and the United States.

Two simultaneous developments enhanced the ease of communication and travel between the village and the outside world. One was the general progress that resulted in lower airfares. The wider availability of automobiles to those working and living abroad made it much easier for the "local boy who made good" to return to his village in a shiny new car, be it a Mercedes, a Cadillac, or a lowly Ford—anything but an Eastern European car, please!—and be the center of admiring glances, surrounded by the pride of parents. The visits made magic out of a feared, hostile and far away world and brought it *in extenso* into the life of the village.

This development has been connected with the relaxation of official policies toward travel both to and from Hungary. The political concession which permitted a greater influx of former Hungarians, with its accompanying result, the sampling of Western life by Hungarian citizens living in Hungary, has been richly rewarded by the lessened social distance between the peasantry and the modern world in general. The sight of peasant women, in traditional multi-layered skirts, sitting on airplanes travelling to visit a son in Munich or New York, or that of a group of peasants stepping out of a tourist bus in Cologne, is no longer a rarity, and this development has succeeded in diminishing the peasant isolation from urban and international life.

Domestically, the influx of nearly two million peasants into the life of the industrial—and at least partially urban—society, however, has already significantly lessened the distance between the cities and villages. With relatives living in the cities, the rural population is no longer so afraid, so totally isolated, hesitant and alien to the cities as it once had been. They are no longer so obviously alien in dress and speech—thanks partially to the equalizing influence of television broadcasts, and the relative ease with which Hungary's few hundred miles of distances to any city can be travelled. At any rate, the process of integrating the rural sphere into the national life through improvements in all aspects of communication once begun cannot be easily reversed.

4. Modernization and Social Restratification

The sweeping structural, economic, educational and social changes of the last three decades brought about a wide social restratification that has fundamentally altered Hungarian society. The very modernization process has also created a new society in the countryside. Not all changes that have taken place were intended or "consciously" desired from above; indeed, many of them have taken place without the support or in direct contradiction to the regime's intended policies.[71]

The starting point for our evaluation should be the examination of changes that have taken place in the occupational sphere; both Marxist and non-Marxist analysts accept this approach because the occupational character of changes clearly reflect both social and economic policy outcomes.[72]

As stated earlier, the most significant alterations in the village sphere have resulted from the occupational restratification of the village. While in 1930, around 85% of people living in the rural sphere were connected with agriculture, in 1976, 58% of the active workers were employed in non-agricultural occupations.[73] Aside from the outmigration of the natural increment and the commuters, roughly two million people have left agricultural jobs and taken up occupations non-agricultural in character.[74] Most of the two million people who left rural occupations have become a part of the industrial working class. Consequently, slightly below 50% of all workers in 1975 were of peasant origin! It would be a mistake, however, to assume that this influx into all strata of the working class has been achieved on an even keel. The truth is far form the fiction of "total openness" of the working class; for various reasons, the numbers of workers originating from the peasantry is the smallest among the skilled laborers (33%), and considerably higher among the semi-skilled (52%) and the unskilled (58%) laborers.[75]

The regime has made determined efforts, specifically during its early years and since the end of the 1960's, to increase the percentage of the peasantry among the political leadership and the intelligentsia. In spite of these efforts among the people serving in leadership positions, only 28.9% comes from the peasantry, and in Budapest, only 7.5% of the leadership comes from this social stratum. In contrast, among the village leadership, 57.1% had originally come from the peasantry itself. Most strikingly, among the intellecturals one finds 20% who claim or admit to be of peasant origin.[76]

But the picture is slightly more confusing if we were to look at the present peasant class, that is, those who are involved in agrarian labor today. It is perhaps the most significant—though not unexpected—to note that there has been practically no influx into the peasantry as a social or economic class; 91% of those who are involved in agricultural activities come from families that had been engaged in agricultural activities before.[77] In short, the mobility has been practically unidirectional, integrating the peasantry into the industrial structure and only very minimally infusing the workers and the intelligentsia—and then only on the leadership level—into the agricultural sphere.

Nonetheless, it is important to restate that the greatest achievement of the regime—and one that was not consciously desired originally by any planner—has been the complete abolition of the uniform, homogeneous peasant village. Of the slightly over five million people who now live in the rural sphere less than 50% are currently engaged in agriculture, giving the village a far more broadly-based social structure. Indeed, in the case of a large number of agricultural families, one or more members are no longer earning their income from agricultural activities but work in other occupations either in the village or in nearby cities.

This change affected also the people of the isolated *tanyas*. For example, in the south of the Great Plain, an area where one of the typical settlement patterns is that of the *tanyas*, only 70% of the inhabitants receive their total income from agriculture, 23% receive income from both agriculture and other sectors, while seven percent have abandoned all agricultural activities.[78]

These changes, however, have resulted not merely in the end of the ancient stratification patterns of peasant society, but in a new restratification. The bases of restratification may be classified (1) according to position of responsibility or occupation and (2) according to wealth and the standard of living.

The restratification of society along occupational and positional lines was inevitable as the system began to develop stable functions. In their present form the positions of responsibility are positions of power. They are, in the Weberian sense, based on the opportunity of an individual to exercise his will even against the opposition of another, "regardless of the bases of the opportunity."[79] Power, combined with influence in affecting the output of producers, results in the division between those occupying the positions of importance and those who do not. The right of directing and controlling the functioning of others separates the village sphere between those exercising power and those upon whom it is exercised.

The most complex examination of the structure of the leaders and the led in Hungarian society has been accomplished by Dr. Ferge in her monumental theoretical work.[80] Suffice it to say that she, too, differentiates between the leadership, the intelligentsia, the middle level specialists who direct the productive work, and the skilled or unskilled agricultural and administrative laborers who are the directed members of the labor force. The distinction between the new leadership cadre and the pre-war leadership in most Communist literature is claimed to be based on the structure of ownership. While in the pre-war rural sphere possessors of significant amounts of land, large estate owners, rich peasants, owners of mills, etc., were said to have exercized power, in the current situation where only one type of ownership exists—socialist or state ownership of land—this criterion is held to be unimportant in the division between the leaders and the led.[81]

It would be useless to debate about terminologies with Hungarian Marxist sociologists in this essay, to point out that, in reality, the representatives or managers of the "owners" of the land hold the leadership positions today to the same extent as the rural leadership represented or ruled in the name of the estate-owners or rich peasants in the pre-war era. Even in attempts at involving the collective-farm peasantry in the decision-making process, there are still distinctions between the multitude of citizens who have no land and the all-powerful collective farm chairman. This relationship is basically similar to that of the formerly landless peasants and the professional managers of large estates of the pre-World War II era.

It is significant to note, however, for the purposes of our examination that leadership positions should not be regarded as narrowly as if they constituted only economic functions. Leadership in the sense of our examination must include positions of economic, administrative and social influence.[82] In this sense, the people who hold leadership positions are all characterized by being engaged in non-physical labor as white collar workers. Therefore, the distinction between those who hold power and those over whom that power is exercized can also be regarded as representing the division of labor in the countryside.[83] In this sense the problem of the leading stratum of the rural sphere is inseparable from the problem of the rural intelligentsia; the intelligentsia plays a leading role in the life of the village and members of this group merely exercize this leading function in different areas.

The following functional differentiation among the rural leadership may be delineated: political-administrative leadership; economic leadership, agricultural, non-agricultural, educational leadership and medical leadership. The political-administrative leadership in the village sphere is composed of the village party-secretary, the president and chief administrative officers of the village council, and the party-secretary or secretaries of the most significant local economic units. Although some overlapping exists with the political-administrative leadership, the economic leadership is composed of the managers of the economic units. Among them are the president, the chief agronomist, the chief engineer, the chief accountant of the local collective or state-farm and, of course, depending on the size of the unit, the number of people holding these positions can multiply like willing rabbits. If there are local industrial establishments, the persons holding similar positions in these also belong to the economic leadership. Very frequently, the manager of the local general store of the collective, the manager and chief engineer of the local mine or mill are also part of this economic-technical intelligentsia. Among the educational leadership one must include the principal of the village school, *some*—though not all—of the teachers, and the manager of the cultural center. The medical leadership structure frequently consists only of the district-physician and, sometimes, the veterinarian of the collective farm.

What percentage of the village population may be included in the rural leadership, the rural intelligentsia, is anybody's guess. At most, the number is around 5%, although in some instances it is probably less. This is a new leadership; the great upheavals of the past four decades had replaced most of its members not just once, but many times. The attrition of the war years alone had accounted for a large group; the defeat of Hungary resulted in the near total disappearance of both the administrative and the economic leadership from the rural sphere with frightening rapidity.[84] Judges and administrative personnel, estate-owners and managers, police and gendarmarie functionaries simply disappeared from the villages as did a large number of other members of the local elites. Teachers and principals, priests and doctors, fled the villages after 1944 in droves, and the new regime had to staff the administrative-political and educational posts with those who were viewed as the most loyal to its new ideology. Frequently, these individuals were not the most able and the best trained; they were often selected for leadership positions strictly on the basis of their social origin and expected loyalty to the party. The upheavals of 1956 and the subsequent second collectivization drive resulted in a second restructuring of leadership cadres and, as indicated earlier in this volume, this second restaffing brought a more balanced, better trained leadership to the fore.[85] But the most significant changes were the results of the introduction of the NEM and the demands for economic profitability in the rural sphere; ability and education since 1968 were prerequisites for success though not for mere survival.

However, it is obvious even today that leaders coming from a peasant background dominate among the office-holders in the villages. In 1975, for example, 57.1% of the rural elite and 33.8% of all members of the rural intelligentsia were of peasant background.[86] It should also be pointed out that the percentage of those who came from intellectual backgrounds and who today occupy leadership positions in the rural sphere remains surprisingly low, in 1975 it amounted to only 4.8%.[87]

The rural intelligentsia and leadership stratum cannot be differentiated merely on the bases of economic benefits received, for the income dispersal among its members is widely varied. Theoretically, the president of the local village council is the most important person of the village. But this is probably not true in terms of the value accorded to the importance of functions by members of the village.

> Today a council president has about one-half of the prestige pssessed by a collective-farm president—complains the president of a local council. "I have no expense account, the only people who come to visit me from Budapest are those who need more workers for a construction firm, while the president of the collective farm is able to entertain guests and goes in his car to any place he wishes to. I have worked in the council administration since 1953, and my salary is 2300 forints a month; the average collective farm president makes at least 6000. This income gives him such an advantage in performance and self-assurance that I am unable to conduct a meeting with him on an equal footing, even if he has only finished six grades of the elementary school. And I cannot even state that I receive greater respect or affection from the residents

> than he does. One can understand the people; the council is poor, I always have to ask them to help out with voluntary work or public assistance, but the collective farm can offer benefits.[88]

The tension between the collective farm and the village is a natural result of the functional differentiation in the importance of the two units. The excessive role-importance of some collective farm presidents has indeed been caricatured because of such excesses. The picture of a collective farm president, who travels in his Chevrolet, hunts, fishes together with the high mukety-mucks, embezzles, and lives the life of a *nouveau-riche* with all the allures of the former aristocrat, has been slightly overdrawn by the brutally perceptive writings of Antal Vegh, but there is a great deal of truth to this characterization.[89] This tension between the haves and have-nots is natural, and we will deal with this problem below. It is important, however, to remember that in spite of the income differentiation, the leadership stratum—or class, if one wishes to designate it as such—is a relatively unified and closed group.

This conclusion has been backed up by an interesting study by the Institute of Social Sciences of Hungary. This study resulted in the publication of a four-volume study entitled the *Situation of the Rural Intelligentsia.*[90] According to the findings of this study the peer-groups or friendship circles of the current leadership in the villages contain only 11.8% persons who are currently physical laborers, and work either as workers or peasants.[91] Moreover, among the village leaders there are very few people whose spouses continue to work as manual laborers of any sort: only 4.5% of the representative sample do so.[92] They have become a closed group whose contacts with one another, while probably somewhat more open than they were in the pre-war years, are still characterized by intra-rather than inter-group contacts.[93]

The isolation of the village intelligentsia is not a new phenomenon: it has been discussed above in Joseph Held's study. In the interwar period, Hungary's rural intelligentsia was well-trained. But, as it was noted:

> "they were unable to find their place because the people of the villages were unable to use them. Precisely because they had gained great knowledge, a world separated them from the world of the peasants and they were neither able to assimilate the world of the village, nor able to transmit their knowledge to the rest of the residents of the village."[94]

Even today, a "stranger" and "outsider" is not readily accepted by the village. It is not by chance that today, just as in the past, the leadership and the intellectual elite view themselves as being surrounded by hostile people for whose future they have a responsibility.[95] They seem to believe that they are *of* the people and *for* the people, but not *with* them. They make frequent attempts, especially after they go to a new position, to act as if they were part of the people, members of the village community. There are many models of behavior among these rural intellectuals:

> "the agricultural engineer who drinks with everyone, who is present and funny at every merry making opportunity; the person who sticks to his own immediate circle and drinks a toast only with the village leaders; those who are able to mingle even with the more important blue-collar members of the collective farm; those who never participate in a wedding, but who are always present at funerals; and those who have a mistress and live their social life only in a far away village."[96]

As varied as the leadership is, its members continue to be set apart by their position, influence, and functions from the rest of rural society.

A second type of restratification has occurred along somewhat more traditional lines in the village-sphere; namely, according to income differentiation. Our consideration, however, cannot be simply based on linear measures, because many elements play a part in the makeup of this restratification between rich and poor. The amount of land possessed, for so long the key determinant of prestige among the village population, has been relegated to the background and the structure of incomes has become variegated. With increasing industrialization and urbanization in society, the traditional sources of income have been altered; by 1976, there were in the rural sphere 654,000 families whose income was derived from both the agricultural and industrial sectors in contrast to the 992,000 and 481,000 households whose incomes were derived solely from agricultural and industrial sources respectively.[97] In other words, 53.4% of all households operating in the rural sphere have received *some* of their income from industrial sources. The importance of the industrial income and the benefits derived from it also shows up in the fact that the annual income of households that were characterized by dual income sources was 23,979 forints in 1976, in contrast to 22,380 for those who received their income only from agriculture.[98]

The spread of the income in the agricultural sphere itself was also dependent upon the amount of time worked in the collective and, even more significantly, on whether the collective farm that operated in the area or in the village was good, average or poor. According to official data in 1970, for example, the monthly income of the at least 10,000 people or 20% of all collective farm membership who were working on the poorest collectives, had failed to reach 500 forints a month from common production activities.[99] While there have been vast improvements in the standard of living of the peasantry since 1970, and the various reform attempts have indeed increased the income of the peasantry in general, there remains a "natural" differentiation between rich and poor even in the same collective. Skill levels, dedication, determination to work, natural endowment, strength: these traits have all contributed to this natural income differentiation. In the Petofi Collective Farm of Jaszalsoszentgyorgy, for example, the annual income differentiation even *among* members was exceedingly significant as is depicted in Table A below.[100]

Table A

Income Differentiation in the Petofi

(Collective Farm of Jaszalsoszentgyorgy)

Annual Income in Forints	Number of Workers Earning That Income	Percentage
1,000- 6,000	63	7.9
6,000-10,000	91	11.4
10,000-15,000	164	20.6
15,000-20,000	85	10.7
20,000-30,000	183	23.0
30,000-40,000	169	21.3
40,000-50,000	30	3.9
50,000 +	10	1.2
TOTAL:	975	100.0

Higher earnings, regardless of the sources of income, the possession of greater material wealth once again became the dividing line among the village populations. We do not wish to imply that the separation between the rich and the poor is as rigid now as it was in the inter-war period or as it had remained in some traditionally highly structured villages such as Soltvadkert, but that the separation does exist should not be denied.[101]

Who are the rural poor? Regionally, they are concentrated largely in the "backward" counties of Hungary, in the Nyirseg, in the Orseg and in regions where industrialization has least affected the area, or where the natural endowments of the land are not very good. The poor in such an area are very poor indeed, and even if they wish to work, they have problems in finding jobs that pay more than those in the local collective. In one such case the father works in construction, the mother rears children. Their monthly income, together with the family assistance program from the state, is 2,200 forints. The father, who works in the nearby town, receives 650 forints a month as his net income; the rest goes for busfare, breakfasts, lunches and dinners of the cheapest possible kind, and for a package of cigarettes a day. The amount that the family can spend for each meal for each child is less than one forint (five cents)! An investigator interviewed the mother of this family:

> "What can you buy with this small amount?" "Potatoes, bread and lard. I cannot buy anything else. The four-month old baby gets crackers for 3.20 forints a day and some milk. The other children snatch away some of the crackers from him. The child cannot nurse. I have no milk because I can't eat better than the other members of the family. From bread and lard and potato soup I cannot produce enough milk for him . . . ."[102]

The woman has never purchased anything in a normal store. She either buys things in the local good-will store or at the used goods market. She has to buy six pairs of shoes, six shirts, so that at least each will have one outfit... and one pair of shoes a year isn't enough even if they go barefoot in the summer. And if by chance the shoe is not worn out, it is passed on to the next child. There are no outgrown clothes here, only tattered rags. There are no spare sheets; if the mother washes them, they have to sleep on a bare bed until they dry. The woman sleeps with the baby and with the three-year old in the same bed. "But it is impossible to sleep like this! I am not used to sleeping, I just get dizzy and sort of faint." The lunch—the main meal in Hungary—is always one course. Potatoes are eaten at least three times a day. They have one knife, one soup plate, nine soup spoons, no fork, a couple of pots and pans.[103]

The village poor have many "reasons" to be poor, among which drunkenness and alcoholism, stupidity and ignorance are not the least, though not the most important determinants. The wife-beating drunken peasant is less prevalent today than before; those who are old, lonely, unable to work and eke a living out of their small pensions, like the aging woman who was gathering some grass for feed and food near the local cemetery of the small village, are more common. The reporter once again writes:

> She is indifferent to her fate. Her husband was hardly pensioned off when he got sick and she merely accepts her role without any complaining as she takes care of him. How many thousands of women fall in this category! It is a generation that has been robbed and exploited and joyless; their bitter fate has been the same for years, their misfortunes continuous and unsparing. Even if they try hard, their efforts go to naught. They live in the deepest depths of the village, hiding behind the combines, the fodder plants, and behind the developing image of the village. They do not wish to be a burden on anyone's back. They have been left out of everything good, of the mechanized housework, and the total comfort . . . .[104]

The village poor includes some 30,000 Gypsies, who continue to roam the countryside in ever-growing numbers. Their plight is not just backwardness or poverty, the lack of education, and the many children, but also their difficulty in adjusting to urban and modern ways of life. For the Hungarian authorities, the Gypsies represent a version of the American Indian question, the unsolved and insoluble dilemma of ancient lifestyles and a lack of desire to coexist with modernity. This is not the place to deal with the question of the "Gypsy problem" of Hungary's rural sphere. Suffice it to say that the problem of escape from poverty for the Gypsies remains difficult in spite of individual and state efforts to accomplish the integration process.

The rural poor are conspicuous in their inability to escape their poverty; but just as conspicuous are the rural rich by their very presence in the villages. They, too, come in many stripes, many colors: the president of the rich collective farm, the peasants who produce large quantities of goods on the household plot, the market-oriented small producers who defy the age-old dictum of peasant life, "nihil hic emitur, omnia domi gignuntur,"[105] and the industrial worker who only works on his land on weekends. Their consumption is enormous, they build modern, new houses with built-in, and most frequently unused, toilets and bathrooms for themselves and their children. They buy brand new automobiles that are kept in garages, new color television sets, kitchens and real buys at the annual fair; they travel and they spend with great abandon. Among them there are those who rarely work anymore, and those "who have 50 sows providing amply for themselves and the state—those who have less than that are not considered to be human beings at all."[106]

They spend hundreds of thousands of forints on weddings, inviting hundreds of people. At one wedding in June, 1975, for example, a few miles from Budapest in a small village:

> "120 people were invited to take part in the reception following the civil ceremony. The "feeding" began with chicken soup filled with liver dumplings. It was followed by hot sausages, various kinds of wursts and spareribs, pickles, cabbage and tortes. It was washed down with ample amounts of cold white wine. After a short respite for the church wedding, the sit-down dinner continued with chicken stew, fried pork cutlets, rice and chicken with gravey, stewed cabbage, torte, coffee, wine, beer and home brewed brandies. Two hundred and fifty chickens and two pigs totaling 900 pounds were prepared for the feast. Nearly 1000 liters of wine, 300 liters of beer, and an unspecified, though equally fantastic amount of brandy was consumed."[107]

Spending extravagances can also be easily documented. Peasants who have the money and spend it lavishly show great ingenuity as to the most visible places for their investment. Since they cannot buy land anymore, and since they have already built their home, bought their car, made their trip to visit Uncle Gyurka in Australia or brother Janos in Cologne, and still have money left over, they put it in the most logical place, where their eternal rest will be hopefully undisturbed, the cemeteries:

> Walking through the village cemeteries among the graves of the "simple" people was as if we walked among the pyramids of peasant pharaohs. Their owners are largely still alive today. My mother points out 50,000-100,000 forint stone memorials whose owners were still drinking this morning in the "Golden Throng." Two bricklayers and a stone mason got together and they have been millionaires for a long time, because they can ask any amount of money for a memorial the like of which has not yet been built for anybody else.[108]

The growing wealth of the villages, the growing embourgeoisment of the peasantry, especially the rich and the super-rich peasants, reflects such ostentatious forms of exhibitionism, just as the slowly growing richness in earlier times was manifest in the purchase of a gaudy kitsch, a picture of saints, or of a smiling woman bustling around a well-stocked kitchen, embroidered on white linen. As more wealth became available, it was spent first on those aspects that were intangible but significant: on food and drink, on modern and ugly functional furniture — the old, timeworn benches, the magnificently hand-painted chests of drawers or hanging wardrobes were discarded. The radio, the refrigerator, the new house and the new car came along, and then the trip abroad, the "vacation" taken in faraway places. And when all that was accomplished for the rich of the village," then came the cemetery, the heavenly copy of today's village:"[109]

> "It is an image that makes us angry, approximately 20% of the rural population sets spending patterns that seem to be viewed as examples to be emulated by the others, the not so fortunate, the not so rich the average,

> the poor. But the restratification of the village is a fact and the example of this type of spending causes problems for the authorities as well who also 'try to mold the consciousness of men.'"[110]

The new houses that are being built in the villages today stand not simply as shelters but as clear examples of the owners' ability to afford all the superfluous decorations that are needed like a hole in the head.[111] The ostentatious spending is obviously unnecessary. But the regime feels, with a maturity that speaks well of its development, that the hard-earned money of those who work for it is theirs, and that they should be able to do with it whatever they desire.

Since 1968, the villages have become modern places to live, especially in the more highly developed counties. The excess income, the excess money is saved or spent in accordance with the desires of the individual families in these counties; and most of the peasants today believe that they never had it so good. On the other hand, people who live in poorly developed regions away from large cities, work alone or collectively on poor land, and the old, the pensioneers, the sick and the "unfortunate" are not so sure that modernization has had positive and beneficial results. The "class struggle" among the rich and the poor of the village continues; the tools of the poor are envy, hatred, distrust, and hostility toward the rich and the powerful. The regime's singular achievement has been its ability to reverse the ratio of the rich and the poor; in Hungary in the 1970's there are far more "rich" or well-off peasants and far fewer poor ones than there had been before. But the regime has not succeeded in abolishing rural poverty; it has not succeeded in equalizing living conditions in the rural and urban spheres and has not succeeded in eliminating regional disparities. These are heavy tasks that will take a far longer time than was originally anticipated.

5. Tradition and Modernity: A Clash of Family Values

General modernization, though it fundamentally altered the pattern of rural society, wrought great havoc with the social structure of the family, created a clash of family values, brought about alterations of roles and resulted in value and behavioral changes within and outside the family. It must be pointed out that the basis of the agrarian economy in Hungary had traditionally been the rural family. Unlike the urban family, the rural family had a specific economic function as a productive unit that combined the work place and the concept of the home under the same roof. The members of the family in traditional times had been kept together by a unity of purpose and interest. The family unit lived under the same roof, their life based on strict, unwritten laws. The economic division of labor defined the social and economic hierarchy of the individual members of the village. The role of the head of the household was clearly delineated and the economic hierarchy was strictly based on the amount of contribution the wife, the sons or the daughters made to the economic well-being of the family.[112]

The choice of a mate, therefore, in the establishment of a family was exceedingly important; this choice depended largely on the amount of land a woman could bring into the marriage and upon the ability, and desire, of a future wife to be an industrious, hard-working member of the family unit.[113]

The basis of the village morality, of the ethical behavior of the community, lay deep in the traditions of the family and the sanctions of the community that approved or disapproved of the actions of the individual in accordance with the values that stemmed from the family orientation of the community itself. Actions that were contrary to those values were regarded as reprehensible and intolerable, while "family oriented activities" were approved.

The depression of the 1930's and the economic disasters that befell the countryside began the process leading to the deterioration of the family structure; as men were unable—

because of the lack of land, lack of work or lack of employment opportunities—to fulfill their traditional roles women were called upon to act responsibly in their places.[114]

The process of change was strengthened and quickened by the industrialization and collectivization drives after 1945. As the value of the land decreased in the creation of basic economic wealth, so did that of the cohesiveness of the family based on an earlier value structure. As the process of industrialization claimed more and more labor, —and we must remember that in some regions of Hungary this process has been going on for more than a century—more and more men, heads of their families, were employed in non-agricultural work. Regardless of the retention of their residence in the village, regardless of the frequency or irregularity with which they came home as commuters, their role as heads of families could not possibly have been as strong as it had been while they stayed permanently in the village, worked the land and derived major income from it.

The loss of prestige/status, of course, had not occurred uniformly. Indeed, the prestige of the industrial worker, working somewhere away and bringing in good money, especially at the time when agricultural work was very unprofitable, remained relatively high. But even then, the major and minor family decisions that had been made before by the father, increasingly shifted to the shoulder of the family member who had remained in the homestead; the wife. And as agriculture became more and more profitable as an occupation after 1968; and as the connection of the family with agriculture was largely manifest through the collective farm membership of the wife, her role took on an added economic importance. In this sense the prestige of the family can be registered as a zero-sum game; any loss in the prestige of the head of the household inevitably accrued to the role played by others within the familial division of labor.[115]

The progress of the altered role of women was somewhat retarded and suffered serious drawbacks by two considerations: their general lack of special skills and the difficulties in acting both as a productive laborer and fulfilling the traditional roles ascribed to them. The first problem in the productive sphere caused great difficulties. The technical education of women to date remains far below that of the men. Even if they are very good at their work, they cannot be sent away for months to faraway schools to acquire special skills; who would take care of their families while they were away? The resulting gap dooms them to largely manual labor, semi-skilled at best. Thus, in 1975, there were only six women presidents out of 1,591 collective farms' presidents (0.4%), only 386 women vice-presidents out of a total of 4,407 vice-presidents (9.2%), and the percentage of women among the holders of such positions as agricultural engineers, brigade or production leaders ranged only between 1.7% and 6.5%.[116]

The urban services frequently available to ease the work of city women on the "second shift" are generally not available in the rural spheres. This fact aggravated the problems for advancement of rural women.[117] They have rarely been able to take advantage of the social legislation that allows young mothers to remain home with their newborn children for three years with reduced pay; they have no kindergarten facilities, few nurseries and the social services in the village are clearly inadequate.[118]

As a result of these considerations (and because the economic importance of owning land has nearly disappeared), passing on and accumulating land for the next generation became far less important. Parallel with these developments, the size of the individual peasant families has also begun to decrease.[119] The role of the young, occupying well-defined places in the family structure as goose-herders, swine-herders, harvesters of wheat, etc., has become economically less important and thus the family size—especially among the more educated peasants—began to decrease. Scores of studies detail in many regions of Hungary, specifically in the southern part of Transdanubia, how the number of offspring rapidly declined until, in many places, the "only child syndrome" became accepted and desired. The decrease in the average size of the rural family from 1960 on became clearly reflected in the statistical indices; from 3.36 in 1960, the average dipped to 3.18 in 1965 and 3.09 in 1970.[120]

Significant alterations have taken place also within the family structure regarding the separation of generations into independent living units. Due to the changes in the occupational structure, the need for the three-generational family began to break apart. Increasing rural prosperity made it possible for the generations to live their own independent existence; the mobility of the younger generation, their faraway work places and their altered social status, made living with parents and grandparents impractical and unnecessary. Only in families where the problem of obtaining or building separate dwelling places, houses or apartments has not been financially possible, do the three-generational families stay together. It is especially noteworthy that the type of modern houses that has been built during the 1970's is not usable for, and cannot be adapted simply for three-generational living; there is just not enough room for the grandparents.

As a consequence of these developments, the role of the older and younger generation has also been altered. The loneliness of the old, their lack of desire to move out of the old house in which they have lived for so many years, is well known. As the family grows old, it needs more and more assistance "and sometimes the children help to do the work. They bring home and stack the wood for the winter . . . but they no longer live with the older generation."[121] More frequently than not the old people can generally rely only on themselves and their own care; the traditional extended family in most of the developed countryside is a remnant of the past.

The role of the younger generation has also been significantly altered. As the land lost its importance as the basis of the traditional economic family structure, most of the families, especially those in the economically most developed regions, excluded the young from the traditional division of labor. Their role in the agrarian basis of creating the family's wealth became more and more limited as their family tried to encourage them to get an education, get a specialization, one that would take them out of the drudgery and relentlessness of agrarian labor. The prestige of agricultural work, in spite of the significant benefits that may be derived from it, remains low and young people who remain in agriculture are usually young women without any special skills. This fact alone would tend to reinforce the low percentage of women among the leaders of agrarian production activities, and insure that in some instances these women would attempt to maintain relatively traditional households.

Until the 1950's, the influence of the church as the reinforcer of traditional values in the countryside was strong. The church organized and and defined the major celebrations of life from birth, to baptism, to marriage, to death, and to funerals. Without the church, one could hardly imagine village life, and it mattered little if that church was Catholic, Protestant, or even a Jewish synagogue. The church also had special functions that were connected with education and the maintenance of nationhood; for many a young peasant lad the only route to upward mobility was through religious education and opportunities provided by the church.

The inter-war period, the isolation, misery and backwardness of the village contributed greatly to the psychological importance of the church in the rural sphere; great numbers sought solace from heavenly sources for earthly ills. The churches, especially the Catholic church, however, were clearly tied to the power structure, not merely through their support of the *status quo,* but also by their huge landholdings. As a result, while peasant attitudes toward the church as an organizer of daily life continued, attitudes toward the church as a landowner were at best ambivalent.

One must mention briefly the Jews of the countryside as a special case. Unlike in Poland, the Jews in Hungary were largely an urban people. Although only three precent of the Jews were employed in agriculture—because of the historical prohibition against the ownership of land by the Jews—the number of Jews living in the countryside can still be estimated to be around 25% of the Jewish population, or approximately 150,000 people. They were largely exterminated between 1942 and 1945.[122]

When the Communists came to power, the primitive anti-religious atheism they preached resulted in a great many horror stories and reinforced the traditional mutual antagonism between the church and Communists. Churches were closed, priests defrocked and often beaten, the believers at best persecuted, at worst, physically harassed and humiliated. The "peace priests" usually designated by the secret police, made a mockery of the religious activities over which they were supposed to preside, rendering unto Rakosi, the Communist dictator, even that which was due to the Lord. Church attendance officially dwindled, although it is little known how important even in these years the faith of the peasants remained as they now sought an escape from the coercive authority of the state. For the first time the unity of the church and the peasantry became evident; that which the *ancien regime* with its ties to the land-owning church was unable to accomplish, the Communists in the 1950's succeeded in attaining by their own new restrictive policies.

The much more liberal policies of the Kadar regime in the middle of the 1960's and 1970's sought a corrective measure of these "errors." The churches were once again able to function, and though attendance dropped as a direct consequence of industrialization, locational and occupational mobility, the churches were once again allowed to become organizers of the religious-ceremonial functions of the village. Weddings and funerals remain sanctified by the churches, and there is resentment when the local functionaries attempt to coerce the population—contrary to official orders—or use "administrative measures" to decrease the influence of the church.[123] Although the number of civil ceremonies and non-church weddings held by the Communist Youth League is on the increase, the influence of the church in the villages remains relatively strong.

We should also point out that the 1960's resulted in a revival of some of the more extreme religious sects, such as the Church of the Nazarene, Pentecostals, Baptists, Evangelical Christians of various denominations, Jehovah's Witnesses and Sabbatarians.[124] These sects with their promotion of intensive individual experience and participation in church life, play surprisingly strong roles, especially in the isolated villages of Transdanubia, although they are also present in other parts of Hungary.

The Hungarian family has indeed undergone a great deal of transformation moving from tradition to modernity. The transformation of the value-system that held the land to be the center of its structure has done much to create a new, much more open, set of attitudes. The youth in the villages take after new urban models, the values of their life are far more modern, far less family oriented. The traditional family values are preserved in the smaller, less developing communities, and are the least observed in the quickly-growing large villages located in the vicinity of towns and cities. The clash of the two value-structures is likely to continue and perhaps a new, more dynamic structure that incorporates many of the elements of the old and the new is slowly emerging as the basis of the "new peasantry" in the last quarter of the twentieth century.[125]

What Is A Peasant Now?

"In the little village of Szentlorinc where I was born, in the restless little agrarian town where I grew up, in the gardens and fields of Mako where I learned the work of the peasant, the word was never uttered. We lived and sometimes rested according to the laws of the peasantry, but like the Jews with the name of the Lord, we never pronounced the name of our fate. Only once was the word uttered in my parents' home, and when it was uttered we froze as if the gods had entered into our hearts upon its pronounciation . . . . I was already in secondary school and frequently had to miss school because of the work in the fields that needed immediate attention, when my grandfather attacked my father with a great deal of gloominess. As if we had pronounced the ultimate curse, he bellowed at us: 'Is this the way you are going to be a gentleman?' Fear grabbed a-hold of us, and my father—who had a long time before rebelled against our fate—dared to respond to my grandfather only with the weakest negation: 'He isn't going to be a gentleman! Doesn't he work like us? Isn't he a peasant now?' 'No!" boomed my grandfather and he turned his cold peasant face away from us. He knew that I was no longer a peasant, my father knew it as well, I knew it too and in our hearts stark determination and cold fear found their resting places. Since then I have known what it was to be a peasant."[126]

As this eloquent passage from the writing of a former peasant shows, to be a peasant in Hungary has been a curse, but also a cause for pride, a blessing—and a social category. It meant far more to be, as Eric Wolf has defined:

> "rural cultivators whose surpluses are transferred to a dominant group of rulers that uses the surpluses both to underwrite its own standard of living and to distribute the remainder to groups in society that do not farm, but must be fed for their specific goods and services."

It meant more than was implied by Wolf's later definition as "populations that are existentially involved in cultivation and make autonomous decisions regarding the processes of cultivation."[127] It meant far more than being "practicing peasants" who are tied to a market as Redfield[128] views them, or provincials with ties strictly to the land as Krader and Moore imply in their studies.[129] To be a peasant in Hungary meant more than to say that the peasants existed simply as a social category, because they shared a common attitude toward the "limited good" as George Foster posited,[130] implying that the peasants believed "that desired things existed in finite quantities and always in short supply" so that they may improve themselves only by attempting to possess these goods.

To be a *paraszt* (peasant) in Hungary meant to be an individual closely tied to the land, to the agricultural occupation, to the closed society of the rural sphere, but it also meant to be an undesirable social category from the perspective of the urban, the refined, the cosmopolitan, the ruling classes.[131] Though Slavic in origin, the word *paraszt,* unlike its Slavic counterparts today, or the German word "Bauer," implies this negative connotation. But in Hungary, even the self-definition of "peasant" implies this deprecation; "the statement that you are a peasant meant that all that was called freedom and free flight was prohibited for you. Everything: the beauty of the sea and the mountains, the intoxication of knowing many things, the recognition of the fields and the sky, in short, everything that is called freedom. You are a peasant, captive and tethered."[132]

It was not a uniform expression in use, not even in such a small country as Hungary. In the Great Plain the term was viewed positively, it was accepted and even regarded with pride. In Transdanubia it was a depracating and offensive term, just as it was so regarded in Lower Slovakia. It was not used uniformly at all times: in the inter-war period it was rarely used even in official Hungary and its use only became widely accepted in the current jargon after 1938. People referred to one another and to themselves as day laborers, cultivators, small-holders, servants or wage-laborers during these twenty years, but rarely as peasants.[133]

I would not wish to enter the arguments as to whether the term is correct, well used, or its implications derogatory; the literature on this subject has been so great that one would have a hard time selecting the "correct" definition that fits the prevailing tides of scholarship. From my own perspective, "peasant society" can be characterized by some specific attributes and these are definable rather clearly. Thus, if we are to examine the changes in the attributes that can be delineated, we could perhaps make some tentative conclusions as to how during the last three decades the prevailing rural transformation affected the people whose lives were transformed so radically. Consequently, in this segment we shall briefly reiterate the changes that have taken place among the rural population in land-ownership and occupational structure, rural residence, lifestyles, and in the attitudes toward their own society. These changes have determined the peasants' attitudinal orientations toward society as a whole.

The most significant factor in the alteration of peasant life from the prewar period to date has been the fundamental change in the ownership structure of land. As it has become clear that the peasants cannot, by governmental decision, own significant amounts of land, the importance of the land as a determinant both of productive activities and social status has nearly disappeared. For today's peasant the ownership of land is no longer important; what is important is that he can *reap the benefits of using some land,* whether that which is his as a household plot or that of the collective farm. Reaping the benefits of his own production and that of the commons becomes the basis of his views and his outlook; all efforts to limit these benefits would be viewed as hostile and would be resisted with the best tools available.

The change in the occupational structure has also played significant roles in the altered society of the rural sphere. The overwhelming domination of the agricultural sector seems to have disappeared, and the ever growing percentages of rural industrial employment, the growth of the tertiary and administrative sectors, have dealt severe blows to the homogeneity of peasant society. But more than that; the rapid modernization of agricultural work rendered the term "peasant" as an occupational description obsolete. The highly specialized practitioners of agriculture today must be far better trained both in their personal as well as collective efforts than their progenitors; to call people who work on huge combines, use the most sophisticated Chicago-Corn Production System, or set the automatic dial on the automatic feeder "peasants" would render the use of the term meaningless. On these bases one might as well call the American farmers peasants. Moreover, the brutality of peasant labor—the work of the man who pulls the yoke in plowing the land, who cuts the wheat with hand-held scythes—largely belongs to the past; mechanization has abolished this type of labor so typical of a "peasant" society.

The village, in its tradition as the place of rural residence also changed. It is no longer merely agrarian; among the residents are workers who commute, who live in town. These are the rural school teachers, administrators, doctors, nurses and engineers. The outward shape of the village changed radically; the traditional style of houses is rapidly disappearing. The houses that are being built now follow a few basic mass-produced groundplans; they are not "peasant" houses any more, but replicas of urban living, through which the residents make a clear "symbolic announcement that they have denied the peasant way of life."[134]

The village structure has also changed. New centers of activity were created around the collective farm at the end of the village, away from the traditional center near the church; the cross on the church and the red star on the collective have now coordinated the settlement pattern of the village.[135]

The lifestyle of the new peasantry is no longer similar to that of the old. They no longer go to bed at dusk, no longer procreate for the sake of having enough children to feed the family and work the land, no longer live with parents or children, no longer skimp and save, or go hungry to be able to afford an additional small plot of land. Instead, they stop by the village coffeehouse and drink expresso cafe—chased by rum or brandy—they go to the movies, take trips to the places where the husbands, children or parents work, drive cars and motorcycles, and curse out the state when their television sets go on the blink. They desire an education for their children, refuse to work them like their parents taught them to work before, and believe that the days when one was "doomed" to be a peasant are past.

The peasants of Hungary are no longer at the total mercy of the state and hence not of society as a whole. They have their own interest group in the National Council of Cooperatives which—although it is regarded as a transmission belt of the party—is still representative of their interests and has spoken out strongly in their defense. They are the shareholders of the General Consumption and Distribution Cooperative (Altalanos Fogyasztasi es Ertekesitesi Szovetkezet, AFESZ) that organizes their marketing and distribution networks. They play significant roles in local decision-making, in the allocation of infrastructural improvements and the type of programs they desire to see in their local cultural centers, significantly *minimizing* the role of the state. In turn, they play significant roles in the activities of the National Patriotic Front which, although it plays an insignificant role in national political life, is still important in local organizations. The Front provides a framework for the activism of the peasants, and allows them to play a strong and positive role in finding solutions to rural problems. Unlike all other functional organizations (generally tied to the place of work), the Front in the rural sphere is tied to the place of residence, and it offers an attractive and well-used outlet for an interchange between the rural and urban spheres of life.

I would not hesitate to agree with Ralph Turner that all these changes have altered the peasants' attitude toward the cities, the centers of power, the centers of culture which they had feared, distrusted and rejected so long in their historical existence.[136] Hungary's peasant culture has disintegrated; there is no more large-scale tranditionalism, provincialism and localism; peasants are more willing to accept the urban ways of life that have replaced traditionalism,with modernity, provincialism with more open outlooks, and localism with becoming a part of the larger whole, the larger community, the nation. The geocentrism of their only known and recognized world has been shattered largely by the aggressive and enticing media with its multi-centralism. They are also affected by the "cult of uniformity" as regional variations and dialects merge under the powerful influence of uniformalizing media language. Their behavior becomes more diverse, their reaction to particular events more varied, less predictable and more complex, unburdened by the eternal hold and tie to the land. Other foci and ideas appear and hold their attention, allegiance and interests.

The process of change has not been and can never be regarded as even or final. There are still backward regions where the traditional peasant is an everyday reality and dominates the milieu. There are also regions where villages are miniature replicas, frequently even caricatures, of the urban centers, where the "peasants" are urban citizens who happen to live in a rural locus, much the same way as a repair mechanic or a business executive live in a rural location a few miles from their work in a city of the U.S. There are places where the peasants still hold to the traditional structure of the family, maintain themselves as a unit with three generations under one patched, thatched roof, and there are contrasting places where row-houses built in modernistic early Swedish bad-taste are designed to house single, and quite small families with English-type tiny gardens in the back.

And in all this process, the regime must take the blame and the responsibility as well as the praise for all that has been accomplished. In a Communist state, where there is really only one party, one real center of power, it is the party and the leadership that is blamed, or praised, for all things ugly and beautiful; for good weather and floods, for greater profits and higher world prices, for inflation and the death of a cousin at the wheel of his car. It is unfair, but that's the way the regime wanted it originally and now there is no way to change it. The regime has depoliticalized the polity, but it has to expect the blame of those who have failed to strike it rich. They have insured the passive loyalty of the peasants, but have yet been unable to earn the respect from those they had once dispossessed.

The peasants accept that the old way of life is over, that the former smallholders who stuck to their property, like the old peasants in one of Kunszabo's short stories, have no future in the present as the owners of the land. The old man in the story dies not "blaming anyone for what has happened:"

> That's the way you wanted life to turn out for us, so that's the way it is . . . . But to create for others? I have only worked and thought about things and worked again. In the previous world that was the way, that was the custom. But my sons are all in industry; engineer, clerical worker, industrial worker . . . Let them do the creation.[137]

There are still many whose will and life have been destroyed in order to accomplish the great goal of modernizing the Hungarian countryside. They rarely share in the great joy of prosperity affecting the transformed rural sphere.

There are victims and victors, poverty-stricken and rich, drunks whose last *fillers* are spent on booze and farmers who have made enough to last three lifetimes. There are agricultural engineers and untrained field hands, urban peasants and peasant urbanites, thatched roofed houses with television antennas and muddy huts that flood when it rains. There are commuters on black trains, drunk and tired, and workers who drive their own Zhigulis home through muddy streets. But there is no doubt that the rural sphere of Hungary has been transformed forever; modernization with all its consequences both positive and negative, has struck the peasantry and the Hungarian countryside with a vengeance during the last thirty years.

NOTES

1. *Evkonyv, 1977,* 27.
2. *Ibid.*
3. *Gyorgy Moldova, Az Orseg panasza* (Lament of the Orseg) (Budapest, 1974), 158.
4. *Adattar,* 11:405.
5. *Ibid.,* 5.
6. Enyedi, "The Transformation," *op. cit.,* 70-1.
7. In Hungary, villages with less than 1,000 inhabitants each are predominant in about 50% of the country. *Ibid.,* 70.
8. Calvin Beale and Donald Bogue, *Recent Population Trends in the U.S. with Emphasis on Rural Areas* (Washington, D. C., 1969), and Dale E. Hathaway and James D. Traver, "Testimonies" before the National Manpower Conference held at Stillwater (Oklahoma, May 17-18, 1968). Unpublished ms.
9. Bela Beluszky, "Functional Types of Rural Settlements in Hungary," in Enyedi, *Rural Transformation, op. cit.,* 45-54, and Viktor Kulcsar, *op. cit.,* 91-129.
10. Pal Romany, *A tanya rendszer ma* (the Tanya-System Today) (Budapest, 1973), 31 and following. See also, Erdei, *Magyar tanyak, op. cit.;* Edit Lettrich, "The Hungarian Tanya-system: History and Present Problems," in Bela Sarfalvy, ed., *Research Problems in Hungarian Applied Geography* (Budapest, 1969), and Nancy Volgyes, "The Hungarian Tanyas: Persistence and Change of an Anachronistic Settlement Pattern," in Ivan Volgyes et al. eds., The process of *Rural Transformation* (New York, Oxford, 1980), 175-191.
11. Romany, *op. cit.,* 39.
12. Zam, *op. cit.,* 3.
13. On the latest changes in government policy in favor of supporting the *tanyas* see *Magyar Nemzet,* October 28, 1977.
14. Nancy Volgyes, "The Hungarian Tanyas," *op. cit.,* 10.

15. Tatai, "The Growth . . . ." *op. cit.,* 72.
16. *Ibid.,* 71.
17. Kulcsar, *op. cit.,* 129-48.
18. Enyedi, "Transformation . . . ." *op. cit.,* 80.
19. Jozsef Sarandi, "Ivoviz," (Drinking Water), *Elet es Irodalom* (October 30, 1977) 3.
20. Agoston Szekelyhidi, "Ki lesz a gazda? (Who is Going to be the Owner?) *Ibid.,* (December 17, 1977), 1.
21. Enyedi, "Transformation," *op. cit.,* 72.
22. Vegh, *Erdohaton, op, cit.,* 137-8.
23. Laszlo Siklos, *Picasso a gyarban* (Picasso in the Factory) (Budapest, 1976), 13.
24. Alice R. Malyusz and Sandor Veress, "Falusi lanyok Pesten," (Village Girls in Pest) *Valosag,* 1 (1976), 96-107.
25. Adam Wazyk, "A Poem for Adults," in Edmund Stillman, ed., *Bitter Harvest* (New York, 1959), 131.
26. Simon Serfozo, "MS ujsag otthon?" (What is the News at Home?), *Elet es Irodalom* (October 1, 1977) 16.
27. Judit Fenakel, "Videkinek lenni," (To Be From the Country), *Ibid.,* (July 23, 1977) 3.
28. E. Takti/Mrs. Vorosmarti, "Demographic Characteristics of Rural Settlements," in Enyedi, *Rural Transformation, op. cit.,* 39.
29. Zsuzsa Ferge, "A szocialista tarsadalmi struktura dinamikaja," (The Dynamics of the Structure of Socialist Society) *Valosag,* 11 (1976) 21-5.
30. Kalman Benda, "A felvilagosodas es a paraszti muveltseg a XVIII. szazadban Magyarorszagon," (The Enlightenment and Peasant Culture in 18th Century Hungary) *Ibid.,* 4 (1976) 54.
31. Janos Herbert, "Egy alfoldi kozseg tarsadalomrajza," (Description of the Society of a Village of the Great Plain) *Tarsadalomtudomany* 6-8 (1927), 23-24.
32. Kulcsar, *op. cit.,* 246.
33. Sandor Zsarnoczai, *Tanulmanyok a mai falurol* (Studies about Today's Village) (Budapest, 1964), 130.
34. Moldova, *Az Orseg, op. cit.,* 79-80.

35. *Ibid.,* 226.
36. Gulyas, "Cserhati . . . ." *op. cit.,* 53.
37. Laszlo Magyar, "Ibafa," *Valosag,* 12 (1977), 74.
38. Vegh, *Erdohaton* . . . . 109. Since 1976, the salaries of all teachers have been raised by 20-30%, but the inequality has remained as farm incomes—and inflation—followed suit.
39. *Ibid.,* 113.
40. *Ibid.,* 64-5.
41. *Ibid.,* 66.
42. Istvan Lazar, "Fa az erdon," (Trees in the Forest) *Elet es Irodalom,* (November 19, 1977) 3.
43. *Hazank, Magyarorszag* (Our Country, Hungary) (Budapest, 1975), I:461.
44. *Evkonyv, 1977,* 47, 48.
45. *Hazank, Magyarorszag,* I:462.
46. *Evkonyv, 1976,* 49.
47. *Ibid.,* 47.
48. *Zsebkonyv, 1977,* 164.
49. *Hazank, Magyarorszag,* I:471 and *Zsebkonyv, 1977,* 168.
50. *Evkonyv, 1976,* 353.
51. Laszlo Levendel, "Feszultsegek az egeszsegugyben" (Tensions in Health Care) *Valosag* 3 (1978), 54.
52. Zsuzsa Solymosi, "Orvosok es telepulesek,: (Medical Doctors and Settlements) *Ibid.,* 10 (1977), 73.
53. Katalin Sulyok, "Fiatal orvosok Szabolcsban" (Young Physicians in Szabolcs), *Ibid.,* 4 (1969), 79.
54. Solymosi, *op. cit.,* 83.
55. Sulyok, *op. cit.,* 78.
56. *Evkonyv, 1976,* 354.
57. Katalin Sulyok, "Vedonovel a tanyakon," (With a District Nurse on the Tanyas) *Elet es Irodalom,* (October 31, 1976), 16.
58. Vegh, *Erdohaton* . . . . , *op. cit.,* 27-8.
59. Ivan Volgyes, "Political Socialization: A Comparative Framework," in Volgyes, ed., *Political Socialization in Eastern Europe* (New York, 1975), 18.

60. *Zsebkonyv, 1977,* 189.
61. Gyorgy Sandor, *A televizio es a kozonseg* (Television and the Audience) (Budapest, 1973), 7.
62. *Zsebkonyv, 1977,* 189.
63. Zsarnoczai, *Tanulmanyok, op. cit.,* 117-43.
64. Moldova, *Az Orseg . . . . , op. cit.,* 72.
65. Erzsebet Galgoczi, *Nadtetos szocializmus* (Socialism with Thatched Roofs) (Budapest, 1970), 272-3.
66. Ferenc Erdei, *Mezogazdasag es szovetkezet* (Agriculture and Cooperative) (Budapest, 1959), 56.
67. *Zsebkonyv, 1977,* 113.
68. From the Ministry of Traffic and Post, Directive, January 18, 1972, quoted by Gyorgy Moldova, *Akit a mozdony fustje megcsapott* (Touched by the Smoke of the Engine) (Budapest, 1977), 281.
69. *Evkonyv, 1976,* 243.
70. *Ibid.,* 244.
71. Ferge, *op. cit.,* 25.
72. For an in-depth description of the changes see Tamas Kolosi, *Tarsadalmi struktura es szocializmus* (Social Structure and Socialism) (Budapest, 1974), and Zsuzsa Ferge, *Tarsadalmunk retegezodese* (The Stratification of Our Society) (Budapest, 1969).
73. Enyedi, "Transformation," *op. cit.,* 72.
74. Ivanyi, "Uton . . . ." *op. cit.,* 16.
75. Kulcsar, *op. cit.,* 271.
76. *Ibid.,* 273.
77. Ferge, *Tarsadalmunk . . . . , op. cit.,* 136.
78. Janos Gyenis and Janos Soptei, *Uj faluk, uj emberek* (New Villages, New Human Beings) (Budapest, 1970), 41.
79. Max Weber, *Wirtschaft und Gesellschaft* (Koln-Berlin, 1964), 152.
80. Ferge, *Tarsadalmunk, op. cit.,* 95-101.
81. *Ibid.,* 86-95, and Andras Hegedus, *A szocialista tarsadalom strukturajarol* (Concerning the Structure of Socialist Society) (Budapest, 1966).

82. Antal Gyenes,"Munkasok es parasztok a mezogazdasagi termeloszovetkezetekben," (Workers and Peasants in the Agricultural Cooperatives) *Valosag* 4 (1968), 290.
83. Gyorgy Lukacs, *A tarsadalmi let ontologiajarol* (Con cerning the Ontology of Social Existence) (Budapest, 1976), II:158.
84. Istvan Markus, *Ezt lattam falun* (This is What I Observed in the Villages) (Budapest, 1971), 3.
85. On the results of the upheavals of 1956, see Erzsebet Galgoczi's moving novel, *A kozos bun* (The Common Crime) (Budapest, 1976).
86. Kulcsar, op. cit., 273.
87. *Ibid.*
88. Moldova, *Az Orseg . . . . , op. cit.*, 88.
89. Vegh, "Nyomtato," *op. cit.*
90. *A videki ertelmiseg helyzete* (The Situation of the Intelligentsia of the Countryside) (Budapest, 1976), 4 vols.
91. N.=184 on a representative stratified sample base.
92. Laszlo Garami, "Falusi ertelmiseg—barati kapcsolatok, kulturakozvetites," (Rural Intelligentsia: Friendship Ties and the Transmission of Culture), *Valosag,* 10 (1975), 86.
93. Ferge, *Tarsadalmunk, op. cit.*, 303.
94. Erdei, *Magyar falu, op. cit.*, 195-6.
95. Galgoczi, *Nadetos, op. cit.*, 137-46.
96. *Evkonyv, 1976,* 327.
97. *Zsebkonyv, 1977,* 154.
98. Gyenis and Soptei, *op. cit.*, 45.
99. Table adapted from Lajos Major, "Ujfajta retegzodes" (A New Type of Stratification) *Szabad Fold,* May 11, 1969.
100. Daniel Hatvani, "Egy eletforma szethullasa," (The Falling Apart of a Life Style) *Valosag,* 11 (1974), 34-44.
101. Vegh, *Erdohaton, op. cit.*, 38-9.
102. Peter Szekulity, "Szerencsetlen oraban szulettem"(I was Born at an Unfortunate Hour) *Elet es Irodalom* (September 2, 1977) 16.

103. Istvan Messinger, "Nagypenteki piacnap" (Market Day on Good Friday) *Ibid.* (December 31, 1977) 16.
104. Mate Nagyszenasi, "Parokat Bozsinknek," (A Wig for Our Bozsi) *Ibid.*, (July 9, 1977) 16.
105. "They buy nothing and produce everything at home. . . ."
106. Ivan and Nancy Volgyes, *The Liberated Female: Life, Work and Sex in Socialist Hungary* (Boulder, Colorado, 1977), 120.
107. *Ibid.*
108. Istvan Lazar, "Oszi utazas halottak napjan, auton" (An Autumn Trip by Car on All Saints' Day), *Elet es Irodalom* (November 12, 1977) 1.
109. Minister of Justice Mihaly Korom, in *Nepszava* (January 1, 1978).
110. *Nepszava* (December 2, 1977).
111. On the traditional family structure see Tamas Hofer and Edit Fel, *Proper Peasants* (New York, 1974) and the chapters on the traditional peasant family in the previous sections of this book.
112. Katalin Javor, "A parasztcsalad munkamegoszlasa egy nyirsegi faluban," (The Division of Labor in a Peasant Family in a Village of the Nyirseg) (Debrecen), Monograph 19, in a Folklore Series, and Erzsebet Orszeghy, "Hevizgyork part valaszt"(Hevizgyork Chooses a Mate) *Valosag* 12 (1977), 67.
113. Ferenc Erdei, *Futohomok, op. cit.*
114. On the role of women in the contemporary situation see Zsuzsa Orolin, *A falusi nok helyzete* (The Condition of Women in the Countryside) (Budapest, 1970), and Ibolya Halacs, "Sociological Survey of the Situation of Women in the Southwestern Transdanubian Region," Keszthely, *Studies,* No. 4 (1971).
115. *Evkonyv, 1976,* 39.
116. Mrs. Lajos Feher, "A falusi asszonyok helyzete," (The Situation of Village Women) *Partelet,* 11 (1969), 19-25.
117. Szekelyhidi, "Ki lesz," *op. cit.*, 1.

118. Ibolya Halacs, "A Cooperative Peasant Family," Keszthely, *Studies No. 3,* 1971.
119. Kulcsar, *op. cit.,* 267.
120. Szekulity, "Szerencsetlen," *op. cit.,* 16.
121. Ivan T. Berend and Gyorgy Ranki, *East Central Europe, op. cit.,* 115-31.
122. For a moving account of the destruction of Hungarian Jewry from the rural sphere see Maria Ember, *Hajtukanyar* (Hairpin Bend) (Budapest, 1976), and Istvan Lazar, *Kialt Patak vara* (The Fort of Patak Yells) (Budapest, 1974), *passim.*
123. Kulcsar, *op. cit.,* 268.
124. On the sects see Sandor Meszaros, "Sotetben maradtak" (They Remained in Darkness), *Vilagossag,* 2 (1968), 28-33; Benedek Toth, "Szektak a Bakonyaljan," (Sects at the Foot of the Bakony) *Nepszabadsag* September 16, 1960, and by the same author, "Punkosdistak Csetenyben" (Pentecostals in Cseteny), and Lazar, *Kialt Patak vara, op. cit.,* 46-50. For a major study, see Laszlo Kardos, *Egyhaz es vallasos elet egy mai faluban* (Church and Religious Life in a Contemporary Village) (Budapest, 1969).
125. Erdei, *Parasztok, op. cit.,* 5.
126. Eric Wolf, *Peasants* (Englewood Cliffs, NJ, 1966), 3-4.
127. Eric Wolf, *Peasant Wars of the Twentieth Century* (New York, 1970), xvi.
128. Redfield, *Peasant Society . . . , op. cit.,* 156.
129. Lawrence Krader, "The Transition from Peasant to Serf in Eastern Europe" *Anthropological Quarterly,* 33 (January, 1960), 76-7, and Barrington Moore, Jr., *op. cit.,* 111.
130. Foster, "Peasant Society . . . ." *op. cit.*
131. Tamas Hoffman, "Parasztok," (Peasants) *Valosag,* 12 (1977), 34-52, and Erdei, *Parasztok, op. cit.,* 7.
132. Laszlo Komlo, "Parasztok vagyunk—parasztok maradunk?" (We Are Peasants—And Are We to Remain Peasants?) *Valosag,* 12 (1977), 53-60.

133. Tamas Hofer, "What is a Peasant?" Paper presented at the symposium on the East European Peasantry, January 7-10, 1977, Boston, Mass, p. 8.
134. Enyedi, "Transformation," *op. cit.*, 75-7.
135. Ferenc Kunszabo, "Talalkozasok," (Meetings), *Elet es Irodalom* (October 8, 1977), 16.
136. Ralph E. Turner, "The Industrial City: Center of Rural Change" in Caroline F. Ware, ed., *The Cultural Approach to History* (New York, 1940), 138-41.
137. Szekulity, "Szerencsetlen . . . ." *op. cit.*, 16.

EAST EUROPEAN MONOGRAPHS

The *East European Monographs* comprise scholarly books on the history and civilization of Eastern Europe. They are published in the belief that these studies contribute substantially to the knowledge of the area and serve to stimulate scholarship and research.

1. *Political Ideas and the Enlightenment in the Romanian Principalities, 1750–1831.* By Vlad Georgescu. 1971.
2. *America, Italy and the Birth of Yugoslavia, 1917–1919.* By Dragan R. Zivojinovic. 1972.
3. *Jewish Nobles and Geniuses in Modern Hungary.* By William O. McCagg, Jr. 1972.
4. *Mixail Soloxov in Yugoslavia: Reception and Literary Impact.* By Robert F. Price. 1973.
5. *The Historical and National Thought of Nicolae Iorga.* By William O. Oldson. 1973.
6. *Guide to Polish Libraries and Archives.* By Richard C. Lewanski. 1974.
7. *Vienna Broadcasts to Slovakia, 1938–1939: A Case Study in Subversion.* By Henry Delfiner. 1974.
8. *The 1917 Revolution in Latvia.* By Andrew Ezergailis. 1974.
9. *The Ukraine in the United Nations Organization: A Study in Soviet Foreign Policy. 1944–1950.* By Konstantin Sawczuk. 1975.
10. *The Bosnian Church: A New Interpretation.* By John V. A. Fine, Jr., 1975.
11. *Intellectual and Social Developments in the Habsburg Empire from Maria Theresa to World War I.* Edited by Stanley B. Winters and Joseph Held. 1975.
12. *Ljudevit Gaj and the Illyrian Movement.* By Elinor Murray Despalatovic. 1975.
13. *Tolerance and Movements of Religious Dissent in Eastern Europe.* Edited by Bela K. Kiraly. 1975.
14. *The Parish Republic: Hlinka's Slovak People's Party, 1939–1945.* By Yeshayahu Jelinek. 1976.
15. *The Russian Annexation of Bessarabia, 1774–1828.* By George F. Jewsbury. 1976.
16. *Modern Hungarian Historiography.* By Steven Bela Vardy. 1976.
17. *Values and Community in Multi-National Yugoslavia.* By Gary K. Bertsch. 1976.
18. *The Greek Socialist Movement and the First World War: the Road to Unity.* By George B. Leon. 1976.

19. *The Radical Left in the Hungarian Revolution of 1848.* By Laszlo Deme. 1976.
20. *Hungary between Wilson and Lenin: The Hungarian Revolution of 1918–1919 and the Big Three.* By Peter Pastor. 1976.
21. *The Crises of France's East-Central European Diplomacy, 1933–1938.* By Anthony J. Komjathy. 1976.
22. *Polish Politics and National Reform, 1775–1788.* By Daniel Stone. 1976.
23. *The Habsburg Empire in World War I.* Robert A. Kann, Bela K. Kiraly, and Paula S. Fichtner, eds. 1977.
24. *The Slovenes and Yugoslavism, 1890–1914.* By Carole Rogel. 1977.
25. *German-Hungarian Relations and the Swabian Problem.* By Thomas Spira. 1977.
26. *The Metamorphosis of a Social Class in Hungary During the Reign of Young Franz Joseph.* By Peter I. Hidas. 1977.
27. *Tax Reform in Eighteenth Century Lombardy.* By Daniel M. Klang. 1977.
28. *Tradition versus Revolution: Russia and the Balkans in 1917.* By Robert H. Johnston. 1977.
29. *Winter into Spring: The Czechoslovak Press and the Reform Movement 1963–1968.* By Frank L. Kaplan. 1977.
30. *The Catholic Church and the Soviet Government, 1939–1949.* By Dennis J. Dunn. 1977.
31. *The Hungarian Labor Service System, 1939–1945.* By Randolph L. Braham. 1977.
32. *Consciousness and History: Nationalist Critics of Greek Society 1897–1914.* By Gerasimos Augustinos. 1977.
33. *Emigration in Polish Social and Political Thought, 1870–1914.* By Benjamin P. Murdzek. 1977.
34. *Serbian Poetry and Milutin Bojic.* By Mihailo Dordevic. 1977.
35. *The Baranya Dispute: Diplomacy in the Vortex of Ideologies, 1918–1921.* By Leslie C. Tihany. 1978.
36. *The United States in Prague, 1945–1948.* By Walter Ullmann. 1978.
37. *Rush to the Alps: The Evolution of Vacationing in Switzerland.* By Paul P. Bernard. 1978.
38. *Transportation in Eastern Europe: Empirical Findings.* By Bogdan Mieczkowski. 1978.
39. *The Polish Underground State: A Guide to the Underground, 1939–1945.* By Stefan Korbonski. 1978.
40. *The Hungarian Revolution of 1956 in Retrospect.* Edited by Bela K. Kiraly and Paul Jonas. 1978.
41. *Boleslaw Limanowski (1835–1935): A Study in Socialism and Nationalism.* By Kazimiera Janina Cottam. 1978.
42. *The Lingering Shadow of Nazism: The Austrian Independent Party Movement Since 1945.* By Max E. Riedlsperger. 1978.
43. *The Catholic Church, Dissent and Nationality in Soviet Lithuania.* By V. Stanley Vardys. 1978.

44. *The Development of Parliamentary Government in Serbia.* By Alex N. Dragnich. 1978.
45. *Divide and Conquer: German Efforts to Conclude a Separate Peace, 1914–1918.* By L. L. Farrar, Jr. 1978.
46. *The Prague Slav Congress of 1848.* By Lawrence D. Orton. 1978.
47. *The Nobility and the Making of the Hussite Revolution.* By John M. Klassen. 1978.
48. *The Cultural Limits of Revolutionary Politics: Change and Continuity in Socialist Czechoslovakia.* By David W. Paul. 1979.
49. *On the Border of War and Peace: Polish Intelligence and Diplomacy in 1937–1939 and the Origins of the Ultra Secret.* By Richard A. Woytak. 1979.
50. *Bear and Foxes: The International Relations of the East European States 1965–1969.* By Ronald Haly Linden. 1979.
51. *Czechoslovakia: The Heritage of Ages Past.* Edited by Hans Brisch and Ivan Volgyes. 1979.
52. *Prime Minister Gyula Andrássy's Influence on Habsburg Foreign Policy.* By János Decsy. 1979.
53. *Citizens for the Fatherland: Education, Educators, and Pedagogical Ideals in Eighteenth Century Russia.* By J. L. Black. 1979.
54. *The History of the "Proletariat": The Emergence of Marxism in the Kingdom of Poland, 1870–1887.* By Norman M. Naimark. 1979.
55. *The Slovak Autonomy Movement, 1935–1939: A Study in Unrelenting Nationalism.* By Dorothea H. El Mallakh. 1979.
56. *Diplomat in Exile: Francis Pulszky's Political Activities in England, 1849–1860.* By Thomas Kabdebo. 1979.
57. *The German Struggle Against the Yugoslav Guerrillas in World War II: German Counter-Insurgency in Yugoslavia, 1941–1943.* By Paul N. Hehn. 1979.
58. *The Emergence of the Romanian National State.* By Gerald J. Bobango. 1979.
59. *Stewards of the Land: The American Farm School and Modern Greece.* By Brenda L. Marder. 1979.
60. *Roman Dmowski: Party, Tactics, Ideology 1895–1907.* By Alvin Marcus Fountain II. 1980.
61. *International and Domestic Politics in Greece During the Crimean War.* By Jon V. Kofas. 1980.
62. *Fires on the Mountain: The Macedonian Revolutionary Movement and the Kidnapping of Ellen Stone.* By Laura Beth Sherman. 1980.
63. *The Modernization of Agriculture: Rural Tranformation in Hungary, 1848-1975.* Edited by Joseph Held. 1980.
64. *Britain and the War for Yugoslavia, 1940-1943.* By Mark C. Wheeler. 1980.